PERFORMANCE MEAS
AND EVALUATION

The Open University Business School

The Open University Business School offers a three-tier ladder of opportunity for managers at different stages of their careers: the Professional Certificate in Management; the Professional Diploma in Management; and the Master of Business Administration. If you would like to receive information on these open learning programmes, please write to the Open University Business School, The Open University, Milton Keynes MK7 6AA, UK.

This volume is a Course Reader for the Open University Business School's MBA course *Performance Measurement and Evaluation* (B889).

PERFORMANCE MEASUREMENT AND EVALUATION

edited by

Jacky Holloway, Jenny Lewis and Geoff Mallory

at the Open University Business School

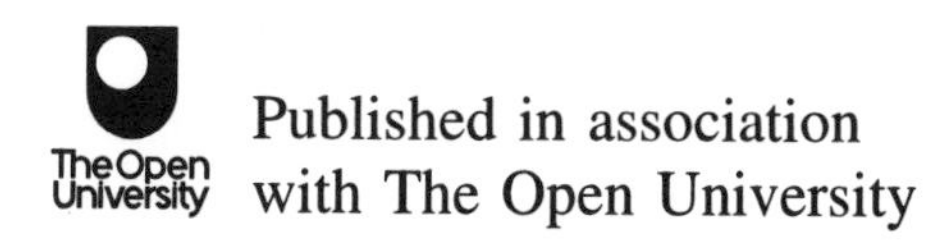

Published in association with The Open University

London · Thousand Oaks · New Delhi

First published 1995

SAGE Publications Ltd
6 Bonhill Street
London EC2A 4PU

SAGE Publications Inc.
2455 Teller Road
Thousand Oaks
California 91320

SAGE Publications India Pvt Ltd
32, M-Block Market
Greater Kailash – I
New Delhi 110 048

British Library Cataloguing in Publication data
A catalogue record for this book is available from the British Library
ISBN 0-8039-7958-4
ISBN 0-8039-7959-2 pbk
Library of Congress catalog card number 94-074795

Typeset by The Open University
Printed in the United Kingdom by The Cromwell Press Ltd, Broughton Gifford, Melksham, Wiltshire

Contents

Acknowledgements

We are grateful to the following for permission to reprint articles:

Article 1: Reprinted by permission of *Harvard Business Review*. 'The performance measurement manifesto' by Robert G. Eccles, January/February 1991, Copyright © 1991 by the President and Fellows of Harvard College, all rights reserved; *Article 2*: Dent, J. and Ezzamel, M. (1987) 'Organisational control and management accounting', in Ezzamel, M. and Hart, H. (eds) *Advanced Management Accounting: An Organisational Emphasis*, Copyright © 1987 Cassell Educational Ltd; *Article 3*: Reed, M. and Anthony, P. (1992) 'Professionalizing management and managing professionalization: British management in the 1980s', *Journal of Management Studies*, pp. 591–613, Vol. 29, No. 5, Basil Blackwell Ltd; *Article 4*: Longenecker, C. and Ludwig, D. (1990) 'Ethical dilemmas in performance appraisal revisited', *Journal of Business Ethics*, Vol. 9, pp. 961–9 Kluwer Academic Publishers; *Article 5*: © The Open University; *Article 6*: Fornell, C. (1992) 'A national customer satisfaction barometer', *Journal of Marketing*, Vol. 56, American Marketing Association, pp. 6–21; *Article 7*: © The Open University; *Article 8*: Reprinted with the permission of The Free Press, an imprint of Simon and Schuster from *Dynamic Manufacturing: Creating the Learning Organization* by Robert H. Hayes, Steven C. Wheelwright and Kim B. Clark. Copyright © 1988 by The Free Press; *Article 9*: Oliver, N., Delbridge, R., Jones, D. and Lowe, J. (1994) 'World class manufacturing: further evidence in the lean production debate', *British Journal of Management*, Vol. 5, Special Issue S53–S63, June 1994, © 1994 by John Wiley and Sons Ltd. Reproduced by permission of John Wiley and Sons Ltd; *Article 10*: Smith, P. (1993) 'Outcome-related performance indicators and organizational control in the public sector', *British Journal of Management*, Vol. 4, pp. 135–151, John Wiley and Sons Ltd, reproduced by permission of John Wiley and Sons Ltd; *Article 11*: Simmonds, A. and Azières, O. (1989) *Accounting for Europe – Success by 2000 AD?*, courtesy of Touche Ross; *Article 12*: Chakravarthy, B.S. (1986) 'Measuring strategic performance', *Strategic Management Journal*, Vol. 7, © 1986 by John Wiley and Sons Ltd. Reproduced by permission of John Wiley and Sons Ltd.; *Article 13*: © John Kay 1993. Reprinted from *Foundations of Corporate Success* by John Kay (1993) by permission of Oxford University Press; *Article 14*: Johnes, J. and Taylor, J. (1990) 'Degree results: differences between universities', *Performance Indicators in Higher Education*, The Society for Research into Higher Education/Open University Press, © Jill Johnes and Jim Taylor 1990; *Article 15*: Schefczyk, M. (1993) 'Operational performance of airlines: an extension of traditional measurement paradigms', *Strategic Management Journal*, Vol. 14, © 1993 by John Wiley and Sons Ltd. Reproduced by permission of John Wiley and Sons Ltd.

Figures

Article 7, Figure 2: adapted by permission of HSA (UK); Article 7, Figure 3: Courtesy of Bain and Company.

Tables

Article 7, Table 3: Courtesy of Martin Deda/PA Consulting Group; Article 7, Table 4: Courtesy of Kaiser Associates Inc.

Preface

This book has been produced for the Open Business School's course *Performance Measurement and Evaluation.* The course is an elective within the MBA programme and started in 1994, attracting in its first year over 600 students from the UK and continental Europe. The course is multidisciplinary in scope and has been studied by managers from almost every sort of organization. Managers increasingly have direct responsibility for the assessment of organizational performance, as well as making a contribution to that performance itself, and the Reader has been produced to support them in this work.

The overall focus both of this book and of the associated course is on organizational performance. However, it would be impractical and inappropriate to neglect both the organization's environment, and its sub-systems which are made up of individuals and groups. Thus for instance, we have included a critical study of staff appraisal systems as well as studies of the impact of the strategic context and physical environment within which organizations operate.

While some articles concentrate on the contribution to be made by particular management disciplines or functions, others assume a multidisciplinary view. 'Performance' is seen as multidimensional – the overall status of an organization in relation to its competitors, or against its own or external standards, should generally be gauged across a profile of measures. The profile may reflect the nature of the business or industry. A popular shorthand is 'the three Es' – economy, efficiency and effectiveness being the most frequently cited – but, for instance, public services are often assessed against criteria of equity, and medical professionals on the efficacy of their clinical interventions.

Intra- and inter-sectoral differences in performance priorities are often shaped by the interests and power balances of their major stakeholders. While this theme is often implicit rather than being the focus of explicit attention by authors, it is one which repays consideration from time to time in any exploration of performance assessment. Powerful stakeholders tend to set the performance evaluation agenda, determining the measures to be used or the results of assessment. Sometimes this has unintended consequences. For instance, Johnes and Taylor draw our attention to the effect on institutional performance which could result if, because of government policy, university funding becomes linked to degree results. The recognition of differences in perspective and priorities among stakeholders can, however, provide the basis for positive developments in performance which, in the best of all worlds, can leave all (or most) stakeholders as winners. This somewhat idealistic rationale lies behind total quality management and comprehensive approaches to environmental management which are exercising the energies of many managers today.

A further underlying theme in this book (and in the Open Business School course) is the need for careful design and development if performance measurement and evaluation systems are to operate effectively. Approaches developed in the commercial sector are increasingly being applied in non-profit organizations; best practices benchmarking is just one example. Public services have led the way in areas such as equal opportunities policy monitoring, now seen as a component of 'social responsibility' and ethical management which is gaining ground in parts of the private sector. And techniques of performance measurement developed in Western market economies have been integral parts of the 'knowledge aid' offered to the former Eastern bloc. However, we cannot assume that these forms of diffusion will be without their difficulties. While writers such as Eccles urge all organizations to adopt a new approach to performance measurement, others like Dent and Ezzamel counsel caution. Contingency factors may play a major part in the effectiveness of performance management, yet the precise nature and role of such factors have yet to be fully researched.

The articles in this book contain a mix of description, prescription and reflection. They have been chosen because, in the view of the editors, they provide good examples within their relevant fields, which may be functional, philosophical or speculative. We do not claim that the book provides a comprehensive review of what is, after all, a field unbounded by the constraints of a recognized management discipline or school of thought. Furthermore, the practices of performance measurement and evaluation are growing in popularity and the volume of relevant written material is proliferating. However, we have tried to select articles which are thought-provoking and reasonably accessible in style to a wide audience.

The book is arranged in three parts, each of which has a loose theme. The articles in Part 1 each take a fairly broad view of themes in management which, in the opinions of their authors, require a critical appraisal. Some also present analytical frameworks which can be of wider relevance.

Part 2 brings together overviews of several comprehensive approaches to performance measurement and examples of sector-specific approaches.

The articles in Part 3 explore components of strategic performance in a range of economic sectors, with an emphasis on the impact of measurement for policy or practice. The implications of the use of performance measures which are unquestioned or only partly understood become clear, and the reader is left in little doubt of the complex nature of strategic performance.

PART 1

THEMES AND FRAMEWORKS

Introduction

Jenny Lewis

Part 1 deliberately contains the widest variety of articles, including several on what may be rather unexpected topics, to give the reader an impression of the true breadth of this interdisciplinary academic area before Parts 2 and 3 consider its wide-ranging practical management applications.

The first article, Professor Robert Eccles' *The performance measurement manifesto*, written in 1991, is already a classic. Eccles argues convincingly that financial performance indicators are both too simplistic and too backwardly focused to be sufficient for successful modern competitive organizations. Crucial reasons for the proposed revolution, namely the need for better performance measurement and evaluation in order to improve strategic decision-making and its implementation, are drawn out. Senior managers require 'a decided taste for ambiguity' to enable them to devise better measurement systems. Without far-thinking initiatives from the top, it is argued, the revolution will not be advanced. Complacency and 'what gets measured gets attention' will continue to be the norm. We should note the author's optimism that a real revolution will occur, and question whether this is starting to happen via initiatives such as Total Quality Management. Quality is an issue that is examined further in Part 2.

Eccles argues that businesses must ask what measures truly predict their long-term financial success. There will be no easy recipes: different sectors and sizes will identify different factors. Part 3 tackles this question in more depth. The contingency theory approach which underpins such questions is further expounded in the second article by Jeremy Dent and Mahmoud Ezzamel. Their lucid discussion of the history of organizational control as an academic discipline leads on from Eccles, but in a more cautionary vein. Although purporting to be about management accounting, a narrow viewpoint criticized by Eccles, these authors demonstrate how complex the organizational issues involved really are, and invoke a systems perspective to deal with this richness. Sections IV and V provide the core of their views in relation to performance measurement, although the whole article gives a thorough, if rather densely academic, overview of the organizational control literature.

The third article, by the sociologists Michael Reed and Peter Anthony, is at first sight very different. Its primary focus is on the development of management as a profession. Education is a vital gateway to the professionalization of any occupational group. The authors, while critically evaluating the history and performance of the UK's higher education system for managers, point out in their section on 'Restructuring Managerial Work' that it is essential to reflect on what such a system *should* be like. An evaluation which emphasizes precision in measuring efficiency, they argue, is no substitute for consideration of effectiveness. The conflicting agendas of the various stakeholders are analysed as the fundamental sources of the confusion over objectives. In the section on 'Educating Managers and Managerial Culture' the authors go on to illustrate how they think university academics can best contribute to the education of practising managers. Leadership, responsibility and business ethics emerge as the most desirable subjects.

The remaining two articles in Part 1 illustrate that ethical requirements are pertinent for managers at all levels of performance and decision making. In *Ethical dilemmas in performance appraisal revisited*, Clinton Longenecker and Dean Ludwig challenge the moral assumptions that lie behind individual performance appraisal, an integral part of any organization's performance improvement schemes. Too often, these activities become bureaucratized and taken for granted, although rarely popular. If we cannot (or deliberately will not, according to these authors) accurately assess whether staff are reaching their targets, we omit a crucial form of performance evaluation. However complex the organization and however automated its processes, most work is carried out and co-ordinated by individual human beings. The authors suggest fascinating social, psychological and philosophical reasons why assessing each other is such a difficult process, and demand that we think more deeply about its implications.

John Blunden's article is again very different from the others. Tracing the history of environmental influences on industry, he again raises issues of moral as well as financial performance, and the way in which the interests of more and more key stakeholders are gradually coming to be recognized by large organizations. 'Green' issues now appear in more and more strategic plans, and it is debatable whether their rise is far more than good public relations. Organizations need to know how to weigh up their impact on their external environments – creating a need for new and challenging performance measures.

1
The performance measurement manifesto*

Robert G. Eccles

Revolutions begin long before they are officially declared. For several years, senior executives in a broad range of industries have been rethinking how to measure the performance of their businesses. They have recognized that new strategies and competitive realities demand new measurement systems. Now they are deeply engaged in defining and developing those systems for their companies.

At the heart of this revolution lies a radical decision: to shift from treating financial figures as the foundation for performance measurement to treating them as one among a broader set of measures. Put like this, it hardly sounds revolutionary. Many managers can honestly claim that they – and their companies – have tracked quality, market share, and other nonfinancial measures for years. Tracking these measures is one thing. But giving them equal (or even greater) status in determining strategy, promotions, bonuses, and other rewards is another. Until that happens, to quote Ray Stata, the CEO of Analog Devices, 'When conflicts arise, financial considerations win out.'[1]

The ranks of companies enlisting in this revolution are rising daily. Senior managers at one large, high-tech manufacturer recently took direct responsibility for adding customer satisfaction, quality, market share, and human resources to their formal measurement system. The impetus was their realization that the company's existing system, which was largely financial, undercut its strategy, which focused on customer service. At a smaller manufacturer, the catalyst was a leveraged recapitalization that gave the CEO the opportunity formally to reorder the company's priorities. On the new list, earnings per share dropped to last place, preceded by customer satisfaction, cash flow, manufacturing effectiveness, and innovation (in that order). On the old list, earnings per share stood first and almost alone.

In both companies, the CEOs believe they have initiated a sea change in how their managers think about business performance and in the decisions they make. Executives at other companies engaged in comparable efforts feel the same – rightly. What gets measured gets attention, particularly when rewards are tied to the measures. Grafting new measures onto an old accounting-driven performance system or making slight adjustments in existing incentives accomplishes little. Enhanced competitiveness depends on starting from scratch and asking: 'Given our strategy, what are the most important measures of performance?' 'How do these measures relate to one another?' 'What measures truly predict long-term financial success in our businesses?'

---

* This article was first published in *Harvard Business Review*, January–February 1991, pp. 131–137.

Dissatisfaction with using financial measures to evaluate business performance is nothing new. As far back as 1951, Ralph Cordiner, the CEO of General Electric, commissioned a high-level task force to identify key corporate performance measures. (The categories the task force singled out were timeless and comprehensive: in addition to profitability, the list included market share, productivity, employee attitudes, public responsibility, and the balance between short and long-term goals.) But the current wave of discontent is not just more of the same.

One important difference is the intensity and nature of the criticism directed at traditional accounting systems. During the past few years, academics and practitioners have begun to demonstrate that accrual-based performance measures are at best obsolete – and more often harmful.[2] Diversity in products, markets, and business units puts a big strain on rules and theories developed for smaller, less complex organizations. More dangerously, the numbers these systems generate often fail to support the investments in new technologies and markets that are essential for successful performance in global markets.

Such criticisms reinforce concern about the pernicious effects of short-term thinking on the competitiveness of U.S. companies. Opinions on the causes of this mind-set differ. Some blame the investment community, which presses relentlessly for rising quarterly earnings. Others cite senior managers themselves, charging that their typically short tenure fosters short-sightedness. The important point is that the mind-set exists. Ask almost any senior manager and you will hear about some company's failure to make capital investments or pursue long-term strategic objectives that would imperil quarterly earnings targets.

Moreover, to the extent that managers do focus on reported quarterly earnings – and thereby reinforce the investment community's short-term perspective and expectations – they have a strong incentive to manipulate the figures they report. The extent and severity of such gaming is hard to document. But few in management deny that it goes on or that managers' willingness to play the earnings game calls into question the very measures the market focuses on to determine stock prices. For this reason, many managers, analysts, and financial economists have begun to focus on cash flow in the belief that it reflects a company's economic condition more accurately than its reported earnings do.[3]

Finally, many managers worry that income-based financial figures are better at measuring the consequences of yesterday's decisions than they are at indicating tomorrow's performance. Events of the past decade substantiate this concern. During the 1980s, many executives saw their companies' strong financial records deteriorate because of unnoticed declines in quality or customer satisfaction or because global competitors ate into their market share. Even managers who have not been hurt feel the need for preventive action. A senior executive at one of the large money-center banks, for example, grew increasingly uneasy about the European part of his business, its strong financials notwithstanding. To address that concern, he has nominated several new measures (including customer satisfaction, customers' perceptions of the bank's stature and professionalism and market share) to serve as leading indicators of the business's performance.

Discontent turns into rebellion when people see an alternative worth fighting for. During the 1980s, many managers found such an alternative in the quality movement. Leading manufacturers and service providers alike have come to see quality as a strategic weapon in their competitive battles. As a result, they have committed substantial resources to developing measures such as defect rates, response time, delivery commitments, and the like to evaluate the performance of their products, services, and operations.

In addition to pressure from global competitors, a major impetus for these efforts has been the growth of the Total Quality Movement and related programs such as the Malcolm Baldrige National Quality Award. (Before a company can even apply for a Baldrige Award, it must devise criteria to measure the performance of its entire operation – not just its products – in minute detail.) Another impetus, getting stronger by the day, comes from large manufacturers who are more and more likely to impose rigid quality requirements on their suppliers. Whatever the stimulus, the result is the same: quality measures represent the most positive step taken to date in broadening the basis of business performance measurement.

Another step in the same direction comes from embryonic efforts to generate measures of customer satisfaction. What quality was for the 1980s, customer satisfaction will be for the 1990s. Work on this class of measures is the highest priority at the two manufacturing companies discussed earlier. It is equally critical at another high-tech company that recently created a customer satisfaction department reporting directly to the CEO. In each case, management's interest in developing new performance measures was triggered by strategies emphasizing customer service.

As competition continues to stiffen, strategies that focus on quality will evolve naturally into strategies based on customer service. Indeed, this is already happening at many leading companies. Attention to customer satisfaction, which measures the quality of customer service, is a logical next step in the development of quality measures. Companies will continue to measure quality on the basis of internally generated indexes (such as defect rates) that are presumed to relate to customer satisfaction. But they will also begin to evaluate their performance by collecting data directly from customers for more direct measures like customer retention rates, market share, and perceived value of goods and services.

Just as quality-related metrics have made the performance measurement revolution more real, so has the development of competitive benchmarking.[4] First, benchmarking gives managers a methodology that can be applied to any measure, financial or nonfinancial, but that emphasizes nonfinancial metrics. Second (and less obvious), it has a transforming effect on managerial mind-sets and perspectives.

Benchmarking involves identifying competitors and/or companies in other industries that exemplify best practice in some activity, function, or process and then comparing one's own performance to theirs. This externally oriented approach makes people aware of improvements that are orders of magnitude beyond what they would have thought possible. In contrast, internal yardsticks that measure current performance in relation to prior period results, current budget, or the results of other units within the company rarely have such an eye-opening effect. Moreover, these internally focused comparisons have the disadvantage of breeding complacency through a false sense of security and of stirring up more energy for intramural rivalry than for competition in the marketplace.

Finally, information technology has played a critical role in making a performance measurement revolution possible. Thanks to dramatically improved price-performance ratios in hardware and to breakthroughs in software and database technology, organizations can generate, disseminate, analyze, and store more information from more sources, for more people, more quickly and cheaply than was conceivable even a few years back. The potential of new technologies such as hand-held computers for employees in the field and executive information systems for senior managers, is only beginning to be explored. Overall, the range of measurement options that are economically feasible has radically increased.

Veterans know it is easier to preach revolution than to practice it. Even the most favourable climate can create only the potential for revolutionary change. Making it happen requires conviction, careful preparation, perseverance, and a decided taste for ambiguity. As yet, there are no clear-cut answers or predetermined processes for managers who wish to change their measurement systems. Based on the experience of companies engaged in this revolution, I can identify five areas of activity that sooner or later need to be addressed: developing an information architecture; putting the technology in place to support this architecture; aligning incentives with the new system, drawing on outside resources; and designing a process to ensure that the other four activities occur.

Developing a new information architecture must be the first activity on any revolutionary agenda. Information architecture is an umbrella term for the categories of information needed to manage a company's businesses, the methods the company uses to generate this information, and the rules regulating its flow. In most companies, the accounting system implicitly defines the information architecture. Other performance measures are likely to be informal – records that operating managers keep for themselves, for instance – and they are rarely integrated into the corporate-driven financial system.

The design for a new corporate information architecture begins with the data that management needs to pursue the company's strategy. This may sound like a truism, but a surprising number of companies describe their strategies in terms of customer service, innovation, or the quality and capabilities of their people, yet do little to measure these variables. Even time – the newest strategic variable – remains largely underdeveloped in terms of which time-based metrics are most important and how best to measure them.

As part of this identification process, management needs to articulate a new corporate grammar and define its own special vocabulary – the basic terms that will need to be common and relatively invariant across all the company's businesses. Some of these terms (like sales and costs) will be familiar. Others, however, will reflect new strategic priorities and ways to think about measuring performance. For example, both a large money-center bank and a multidivisional, high-technology manufacturer introduced the use of cross-company customer identification numbers so they could readily track such simple and useful information as the total amount of business the company did with any one customer. It sounds elementary and it is – as soon as you start to look at the entire measurement system from scratch.

Uniformity can be carried too far. Different businesses with different strategies require different information for decision making and performance measurement. But this should not obscure the equally obvious fact that every company needs to have at least a few critical terms in common. Today few large companies do. Years of acquisitions and divestitures, technological limitations, and at times, a lack of management discipline have all left most big organizations with a complicated hodgepodge of definitions and variables – and with the bottom line their only common denominator.

Developing a coherent, companywide grammar is particularly important in light of an ever-more stringent competitive environment. For many companies, ongoing structural reorganizations are a fact of life. The high-technology company described above has reorganized itself 24 times in the past 4 years (in addition to a number of divisional and functional restructurings) to keep pace with changes in its markets and technologies. Rather than bewail the situation, managers relish it and see their capacity for fast adaptation as an important competitive advantage.

A common grammar also enhances management's ability to break apart and recombine product lines and market segments to form new business units. At a major merchant bank, for example, the organization is so fluid that one senior executive likens it to a collection of hunting packs that form to pursue business opportunities and then disband as the market windows on those opportunities close. The faster the company can assemble information for newly formed groups, the greater the odds of success. So this executive (who calls himself the czar of information) has been made responsible for developing standard definitions for key information categories.

How a company generates the performance data it needs is the second piece of its information architecture. Not surprisingly, methods for measuring financial performance are the most sophisticated and the most deeply entrenched. Accountants have been refining these methods ever since double-entry bookkeeping was invented in the fifteenth century. Today their codifications are enforced by a vast institutional infrastructure made up of professional educators, public accounting firms, and regulatory bodies.

In contrast, efforts to measure market share, quality, innovation, human resources, and customer satisfaction have been much more modest. Data for tracking these measures are generated less often: quarterly, annual, or even biannual bases are common. Responsibility for them typically rests with a specific function. (Strategic planning measures market share, for example, while engineering measures innovation and so on.) They rarely become part of the periodic reports general managers receive.

Placing these new measures on an equal footing with financial data takes significant resources. One approach is to assign a senior executive to each of the measures and hold him or her responsible for developing its methodologies. Typically, these executives come from the function that is most experienced in dealing with the particular measure. But they work with a multifunctional task force to ensure that managers throughout the company will understand the resulting measures and find them useful. Another, less common, approach is to create a new function focused on one measure and then to expand its mandate over time.

A unit responsible for customer satisfaction might subsequently take on market share, for example, or the company's performance in human resources.

Unlike a company's grammar, which should be fairly stable, methods for taking new performance measures should evolve as the company's expertise increases. Historical comparability may suffer in the process, but this is a minor loss. What matters is how a company is doing compared with its current competitors, not with its own past.

The last component of a corporate information architecture is the set of rules that governs the flow of information. Who is responsible for how measures are taken? Who actually generates the data? Who receives and analyzes them? Who is responsible for changing the rules? Because information is an important source of power, the way a company answers these questions matters deeply. How open or closed a company is affects how individuals and groups work together, as well as the relative influence people and parts of the company have on its strategic direction and management. Some companies make information available on a very limited basis. At others, any individual can request information from another unit as long as he or she can show why it is needed. Similarly, in some companies the CEO still determines who gets what information – not a very practical alternative in today's world. More often what happens is that those who possess information decide with whom they will share it.

Advances in information technology such as powerful workstations, open architectures, and relational databases vastly increase the options for how information can flow. It may be centralized at the top, so that senior executives can make even more decisions than they have in the past. Or it may be distributed to increase the decision-making responsibilities of people at every level. The advantages of making information widely available are obvious, though this also raises important questions that need to be addressed about the data's integrity and security. In principle, however, this portion of the information architecture ought to be the most flexible of the three, so that the company's information flows continue to change as the conditions it faces do.

Determining the hardware, software, and telecommunications technology a company needs to generate its new measurement information is the second activity in the performance revolution. This task is hard enough in its own right, given the many choices available. But too often managers make it even harder by going directly to a technology architecture without stopping first to think through their information needs. This was the case at a high-tech manufacturing company that was growing more and more frustrated with its information systems planning committee. Then the CEO realized that he and the other senior managers had not determined the measures they wanted before setting up the committee. Equipped with that information, the committee found it relatively easy to choose the right technology.

Once the information architecture and supporting technology are in place, the next step is to align the new system with the company's incentives – to reward people in proportion to their performance on the measures that management has said truly matter. This is easier said than done. In many companies, the compensation system limits the amount and range of the salary increases, bonuses, and stock options that management can award.

In companies that practice pay-for-performance, compensation and other rewards are often tied fairly mechanically to a few key financial measures such as profitability and return on investment. Convincing managers that a newly implemented system is really going to be followed can be a hard sell. The president of one service company let each of his division general managers design the performance measures that were most appropriate for his or her particular business. Even so, the managers still felt the bottom line was all that would matter when it came to promotions and pay.

The difficulty of aligning incentives to performance is heightened by the fact that formulas for tying the two together are rarely effective. Formulas have the advantage of looking objective, and they spare managers the unpleasantness of having to conduct truly frank performance appraisals. But if the formula is simple and focuses on a few key variables, it inevitably leaves some important measures out. Conversely, if the formula is complex and factors in all the variables that require attention, people are likely to find it confusing and may start to play games with the numbers. Moreover, the relative importance of the variables is certain to change more often – and faster – than the whole incentive system can change.

For these reasons, I favor linking incentives strongly to performance but leaving managers free to determine their subordinates' rewards on the basis of all the relevant information, qualitative as well as quantitative. Then it is up to the manager to explain candidly to subordinates why they received what they did. For most managers, this will also entail learning to conduct effective performance appraisals, an indirect – and invaluable – benefit of overhauling the measurement system.

Outside parties such as industry and trade associations, third-party data vendors, information technology companies, consulting firms, and public accounting firms must also become part of the performance measurement revolution. Their incentive: important business opportunities.

Industry and trade associations can play a very helpful role in identifying key performance measures, researching methodologies for taking these measures, and supplying comparative statistics to their members – so can third-party data vendors. Competitors are more likely to supply information to a neutral party (which can disguise it and make it available to all its members or customers) than to one another. And customers are more likely to provide information to a single data vendor than to each of their suppliers separately.

Consulting firms and information technology vendors also have important roles to play in forwarding the revolution. Firms that specialize in strategy formulation, for example, often have well-developed methods for assessing market share and other performance metrics that clients could be trained to use. Similarly, firms that focus on strategy implementation have a wealth of experience designing systems of various kinds for particular functions such as manufacturing and human resources. While many of these firms are likely to remain specialized, and thus require coordination by their clients, others will surely expand their capabilities to address all the pieces of the revolution within a client company.

Much the same thing is apt to happen among vendors of information technology. In addition to helping companies develop the technological architecture they need, some companies will see opportunities to move into a full range of services that use the hardware as a technology platform. IBM and DEC are already moving in this direction, impelled in part by the fact that dramatic gains in price-performance ratios make it harder and harder to make money selling 'boxes'.

Finally, public accounting firms have what may be the single most critical role in this revolution. On one hand, they could inhibit its progress in the belief that their vested interest in the existing system is too great to risk. On the other hand, all the large firms have substantial consulting practices, and the revolution represents a tremendous business opportunity for them. Companies will need a great deal of help developing new measures, validating them, and certifying them for external use.

Accounting firms also have an opportunity to develop measurement methods that will be common to an industry or across industries. While this should not be overdone, one reason financial measures carry such weight is that they are assumed to be a uniform metric, comparable across divisions and companies, and thus a valid basis for resource allocation decisions. In practice, of course, these measures are not comparable (despite the millions of hours invested in efforts to make them so) because companies use different accounting conventions. Given that fact, it is easy to see why developing additional measures that senior managers – and the investment community – can use will be a massive undertaking.

Indeed, the power of research analysts and investors generally is one of the reasons accounting firms have such a crucial role to play. Although evidence exists that investors are showing more interest in metrics such as market share and cash flow, many managers and analysts identify the investment community as the chief impediment to revolution.[5] Until investors treat other measures as seriously as financial data, they argue, limits will always exist on how seriously those measures are taken inside companies.

GE's experience with its measurement task force supports their argument. According to a knowledgeable senior executive, the 1951 effort had only a modest effect because the measures believed to determine the company's stock price, to which incentives were tied, were all financial: earnings per share, return on equity, return on investment, return on sales, and earnings growth rate. He believed that once the financial markets valued other measures, progress within companies would accelerate.

Investors, of course, see the problem from a different perspective. They question whether managers would be willing to publish anything more than the financial information required by the SEC lest they reveal too much to their competitors. Ultimately, a regulatory body like the SEC could untie this Gordian knot by recommending (and eventually requiring) public companies to provide nonfinancial measures in their reports. (This is, after all, how financial standards became so omnipotent and why so many millions of hours have been invested in their development.) But I suspect competitive pressure will prove a more immediate force for change. As soon as one leading company can demonstrate the long-term advantage of its superior performance on quality or innovation or any other nonfinancial measure, it will change the rules for all its rivals forever. And with so many serious competitors tracking – and enhancing – these measures, that is only a matter of time.

Designing a process to ensure that all these things happen is the last aspect of the revolution. To overcome conservative forces outside the company and from within (including line and staff managers at every level, in every function), someone has to take the lead. Ultimately, this means the CEO. If the CEO is not committed, the revolution will flounder, no matter how much enthusiasm exists throughout the organization.

But the CEO cannot make it happen. Developing an information architecture and its accompanying technology, aligning incentives, working with outside parties – all this requires many people and a lot of work, much of it far less interesting than plotting strategy. Moreover, the design of the process must take account of the integrative nature of the task: people in different businesses and functions including strategic planning, engineering, manufacturing, marketing and sales, human resources, and finance will all have something to contribute. The work of external players will have to be integrated with the company's own efforts.

Organizationally, two critical choices exist. One is who the point person will be. Assigning this role to the CEO or president ensures its proper symbolic visibility. Delegating it to a high-level line or staff executive and making it a big piece of his or her assignment may be a more effective way to guarantee that enough senior management time will be devoted to the project.

The other choice is which function or group will do most of the work and coordinate the company's efforts. The CEO of one high-tech company gave this responsibility to the finance function because he felt they should have the opportunity to broaden their perspective and measurement skills. He also thought it would be easier to use an existing group experienced in performance measurement. The president of an apparel company made a different choice. To avoid the financial bias embedded in the company's existing management information systems, he wanted someone to start from scratch and design a system with customer service at its core. As a result, he is planning to combine the information systems department with customer service to create a new function to be headed by a new person, recruited from the outside.

What is most effective for a given company will depend on its history, culture, and management style. But every company should make the effort to attack the problem with new principles. Some past practices may still be useful, but everything should be strenuously challenged. Otherwise, the effort will yield incremental changes at best.

Open-mindedness about the structures and processes that will be most effective, now and in the future, is equally important. I know of a few companies that are experimenting with combining the information systems and human resource departments. These experiments have entailed a certain amount of culture shock for professionals from both functions, but such radical rethinking is what revolution is all about.

Finally, recognize that once begun, this is a revolution that never ends. We are not simply talking about changing the basis of performance measurement from financial statistics to something else. We are talking about a new philosophy of performance measurement that regards it as an ongoing, evolving process. And just as igniting the revolution will take special effort, so will maintaining its momentum and reaping the rewards in the years ahead.

Notes

[1] Ray Stata, 'Organizational learning – the key to management innovation,' *Sloan Management Review,* Spring 1989, pp. 63–74.

[2] Donald A. Curtis, 'The modern accounting system,' *Financial Executive,* January–February 1985, pp. 81–93; and H. Thomas Johnson and Robert S. Kaplan, *Relevance Lost* (Boston: Harvard Business School Press, 1987).

[3] Yuji Ijiri, 'Cash flow accounting and its structure,' *Journal of Accounting, Auditing and Finance,* Summer 1978, pp. 331–348.

[4] Robert C. Camp, *Benchmarking* (Milwaukee, Wisconsin: ASQS Quality Press, 1989).

[5] 'Investors: look at firms' market share', *Wall Street Journal,* February 26, 1990, pp. C1–2.

2

Organisational control and management accounting*

Jeremy Dent and Mahmoud Ezzamel

The notion of organisational control is susceptible to many different interpretations. Different researchers approach the topic from their own particular backgrounds and stress different aspects of the totality of the organisational control process. For the purposes of this article, however, it seems sensible to adopt a broad definition of organisational control, which will then be used to consider the contribution of management accounting.

The need for a mechanism for the internal control of an organisation is self evident. It arises from the fundamental nature of organisations. The organisation embodies a coalition of participants. Each participant may have his own, possibly divergent, demands and some discretion in his choice of actions. Organisational control may be interpreted as the problem of ensuring some consistency in organisational activities. But demands change over time. The operating characteristics of the organisation evolve. Information is unevenly distributed. Participants may engage in strategic manoeuvring. Organisational control is thus complex and multifaceted.

In this article it is argued that the study of organisational control has been only partial. Researchers tend to concentrate on different elements of the control process and often ignore the complexities of the organisational context. Yet it precisely the complex interaction between different controls which gives organisations their coherence in a dynamic evolving world.

Section I of this article contains a description of some traditional approaches to the problems of organisational control, and their influence on accounting research. Section II contains a discussion of a somewhat modified systems approach to characterise the interconnectedness of organisational functioning in an explicit way. Section III considers the ambiguous role of information in organisational control, and section IV presents a framework for analysis. In section V conclusions are drawn, and implications for future research are discussed.

I Some traditional approaches to organisational control

Consider, for a moment, a moderately-sized manufacturing organisation operating in a relatively stable environment. The organisation may be subject to a range

*This article was first published in *Advanced Management Accounting: An Organisational Emphasis*, edited by M. Ezzamel and H. Hart (1987), pp. 86–112.

of conflicting demands. It may market a number of products. It may have a complex technology with production centred at several different locations. It may have a critical flow of resources between production centres. Information about the environment and the operating characteristics of the organisation may be concentrated at localised points. Such data as is transmitted to other members may be biased or randomly inaccurate, and subject to processing delay. The task of coordinating the separate activities of such an organisation is likely to be formidable. Moreover, recognition of environmental/technological change and instability adds a further dimension to the control process. Effective control implies some sensitivity to changing patterns of demand, technology, and economic and social expectations.

The classical approach to control

Not unnaturally writers from different disciplines respond to the complexity of the problem in different ways. For example, in what Arrow (1964) was termed the 'classical businessman's view' emphasis is placed on the need for decentralised coordination. In this approach the problem of control is tackled through the establishment of one integrated plan of action for the organisation as a whole. The plan is devolved into a series of specific coordinated tasks for each segment or participant in the organisation. Formal rules and procedures limit the discretion required at lower levels in the organisation. Emphasis is placed on vertical control through the line of authority. Centralised coordination is seen as essential in the face of the sheer complexity of organisational operations.

Such is the essence of the classical approach to management. The central planners are considered to have superior knowledge of the interrelationship and operating characteristics of the organisation. Moreover they are presumed to be better able to take a corporate view of the organisation and its interrelationship with the environment. Tasks are unambiguously defined. Minimal flexibility is permitted to subordinates. Power, in the sense of the formal authority conferred by the organisational hierarchy, is relied upon. Compliance is engineered through the use of sanctions and rewards.

In contrast, other theorists have tended to argue that the centralised approach to organisational control is potentially sub-optimal (e.g. Williamson, 1975). For one thing it is likely to be inefficient. As the size and complexity of the firm increases the centralised approach may impose a considerable load on the planning authorities. Extra communication channels will be required to transmit organisational and environmental data to the planning officials, and detailed plans to lower organisational levels. Moreover, centralisation may not be particularly effective. Data typically does not flow noiselessly within an information system. Random errors occur, filtering effects take place and biases are introduced. Thus plans may not reflect the underlying circumstances of the firm. Nor is the centralised approach instantaneous. Data communication is subject to delay, plans take time to be prepared. In a dynamic environment adaptation may be impaired.

These researchers have considered the possibility of developing a decentralised alternative to the problem of organisational control. If, it is argued, the firm can be treated as a number of semi-autonomous sub-units, and decision making devolved to those levels in the organisation where information is available at first hand, so it may be possible to increase the efficiency and the effectiveness of control procedures. Data is likely to be more accurate. The load on communication channels is reduced as operating decisions are taken by local managers. Subordinates are also encouraged to adapt to prevailing circumstances.

Of course, there are likely to be problems in coordinating the actions of individual decision makers. Far-reaching interdependencies may exist between sub-units, for example, in the form of resource transfers between units, or in the form of external effects imposed by some units upon others. The full extent of these interdependencies may not be immediately apparent to decision makers at the operating level, neither may there be any incentive for local managers to take them into account. Certain units may be in a position of power relative to others and there may be a temptation to engage in 'unfair practices' detrimental to the organisation as a whole. Various structural and financial controls have been designed to address these problems.

Such a liberal approach to organisational control may be appealing. Nevertheless, on closer inspection one is inclined to focus on potential difficulties in implementation. The problem posed by intraorganisation externalities, for instance, is quite significant. The control of externalities through the price mechanism is known to be feasible (e.g. Collard, 1973), but it will generally necessitate some measure of centralised planning (Davis and Whinston, 1962). The recognition of uncertainty further complicates the issue. Each sub-unit manager will face a choice under uncertainty, and his choices will depend partly on his attitude towards risk. In the absence of insurance against uncertain consequences or specific reward structures such as those discussed in the theory of agency (e.g. Holmstrom, 1979) only by chance will local managers take appropriate decisions.

Neoclassical approaches to control

The efficiency and effectiveness of decentralised control is, therefore, debatable: the optimal strategy in any particular situation is not clear cut. A priori, no particular procedure can be unambiguously defended. To an extent, however, the issues of control are only partially addressed by such mechanistic considerations. Cyert and March (1963), for example, focus on the divergent goals of individual participants, and on the conflict and bargaining that takes place within the organisation. In their analysis, organisations are perceived to exist and thrive with considerable latent conflict of goals. The formal and informal bargaining procedures that are developed are fundamental elements of the organisational control process; hence the attention given to organisational equilibrium (inducements–contribution theory, March and Simon, 1958), and side payments (Cyert and March, 1963). Control, in this sense, is not predominantly a problem of formal structure, but a behavioural or social problem.

This issue is touched upon in the structural analysis. The classical view, for example, is characterised by the assertion that man is naturally lazy and wasteful, and that appropriate behaviour can be bought by an exchange of money. The formal reward structure is an essential element of the classical 'control package'. This presumption forms the basis of the economic analysis of agency theory. On the other hand, much of the economic literature on decentralisation takes conflict as non-problematic (e.g. Marschak and Radner, 1972). The immense diversity of individual needs and aspirations is a distinguishing feature of organisations, and should be recognised in the analysis of organisational control.

This focus on the richer social and psychological aspects of organisations has been the hallmark of neoclassical organisational researchers. Principles of specialisation, hierarchy and impersonality are held to frustrate individual needs for autonomy, responsibility and self-actualisation (e.g. McGregor, 1960; Likert, 1961). Effective performance, these writers have argued, is only obtained when tasks are made intrinsically stimulating and rewarding. Job enlargement and job enrichment programmes are advocated to increase the size, scope and variety of work (e.g. Herzberg, 1966). Participation schemes and management-by-objectives are advocated to encourage ego-identification with corporate goals (e.g. Bennis, 1966). The emphasis on job involvement and self control is central to the human resources analysis of organisational control.

In a slightly different vein, the human relations school, including such writers as Lewin (1947) and Likert (1961), have stressed the role of groups and the informal organisation in influencing organisational activities. Groups, particularly cohesive groups, it is argued, exert a powerful influence on behaviour. Individuals have affiliative needs which can be satisfied by a group, such as a sense of belonging, support, reinforcement, security, encouragement and so on. Membership of a group involves mutual commitment and shared ideals. From these develop attitudinal norms and behavioural expectations. Discipline is enforced through a system of informal sanctions and rewards. Group support may be withdrawn. Members may be ridiculed or ostracised (e.g. Tannenbaum, 1966).

Group pressure is thus a potentially significant source of control which should be harnessed towards organisational effectiveness. According to Likert (1961) intergroup conflict should be handled by explicit incorporation of 'linking pins' in organisational design. Change should be managed through consensus and group acceptance. The creation of a supportive work environment is considered to be central to high morale and efficiency. Thus, it is argued, the consideration and initiating dimensions of leadership are crucial elements in organisational control (e.g. Halpin and Winer, 1957).

The human orientation of neoclassical organisation theory stands in some contrast to the structural and economic orientation. The emphasis on individual aspirations and group cohesiveness adds another dimension to the control process. On the other hand, the position of these researchers is almost ideological. Conflict is treated as evil, symptomatic of poor management, and something to be eliminated. Harmony and consensus are seen as indicative of good health (Baritz, 1960). Yet this proposition is equivocal at best. Unresolved conflict may be good or bad; it may generate functional and dysfunctional consequences (Pondy, 1967). Consensus may breed complacency and an unquestioning acceptance of the status quo. Organisations may need a measure of conflict to stimulate change and innovation.

Implications for accounting

These approaches do illustrate different conceptions of control, and they have each had their impact on accounting thought. The authoritarian approach to organisational control has been the basis for much of the traditional practice of management accounting. Budgetary procedures serve to facilitate control through centralisation. Targets are specified for each functional area of the firm. Variance analysis procedures serve to reinforce the threat of sanctions and rewards. As the firm's environment becomes increasingly hostile or dynamic, or its operations increasingly complex and interdependent, so a greater emphasis is placed on the need for budgetary control. Budgets become tighter; standards become more rigorously enforced and formal authority becomes more in evidence (e.g. Argyris, 1952; Caplan, 1968).

The human orientation of neoclassical theory has led to an impressive volume of accounting research into the motivational impact of budgets (e.g. Hofstede, 1967; Stedry, 1960; Tosi, 1975), covering such issues as the impact of budgets on dysfunctional managerial behaviour (e.g. Schiff and Lewin, 1970; Hopwood, 1972; Otley, 1978), the effects of budgetary participation (e.g. Becker and Green, 1962; Searfoss and Monczka, 1973; Kenis, 1979), the accounting implications of group dynamics (e.g. Flamholtz, 1975) and human resource accounting (e.g. Flamholtz, 1972).

Similarly the research on decentralisation has led to the development of measures for assessing the financial performance of decentralised units (e.g. Solomons, 1963) and evaluations of transfer pricing mechanisms (e.g. Abdel-khalik and Lusk, 1974).

But, underlying this research are implicit assumptions about the nature of organisational control and the role of accounting in organisational functioning. Control is perceived as a homogeneous goal-oriented process. Objectives for accounting are taken as unambiguous. In reality, however, organisations are complex and multi-faceted. Goals may be loosely articulated (March, 1979). Controls may exhibit a measure of inconsistency (Westerlund and Sjostrand, 1979). Accounting may serve in a multiplicity of roles (Burchell *et al.*, 1980). Guided, or perhaps confused, by the conflicting pressures of many interacting forces, organisations sustain a chaotic existence.

Thus there is a need to focus explicitly on accounting in its subtle organisational context to draw out its role in organisational control (Hopwood, 1978; Burchell *et al.*, 1980). A valid model of organisations must at least attempt to integrate the various processes of organisational control in order to portray one organic interacting whole. It must explicitly focus on the richness and diversity of the organisation, its participants and its procedures, both formal and informal. Only such an aggregate view is likely to present a coherent picture of the organisational control process. Such a view seems to be lacking in the accounting literature.

To develop this theme the next section describes first the cybernetic approach to organisational control and then some recent developments in systems thinking. This approach, it is claimed, provides an integrated framework for organisational analysis. The third section examines more specifically the role of accounting in organisational control.

II A systems–cybernetics approach to organisational control

The holistic emphasis is the hallmark of a systems approach to organisational analysis. Within a general systems theory (GST) framework no system is isolated from the universe of systems. The universe is characterised as an indivisible and interacting whole. But it is precisely this highly complex interaction which endows systems with control, which drives them towards a dynamic coherence. Systems rely quite fundamentally on interaction for their viability.

Of course, there may be operational problems in analysing interactions within the universal system. Conceptually it may be difficult to define boundaries between sub-systems. But, in general, sub-systems consisting of less than the whole can be recognised. At any particular level in the hierarchy of systems, boundaries can be drawn round some sets of phenomena and sub-systems and their interactions with their immediate environments can be identified. With an appropriate degree of resolution (Lowe and McInnes, 1971) some arbitrary level of elementary systems (a convenient unit of analysis) can be focused upon. By successively addressing the communication patterns between elementary systems and between systems and their immediate environments, an understanding of the interconnectedness of the whole can be attained. This is the approach of cybernetics. It is claimed to provide a vehicle for reconciling the holistic approach of GST with the practical problems of designing systems for control. By explicitly facing the complexity of the world this philosophy is designed to achieve effective control.

The analysis of Ashby (1956, 1960) identified self-regulation and self-veto as the essential elements for a cybernetic design. A necessary condition for self-regulation is the characteristic error-controlled negative feedback loop: a mechanism capable of continuously monitoring the state of a process and automatically feeding back appropriate corrective signals. This presupposes that the control mechanism exhibits the requisite degree of variety (Ashby, 1956), and has sufficient information carrying capacity (Shannon and Weaver, 1949). The variety of potential control signals must be at least sufficient to control the variety of possible states: 'Only variety can absorb variety'. Now consider two finely-balanced, interacting, self-regulating systems, and let the first system be subjected to some disturbance. If its balance is upset, the self-regulatory mechanism will act to restore its internal equilibrium. But this change in the state of the first system may have some consequential effect on the balance of the second system, whereupon the self-regulatory mechanism of the second system acts to restore its internal equilibrium. But this change in the state of the second system may in turn destroy the balance of the first system, and so the cycle repeats itself.

Loosely speaking, Ashby (1960) has argued that this self-vetoing facility, coupled with requisite variety, is sufficient to ensure ultimate coordination and stability. For, in the absence of intermediate disturbance, the self-vetoing process must inevitably lead to the attainment of a mutually compatible combination of states, even as a consequence of random mutation. This is the operation of the 'homeostat'.

The world, however, is characterised by change, and casual observation suggests that the rate of change tends to increase over time. How then is stability to be engineered? If on average the interval between successive disturbances approaches the time taken for the system to stabilise, then there will be a tendency to oscillate interminably. Indeed, Beer (1966, ch. 16) has argued that Ashby's trial and error hypothesis is simply insufficient to explain the apparent order of the universe. This view is widely accepted by modern systems theorists (e.g. Jantsch, 1980). Certainly, random mutations are an essential prerequisite for adaptation, for it is mainly through experimentation that knowledge is acquired; but some more purposive explanation is required.

In Beer's (1966) analysis this is accomplished through the concept of memory. If the system is endowed with memory, in the sense of some sequential learning device capable of absorbing the past history of the system, then bias is introduced into the random mutations of the self-vetoing process. More specifically, if positive reinforcement is introduced through an approximation to the Bayesian probability revision procedures of statistical decision theory, then, so it is argued, the dynamics of the system can be structured so as to ensure progressive convergence towards a global consistency. As Beer (1966, p. 368) commented:

> Nature does not lead an exact or even closely predictable process here: nor does the cybernetician. It is enough that the mutations of an adapting system should not be entirely hazardous, but should be biased, for positive feedback can be relied upon to steer the progressive bias towards viable behaviour – once the bias exists.

The cybernetic design offers some insight into the problems of organisational control. These essentially simple concepts serve to structure effective stabilisation schemes even for highly complex interacting systems. Layer upon layer of self-regulating mechanisms are tightly knit together in the intricate homeostatic designs created by cyberneticians. Integrated information linkages serve to draw sub-systems into a coherent functional whole.

Cybernetic concepts form the basis for many of the more traditional management controls, for example, the principle of management by exception, or in a more specific context, budgetary control and variance analysis. But the cybernetic model is much richer in its implications than this. Control in the early cybernetic view was not perceived as authoritarian or coercive, rather it was based on principles of self-control and mutual adjustment (Ashby, 1960). Although this basis might appear to have been subverted in the work of later cybernetic theorists, principles of autonomy and flexibility are still claimed to lie at the heart of their designs (Beer, 1972). As systems exhibit a greater degree of variety so they become more difficult to control from without. The cybernetic design emphasises the importance of structuring for control from within.

This emphasis on self control is evident in the organisational literature. For example, it is frequently observed that as an organisation's environment becomes more dynamic or as its technology becomes more complex, so there will be a greater need to decentralise decision making (e.g. Burns and Stalker, 1961). As the degree of decentralisation increases, so there will be a greater need for lateral communications to coordinate interdependent activities (e.g. Lawrence and Lorsch, 1969). In a heavily centralised system, the variety encountered by the organisation will be transmitted hierarchically. Escalating through the system, it will tend to be amplified by interaction. Ultimately such a system might simply collapse from chronic overload. The cybernetic principle of self control, in contrast, absorbs variety 'like a sponge'. Variety is matched with variety.

One response to increasing variety is to increase the capacity of the information system to transmit data (Galbraith 1972, 1977). In situations of low variety this may be feasible. On the other hand, as variety increases beyond some limit, it may become impossible to make sense of the sheer volume of data in the system. At that point the controller becomes over-loaded (Beer, 1966; Kerr *et al.*, 1975). Organisations in fact respond in many ways in the face of variety. For example, they may establish buffer inventories to absorb environmental fluctuations (Thompson, 1967), or they may form cartels to suppress the variety in their environments. These examples are of organisations seeking to absorb variety at source. They are illustrations of structuring for self control.

In the accounting literature there has been some limited discussion of the principle of self control. The long-standing centralisation *v.* decentralisation debate may be interpreted as an attempt to introduce more flexibility at lower levels in the organisational structure. The discussion of responsibility centres – profit centres, investment centres and so on – is perhaps evidence of this development.

Similarly, certain behavioural studies can be considered in a cybernetic light. The interest in motivation is essentially oriented towards obtaining a higher degree of goal congruence between the individual and the organisation. In other words it is an attempt to internalise self control at the atomistic level. Expectancy models, for example, formalise a hypothetical relationship between work goal achievement and organisational reward structures (e.g. Vroom, 1964; Porter and Lawler, 1968; and in an accounting context, Ronen and Livingstone, 1975). The usefulness of this research in a cybernetic sense is to conceptualise the feedback loop at the lowest level. A similar analysis could be applied to some of the group dynamics research including some participation literature (e.g. Vroom, 1964; Becker and Green, 1962).

Nevertheless, despite this limited recognition of the importance of self control it is widely acknowledged that accounting controls in practice are basically coercive and authoritarian. They tend to emphasise control by imposition rather than control by mutual adjustment. For example, Caplan (1966) has argued that budgeting procedures are heavily centralised and rigidly structured. Some empirical evidence supports this observation (e.g. Argyris, 1952; Caplan, 1968). Moreover the hierarchical orientation of accounting information flows may simply be inadequate to cope with the degree of lateral communications necessary for the coordination and integration of decentralised organisational sub-systems (Lawrence and Lorsch, 1969; Galbraith, 1977).

The above discussion might be taken to imply an unqualified endorsement of the cybernetic model, but this is not the view intended here. The cybernetic model is very mechanistic in its conception, and imposes an unduly rationalistic framework for the analysis of organisational control. It posits the existence of a well-defined meta-systemic goal, and at least some degree of goal consensus amongst participants (Lilienfeld, 1978). But organisational goals may be ambiguous, conflicting, ill-defined and fluid (e.g. Hedberg and Jonsson, 1978). Moreover they may not even pre-exist organisational activities. It may be that goals serve only to rationalise past choices (Weick, 1979); or they may be the product of those choices (Lindblom, 1959; March, 1972, 1979). In addition, the cybernetic notion of adaptation is very narrowly conceived. As Ashby's (1960) concept of 'ultra-stability' suggests, the cybernetic design is predominantly concerned with stabilisation. It is dynamic only in the sense that the system is seen to be continually adapting to variety – its overriding emphasis is on the attainment of a predetermined set of goals within a given structure. In this view attention is centred on the equilibrium of the present. But in a dynamic sense the present is nothing more than the product of evolution. The environment not only exhibits variety, but is itself evolving. Adaptation is much more richly endowed. Goals evolve and continue to evolve, structures evolve and continue to evolve. The present is merely transient. Viable systems exhibit self-organising properties to carry them through tomorrow.

Self-organising properties

The cybernetic analysis has certainly furthered our understanding of the stabilisation of given structures within predetermined limits. But the motion of equilibrium which is frequently implied in the cybernetic analysis is restrictive. Equilibrium primarily focuses on the internal relationships in the system. External factors are acknowledged only in so far as they induce disequilibrium (Burrell and Morgan, 1979). The notion of equilibrium is inadequate for the study of socio-cultural systems whose morphogenic properties are distinctly different from those of biological and physical systems (Buckley, 1967). Thus, the dynamics of coherent systems, systems whose structure and form evolve themselves in a coherent way, have been only partially addressed.

The new evolving theory of systems dynamics, in contrast, centres attention on the natural and continuing evolution of disequilibrium systems (Jantsch, 1980) and on the dynamics of the process of change in the system and in its underlying structure (Buckley, 1967). The learning patterns foreseen by Beer (1966) are formalised into a macroscopic theory of evolution. Conflict is seen to reinforce change. Goals themselves become part of the wider evolutionary process. This theory addresses natural, self-organising adaptive capabilities. No longer is interest centred on the solid structure of the present. Equilibrium serves only to define the limiting form of today. The centre of interest is the dynamics of disequilibrium. The only stability observed is the extraordinary coherence induced by disequilibrium forces collectively driving the system towards self renewal and regeneration.

This richer notion of adaptation, with its emphasis on self organisation, is prominent in some of the more recent organisational literature. For example, Hedberg *et al.* (1976) discuss the paradoxical prescription for a self-designing organisation. Similarly Argyris and Schön (1978) emphasise the importance of designing organisational structures which facilitate learning and adaptation. Structure is no longer taken as an immutable given state. Rather it is seen as fluid and evolving.

Yet adaptation is almost antipathetic to the practice of management accounting. Controls, primarily, are centred on the internal order of the present. They emphasise a static state in the internal operations of the organisation. They take the state of the environment as given. They discourage innovation and experimentation. In the analysis of Katz and Kahn (1978) they serve as 'maintaining systems' – they operate to perpetuate the status quo. Their message is resistance and entrenchment. Relatively little attention is directed at change, at forces in the environment, at the evaluation of trends, towards the stimulation of adaptive behaviour.

There is no intention to imply that organisations have no need for maintaining systems. Organisational coherence emerges from the complex interplay of the many conflicting forces shaping organisational behaviour (Katz and Kahn, 1978; Hedberg *et al.*, 1976). There is a need in most organisations, most of the time, both for maintaining systems to soak up variety and preserve some stability, and for adaptive systems to stimulate innovation and experimentation. But this latter role seems to have been almost neglected in accounting practice, and to a great extent in the accounting literature. Not that innovation and experimentation are easy to stimulate; on the contrary, it is not immediately obvious how that may be achieved. Analysis, however, suggests that systems are triggered into adaptive responses; that unexpected outcomes reach some threshold beyond which systems are stimulated into search behaviour (March and Simon, 1958; Jantsch, 1980). There is also some consensus that standard operating procedures tend to filter away environmental inconsistencies and encourage a complacency towards environmental change (Cyert and March, 1963; Hedberg and Jonsson, 1978).

Accordingly, it may be appropriate to counteract this tendency by deliberately introducing ambiguity into accounting controls, for instance, by reporting a more diverse set of quantitative and non-quantitative data. Focusing on environmental inconsistencies in a non-reductionist approach might bring sub-systems into closer contact with their environments. Such 'semi-confusing' information would serve to destabilise the status quo, to trigger search behaviour at a lower threshold of environmental change. In a sense this would be an attempt to shift emphasis from problem solution, the traditional concern of management accounting, to problem identification. As Hedberg and Jonsson (1978) observe,

> there are information systems which offer less discretion to decision makers than others, and which lead to organisational rigidity; and there are information systems which stimulate organisations to experiment and innovate, and which foster organisational flexibility.

This destabilising role is far removed from the received philosophy of management accounting. The significance attached to flexibility, ambiguity and experimentation is in stark contrast to the rigidity and precision of traditional control procedures.

III Information and control

A central theme of the preceding analysis has been the significance attached to information flows. Indeed in the systems-cybernetics approach, effective control relies critically on appropriate information flows. As organisations encounter variety, so information flows support coordination and adaptation. This emphasis is not unique to cybernetic analysis, but recurs in a wide range of management literature. For instance, Lawrence and Lorsch (1969) observed that as organisations encounter increasing variety, for example, as a result of the unpredictability of their environments, so differentiation occurs. As organisations become increasingly differentiated so there is a greater need for integration. Integration in this sense, it might be argued, is primarily an informational phenomenon. Overlaid on the hierarchical structure can be various possible degrees of lateral linkages ranging from temporarily constituted task forces through to fully institutionalised matrix designs. These are considered to increase the lateral flow of information between interconnected sub-systems and so establish (homeostatic) coordinating mechanisms.

Galbraith (1972, 1977), in his information processing characterisation of the firm, has argued that improvement in lateral relations is merely one alternative to investment in the more familiar vertical information system. Faced with variety and interconnectedness firms may seek to encourage control through mutual adjustment by improving lateral information flows; alternatively they may seek to improve the effectiveness of hierarchical control systems. Investment in vertical information systems, for instance, reducing transmission delay and increasing data accuracy, would facilitate more timely revision of corporate plans, thus expediting coordination without the need for on-the-job consultation between interdependent sub-units.

In addition, Galbraith notes, organisations can take steps to reduce their need for information. Creating slack, for example, by establishing buffer inventories or relaxing technical specifications, can have the effect of reducing the degree of connectedness between interdependent sub-units and hence their requirement for communication. Alternatively, organisations may seek to structure self-contained tasks to facilitate resolution of problems without reference to bodies external to the sub-unit. The creation of separate design, manufacturing and marketing departments for each product or product group, and their organisation on a product basis is a common approach to divisionalisation (Ezzamel and Hilton, 1980). Organisations therefore face alternatives, both in terms of strategies for increasing the flow of information, and in terms of strategies for reducing their need for information.

Galbraith's analysis is useful in so far as it highlights some of the interdependencies between organisation structure and information system design. Clearly such interdependencies have important implications for accounting. Yet these are only partially addressed. A more recent development in accounting research has been the attempt to develop a formal contingency framework for the design of management accounting systems. This is discussed below.

The contingency theory of management accounting

The contingency theory of management accounting is a relatively recent development in accounting research. Drawing on the organisational literature (e.g. Woodward, 1965; Lawrence and Lorsch, 1969) this line of research has sought to isolate those variables with implications for design of a firm's information system. Through a combination of a priori reasoning and empirical validation, propositions are developed formalising the relationship between the situational contingencies of a firm and the appropriate nature of its information system. Organisational effectiveness, it is argued, will be improved by attaining an appropriate fit between the characteristics of the organisation's situation (the situational contingencies) and the characteristics of its Management Information Systems (MIS).

MIS are not identical to management accounting systems. Management information systems are typically concerned with the development, design, and implementation of computer-based information systems. Because of their joint concern with information design and flow, the distinction between MIS and management accounting systems is frequently blurred (Macintosh, 1985). Some of the studies reviewed below focus on MIS and others focus on management accounting systems. For convenience of presentation the following discussion focuses on MIS, but it is assumed that the implications for management accounting systems are the same.

The contingency theory of organisational structure identifies four main variables with important implications for organisation design: technology; environment; age and size; and power distribution, both internal and external. The literature on the contingency theory of management accounting, however, has primarily focused on the implications of only technology and environment for the design of MIS. Thus, the implications of age and size have been largely neglected (but see Merchant, 1984). Furthermore, only recently have researchers attempted to investigate the political implications of power on the design of MIS (e.g. Cooper, 1980).

In considering the effects of technology on the design of MIS, researchers have tended to distinguish between (i) certain contingencies, where environment is highly certain and technology is fairly routine, and (ii) uncertain contingencies, where environment is highly uncertain and/or technology is non-routine, with a distinction in each case between independent or interdependent tasks. Dent and Ezzamel (1986) used this classification to summarise and evaluate the contingency research in management accounting. The following discussion draws heavily on their work.

1 The certain contingencies cases Consider first the case of a firm with independent, routine tasks operating in an environment characterised by low uncertainty. With independent tasks, differentiation and integration requirements are expected to be low. This case may be characterised by crystallised standards of desirability (performance) and complete knowledge of cause–effect relationships (Thompson, 1967). This appears to provide a convenient setting for efficient centralisation facilitated by the possible development and use of unambiguous standard procedures (Mechanic, 1962; Thompson, 1967; Lawrence and Lorsch, 1969; Waterhouse and Tiessen, 1978). The nature of information most relevant in this case is likely to be precise and unambiguous, with a clear focus on single rather than multiple solutions to encourage quick and decisive action (e.g. Macintosh, 1981).

Given the above position, Ginzberg (1980) suggested that the relevant MIS design may be labelled 'procedural independent'. This design has two important characteristics. Firstly, it enhances control over tasks by reducing the discretion of task performance and/or making greater use of standard procedures. Secondly, it attempts to reduce the need for information processing, thus achieving a satisfactory match between information processing needs and information processing capacity.

Therefore, with routine, independent tasks and a certain environment, the role of the MIS as seen by the contingency theory is primarily one of exerting hierarchical control, and its nature is precise and unambiguous. Although the small number of unusual operating conditions encountered with routine tasks is systematically analysable (Perrow, 1967), a 'seat of the pants' approach to decision making may be preferred to the analytical approach on the basis of economic efficiency (Gordon and Miller, 1976).

Turning now to the case of routine but interdependent tasks in an environment with low uncertainty, the findings of Lawrence and Lorsch (1969) suggest that the greater the measure of differentiation between organisational sub-units, the greater the need for integrating devices to improve consistency and to minimise intraorganisational conflict. The potential of the MIS as a powerful integrating mechanism has been recognised by many writers, for example, Gordon and Miller (1976); Ginzberg (1980). Thus, given the above setting Ginzberg (1980) argued that the relevant MIS is one of the type 'procedural interdependent'. This system should enhance control and coordination of interdependent tasks by facilitating lateral information flow and information sharing. Thus, since greater task interdependence is like to call for greater sub-unit integration, the MIS should foster this integration by providing data relevant to sub-unit interdependencies (Watson, 1975).

2 The uncertain contingencies cases Consider now the case of a firm with non-routine technology operating in an uncertain environment. Non-routine tasks are usually characterised by many exceptions, with less systematically analysable search processes (Perrow, 1967). The literature suggests that organisational uncertainties, i.e. task non-routineness and environmental uncertainty, have demonstrable effects on the structure and distribution of authority within the organisation. Thus, one of the sources of influence within the organisation is the ability of the individual, or sub-unit, to successfully cope with uncertainty; see for example Burns and Stalker (1961); Thompson (1967); Hickson *et al.* (1971). This depends, at least in part, on the uniqueness of knowledge and skills of the individual, and on the availability of information relevant to the prevailing uncertainties. Thus, for example, Waterhouse and Tiessen (1978), and Mintzberg (1979) point out that technological and environmental uncertainties lead to greater decentralisation. Furthermore, organisation structures which evolve in response to greater uncertainty in contingency factors are typically organic (Burns and Stalker, 1961). Here, a procedural emphasis to the MIS is likely to be inadequate. Such systems emphasise hierarchical control and minimal diffusion of authority (e.g. Pfeffer, 1978). Moreover, they fail to address the diversity of conditions encountered by the organisation.

Various writers have investigated some of the implications of organisational uncertainties for the design of MIS. Amongst them, Khandwalla's (1972) results suggest that the extent of sophistication of the control system of an organisation is highly correlated with the intensity of competition in product markets and the complexity of economic conditions. In such circumstances MIS are called upon to help not only in the problem-solving area but also in integrating and coordinating organizational activities and in assessing performance. Such associations, however, were not observed in the case of marketing and price competition. Similarly, Bruns and Waterhouse (1975) argued that as organisations face uncertain contingencies, so they tend to decentralise decision making. Managers in more decentralised organisations tend to perceive themselves as having more influence and participating more in the budget process than managers in more authoritative and centralised organisations. Furthermore, the findings reported by Daft and Macintosh (1978) suggest that significantly high correlations exist between the extent of technological uncertainty and the style of MIS. Amigoni (1978) observed that environmental discontinuity often necessitates the replacement of obsolete tools by new ones. This point therefore highlights the potential impact of different situational contingencies. thus, in the face of different contingencies, organisations may require significantly different information and control systems.

In this setting, much of the information required is likely to be less precise, and frequently ill-defined with multiple focuses. Gordon and Narayanan (1984) reported that as decision makers perceive greater environmental uncertainty they tend to seek external, non-financial, and *ex-ante* information in addition to other types of information. Similarly, Chenhall and Morris (1986) observed a significant association between environmental uncertainty and broad scope and timely information; the greater the uncertainty, the more managers sought broad scope and timely information. Daft and Macintosh (1981) noted that, in general, greater task variety was associated with greater reported amounts of information-processing activity. Greater task analysability was found to be associated with the reported processing of equivocal information. In the context of a firm with independent tasks and non-routine technology in an uncertain environment, Ginzberg (1980) advocated an MIS design called 'decisional independent'. Instead of attempting to increase hierarchical control, this system emphasises the use of decentralised decision making, the institutionalisation of more effective decision models, and the localisation of information required for performance to minimise the need for sub-unit interaction.

Turning now to the complementary case in which the environment is uncertain and tasks are non-routine but interdependent, the presence of task interdependencies calls for greater use of integrating measures, as indicated earlier. The study by Chenhall and Morris (1986) suggests that broad-scope information, aggregated information, and integrated information were perceived as useful by managers of sub-units with interdependent activities. Macintosh and Daft (1987) reported that departmental interdependence is related to the emphasis placed on three elements in a package of management controls. Standard operating procedures were an important control device when interdependence was low. The budget and statistical reports were used more extensively when interdependence was moderate. When departmental interdependence was high, the role of all three control systems diminished. In this case, Ginzberg (1980) argued that the use of a 'decisional interdependent' MIS facilitates the development and maintenance of decentralised structures by emphasising shared decision models, shared information, and the coordination necessary for decentralised decision making by interdependent sub-units. Thus Ginzberg argued that a 'decisional interdependent' MIS is important for coordinating the activities of highly differentiated sub-units with high integration requirements.

An evaluation of contingency theory

The above outline shows how the contingency theory of management accounting might be seen to provide a coherent conceptual approach towards the design of management information systems. However, such a view might be premature, and there are significant reservations about this literature. As this theory draws heavily on the contingency theory of organisational structure, it seems appropriate first to provide a perspective by referring to some anomalies of the organisational research.

Some of the more technical limitations of the contingency approach to organisation design may be summarised as: (i) lack of precision in defining contingency factors; (ii) misspecification of model parameters and use of perceptual measures as proxies for organisational characteristics; (iii) use of cross-sectional approaches to measure dimensions of variables that can only be meaningfully measured by employing longitudinal approaches; (iv) lack of consideration of the effects of multiple (and possibly conflicting) contingencies on structural configurations; (v) lack of consideration of the implications of intraorganisational heterogeneity, e.g. where the firm deals in different sorts of markets, or has different technologies and (vi) frequent use of defective sampling techniques.

Although several organisation theorists have long been aware of these limitations, e.g. Child (1972a); Pennings (1975); Wood (1979), until very recently there has been little awareness of these issues in the accounting research. It is therefore hardly surprising that these limitations are prominent in the literature on the contingency theory of management accounting. When contingency factors are discussed they are either taken for granted (e.g. Gordon and Miller, 1976) or interpreted differently by different researchers. Further, the MIS literature typically considers only the effects of single contingency factors one at a time (e.g. Gordon and Miller, 1976) or of several contingency factors which are perceived to have a similar impact (e.g Waterhouse and Tiessen, 1978). Thus, the effects of different contingency factors, or of combinations of contingencies with differing and conflicting implications for MIS design, are seldom considered; nor is the possibility that a firm's contingencies may be difficult to classify due to intraorganisational differences.

The techniques used to derive propositions concerning the design implications for MIS also raise considerable doubt about their credibility. Thus, in several cases (e.g. Gordon and Miller, 1976) assertive propositions are derived with neither conclusive empirical evidence nor sound theoretical foundations. In most cases the contingency formulation is taken for granted as the ultimate framework for MIS design. It is implicitly assumed that by achieving an appropriate fit between the MIS and the relevant contingency factors, other things being the same, organisational effectiveness will improve. Yet organisational effectiveness is rarely included as a dependent variable in experimental designs. The empirical evidence suggests little more than the fact that different information systems exist. A link between situational contingencies, MIS design configurations and organisational effectiveness has yet to be established (Otley, 1980).

Organisational effectiveness is a rather elusive concept. Some of the difficulties experienced in the wider organisational literature in measuring effectiveness include:

1 a lack of clarity in the concept of effectiveness

2 the tendency to describe effectiveness along a single dimension, suppressing its multidimensional and possibly conflicting characteristics; and

3 separate problems of research design which have not as yet been resolved, including (i) the need for longitudinal studies to reflect changes in effectiveness over time; (ii) the bias in the perception of effectiveness resulting from the individual researcher/respondent frame of reference; and (iii) the possible need for developing different effectiveness criteria for different organisations.

Daunting conceptual and empirical problems need to be satisfactorily resolved before sensible conclusions about organisational effectiveness can be drawn. Indeed, the existence of these problems has prompted Child (1977) to conclude, in the context of the organisational research, that there is no conclusive evidence that matching organisation structure to contingency factors has an important influence on performance.

The above discussion will have elucidated some of the limitations of the MIS research. But more fundamentally, the contingency framework understates the role of choice in formulating strategies for organisational control. Decisions with regard to organisational structure and MIS design are presumed to be dictated by the need to adapt to contingency requirements; organisations are not permitted to have preferences for outcomes other than those implied by contingency factors. Yet in dealing with uncertainty, organisations may only seek to reduce its extent to manageable levels and in so doing often follow different strategies (Weick, 1979; Miller, 1981). The design implications of contingency theory promote a deterministic view in asserting that under a given set of contingencies there is only one best way to manage. Wood (1979) went even further in arguing that contingency theory not only underplays the scope for choice but also renders such choice redundant. By treating the organisation as a monolithic entity organised by a homogeneous management, the contingency framework ignores the possibility that different organisational participants may have preferences for different strategies.

Thus contingency theory is premised on existing authoritarian concepts of control. Metaphors like Simon's (1977) 'rational man' metaphor and Weick's (1979) 'military' metaphor dominate the contingency framework. The MIS is considered only in its procedural or decision support mode (Gorry and Scott-Morton, 1971). The much wider psychological orientations of organisational control and intraorganisational power considerations are hardly addressed (Cooper, 1980). Information systems are not neutral in their impact on behaviour (Drucker, 1964). All sorts of effects, both functional and dysfunctional, may be stimulated by particular information system characteristics (e.g. Argyris, 1952;

Lawler and Rhode, 1976). Certain characteristics may render an information system more susceptible to strategic manipulation (Schiff and Lewin, 1970) and information may be used to further power and influence within the organisation (Bariff and Galbraith, 1978). March and Simon (1958), for example, refer to the concept of 'uncertainty absorption' whereby subjective inferences are drawn from a body of evidence and fed into an information system, becoming legitimised organisational 'facts'. These 'facts' in turn shape organisational choices. Managers may manipulate information passing to their colleagues to create confusion and ambiguity as a cover for the expansion of their particular empires (Dalton, 1959). Superiors may falsify information passing to subordinates to create dissent and competition (Pondy, 1967). Subordinates may alter and suppress information passing to their superiors in a way compatible with their ends (Thornton, 1974). At all organisational levels participants play a role, whether consciously or unconsciously, in determining the shape, quantity and quality of information flows.

To an extent organisations may instigate formal and informal controls to counteract this phenomenon. But in many cases there may be neither the time nor the knowledge to eliminate, or even reduce, it. Equally important is the possibility that managers may willingly allow information to be suppressed and manipulated by subordinates to reduce ambiguity and overload (Westerlund and Sjostrand, 1979). To the extent that such manipulation facilitates managerial decision making, it may not be entirely undesirable. However, organisational adaptation is likely to be impaired, and it may be appropriate to design information systems which offer less scope for manipulation and suppression, for example, by establishing direct information linkages, and avoiding to some extent standard aggregation procedures. Moreover, multiple channels of communication, providing horizontal as well as vertical linkages, may focus managerial attention on crucial inconsistencies which might otherwise go unobserved.

All in all, the role of accounting in organisation control is little understood (Burchell *et al.*, 1980). How it interacts with other control processes has only been partially addressed in the literature. There is a need for further analysis within a global organisational framework. One such attempt is discussed below.

IV A framework for organisational control

In this section, the framework developed by Dent and Ezzamel (1986) for the analysis of organisational control is discussed. The framework draws on previous research, much of which has already been discussed in this article. In order to facilitate the presentation of the Dent and Ezzamel framework, a brief summary of the relevant points made so far is presented first.

In the first section of this article the nature of the organisational control process was characterised. Several different schools of organisational analysis were identified, each providing insight into the control of organisational activities. Some dimensions of structure were considered briefly, relating to the efficiency and effectiveness of alternative planning procedures. The rationale of the classic prescription for centralisation was discussed. Difficulties associated with such authoritarian procedures were outlined, including the dispersion of essential knowledge, and the noise and filtering effects that occur in the transmission of information. Drawing on the economic literature, it was argued that centralisation was likely to be particularly costly not only in terms of the necessary staff and the information technology, but also in terms of the speed of adjustment to environmental change. On the other hand, difficulties associated with decentralised procedures were noted including those of internalising interdependencies and external effects, and of risk sharing. It was argued that the structural analysis was overly mechanistic. Organisations exist through the efforts of people, and people have divergent goals and aspirations. Conflict and the constant negotiation that takes place within organisations are essential elements of the control process. Recognition of group pressure, and the power of the informal organisation, is crucial to an understanding of organisational functioning. Moreover, issues of structural design are more richly endowed. People look to organisations for satisfaction of a variety of needs. Job characteristics and leadership style may have a significant impact on the quality of individual performance. These social and psychological insights into organisational functioning have provided a different focus for organisational researchers. Their analysis, however, constitutes a complementary view of the organisational control process. Only through integration of the ideas of different management theorists can a coherent and comprehensive framework of organisational control be developed.

To formalise this eclectic approach the discussion was extended to include principles of cybernetic analysis. It was indicated that the homeostatic concept placed emphasis on control through mutual adjustment, conflict being thoroughly embedded in the model, and that organisations constantly evolve in response to internal and external stimuli. The significant contributions of the cybernetic analysis include the recognition of the interconnectedness of the whole; the emphasis on self control; and the nature of organisational adaptation. The organisation was characterised as being subject to continual disequilibrium forces driving it inexorably onwards through time.

Over time, it was argued, an organisation may change its activities, its structure, its personnel and so on. Thus a completely new and expansive concept of organisational control was acquired. Attention was drawn, however, to some of the mechanistic ideas and rationalistic orientations of the cybernetic model.

Drawing on the implicit orientation of the cybernetic analysis, the important role played by information in organisational control was emphasised. Whether the MIS is viewed as a vehicle for enhancing the information processing capacity of the organisation (e.g. Galbraith, 1972), or as a political vehicle for exerting control (e.g. Pfeffer, 1978) or as a decision-support system (e.g. Burchell *et al.*, 1980), information processing is recognised as a key organisational activity. Thus, as organisations encounter increasing variety and interconnectedness, so information plays a crucial role in supporting effective coordination and adaptation. Moreover, both the structure of communication channels and the nature of the data are relevant to MIS design. As the need for organisational adaptation increases, so there may be a need for a more diverse and destabilising set of information.

To formalise this intuitive analysis, the contingency theory of management accounting was considered. It was pointed out that researchers have sought to associate characteristics of the firm's information system with its technology and environment. By achieving a fit, so it is argued, between the contingency factors and the information system, organisational effectiveness will be improved. However, the existing research is incomplete in so far as contingency factors are under-specified. Moreover, organisations face alternatives for coping with internal and external variety. The means of effective organisational control are not necessarily dictated by situational contingencies.

The preceding discussion will have demonstrated that organisational control is a total process. As Westerlund and Sjostrand (1979) point out, it is common in organisations that many controls operate simultaneously. To this extent it is almost impossible to isolate the separate effects of a particular means of control. Only by considering the process as a whole can the significance of one element *per se* be appreciated. The process of organisational control is not susceptible to tidy and precise analysis. Any formal approach will inevitably be incomplete. Nevertheless, drawing on the above ideas, Dent and Ezzamel (1986) identify five elements which can be sensibly incorporated in the framework. These are:

1 *Contingency factors*. Traditionally, this set is said to contain an organisation's environment, its technology, its age and size, its internal and external power distribution, and ownership characteristics. Other factors can be added to this list: for example, organisational goals (Dermer, 1977) and the type of personnel employed by the organisation (Child, 1977).
2 *Information system characteristics*. Here two sets of characteristics can be distinguished: (i) structural characteristics such as the orientation of the information system (internal/external), the sources of data (internal/external), the structure of information linkages (lateral/vertical), the scope of the information system (global/localised); (ii) other characteristics referring to the nature of information, for example, the diversity and ambiguity of information, the extent of predictive data, and the timeliness and frequency of the data.
3 *Structural configuration*. Under this heading three related sets of characteristics can be identified. At the individual level there are such attributes as the degree of job specification and task variety, the definition of individual responsibilities, the organisation of tasks and the degree of differentiation. Organisational attributes would include lines of formal authority (functional/product/matrix orientations), flexibility of formal structure, organisational reward structures, the informal organisation, and the extent of integrating mechanisms. There is also a third category of decision making and leadership characteristics, for example, the extent of formal and informal decentralisation, leadership style and managerial consideration.
4 *Managerial choices*. This set relates to managerial input into the control process. Managerial choices encompass three broad types of decision: strategic choices, structural choices (including information system choices) and tactical choices. These represent the means whereby managers may attempt to influence an organisation's functioning.

5 *Organisational activity*. Given the organisational infrastructure established by the preceding elements of the framework, the term activity is used here to refer to the actual workings of the organisation. Thus it embraces such attributes as the cohesiveness and morale of informal groups, levels of conflict and anxiety within the organisation, and dimensions of organisational effectiveness. Also included are measures of economic efficiency, for example, levels of task performance, productivity, profitability, and stock market performance, as well as

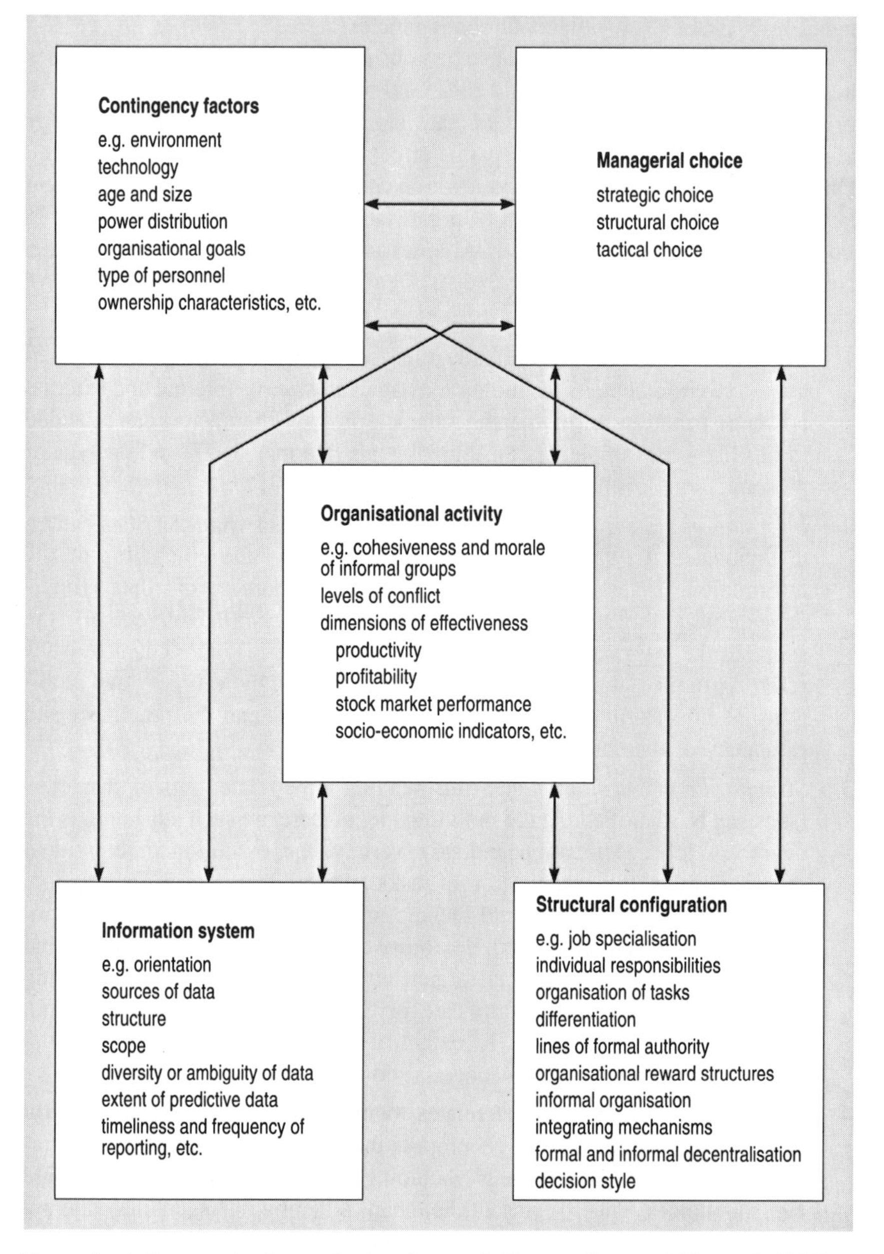

Figure 1 *A framework of organisational control (Source: Dent and Ezzamel, 1986)*

socio-economic indicators, for example employee earnings, satisfaction, and societal benevolence. In addition, it might be appropriate to consider here organisational flexibility and adaptation.

To an extent these elements may be difficult to distinguish precisely. Although important in an empirical context, such precision is not crucial to the present exposition, and might only serve to confuse. In any event, in consistency with the preceding analysis, it is not the elements in isolation that are emphasised here, but rather their interaction. Figure 1 (opposite) offers a diagrammatic representation of the five elements in the framework.

In a contingency approach, the nature of the contingencies facing the organisation would be presumed to dictate the appropriate choice of structural configuration and MIS design. This would be represented by arrows running from the contingency factors to managerial choices, and from managerial choices to structure and information system. Arrows running from these two elements to organisational activity could be used to show the impact on organisational effectiveness of an appropriate fit between these two elements and the contingencies. Such a characterisation would, however, be incomplete and potentially misleading. As indicated earlier, a more realistic representation would reveal a great deal more interaction amongst the elements.

Interactions between the five elements

Consider first the relationship between the organisation and its contingency factors. Traditionally, contingency theorists have tended to perceive the organisation as a *passive* adaptor to its situation. The behaviour of the organisation is seen by them as being fully dictated by the nature of its contingencies. However, it has been argued that managers face alternatives in coping with their contingencies. Moreover, the interaction between the organisation and its contingencies is not one-sided, but rather each exerts a measure of influence over the other.

Take, for example, the influence of the environment. Many authors have commented on the role of the organisation in *managing* its environment. Thus Cyert and March (1963) advanced the concept of a 'negotiated environment'. In their view, organisations negotiate with their competitors, suppliers, customers and so on to control the uncertainty in their environments. Similarly Thompson (1967) spoke of smoothing policies (e.g. advertising, off peak pricing), and observed that organisations attempt to place their boundaries around activities which would otherwise be crucial contingencies. Stronger propositions have been advanced by Weick (1979) who seemed to suggest that through a process of enactment, organisations literally create the environments they observe. Indeed Ackoff (1979) went so far as to suggest that the dominant 'predict and prepare' philosophy is symptomatic of a mechanistic age, and proposed a proactive philosophy of 'redesigning the future'. Thus, to some extent at least, organisations play a role in shaping the environments in which they operate.

Similar propositions could be made with respect to the other contingency factors. Thus the nature of the firm's technology is in part controlled by managerial choices, and the size of organisational units will be influenced by policies of vertical and horizontal integration, growth and divisionalisation. Moreover, both information system characteristics and structural configuration may have a direct impact on the nature of the firm's contingencies. Thus, for example, the information released by the organisation will influence its public image and its financial prestige; and the extent of vertical and horizontal integration will affect the degree of environmental variety. Similarly, the nature of organisational activities will also impinge directly on the situational contingencies. Thus situational contingencies are not exogenous 'given' factors in the control process. Rather the organisation may exert a significant measure of control over these factors, and proactive management may be at least as important as skilful adaptation (Ackoff, 1979).

No intention is made here to imply that situational contingencies are without significance to the organisation. Contingency factors, however defined, exert at least a constraining influence on managerial choices. For example, contingency factors may constrain top management's choice of, say, one particular strategy from a set of potentially available strategies. Alternatively, the long-term plans of the organisation may have to be modified to accommodate the requirements of some specific contingencies. Similarly, situational contingencies may exert a constraining influence on managerial choice of information system characteristics, structural configuration and organisational activities.

Moreover, contingencies may have a direct impact on the other elements of the framework. Thus, as an organisation's technology becomes more complex, for example, so individuals may become more specialised and increasingly feel the need for different types of information. Hence there may be a direct information system effect. Further, owing to the inevitable increase in specialisation in the above setting, subordinates are likely to find it easier to manipulate information passing to their superiors. This will have important implications for the formal and informal power distribution within the organisation, and in particular it may lead to an increasing extent of formal and informal decentralisation: hence a direct structural effect may be observed. Furthermore, an increase in uncertainties caused by situational contingencies may directly constrain the scope of organisational activities and the indices of its effectiveness.

Consider, next, managerial choices over structural configuration and information system. Traditionally, it has been assumed that managerial choices with respect to these two elements are homogeneous and congruent. This assumed unilateral planning by top managers of choices under their control reflects the traditionally dominant view of imposed control. However, management's ability to exert control within the organisation is likely to be conditioned by many factors. These may include the extent to which the organisation is internally or externally constrained, past and present organisational activities, existing organisational structures, the information made available to managers, managerial competence and the extent of control exercised by subordinates over their managers. Notice also that the framework shows patterns of bi-directional influence between structural configuration and information system. Thus, one would expect that the nature of the firm's information flow may constrain the choice of organisational structure, whilst the existing organisational structure could have specific design implications for the information system.

Finally, consider the interactions involving organisational activity. The figure shows contingency factors, managerial choices, structural configuration and the MIS all influencing organisational activities. Notice, however, that in view of the resultant organisational activities top managers may introduce changes into organisational strategies, structure and information system. Moreover, organisational activities may have a direct impact on structural configuration and MIS characteristics as well as on the situational contingencies.

Even though Figure 1 is a simplified abstraction from reality, it still exemplifies the difficulties of understanding organisational control processes. Organisations are extremely complex. The diagram conceals a mass of detailed interaction as well as the dynamic nature of organisational processes. For obvious reasons it was not possible to show the passage of time along a third dimension. Yet organisational processes are dynamic. They change over time, and over time they induce changes in organisational activities. Driven by conflicting forces through time organisations follow different paths, and they adopt different strategies for control. The framework is also fairly general. It depicts a number of interactions, and deliberately refrains from ranking them in any order of importance. Nevertheless, organisations do differ, both amongst themselves and over time, and it may not be unreasonable to expect to observe differences in their control strategies. For some organisations managerial choices may be crucially important, whereas for others, structure or information system characteristics may be paramount. Moreover, some organisations may place more emphasis on strategic management, seeking to manipulate and pre-empt their environments, whereas others may seek to consolidate their position by concentrating on existing activities and improving their efficiency (Gordon and Miller, 1976; Miles and Snow, 1978).

Some accounting implications of this perspective have been explored in the literature. For example, Hedberg and Jonsson (1978) have discussed self-annihilating information packages. They suggested that information should be coded with an expiry date to shake organisations out of their complacency. Decision makers should be required to test, periodically, the validity of their premises and beliefs. More specifically Earl and Hopwood (1980) have discussed how differences in the consensus of beliefs might influence information use. Drawing on Thompson and Tuden's (1959) classification they distinguished differences in the certainty of cause and effect relationships from differences in the certainty of objectives. Given high uncertainty of objectives and cause and effect relationships, they argued, organisations need 'idea machines' to promote creative experimentation. On the other hand, given a consensus on objectives and cause and effect relationships organisations are considered to need 'answer machines' to promote informed and rational decision making. In the intermediate case of consensus on objectives but the uncertainty of cause and effect, they advocated 'learning machines' to assist in the process of discovery and judgement. Finally, in the case of agreement on cause and effect but minimal consensus on objectives, they advocated 'dialogue machines' to promote informed compromise.

In practice, however, the MIS may be used in different roles. Given high uncertainty on both dimensions, for example, the MIS may serve principally to rationalise decisions. Or given low uncertainty of cause and effect relationships but high uncertainty of objectives, the MIS may be used as 'an ammunition machine'. Such behaviours do occur and may not be difficult to rationalise. But rather than dismissing them as manifestations of dysfunctional behaviour, we should seek to understand the part such behaviours play in shaping organisational activities and their evolution over time. As yet there is no framework in which such phenomena may be functionally interpreted.

V Conclusions and implications for research

This article attempted to describe the process of organisational control, and some of the ambiguous roles which accounting may play. The subtle interplay of the various mechanisms which shape organisational activities and stimulate their evolution over time has been emphasised. It has been argued that this process is not susceptible to tidy and precise analysis. Organisational control is immensely more complex than is generally recognised. Simplistic characteristics are potentially misleading. Briefly, the above arguments may be summarised as follows.

Firstly, organisations are not merely passive adaptors to their situation: they influence and are influenced by that situation. This implies that the management of contingencies may assume at least as much significance in organisational control as the management of the internal functioning of the organisation. Secondly, organisational control is a broad concept. Thus, the presence of intra-organisational conflict and power, and the phenomenon of information manipulation need to be explicitly recognised. Such an approach is consistent with the view expressed by Westerlund and Sjostrand (1979, p. 109) when they pointed out that 'all action taken in an organisation can be regarded as means of control as long as it influences members' activities. Thirdly, organisational control is a much more liberal concept than is traditionally believed. Thus, self control and mutual adjustment are at least as important as control through dominance. Fourthly, the various elements of the organisational control process are linked in a complex set of interrelationships. Although some useful insights can be gleaned from studying each subsystem in isolation, it is important to adopt a global approach to organisational analysis if a fuller understanding of organisations is sought. Fifthly, organisational activities are not static but dynamic and stochastic and are also characterised by renewal and regeneration. This has obvious implications for the interpretation of effectiveness. Sixthly, notions of rationality and consensus are not always useful in interpreting organisational processes. Such processes are often inconsistent, and functionally so. Conflict may stimulate organisations into innovative behaviour. Seventhly, organisational means for control are in themselves equivocal: different organisations facing similar contingencies can, and do, successfully promote dissimilar strategies and structures. Finally, in formalising the framework, variables were deliberately not classified into sets of dependent and independent variables, nor was a greater weight attached to the effects flowing from any one particular element. Instead, lines of multiple causality were depicted. The pre-eminence of any one particular element in the control process can only exist with reference to a focal organisation at a particular point in time.

It seems that at least two sets of questions need to be asked.

1 How does accounting fit in the totality of organisational activities? How do observed abuses of accounting interact with other organisational mechanisms?

2 What forces shape the accounting function in organisations? Why do accounting practices take the form they do? How do accounting practices evolve over time? Such questions should, perhaps, be addressed before deriving normative accounting propositions.

These conclusions may be familiar. Nevertheless they do not seem to have been widely recognised in accounting research. Notions of causality, rationality and separability pervade the literature. Interactions are suppressed: consensus is perceived as intrinsically desirable, organisational objectives are presumed. Prescriptions typically fail to address the dynamic evolving nature of organisational activities. The wisdom of such approaches has been questioned here. A false sense of order and coherence is created. In reality the role of accounting in organisational control is little understood. How do we proceed from here?

One possibility would be to concede the impossibility of modelling organisational functioning and to argue that the process of organisational control is a gigantic mess that is not susceptible to any form of structuring or analysis. But research along the notions of ambiguous goals, evolving life cycles, and dynamic interacting systems may require a revolution in methodology. To argue along these lines, however, would be to accept that partial knowledge is as good as may be hoped for, or, at the extreme, that research into organisational control is a fruitless endeavour. This is not an appealing argument.

Another possibility would be, in the first instance, to raise the level of resolution of existing research: that is to say, to lift the focus of our attention from the minutiae of accounting to the interaction of accounting in aggregate with other aggregates of organisational processes. This approach has been advanced by Simon (1962). He argued that complex systems may tend in their dynamics to display the property of 'near decomposability'. In a nearly decomposable system: (i) the short-run behaviour of each element is approximately independent of the short-run behaviour of the other elements, and (ii) the long-run behaviour of any element depends in only an aggregate way on the behaviour of other elements. Because elements only interact with one another in an aggregate fashion, the details of their internal interactions can be largely ignored in macro research: the behaviour of the whole can be understood in terms of the interactions amongst aggregate sub-systems.

Clearly, the plausibility of this argument will depend upon whether the interactions within even a nearly decomposable system are simple enough to be captured by an investigation process which ignores the detailed functioning of the elements. Not all the researchers would endorse this view. Yet it does simplify the task, in that we may be able to further our understanding of the role of accounting in organisational control by aggregating organisational processes into several large bundles and initially focusing only on the interactions between the bundles. In this manner it may be possible to make some sense of the problem, gradually lowering the level of resolution until a useful picture emerges.

Such a 'top-down' strategy may be criticised for being similar to what Lindblom (1959) has, in a different context, described as a root (comprehensive) approach, with all the problems thereby entailed. It is argued here, however, that the proposal is more in line with the 'soft-systems' approach advocated *inter alia* by Checkland (1981). At least in the analysis of human systems, it may be necessary in the first instance to adopt a higher level of resolution to obtain some perspective of the totality of the problem. As Checkland (1981, p. 165) commented:

> it has been found most useful to make the initial expression of a building up of the *richest possible picture* of the situation being studied. Such a picture then enables selection to be made of a viewpoint (or viewpoints) from which to study further the problem situation.

Certainly, the extant incremental (branch) approach has contributed significantly to our knowledge of accounting, and we are moving gradually towards a better understanding of the whole. On the other hand, the phenomena to be studied are so immensely complex that the overall picture may never emerge, or may tend to be obscured by the detail. The soft-systems approach, in contrast, places the overall picture in its ambit in the first instance, and keeps it there.

The discussion above suggest that if meaningful insights are to be obtained, then systems dynamics must be explicitly captured in research design. The control process described earlier is inextricably linked with notions of disequilibrium, change, and evolution. This suggests the limited usefulness of cross-sectional analysis *per se*. Yet the methods of longitudinal research are comparatively underdeveloped. For example, is historical time an adequate substitute for real time? How can we control for the vagaries of chance? How can comparative case studies be designed? These questions are yet to be adequately addressed in the literature.

In conclusion, accounting research needs to be reoriented away from the tradition of partial analysis towards the totality of its organisational context, and away from the tradition of statics towards the dynamics of organisational functioning. There is a desperate need to improve our understanding of the way in which organisational activities evolve over time and how organisational processes interact to shape these activities. Only such a total approach will explain why and how accounting is intertwined with organisational functioning.

References

Abdel-khalik, A.R. and Lusk, E.J. (1974) 'Transfer pricing – a synthesis', *Accounting Review*, January, pp. 8–23.

Ackoff, R.L. (1979) 'The future of operational research is past', *Journal of the Operational Research Society*, Vol. 30, No. 2, February, pp. 93–104.

Amigoni, F. (1978) 'Management planning and control systems', *Journal of Business Finance and Accounting*, Autumn, pp. 279–291.

Argyris, C. (1952) *The Impact of Budgets on People*. Controllership Foundation.

Argyris, C. and Schön, D.A. (1978) *Organizational Learning: A Theory of Action Perspective*. Addison-Wesley.

Arrow, K.J. (1964) 'Control in large organizations', *Management Science*, April, pp. 397–408.

Ashby, W.R. (1956) *Introduction to Cybernetics*. Chapman & Hall.

Ashby, W.R. (1960) *Design for a Brain*, 2nd edn. Chapman & Hall.

Bariff, M.L. and Galbraith, J.R. (1978) 'Intraorganisational power considerations for designing information systems', *Accounting, Organizations and Society*, pp. 15–27.

Baritz, L. (1960) *The Servants of Power*. Wesleyan University Press.

Becker, S. and Green, D. (1962) 'Budgeting and employee behaviour', *Journal of Business*, October, pp. 392–402.

Beer, S. (1966) *Decision and Control*. John Wiley.

Beer, S. (1972) *Brain of the Firm*, 2nd edn. Allen Lane, The Penguin Press.

Bennis, W. (1966) *Changing Organizations*. McGraw-Hill.

Bruns, W.J. and Waterhouse, J.H. (1975) 'Budgetary control and organizational structure', *Journal of Accounting Research*, Autumn, pp. 177–203.

Buckley, W. (1967) *Sociology and Modern Systems Theory*. Prentice-Hall.

Burchell, S., Clubb, C., Hopwood, A.G., Hughes, T. and Nahapiet, J. (1980) 'The roles of accounting in organisations and society', *Accounting, Organizations and Society*, Vol. 5, No. 1, pp. 5–27.

Burns, T. and Stalker, G.M. (1961) *The Management of Innovation*. London, Tavistock.

Burrell, G. and Morgan, G. (1979) *Sociological Paradigms and Organisational Analysis*. Heinemann.

Caplan, E.H. (1966) 'Behavioural assumptions of management accounting', *Accounting Review*, July, pp. 496–509.

Caplan, E.H. (1968) 'Behavioural assumptions of management accounting – report of a field study', *Accounting Review*, April, pp. 342–362.

Checkland, P.B. (1981) *Systems Thinking, Systems Practice*. Wiley.

Chenhall, R.H. and Morris, D. (1986) 'The impact of structure, environment and interdependence on the perceived usefulness of management accounting systems', *Accounting Review*, January, pp. 16–35.

Child, J. (1972a) 'Organizational structure, environment and performance: the role of strategic choice', *Sociology*, pp. 2–22.

Child, J. (1972b) 'Organization structure and strategies of control: a republican of the Aston study', *Administrative Science Quarterly*, June, pp. 163–176.

Child, J. (1977) *Organisations: A Guide to Problems and Practices*. London, Harper and Row.

Collard, D.A. (1973) 'External effects', in Amey, L.R. (ed.) *Readings in Management Decision*. Longman.

Cooper, D.J. (1980) 'A social and organisational view of management accounting', in Bromwich, M. and Hopwood, A.G. (eds) *Essays on British Accounting Research*. Pitman.

Cyert, R.M. and March, J.G. (1963) *A Behavioural Theory of the Firm*. Prentice-Hall.

Daft, R.L. and Macintosh, N.B. (1978) 'A new approach to design and use of management information', *California Management Review*, pp. 82–92.

Daft, R.L. and Macintosh, N.B. (1981) 'A tentative exploration into the amount and equivocality of information processing in organizational work units', *Administrative Science Quarterly*, Vol. 26, pp. 207–224.

Dalton, M. (1959) *Men Who Manage*. Wiley.

Davis, O. and Whinston, A. (1962) 'Externalities, welfare and the theory of games', *Journal of Political Economy*, June, pp. 241–262.

Dent, J.F. and Ezzamel, M.A. (1986) 'Organisational control and management accounting: a contingency critique', forthcoming.

Dermer, J. (1977) *Management Planning and Control Systems*. Irwin.

Drucker, P.F. (1964) 'Controls, control and management', in Bonini, C.P., Jaedicke, R.K. and Wagner, H.M. (eds) *Management Controls, New Directions in Basic Research.* McGraw-Hill.

Earl, M.J. and Hopwood, A.G. (1980) 'From management information to information management', in Lucas, H.C., Jnr *et al.* (eds) *The Information Systems Environment.* North Holland.

Ezzamel, M.A. and Hilton, K. (1980) 'Divisionalisation in British industry: a preliminary study', *Accounting and Business Research*, Spring, pp. 197–214.

Feldman, M.S. and March, J.G. (1981) 'Information in organizations as signal and symbol', *Administrative Science Quarterly*, Vol. 26, June, pp. 171–186.

Flamholtz, E.G. (1972) 'Towards a theory of human resource value in formal organizations', *Accounting Review*, October, pp. 666–678.

Flamholtz, E. (1975) 'Small group interaction and task performance: its implications for managerial accounting', in Livingstone, J.L. (ed.) *Managerial Accounting: The Behavioural Foundations.* Grid.

Galbraith, J.R. (1972) 'Organisation design: an information processing view', in Lorsch, J.W. and Lawrence, P.R. (eds) *Organisation Planning: Concepts and Cases.* Irwin.

Galbraith, J.R. (1977) *Organisation Design.* Addison Wesley.

Ginzberg, J. (1980) 'An organizational contingencies view of accounting and information systems implementation', *Accounting, Organizations and Society*, pp. 369–382.

Gordon, L.A. and Miller, D. (1976) 'A contingency framework for the design of accounting information systems', *Accounting, Organizations and Society*, pp. 59–70.

Gordon, L.A. and Narayanan, V.K. (1984) 'Management accounting systems, perceived environmental uncertainty and organization structure: an empirical investigation', *Accounting, Organizations and Society*, Vol. 9, No. 1, pp. 33–47.

Gorry, G.A. and Scott-Morton, M.S. (1971) 'A framework for management information systems', *Sloan Management Review*, pp. 55–70.

Halpin, A. and Winer, B. (1957) 'A factorial study of the leader behaviour descriptions', in Stogdill, R. and Coons, A. (eds) *Leader Behaviour: Its Description and Measurement.* Ohio State University.

Hedberg, B. and Jonsson, S. (1978) 'Designing semi-confusing information systems for organisations in changing environments', *Accounting, Organizations and Society*, pp. 47–64.

Hedberg, B., Nystrom, P.C. and Starbuck, W.H. (1976) 'Camping on seesaws: prescriptions for a self-designing organization', *Administrative Science Quarterly*, Vol. 21, March, pp. 41–65.

Herzberg, F. (1966) *Work and the Nature of Man.* Cleveland, OH, World.

Hickson, D.J., Hinnings, C.R., Lee, C.A., Schneck, R.E. and Pennings, J.M. (1971) 'A strategic contingencies' theory of intraorganisational power', *Administrative Science Quarterly*, June, pp. 216–229.

Hofstede, G.H. (1967) *The Game of Budget Control.* Van Gorcum.

Holmstrom, B. (1979) 'Moral hazard and observability', *Bell Journal of Economics*, Spring, pp. 74–91.

Hopwood, A.G. 1(972) 'An empirical study of the role of accounting data in performance evaluation, empirical research in accounting: selected studies', Supplement to *Journal of Accounting Research*, Vol. 10, pp. 156–182.

Hopwood, A.G. (1978) 'Towards an organizational perspective for the study of accounting and information systems', *Accounting, Organizations and Society*, pp. 3–14.

Hunt, J.W. (1972) *The Restless Organization.* Wiley International.

Jantsch, E. (1980) *The Self-Organizing Universe.* Pergamon.

Katz, D. and Kahn, R.L. (1978) *The Social Psychology of Organisations*, 2nd edn. John Wiley.

Kenis, I. (1979) 'Effects of budgetary goal characteristics on managerial attitudes and performance', *Accounting Review*, October, pp. 707–721.

Kerr, S., Klinoski, R.J., Tolliver, J. and Von Gunov, M.A. (1975) 'Human information processing', in Livingstone, J.L. (ed.) *Managerial Accounting: The Behavioural Foundations*. Grid.

Khandwalla, P. (1972) 'The effect of different types of competition on the use of management controls', *Journal of Accounting Research*, Autumn, pp. 276–285.

Kimberly, J.R. and Miles, R.H. (1980) *The Organizational Life Cycle*. Jossey-Bass.

Lawler, E.E. and Rhode, J.G. (1976) *Information and Control in Organizations*. Goodyear.

Lawrence, P.R. and Lorsch, J.W. (1969) *Organization and Environment*. Irwin, first published 1967.

Lewin, K. (1947) 'Group decision and social change', in Newcomb, T.M. and Hartley, E.L. (eds) *Readings in Social Psychology*. Holt.

Likert, R. (1961) *New Problems of Management*. McGraw-Hill.

Lilienfeld, R. (1978) *The Rise of Systems Theory: An Ideological Analysis*. Wiley.

Lindblom, C.E. (1959) 'The science of muddling through', *Public Administration Review*, Spring, pp. 79–88.

Lowe, E.A. and McInnes, J.M. (1971) 'Control in socio-economic organisations: a rationale for the design of management control systems', *Journal of Management Studies*, May, pp. 213–227.

McGregor, D. (1960) *The Human Side of Enterprise*. McGraw-Hill.

Macintosh, N.B. (1981) 'A contextual model of information systems', *Accounting, Organizations and Society*, pp. 39–53.

Macintosh, N.B. (1985) *The Social Software of Accounting and Information Systems*. Wiley.

Macintosh, N.B. and Daft, R.L. (1987) 'Management control systems and departmental interdependencies: an empirical study', *Accounting, Organizations and Society*, Vol. 12, No. 1, pp. 49–61.

March, J.G. (1972) 'Model bias in social action', *Review of Educational Research*, pp. 413–429.

March, J.G. (1979) 'The technology of foolishness', in March, J.G. and Olsen, J.P. *Ambiguity and Choice in Organizations*, 2nd edn. Universitetforlaget.

March, J.G. and Simon, H.A. (1959) *Organizations*. John Wiley.

Marschak, J. and Radner, R. (1972) *Economic Theory of Teams*. Yale University Press.

Mechanic, D. (1962) 'Source of power of lower participants in complex organisations', *Administrative Science Quarterly*, December, pp. 349–364.

Merchant, K.A. (1984) 'Influences on departmental budgeting: an empirical examination of a contingency model', *Accounting, Organizations and Society*, Vol. 9, No. 3/4, pp. 291–307.

Miles, R.E. and Snow, C.C. (1978) *Organizational Strategy, Structure and Process*. McGraw-Hill.

Miller, D. (1981) 'Towards a new contingency approach: the search for organizational', *Gestalts, Journal of Management Studies*, pp. 1–26.

Mintzberg, H. (1979) *The Structuring of Organizations*. Prentice-Hall.

Otley, D.T. (1978) 'Budget use and managerial performance', *Journal of Accounting Research*, Spring, pp. 122–149.

Otley, D.T. (1980) 'The contingency theory of management accounting: achievement and prognosis', *Accounting, Organizations and Society*, pp. 413–428.

Pennings, J.M. (1975) 'The relevance of the structural–contingency model for organizational effectiveness', *Administrative Science Quarterly*, September, pp. 393–409.

Perrow, C. (1967) 'A framework for the comparative analysis of organisations', *American Sociological Review*, pp. 194–208.

Pfeffer, J. (1978) *Organizational Design*. Arlington Heights, IL, AHM Publishing.

Pondy, L.R. (1967) 'Organizational conflict: concepts and models', *Administrative Science Quarterly*, September, pp. 296–320.

Porter, L.W. and Lawler, E.E. (1968) *Managerial Attitudes and Performance*. Irwin.

Ronen, J. and Livingstone, J.L. (1975) 'An expectancy theory approach to the motivational impacts of budgets', *Accounting Review*, October, pp. 671–685.

Schiff, M. and Lewin, A.Y. (1970) 'The impact of people on budgets', *Accounting Review*, April, pp. 259–268.

Searfoss, D.G. and Monczka, R.M. (1973) 'Perceived participation in the budget process and motivation to achieve the budget', *Academy of Management Journal*, pp. 541–554.

Shannon, C. and Weaver, W. (1949) *The Mathematical Theory of Communication*. University of Illinois Press.

Simon, H.A. (1962) 'The architecture of complexity', *Proceedings of the American Philosophical Society*, Vol. 106, No. 6, December, pp. 467–482.

Simon, H.A. (1977) *The New Science of Management Decision*. Prentice-Hall.

Solomons, D. (1963) *Divisional Performance: Measurement and Control*. Irwin.

Sorter, G.H. and Becker, S.W. (with the assistance of Archibald, T.R. and Beaver, W.H.) (1964) 'Corporate personality as reflected in accounting decisions: some preliminary findings', *Journal of Accounting Research*, Autumn, pp. 183–192.

Stedry, A. (1960) *Budget Control and Cost Behaviour*. Prentice-Hall.

Tannenbaum, A. (1966) *Social Psychology of the Work Organization*. Wadsworth.

Thompson, J. (1967) *Organizations in Action*. McGraw-Hill.

Thompson, J.D. and Tuden, A. (1959) 'Strategies, structures and processes of organizational decision', in Thompson, J.D. *et al.* (eds) *Comparative Studies in Administration*. University of Pittsburgh Press.

Thornton, R. (1974) 'Controlling the technician: the adversary approach', *MSU Business Topics*, Summer.

Tosi, H. (1975) 'The human effects of managerial budgeting', in Livingstone, J.L. (ed.) *Managerial Accounting: The Behavioural Foundations*. Grid.

Vroom, V.H. (1964) *Work and Motivation*. Wiley and Sons.

Waterhouse, J.H. and Tiessen, P. (1978) 'A contingency framework for management accounting systems research', *Accounting, Organizations and Society*, pp. 65–76.

Watson, D.J.H. (1975) 'Contingency formulations of organisational structure: implications for managerial accounting', in Livingstone, J.L. (ed.) *Managerial Accounting: The Behavioural Foundations*. Grid.

Weick, K.E. (1979) *The Social Psychology of Organising*, 2nd edn. Addison-Wesley.

Westerlund, G. and Sjostrand, S.E. (1979) *Organizational Myths*. Harper and Row.

Williamson, O. (1975) *Markets and Hierarchies: Analysis and Antitrust Implications*. Free Press.

Wood, S. (1979) 'A reappraisal of the contingency approach to organisation', *Journal of Management Studies*, October, pp. 334–354.

Woodward, J. (1965) *Industrial Organisation: Theory and Practice*. London, Oxford University Press.

3
Professionalizing management and managing professionalization: British management in the 1980s*

Michael Reed and Peter Anthony

The purpose of this article is to analyse the strategy of managerial professionalization through educational reform as it has been attempted in Britain during the course of the 1980s. This strategy – whatever its internal contradictions and inherent weaknesses – is located within the longer-term historical context in which British management has developed. In turn, this brief historical analysis is complemented by an assessment of the feasibility of the strategy of professionalization in relation to some of the most recent work carried out on the sociology of the professions/expert knowledge. Finally, we discuss the broader implications of this analysis for current debates concerning the reality of managerial work and management culture, as well as the pedagogical principles and practices thought most appropriate to the latter – that is, how managers ought *to be educated and developed.*

Introduction

During the 1980s the state of British management education and training again became a matter for public concern, debate and action. A number of reports (Constable and McCormick, 1987; Handy, 1987; Mangham and Silver, 1986) indicated that both the range and quality of provision in this area fell well below that of our major economic competitors in America, Europe and Japan:

> The conclusion is inescapable that in Britain management education and training is too little, too late for too few. The British have rationed something which should be universally available and turned a potential common good into a special reserve. What should be a prerequisite for all managers has become a perk for the minority. The result is, in some areas, a spurious elite.
>
> (Handy *et al.*, 1988, p. 168)

The Cassandra-like warnings of accelerated economic decline galvanized 'leading providers' to undertake a number of initiatives aimed at producing a more coherent, extensive and integrated system of management education and development (Drewsmith *et al.*, 1989). These initiatives were directed at transforming the culture, competence and co-ordination of British management in the

*This article was first published in *Journal of Management Studies*, Vol. 29, No. 5, pp. 591–613, September 1992.

direction of a more 'enterprising' value system and a more 'professional' mode of occupational accreditation and control. The underlying ideological tensions and contradictions between an enterprising or entrepreneurial value system on the one hand, and a professional or status and control-oriented strategy on the other, were hardly recognized, much less debated or resolved. The organizational problems and political conflicts likely to accrue from these underlying tensions were also left unresolved. For the most part, they were sublimated within a pragmatically-oriented drive 'to do something' about the parlous state of management education, development and training in the UK as quickly as possible, while ensuring that the initiatives undertaken were soaked in the rhetoric of the 'enterprise culture' and the ideological and political sensitivities it catered for within governing institutions.

The fact that some of the major actors or agencies charged with transforming the depth and quality of management education and training would have very different ideas as to how this objective was to be achieved was also glossed over in the rush to 'get a slice of the action'. While less ambitious initiatives of this kind had been attempted between the 1950s and 1970s (Thomas, 1980; Wheatcroft, 1970; Whitley *et al.*, 1981), and more limited developments had occurred in relation to particular functional specialisms within management (Armstrong, 1987), the 1980s witnessed a more concerted strategy of educational reform in which the ideology and practice of 'professionalization' played a central political and organizational role.

Making managers

The position and standing of management within British society seems to have changed relatively little since the industrial revolution. Pollard's analysis of the genesis of modern management between the 1780s and 1850s suggests the emergence of a highly differentiated, not to say fragmented, group that had a poorly developed sense of its distinctive identity and existence as a separate class, profession or even occupation.

> A common body of knowledge and code of behaviour, as far as they existed, were valid only for each industry separately and hardly for an industrial manager's class as such ... there was thus virtually nothing to link the groups of management across the boundaries of their industries.
>
> (Pollard, 1965, pp. 87–8)

The vision of Britain as a cohesive and meritocratic professional society became a powerful ideological construction from the latter half of the nineteenth century onwards (Perkin, 1989). Yet, the power and status of management within this system was weak and indeterminate. The managerial 'class', such as it was, had become deeply embedded in a centuries-old technique and culture of rule which emphasized stability at the expense of innovation, and compromise at the expense of confrontation (Fox, 1983, p. 33). Not only this, but British managers seemed to lack the entrepreneurial zeal and thrust, as well as the basic technical competence, of managerial elites elsewhere. This led to a succession of promptings from governments of both major parties aimed at generating enhanced managerial dynamism and leadership. But management remained an essential institutional component of a political history and culture steeped in instrumental, pragmatic, individualistic values, and dominated by sectional tensions and conflicts (Middlemass, 1979). In so far as management was regarded as a constituent member of an embryonic 'service' or 'professional class', then it remained internally divided and unable and/or unwilling to develop and extend its 'causal powers' in such a way that it could remake British society according to its own values and interests. As Urry has argued:

> Management did not develop in Britain as a relatively autonomous set of interrelated professions, able to force through further widespread educational, technical and organisational reforms ... the service class in Britain before the Second World War did not possess sufficient organisational and cultural resources to produce a substantial restructuring of British society.
>
> (Urry, 1984, p. 43)

In this respect, the political and organizational weakness of British management was reflected in its reliance on a model of 'status', rather than 'occupational', professionalism. The former militated against the development and acceptance of an ideology of managerial professionalism for it legitimated intra-occupational specialization of an extreme kind, and the internal divisions which this encouraged (Child *et al.*, 1983). Status-oriented professionalism facilitated and supported an expert division of labour *within* management that fostered distinctive occupational entry and mobility in specific functional areas. It also encouraged and legitimated hierarchical differentiations within each specialism of a particularly rigid kind. Segmentalism between and within distinctive managerial specialisms became the dominant organizational motif in the development of British management (Armstrong, 1984; Child, 1969; Lash and Urry, 1987).

The historical and ideological trajectory (Fox, 1983; 1985) exerted a profound influence on its relationship with higher education. The development of institutions concerned with advanced management education was late and extremely circumspect; it was regarded with deep-seated scepticism, not to say hostility, by business, the universities and the state. Instead of an effective partnership between the three central actors, the evolution of management education in Britain followed a much more conflictual path in which it became – and continues to be – an agenda to be struggled over by contending interests and groups who lack any shared sense of strategic objectives and the means required to realize them (Thomas, 1980). Consequently, the expansion and consolidation of advanced management education was more often than not perceived as a threat to established business and academic imperatives and practices, rather than an expression of a shared political project (Locke, 1989). It is against this crippling educational heritage and the wider socio-political context in which management education became institutionalized that the developments of the 1980s must be interpreted.

During the course of the 1980s the condition of management education became one focus in the national debate concerning the state of the economy within an increasingly unstable global economic system. By the mid-to-late 1980s several commentators suggested that this 'surge of interest' in the contribution that a poorly resourced and developed system of management education was making to national economic decline had achieved a 'critical momentum' so that

> demand and provision are unlikely to fall back in the foreseeable future; that the commitment of many employers will be sustained and that those uncommitted at present will increasingly review their position and policies: and that interest by individual managers in their education, training and development will continue to expand.
>
> (Drewsmith *et al.*, 1989)

The key reports issued over this period maintained that British managers lacked the developmental, educational and training opportunities of their major international competitors. The British 'system', such as it was, was poorly organized, under-resourced and bereft of sustained cultural and political support from significant segments of British society:

> The lack of a clear, relevant and prestigious route into business and management may be one reason why fewer of the best of the British go into careers in business and management compared with their counterparts ... The 70,000 students on courses in the public sector provide good evidence of the general interest today in business and management, but these cannot in themselves constitute a prestigious professional formation.
>
> (Handy, 1987, pp. 11–12, emphasis added)

Thus, Handy's conclusion that the deficiencies of management education could only be corrected if a national system were to be initiated by government, industry and academia working together emerged as the overriding strategy to be followed through by interested parties. But Handy tied his proposals to a professional model of educational development and occupational advancement very much in keeping with the established tradition of 'status professionalism':

> Were these (a tradition of apprenticeship followed by corporate-based enhancement) all to happen, Britain would have developed an approach to the formation of her managers remarkably similar to the ways in which all the professions in Britain, including the armed services, develop their members in their desire to maintain a proper professionalism. Doctors, architects, accountants, lawyers, nowadays spend up to seven years (like managers in West Germany or in Japan) from the time of entry to a degree course, through a period of apprenticeship and further study, before they are allowed to practice without supervision, at which stage they have important responsibilities. ... It is, on the face of it, odd that the British never applied the procedures of professionalism to management.
>
> (Handy, 1987, pp. 15–16)

Initially, the Management Charter group became the agency through which this professionalizing project was to be implemented. This drive towards the professionalization of management was received very coolly, to say the least, by a majority of employers and other professional bodies concerned with these proposals (Drewsmith *et al.*, 1989). The strategy was perceived as driving a wedge between the individual manager and the employing organization: the wider commitments to a professional body and the enhanced possibilities for labour market mobility within the management field outside corporate monitoring or control sat very uneasily with the ingrained instincts of British business elites and the entrepreneurial and individualistic ideological prejudices of the government

(Whitley *et al.*, 1981). Consequently, the National Forum for Management Education and Training – the successor body to the Charter Initiative – very quickly reproduced within itself many of the philosophical and organizational conflicts which have bedevilled the history of management education in the UK for more than a century. Eventually, these boiled down to a conflict between those who wished to press the 'competencies-based' training approach and those who argued for a much broader and, in many respects, 'academic' view of the educational needs of British managers.

The National Forum very quickly encountered the well-established resistance of employers to any educational initiatives likely to dilute their traditional control over managerial recruitment and development. It also began to experience the pervasive impact of a government determined to absolve itself of any far-reaching financial or political responsibility for improving the depth and range of provision, as well as attempting to ensure that developments were under the aegis of the Training Enterprise Councils. At the same time, the universities – in the shape of the Council of University Management Schools – began to distance themselves from this emerging strategy which seemed to entail a substantial diminution in the knowledge-based/academic-cum-professional ethos which informed Handy's analysis. Burgoyne attempts to encapsulate this struggle of educational philosophies and practices in the following way:

> Those concerned with managing are clearly searching at the moment for an appropriate degree and form of professionalization for its conduct and execution ... Dealing with managing simply through listing managerial competencies tends to emphasize the technical. If competency approaches are to become a main foundation for management development, then ways must be found to expand and to accommodate the moral and ethical dimensions ... any effective scheme must recognize the holistic nature of management, the inevitability of a large element of judgement in its assessment, the variability of management across situations, the need to incorporate the moral/ethical element, the need to acknowledge that effective managing changes the nature of managerial competencies.
>
> (Burgoyne, 1989, pp. 59–6)

At one level, this struggle for pedagogical hegemony between the technical competencies-based approach and the creative professions/ethical approach is based on very different views concerning the reality of managerial work and the educational process thought most appropriate to producing better educated and skilled managers. At another level, it simply symbolized another phase in the perennial conflict between a technocratically oriented view of management education and training which is directly under the purview and control of employer/governmental agencies and a professionally-oriented conception that finds support from the latter, but is under the effective monitoring and tutelage of the major educational providers. The National Forum and the Training Agency seem determined to fight for the technocratic vision and support the drive for qualifications based on workplace in-company competencies, monitored and accredited by the Charter Network/TECs. However, the Council for University Management Schools seems to be pulling away from this strategy of accreditation and control. It is calling for a clearer and well-negotiated division of labour between employers and providers, in which the latter exercise a much higher degree of autonomy and control in shaping the content and form of educational accreditation for managers. The institutions of higher education see their primary 'mission' as providing a much larger pool of well-educated and qualified younger people from which British business can select their future generations of managers. In contrast, employers and state agencies charged with some kind of residual responsibility for supporting the expansion of vocationally oriented education and training are looking for pedagogical packages and organizational mechanisms to upgrade basic technical skills and competencies. They are required to achieve this without diminishing in any way the tight control exerted over initial selection, retention and mobility within the corporate hierarchy.

Underlying this conflict for control over the content of management education and training is the issue as to whether 'management' is, can be, or ought to be, regarded as a profession with a defined area of expertise. Those who support a professional model have tended to emphasize the universality and transferability of managerial knowledge and skill. Critics have stressed the particularistic nature of managerial competencies and the organizationally dependent qualities of management as a highly diverse occupational group. But advocates of both views have failed to examine the form of professionalization that may be most appropriate for management or the educational needs which this generates.

Managing professionalization

Professionalism has been used as a rhetorical device and ideological resource to legitimate the claims various expert groups and their representatives make on society's material and cultural resource base. In the case of management, there has been little or no systematic analysis of the relevance of professionalism to the work situation, organizational position and societal location of managers within advanced industrial societies. However, some of the most recent work on professionalism and professionalization suggests we need to reconsider conventional views as to their relevance in the managerial sphere.

Recent analyses of professionalization highlight the strategic role and significance of higher education in providing the primary institutional locale for constituting 'expertise' in advanced industrial societies:

> That link between higher education and the social division of labour that we call 'profession' has become, at least in capitalist societies, an almost ubiquitous way of *constituting expertise*; that is, creating, organizing, representing to both actors and spectators (or practitioners and clients) that here, vested in a person identified by particular badges, there is available specialized knowledge superior to that of other persons, who may well be even more knowledgeable and well trained *but in other domains*.
>
> (Larson, 1990, p. 36, emphasis added)

Larson's comment suggests that higher education is likely to become of even greater importance for the self-constitution of professions as coherent, authoritative and stable occupational entities with discursive fields and knowledge bases of their own. This is the case in so far as it provides the major source of cultural capital and theoretical knowledge through which professionalization can be mobilized and sustained (Collins, 1990). Abstract academic knowledge defines and legitimates 'professional work' and the systems of occupational control which crystallize around it (Abbott, 1988).

Second, recent work on the professions emphasizes the symbiotic link between educational credentialism, occupational closure and knowledge monopolization and control. These interlinked processes of collective exclusion provide the institutional and ideological foundations of occupational expertise and power (Murphy, 1990). Third, the ability of an occupational group to establish an effective 'jurisdictional claim' over task-based expertise is crucial in determining its success in achieving professional status within the expert division of labour:

> Public jurisdiction, in short, is a *claim of both social and cultural authority* ... abstract knowledge is the foundation of an effective definition of professions. Many occupations fight for turf, but only professions expand their cognitive dominion by using abstract knowledge to annex new areas, to define them as their own proper work.
>
> (Abbott, 1988, pp. 60–102, emphasis added)

Finally, the type of knowledge 'system' which professions rely on must lend itself to institutionalization as 'expertise' and occupational power and authority. Thus, 'a deliberate creation of an aura of indetermination about their activities that denies the possibility of rationalization and codification' (Boreham, 1983, p. 697) becomes crucial for successful professionalization. A judicial blend of formalized knowledge and expertise, mixed with tacit or 'sacred' practices and the inaccessibility which they promote, establishes the ideal knowledge base on which a successful professionalization project can be mobilized and sustained.

The failure of British management to mobilize and sustain an effective professionalization project has been well-rehearsed and documented elsewhere (Reed, 1989). The former exhibits an occupational structure that is socially fragmented, economically polarized and culturally stratified. This is unlikely to provide the appropriate institutional foundations for monopolization, exclusion and control. A high degree of organizational dependence for employment, remuneration, status and authority exposes managers to rationalization processes which drastically limit and reduce the degree of self-managed autonomy and discretion usually associated with established professions (Child, 1982). The lack of any effective monopoly over the knowledge base of managers and the subservience of managerial performance to the normative codes of corporate governance (Raelin, 1990), as well as the 'morality in use' of the organizational hierarchy (Jackall, 1988), prevents effective occupational closure. Finally, the nature of managerial work and the knowledge base on which it draws for task performance militates against the formation of high discretion, indeterminate and expert discursive domains from which effective jurisdictional claims and territories can be constructed and defended against predatory groups:

> ... the real problem with business management is the tenuous connection between the various abstractions applied to the area and the actual work of managers. As a result of this disconnection, the management area has numerous claimants, a degree (MBA) that covers extremely diverse forms of training and knowledge, and an equally diverse body of abstractions, about how the work ought to be done. Psychology, sociology, administration, economics, law, banking, accounting and other professions all claim some

jurisdiction in business management, each by extending its own abstractions, emptying them of content, and claiming that they cover the whole field.

(Abbott, 1988, p. 103)

Indeed, the successive attempts made to professionalize management through educational credentialism since the Second World War stand as testimony to the formidable – some would say insurmountable – obstacles which stand in the way of managerial professionalization. The traditional division between 'theory and practice' that has dogged management educational provision (Bain, 1990), the inability to forge an effective 'community of interest' behind higher management education (Weir, 1990), and the internal social, economic and cultural divisions within a fragmented service class (Savage *et al.*, 1988) all seems to reinforce the accepted view that management studies is a 'fragmented adhocracy' (Whitley, 1988). Managerial practice remains a highly diversified activity bereft of the basic occupational organization and control required to generate effective professional authority and closure (Whitley, 1989).

However, there is another way of reading this situation which suggests that a 'professional model' of management education and occupational formation may be more feasible than the critics imply. Indeed, one might argue that *the form* of professionalization and professionalism appropriate to management is prototypical of the general strategies and structures of professional power and control emerging in advanced industrial societies. Managers are both agents and victims of a process of formal rationalization which is a permanent threat to professional monopoly, closure and control. But, at the same time, the process of rationalization generates opportunities for the creation of 'new professions'; of forms of expert knowledge and control from which managers as a professional group can benefit. As Abbott has recently argued:

At present, professionalism seems to hold its own. It has stayed ahead of commodification, although many professions and their subgroups have been destroyed in the process. But it may ultimately lose out to organizations. The new hiring patterns of the major information firms and the loose forms of *organizational professionalism* point to a much weaker control of work by the professions themselves.

(Abbott, 1988, p. 325, emphasis added)

In Abbott's terms, management (and its political advocates or representative agencies) may be able to construct a form of occupational control and substantive work content that is an organizational hybrid of professionalism and craft modes of closure. This is much in keeping with the processes of formal rationalization and bureaucratization inherent within the trajectory of institutional development followed by all advanced industrial societies. As Murphy has maintained:

The later phase of formal rationalization, in which bureaucratization was more advanced, drew [the early professions] into bureaucratic organizations and created new professions which were born into bureaucracy ... Groups of credentialled experts differ from the autonomous liberal professions in the early phase of formal rationalization in that they have increasingly come under bureaucratic control ... The process of formal rationalization has resulted in specific resources which the credentialled mobilize and in opportunities which they seize in the structured system of closure and power of which they are a part.

(Murphy, 1990, pp. 91–2)

This reinforces Larson's hypothesis that the bureaucratization of professions will produce a type of 'organizational professionalism' that will become increasingly prevalent, not to say dominant (Larson, 1979) with the central role of state support facilitating the institutional and ideological preconditions in which such organizational professions can become more securely founded and protected. This envisages a kind and degree of state support of which there is admittedly little or no sign within the more recent initiatives reviewed above. Nevertheless, the *potential* for such a strategy of social closure and occupational control amongst managers should not be ignored; even if the major supportive agencies (and particularly the British state) have consistently failed to provide adequate support or action for this project when compared to most of their European (Lane, 1989) and North American counterparts (Roomkin, 1989).

As a prototype of the 'organizational professions', management may be said to display the following characteristics:

(i) a relatively high degree of organizational dependence;

(ii) a relatively high degree of work-related and occupationally-related heterogeneity;

(iii) a knowledge base and task repertoire that are organizationally diverse and resist complete codification of a highly formal kind, but are also dependent on an appreciation of complex relationships and the practice of craft skills embedded in systematic, reflective understanding (Whitley, 1989);

(iv) a limited degree of monopoly control over that knowledge base and the partial strategies of occupational closure and control which this makes available;

(v) significant contextual or external constraints and internal limitations upon the exercise of discretion and autonomy concerning the context and performance of work tasks;

(vi) internal functional differentiation and hierarchical stratification *within the occupational group* that militates against the emergence and maintenance of a strong and cohesive occupational identity and culture firmly resistant to the challenge of competitor groups.

These structural and operational characteristics are to be found amongst an increasing number of expert groups (Reich, 1991; Wilson and Rosenfield, 1990) that compete to establish the uniqueness of their specialist contribution with advanced industrial societies. In relation to both state policy and corporate strategies, the potential ideological and organizational power available to management – *if* it can develop and control an expert knowledge base resistant to easy intrusion from competitor groups – is considerable, and could provide the foundation for an effective professionalization project. That control will be more limited than *was* the case with the 'liberal professions', but it could provide the basis for a form of managerial professionalism akin to that emerging in other specialist domains.

This potential for a viable professionalization project is reinforced by long-term trends in the restructuring of managerial work and organization. Taken together, they also raise some interesting questions as to the kind of education needed by future managers. It may prove to be the case that, with respect to higher education, the form and content of managerial education which ought to be available differs fundamentally from that currently being advocated.

Restructuring managerial work

The educational initiatives undertaken to enhance management in the 1980s have been advanced with little or no regard for recent research on the complexities of managerial work. Neither has any serious attempt been made to consider the ways in which managerial work is being transformed as a result of technological, economic, political and cultural changes occurring within all advanced industrial societies. Hence, there is a very real danger that the diagnoses of the 'problem' of management education, and the proposed treatment, are based upon a specification of firm-specific needs and skills which will become effectively obsolete before they can be operationalized in practice. As Locke has recently demonstrated, the predilection of British employers, politicians and educators to pursue a relatively rigid and mechanistic conception of management educational and training 'needs', at a time when enhanced flexibility and adaptability are called for, is in danger of being repeated once more (Locke, 1989). There is the additional problem that they will resort to the traditional liberal or autonomous model of professionalism (Siegrist, 1990). But the latter is inappropriate to the present environmental and organizational context which requires a more reflective consideration of the social, political and ethical aspects of managerial work. Any evaluation of the latter, and their wider pedagogical implications, will need to focus on the creative and innovative aspects of managerial work in a rapidly changing environment. As Locke contends:

> To succeed, a modern business community and a modern business firm within that community have to mould a lot of disparate functions into a self-supporting whole. That, at least, is what the American firms and then the Japanese taught the managerial world.
>
> (Locke, 1989, p. 217)

All too often, the educational community has retreated into a narrow vocationalism in which the overriding emphasis is given to functional and technical skills which crowds out any sustained concern with the social, moral, political and ideological ingredients of managerial work and the form of educational experience most appropriate to their enhancement and development (Anthony, 1986). This would seem to be doubly inappropriate at a time when the nature of managerial work, and the constantly shifting environment in which it is practised, are likely to undermine and subvert the rigid application of technical skills or 'competencies', which are divorced from the social and organizational context in which they have to be applied. Indeed, there is every reason to think that the building and maintenance of strong community traditions and structures within business is even more of a prerequisite for economic success in the conditions presented by 'disorganized capitalism' (Reed, 1991).

The cumulative findings of the empirical research on managerial work over the last three decades has suggested a clear rejection of the comforting, but misplaced, simplicities of the rational/technocratic view of such a vital social practice. It has also led to [a] conception of management which suggests that '... because they [managers] are concerned with social and political relationships in organizations, they have a real concern with moral relationships' (Anthony, 1986, p. 186).

This latter view places the 'negotiation of order' within complex organizations and the wider society at the core of the managerial task. It locates managerial practices and skills within a broader concern for the ethical foundations and moral quality of the social relationships that managers construct and reconstruct in their attempt to forge order out of chaos. At the same time, it recognizes the structural and ideological constraints within which the fashioning of 'organizational communities' has to take place.

However, research on contemporary management indicates contradictory trends. On the one hand, there is the view that technological and structural change will facilitate the development of a hybrid form of managerial practice encapsulating the knowledge and skills of the professional politician and the craftsman artist (Sabel, 1990). The jurisdictional divisions between the traditional professions and experts will break down under the constant pressure for innovation and diversity exerted by more flexible technologies and more fluid corporate structures (Best, 1990). In their place will emerge new groups of managers who will apply their expertise in such a way that cognitive diversity and collective learning will be enhanced. The reintegration of conception and execution within the 'mega-corporation', made possible by information technology and its organizational consequences, will produce new foundations for managerial authority based on a commitment to expand collective intellectual knowledge and skills, rather than to re-establish control over the organization's knowledge base so as to preserve hierarchical power (Zuboff, 1988).

On the other hand, there is a darker, more pessimistic, view which interprets the underlying dynamic of change as reinforcing organizational and occupational polarization within an ideological climate dominated by instrumental values (Armstrong, 1989; Child, 1984, 1987; Scase and Goffee, 1989):

> ... it can be argued that there are tendencies polarizing the structure of modern management ... the commitment, motivation and job satisfaction of middle and junior managers may be severely eroded as they become even more excluded from participation in the decision-making processes surrounding the specification of major corporate objectives ... they may be now developing more instrumental and calculative attitudes towards their employing organizations ... there is an increasing polarization of management tasks within large-scale organizations ... [this has] reinforced the concentration of decision-making among limited numbers of senior managers responsible for longer-term corporate strategy. ... These experiences suggest a growing divide between, on the one hand, senior executives and, on the other, middle and junior managers. The former increasingly appear to monopolize strategic decision-making, while the latter are delegated routine administrative duties which are subject to tighter measures of performance.
>
> (Scase and Goffee, 1989, pp. 12–28)

This polarization between a knowledge-based elite and a machine-minding mass, within a low-trust managerial culture dominated by power interests and the elaborate system of organizational and ideological controls that it generates (Jackall, 1988), is also seen to be reflected at the level of occupational restructuring within management – particularly with regard to British management (Bamber and Snape, 1987; Crompton, 1990; Savage *et al.*, 1988). The capacity of British management to form a 'third force' within British society, where managers are 'seen as a distinct social grouping whose interests may differ from those of owners and other workers' (Bamber and Snape, 1987, p. 51), is thought to be pre-empted by long-standing internal divisions and conflicts which have been exacerbated by more recent structural and ideological trends. Hierarchical and functional divisions at the corporate level are seen to be overlain by labour market and sectoral splits at the occupational level to produce a British 'service class' divided into a traditional public sector/large companies group, and an embryonic private sector/self-employed group. This leads to a fragmented managerial culture and a fractured occupational politics in which internal cleavages outweigh any residual potential for collective mobilization and action (Savage *et al.*, 1988).

Whichever of these interpretations one chooses – and the 'jury is still out' and is likely to remain so for some time – they make available considerable intellectual, and possibly institutional, space in which a fundamental re-evaluation of management education and its links with the professionalization of managerial work and its associated occupational structures is now possible. So far this opportunity seems to have been missed by those engaged in the attempt to enhance the range and quality of management education and development within the UK. We need to consider how the space opened up by contemporary developments can be utilized profitably to develop a more coherent and realistic philosophy of management education and the managerial culture in which it is most likely to be nurtured. Some consideration of the more prescriptive implications of the previous analysis is attempted in the subsequent sections of this article.

Educating managers and managerial culture

The space to be filled is the difference between the established educational provision for managers, based upon what is believed to be required or what is marketable, and what is emerging from research as the reality of management. A necessary competence in analytic skills and techniques does nothing to encourage a reflective understanding of the complexities and nuances of organizational relationships and distributed power, nor does it do much to develop a critical response to the vagaries of organizational and personal authority. Perhaps it is the needs of teachers rather than managers that has encouraged a concentration on the strict mechanisms of rational bureaucracy instead of the uncertainties and subtleties of negotiated order. Our contention that management education should explore this space is based upon three propositions:

(i) that the negotiation of organizational order is the abode of the actual but often unrecognized concerns and problems of practising managers in the real world – it is practical rather than abstracted;

(ii) that management practice is about moral issues and requires ethical examination because these are fundamentals upon which any organizational reality rests;

(iii) that any educational process must develop and encourage critical and sceptical responses and that the failure of management education to do so will contribute to its own redundancy.

We have suggested that new and less determinate views of managerial relationships have emerged from research and we have argued elsewhere that these form the basis of actual conduct in the management of the delivery of health care in the hospital service (Anthony and Reed, 1990). This view is reinforced by recent, but perhaps less reliable, predictions as to the nature of the management process in the widely heralded new, flat, flexible, non-hierarchical, knowledge-based enterprises. One of several emerging contradictions is that the successful enterprise of the twenty-first century will be more like a university (Sadler, 1988) whilst the universities insist not only that management is essentially bureaucratic, but also sedulously ape Detroit management in the direction of their own affairs.

There is some evidence that management education is beginning to respond thoughtfully to these changes. The present and predicted condition of organizational management and the demand for excellence in an unstable environment explain the recent return to an interest in leadership and an advance to the frontiers of organizational culture. These developments are associated with an explosion of interest in business ethics in the USA and a barely audible echo of it in this country. They are, on the face of it, just the sort of changes we should welcome but they could turn out to be a false promise to reinforce, rather than remove, the errors of management education. Let us examine them.

Leadership, one of the original and then discarded shibboleths of early management education, has returned to the agenda because of its close association with the management of culture and cultural change. In some respects they are synonymous:

> Organizational cultures are created by leaders and one of the most decisive functions of leadership may well be the creation, the management and – if and when they may become necessary – the destruction of the culture. ... Culture and leadership are ... two sides of the same coin.
>
> (Schein, 1985, p. 2)

Their identity arises from the two broad senses in which organizational culture is defined; as what exists (in the anthropological sense) and as what may be deliberately influenced or changed (the managerial sense). In the former, organizational culture is observed behavioural regularities (Goffman, 1959), the rules of the game of getting along in the organization, the ropes that a newcomer must learn in order to become an accepted member, the way we do things here. In the latter case, culture concerns the philosophy that guides an organization's policy towards employees or customers (Ouchi, 1981; Pascale and Athos, 1982) and, although Schein distinguishes culture from overt behaviour patterns which can be as much a reflection of the environment as of the culture (Schein, 1985, p. 9), Ogbonna and Wilkinson (1990) point out the difficulty of distinguishing cultural response from resigned behavioural compliance which is the result of instrumental motives or the threat of sanctions rather than the internalization of espoused values. The current interest in leadership and organizational culture arises from a belief in its utility in achieving ends rather than in any academic or anthropological concern to better understand the behaviour and values of the natives. The association of leadership with the management of organizational culture represents an advance from the older belief in the provision of personal meaning by organizational adjustment to the adjustment of personal meaning for organizational ends (Anthony, 1990).

The concern continues to be utilitarian rather than disinterested, but the pursuit of compliance and co-operation through culture certainly serves to broaden the interest of management theory and education. When the subject takes us into rhetoric, narrative, symbolic or emblematic meaning, metaphor and magic (Cleverley, 1973; Daudi, 1986; Gambling, 1977; Gowler and Legge, 1983; Pondy, 1983) we are far adrift from the mechanisms of bureaucracy and, at the same time, in seas long since charted by critical ancient mariners. Management education, in short, has to begin to think.

Organizational culture, if managers can begin to understand it, let alone influence it, demands some philosophical awareness of the importance of values, a complexity sometimes eschewed by the older generation of analysts of organizations. Cultures are not homogeneous; sub-cultures need to be recognized (Turner, 1971) if their influence is to be understood or overcome. To the extent that cultural management is to be successful rather than cosmetic or deceptive, it will have to comprehend comparative values and belief systems.

The concern with leadership, too, raises issues of an abstract and indeterminate complexity rare in management education. If by leadership we mean anything beyond charismatic mystery; if, in short, we believe that it can be taught, then we are concerned with both political and moral theory, with questions of jurisprudence and justice, moral and social reciprocity, with the proper loyalty owed to a leader in return for the proper care and responsibility that the leader owes to those who follow.

These developments, along with speculations about new forms of post-Fordist organizations, concerning leadership and culture, the nature of authority and its relationship to ethics, take management into conceptual areas beyond the precision of bureaucratic and technical primary control. They are not so much reactions against the environments of new information technology and competitive markets, as implied and necessary adjustments to them. We would argue, in a sense both normative and prescriptive, that they have always been the concern of managers but that management theory and education have hitherto avoided them. The reasons for the obfuscation of realities long recognized in the spheres of social and political relations by management educators are complex. They concern, in part, the belief that such immeasurable abstractions, the very core of interaction in any other field of human endeavour, were made irrelevant by the power exercised over both employer and customer: where coercion suffices there is no call for subtlety. Management education could safely confine itself to techniques of control, explanations of their efficacy and nostrums designed to make them seem acceptable.

If anything supports the present movement beyond these charades into a real concern with reflective responsibility it is surely the attention now being given to business ethics. There are suggestions that this attention reflects a real attempt to come to terms with abiding managerial problems. Donaldson, for example, tells us of American evidence to the effect that ethical concerns are part of the routine practices of management. They are characterized less frequently by legal issues than by concerns about relationships and responsibility, and while they deal with right and wrong decisions, they frequently involve factors that make the right and wrong less than patently clear (Donaldson, 1989, p. 54). The difficulties seem to arise over differences of interest (between family and business reputation), conflicts over the application of a value (loyalty to the group versus loyalty to the head of the group), conflicts between values (truth versus human welfare) or conflict between codes of conduct (company policy versus professional standards). Managers report that such issues are typical and difficult.

Such accounts seem to support our contention that the reality of management has always involved wider areas of conceptual attention than the perspective conventionally afforded it in orthodox management education. But, we should not be over hasty in concluding that business education has filled the gap; doubts exist concerning both motive and method. The motive for the attention to business ethics is, in part, prudential, a recommended adherence to published statements of good attention and social responsibility. Codes of conduct may serve as guides to conduct and they may also demonstrate sound public relations, advertisements of reliability and trustworthiness intended to extend sales or to avoid legal constraint or public investigation. If the city or the banks or soccer clubs do not reform themselves they will be subject to control; so, if they are wise, they take up business ethics.

The method is questionable in so far as it abandons the very difficulties attending the 'ethical routine practices of management' by proffering a routine bureaucratic response: the elaboration of codes of practice. Codes of practice have their uses: they set out the requirements of the law; they prescribe the limits of discretionary decision (redundancy will be determined by seniority); they outline general good intentions. They are attractive but not necessarily useful in helping managers to avoid moral dilemmas because their purpose is to substitute for the essential difficulties of moral issues, simple, understandable, definitional rules: they help to avoid painful thought. Jackall (1988) further implies that policy statements and codes may be of no great practical help to managers in guiding their conduct in situations where they have to be expedient; in these circumstances they may even add to a degree of managerial cynicism.

Such difficulties lead to questions about business ethics and about the reasons for their inclusion in educational programmes. Morality sometimes seems to be swallowed up in notions of corporate good, the result of the convenient recruitment of utilitarian ethical theory. The parent who reprimands untruthfulness in children at the breakfast table takes the same moral values to work but, once there, strange confusions occur. Corporate good is claimed to outweigh the good of the individual: the company represents great interests which must not be damaged because of the great suffering that will follow; the economy of the country will suffer; employees will be put out of work; other and less morally responsible companies will prosper, customers or clients will be harmed; pretzels are more important than people. In extreme cases, the worst practices can be defended, as they were at Nuremburg: loyalty and allegiance to the leader require that orders be obeyed; refusal entails an abnegation of duty and duty is a moral virtue.

Jackall's account in his book *Moral Mazes* (1988) goes some way to explain a state of moral breakdown. His corporate managers behave like characters in Jacobean revenge tragedy. They exhibit a 'bureaucratic alertness to expediency' (Jackall, 1988, p. 123), governed by the overriding influence of institutional logic, tactical means, the suppression of criticism and professional debate allied, ultimately, to individual self-interest. The result is that the manager 'comes to see himself as an object, a commodity and to the extent that self-objectification is incomplete ... to that extent do managers experience moral dilemmas ... The logical result of alertness to expediency is the elimination of any ethical lines at all' (Jackall, 1988, p. 133).

And here we come to the ultimate objection to any proposal to educate managers in reflective responsibility: that it will not work because it is irrelevant, unreal and impractical. It would interfere with the bureaucratic process of commodification and would contradict the essential tenet of utilitarianism; it would cause managers pain rather than pleasure and would therefore be avoided. This is a philosophical explanation of the difficulty in answering the question 'how is managerial behaviour to be improved by education?' The practical version is that responsibility seems to be driven out by competition with ruthless and self-interested opponents or, as Jackall puts it, 'the fundamental requirements of managerial work clash with the normal ethics governing interpersonal behaviour' (Jackall, 1988, p. 195).

The first objection to this implacable conclusion is that it is intolerable. MacIntyre (1981) directs his coruscating attack against the moral vacuity of management ('the best managers are the best actors') because managers are the most influential central characters of our time. Jackall agrees; given their pivotal role in our epoch, they help create and recreate, as one unintended consequence of their personal striving, a society where morality becomes indistinguishable from the quest for one's own survival and advantage (Jackall, 1988, p. 204). It has been argued elsewhere that at no other time in history has power been exercised without some educational attempt to impose upon it responsibility and that, if we are the first exception, we are contributing to the creation of a barbarian elite (Anthony, 1986). Whether management can be brought into civilized intercourses is, finally, a problem for society which, if it cannot succeed, is likely to break down because the ultimate defence of morality is that it is necessary: if we do not tell the truth, no one can be trusted and all will suffer. Our problem, as teachers, is simpler: if managers insist on going to hell we have no business helping them. The lesser consequence is that if teachers abandon the essential core of education they are likely to be regarded as contemptible, to their own ultimate disadvantage. While the demand for management education is sustained by the belief that improved economic performance requires more of it, more business schools, more MBAs, more certificated or chartered managers, the evidence of improved competence is not easy to find. But education, even for management, must ultimately be a matter of faith, or belief in values that are fundamental. That, after all, is why the universities are the indispensable providers, because they enshrine the virtues of objectivity, concern for truth, reflective understanding, sceptical enquiry and research as ends in themselves which may (or may not) turn out to be useful.

If that was the 'idea of a university' that concerned Newman and Arnold, we teachers know it to be an idea which is never realized. But we are taught to try despite the evidence of imperfection. The present question is whether we can continue to try or, rather, whether we are being taught not to try in the field of management education which promises or threatens to command the nature of universities themselves. The present question is whether we are concerned with the education of managers at all.

The second objection to the view that management education can do nothing to address the fundamental problem of management, that it is exempt from the rules of social intercourse, is that it is unrealistic and impractical. Accumulating evidence shows that managers (real managers, below the level of corporate manipulation; the difference goes back to the old distinction between financial and productive management) depend for their effectiveness upon norms of reciprocity, upon trust, obligation and the maintenance of defensible social relationships (Burns and Stalker, 1961; Dalton, 1959; Kotter, 1982; Mintzberg, 1973; Stewart, 1983). To the extent that management education avoids areas of reflective responsibility, it constructs a conceptual astigmatism which distorts reality so as to make it conform to its own myopia. Reality, both social and economic, resides in the production and exchange of goods and services and that depends on the dialectics of control and co-operation, on leadership and community and, finally, upon authority, which is essentially moral.

How we incorporate reflection, thoughtfulness and responsibility into the curriculum is a matter for debate (Leavitt, 1983). The programme should probably avoid (to paraphrase Jackall) management texts. At least one Professor of Administration (Wilkie, 1989) begins with literary criticism. Business history would be useful because it seems safely remote from present preoccupations, while at the same time developing a relevant spirit of enquiry. Journalism, particularly of the financial kind, is likely to be more valuable than the pursuit of managerial excellence. Industrial relations should be rescued before it is too late, because it requires attention to differences in power, perspective and values.

It may not matter too much what the subject matter is as long as we encourage our students and our managers to think and as long as we believe that what we are doing is valuable rather than profitable. Prescription as to the content of a reformed management education, however, is neither valuable nor necessary. What is important is that it should *become* an education. In the present circumstances it seems that statement can no longer be regarded as axiomatic. One sufficient justification is that an activity residing in academic institutions should be a practice concerned with values and with critical examination beyond the purpose of its own sustenance. If it fails, then it ceases to meet the needs of its client; it becomes entirely dependent on the market which will quickly discover that the universities are valueless and that it can better provide for itself.

That might be no matter for regret beyond the protection of the career prospects of management teachers. The second justification is of wider significance: it concerns the lives and responsibilities of managers who, we are persuaded, are among the central characters of the contemporary world. It becomes, therefore, a matter of social and political importance.

The organizations which conduct business enterprise and the provision of services, private or public, are themselves communities. The networks that compose them engage in activities and dependencies which are not susceptible to mechanistic description and measurement. The processes of bureaucratic control, of prescribed subordinate performance, never did entirely account, even in the most coercive extremes, for the way organizations work. They are even less relevant in higher-order, knowledge-based and necessarily more open organizational structures. Organizations always were, and are increasingly becoming, dependent on collaboration and exercised discretion. As they become more voluntaristic and co-operative in order to become more effective and profitable, so their influence on society increases. The real need for a reformed management education rests on the requirement for managers to be helped to an awareness of their own significance and responsibility by encouraging in them a consciousness of the difficulties with which they are engaged. They must be encouraged to think about the unprogrammable complexities which face them without the distracting and specious assistance of codes, competencies, catch phrases and mission statements. Managers must begin to reflect upon the real world which they know they inhabit. Paradoxically, when management education begins to give them serious academic attention it may at last have some prospect of entering the real world itself.

Conclusion

We have argued in this article, both on sociological and pedagogical grounds, that the education of managers should take a rather different form and content to that proposed by advocates of a competencies-based or technically oriented approach. As an organizational profession, we have argued that management must take its responsibilities to the organization seriously; that is, it must be prepared to protect the long-term interests and viability of the organization against short-term environmental pressures of one kind of another. If managers are to maintain the integrity of the organization as a viable community, and the ethical and political foundations on which it rests, then their education must provide crucial assistance to them in performing this role. In short, it must help in preparing them to cope with the contradictory pressures and conflicting priorities which they will inevitably confront as professionals working within, and to some extent dependent on, complex organizations.

The prevailing political climate and situation in Britain may be hostile to the 'professional state' (Marquand, 1990). However, management educators have a responsibility to develop and promulgate a view of their practice that is more appropriate to the social realities and moral dilemmas that managers face. The fulfilment of this may require a fundamental break with the historically sedimented 'traditions' which have accrued within the educational and managerial cultures of British society since the time of the industrial revolution. Yet, it is only by challenging the ideological and intellectual constraints implicit within these 'traditions' – which are grounded in an unreflective pragmatism or 'hucksterism' poorly suited to the spirit and condition of the times – that educators and managers will be placed in a better position to shape their own destinies.

The pivotal role of higher education – and universities in particular – in the formation of management as an organizational profession demands that it plays a much more prominent part in determining what and how managers will be taught. The inherent – some would say debilitating – weaknesses of British management education revealed in this article will only change for the better if institutions of advanced learning begin to take a much more proactive, coherent and independent line in determining both the form and content of the educational experience that they provide for managers. They need to recover their institutional and pedagogical nerve.

References

Abbott, A. (1988) *The System of Professions*. Chicago, University of Chicago Press.

Anthony, A. (1986) *The Foundation of Management*. London, Tavistock.

Anthony, A. (1990) 'The paradox of management culture or he who leads is lost', *Personnel Review*, Vol. 19, No. 4, pp. 3–8.

Anthony, A. and Reed, M. (1990) 'Managerial roles and relationships in a district health authority', *International Journal of Health Care and Quality Assurance*, Vol. 3, No. 3, pp. 20–31.

Armstrong, P. (1984) 'Competition between the organizational professions and the evolution of management control strategies', in Thompson, K. (ed.) *Work, Employment and Unemployment*, pp. 97–120. Milton Keynes, Open University Press.

Armstrong, P. (1987) 'Management control strategies and inter-professional competition: the cases of accountancy and personnel management', in Knights, D. and Willmott, H. (eds) *Managing the Labour Process*. Aldershot, Gower.

Armstrong, P. (1989) 'Limits and possibilities for HRM in an age of management accountancy', in Storey, J. (ed.) *New Perspectives on Human Resource Management*, pp. 154–63. London, Routledge.

Bain, G. (1990) 'A vocational vortex', *Times Higher Educational Supplement*, 23 February.

Bamber, G. and Snape, E. (1987) 'Managerial and professional employees in Britain', *Employee Relations*, Vol. 9, No. 3.

Best [no initials given] (1990) *The New Competition*. Cambridge, Polity Press.

Boreham, P. (1983) 'Indetermination: professional knowledge, organization and control', *Sociological Review*, Vol. 31, No. 4, pp. 693–718.

Burgoyne, J. (1989) 'Creating the managerial portfolio: building on competency approaches to management development', *Management Education and Development*, Vol. 20, pp. 56–61.

Burns, T. and Stalker, G.M. (1961) *The Management of Innovation*. London, Tavistock.

Child, J. (1969) *British Management Thought*. London, Allen & Unwin.

Child, J. (1982) 'Professionals in the corporate world: values, interests and control', in Dunkerley, D. and Salaman, G. (eds) *The International Yearbook of Organization Studies*, pp. 212–41. London, Routledge.

Child, J. (1984) *Organization: A Guide to Problems and Practice* (second edition). London, Harper and Row.

Child, J. (1987) 'Microelectronics and the quality of employment in services', in Marstrand, P. (ed.) *New Technology and the Future of Work and Skill*, pp. 163–40. London, Frances Pinter.

Child, J., Fores, M., Glover, I. and Lawrence, P. (1983) 'A price to pay?: professionalism and work organization in Britain and West Germany', *Sociology*, Vol. 17, No. 1, pp. 63–78.

Cleverley, G. (1973) *Managers and Magic*. Harmondsworth, Pelican.

Constable, J. and McCormick, R. (1987) *The Making of British Managers*. London, British Institute of Management.

Collins, R. (1990) 'Changing conceptions in the sociology of the professions', in Torstendahl, R. and Burrage, M. (eds) *The Formation of Professions*, pp. 11–23. London, Sage.

Crompton, R. (1990) 'Professions in the current context', *Work, Employment and Society,* Special Issue, 'A Decade of Change?', pp. 147–66.

Dalton, M. (1959) *Men Who Manage*. New York, Wiley.

Daudi, P. (1986) *The Discourse of Power in Managerial Praxis*. Oxford, Blackwell.

Donaldson, J. (1989) *Key Issues in Business Ethics*. London, Academic Press.

Drewsmith, S., Pell, C., Jones, P., Sloman, M. and Blacknell, A. (1989) *Management Challenge for the 1990s*. London, Training Agency, Deloitte, Haskins and Sells.

Fox, A. (1983) 'British management and industrial relations: the social origins of a system', in Earl, M.D. (ed.) *Perspectives on Management*, pp. 6–39. Oxford, Oxford University Press.

Fox, A. (1985) *History and Heritage: The Social Origins of the British Industrial Relations Systems*. London, Allen & Unwin.

Gambling, T. (1977) 'Magic, accountancy and morale', *Accountancy, Organizations and Society,* Vol. 2, No. 2, pp. 141–51.

Goffman, E. (1959) *Asylums*. Harmondsworth, Penguin.

Gowler, D. and Legge, K. (1983) 'The meaning of management and the management of meaning: a view from social anthropology', in Earl, M.D. (ed.) *Perspectives on Management*, pp. 187–233. Oxford, Oxford University Press.

Handy, C. (1987) *The Making of Managers*. London, Manpower Services Commission/National Economic Development Council, British Institute of Management.

Handy, C., Gordon, C., Gow, I. and Randlesome, C. (1988) *Making Managers*. Oxford, Pitman.

Jackall, R. (1988) *Moral Mazes: The World of Corporate Managers*. Oxford, Oxford University Press.

Kotter, J.P. (1982) *The General Managers*. New York, Free Press/Collier Macmillan.

Lane, C. (1989) *Management and Labour in Europe: The Industrial Enterprise in Germany, Britain and France*. Aldershot, Edward Elgar.

Larson, M.S. (1979) *The Rise of Professionalism: A Sociological Analysis*. Berkeley, University of California Press.

Larson, M.S. (1990) 'In the matter of experts and professionals', in Torstendahl, R. and Burrage, M. (eds) *The Formation of Professions*, pp. 24–50. London, Sage.

Lash, S. and Urry, J. (1987) *The End of Organized Capitalism*. Cambridge, Polity Press.

Leavitt, H. (1983) 'Management and management education in the west: what's right and what's wrong', The Stockton Lecture, London Business School.

Locke, R. (1989) *Management and Higher Education since 1940*. Cambridge, Cambridge University Press.

MacIntyre, A. (1981) *After Virtue: A Study in Moral Theory*. London, Duckworth.

Mangham, I. and Silver, M. (1986) *Management Training: Context and Practice*. London, Economic and Social Research Council.

Marquand, D. (1990) 'Smashing times', *New Statesman and Society,* 27 September, pp. 18–20.

Middlemass, K. (1979) *Politics in Industrial Society: The Experience of the British System since 1911*. London, Andre Deutsch.

Mintzberg, H. (1973) *The Nature of Managerial Work*. New York, Harper and Row.

Murphy, R. (1990) 'Proletarianization or bureaucratization: the fall of the professional?', in Torstendahl, R. and Burrage, M. (eds) *The Formation of Professions*, pp. 70–96. London, Sage.

Ogbonna, E. and Wilkinson, B. (1990) 'Corporate strategy and corporate cultures: the view from the checkout', *Personnel Review*, Vol. 19, No. 4, pp. 9–15.

Ouchi, W. (1981) *Theory z: How American Business Can Meet the Japanese Challenge*. Reading, Mass., Addison-Wesley.

Pascale, R. and Athos, A. (1982) *The Art of Japanese Management: Applications for American Executives*. Harmondsworth, Penguin.

Perkin, H. (1989) *The Rise of Professional Society: England since 1880*. London, Routledge.

Pollard, S. (1965) *The Genesis of Modern Management*. Harmondsworth, Penguin.

Pondy, L.R. (1983) 'The role of metaphors and myths', in Pondy, L.R., Frost, P.J., Morgan, G. and Dandridge, T.C. (eds) *Organizational Symbolism*, p. 164. Greenwich, Conn., JAI Press.

Raelin, J. (1990) 'Let's not teach management as if it were a profession', *Business Horizons*, Vol. 33, No. 2, pp. 23–8.

Reed, M. (1989) *The Sociology of Management*. London, Harvester.

Reed, M. (1991) 'The end of organized society: a theme in search of a theory?', in Blyton, P. and Morris, J. (eds) *A Flexible Future? Prospects for Employment and Organisation*, pp. 23–37. Berlin, De Gruyter.

Reich, R. (1991) *The Work of Nations*. London, Simon & Schuster.

Roomkin, M.J. (1989) *Managers as Employees: An International Comparison of the Changing Character of Managerial Employment*. Oxford, Oxford University Press.

Sabel, C. (1990) 'Skills without a place: the reorganization of the corporation and the experience of work', British Sociological Association unpublished paper, April.

Sadler, P. (1988) *Managerial Leadership in the Post-Industrial Society*. Aldershot, Gower.

Savage, M., Dickens, P. and Fielding, T. (1988) 'Some social and political implications of the contemporary fragmentation of the "service class" in Britain', *International Journal of Urban and Regional Research*, Vol. 12, pp. 455–75.

Scase, R. and Goffee, R. (1989) *Reluctant Managers: Their Work and Lifestyles*. London, Unwin Hyman.

Schein, E.H. (1985) *Organizational Culture and Leadership*. San Francisco, Jossey-Bass.

Siegrist, H. (1990) 'Professionalization as a process: patterns, progression and discontinuity', in Burrage, M. and Torstendahl, R. (eds) *Professions in Theory and History*, pp. 177–97. London, Sage.

Stewart, R. (1983) 'Managerial behaviour: how research has changed the traditional picture', in Earl, M.D. (ed.) *Perspectives on Management*, pp. 82–96. Oxford, Oxford University Press.

Thomas, A. (1980) 'Management and education: rationalization and reproduction in British business', *International Studies of Management and Organization*, Vol. 10, No. 1–2, pp. 71–109.

Torstendahl, R. and Burrage, M. (eds) (1990) *The Formation of Professions*. London, Sage.

Turner, B. (1971) *Exploring the Industrial Sub-Culture*. London, Macmillan.

Urry, J. (1984) 'Scientific management and the service class'. Lancaster Regionalism Group, Working Paper 12, Lancaster University.

Weir, D. (1990) 'The boys from the B schools', *Times Higher Educational Supplement*, 29 June.

Wheatcroft [no initials given] (1970) *The Revolution in British Management Education*. London, Pitman.

Whitley, R. (1988) 'The management sciences and managerial skills', *Organization Studies*, Vol. 9, No. 1, pp. 47–68.

Whitley, R. (1989) 'On the nature of managerial tasks and skills, their distinguishing characteristics and organization', *Journal of Management Studies*, Vol. 26, No. 3, pp. 209–23.

Whitley, R., Thomas, A. and Marceau, J. (1981) *Masters of Business?* London, Tavistock.

Wilkie, R. (1989) 'Values and decisions'. Unpublished conference paper, British Academy of Management, Annual Conference, Manchester Business School.

Wilson, D.C. and Rosenfield, R.H. (1990) *Managing Organizations: Texts, Readings and Cases*. London, McGraw-Hill.

Zuboff, S. (1988) *In the Age of the Smart Machine*. London, Heinemann.

4

Ethical dilemmas in performance appraisal revisited*

Clinton Longenecker and Dean Ludwig

Abstract

In managers' dynamic, real-world environments, they often feel it is necessary to exercise some creative discretion over employee ratings. Most managers do not describe their ratings of subordinates in performance appraisals as completely honest or accurate. The inaccuracy is often in the form of inflated ratings. They justify the inaccuracy by citing, among other things, the need to avoid confrontation with subordinates, damaging working relationships, and creating permanent written documents which may later harm a subordinate's career. Many of these motives are not only well intentioned, but are designed to enhance individual, unit, and organizational performance (some of the ultimate objectives of performance appraisal systems). This paper examines the ethics of this sort of deliberate manipulation of performance appraisal systems. It suggests that at the organizational level, performance appraisal is usually seen as an end in itself, and a formalist ethical critique is applied. At the managerial level, performance appraisal is usually seen as a means to an end, and a utilitarian critique is applied. Since both perspectives are essential, we conclude that a Janus-Headed analysis is needed. We suggest some duties and obligations for both the organization and the manager engaged in performance appraisal.

Introduction

Performance appraisal has become a widespread formal organizational procedure with managers measuring and evaluating subordinates' performance using formal rating instruments on an annual or semi-annual basis. It has been estimated that over 92% of all organizations in the US use some form of this process (Locher and Teel, 1988). Performance appraisals continue to be a very hot topic these days for both the academician as well as the practitioner as organizations attempt to use the formal appraisal process as a critical human resource management tool (Landy and Farr, 1983).

Researchers have continually looked for the optimal rating instrument and presently seek to better understand the cognitive and interpersonal dynamics of the appraisal process (Cascio, 1987; Feldman, 1981). Practitioners are continually seeking to increase overall effectiveness and acceptance of the appraisal process

* This article was first published in *Journal of Business Ethics* (1990), Vol. 9, pp. 961–969.

since a host of human resource decisions surround any organization's formal appraisal process (wage and salary administration, promotional decisions, training needs, etc.) (Bernardin and Beatty, 1984; Latham and Wexley, 1981).

The research community's driving concern has traditionally been the issue of rating *accuracy*. That is to say, the written evaluation of a subordinate's performance should indeed be an accurate testimony to the subordinate's actual performance during a particular period of time. The bulk of the research efforts during the past fifty years have focused on the issue of rater accuracy in the appraisal process (Bernardin and Beatty, 1984; Landy and Farr, 1983). Efforts to increase rater accuracy typically focused on the rating instrument and the procedure used to evaluate a subordinate.

The belief was that if the right rating instrument and procedure were found, accurate ratings would follow (Feldman, 1981). Thus, researchers and organizations focused an inordinate amount of energy on developing the 'right' rating format and procedure to increase rater accuracy and reduce the likelihood of a host of rater errors (e.g., halo effect, central tendency, recency effect, contrast effects, etc.) (Landy and Farr, 1983).

The goal of increasing rater accuracy is indeed a noble one because the whole issue of inaccuracy in performance ratings raises a host of ethical and managerial problems for all parties concerned with the process. However, is focusing on the rating instrument and the appraisal procedure the key to reducing ethical and managerial dilemmas associated with the appraisal process? Some researchers think so. We will first examine what these authors have to say and then explain why we believe their analysis is incomplete.

A moral justification of performance appraisal?

In a recent article in the *Journal of Business Ethics*, entitled 'Ethical Dilemmas in Performance Appraisal', Banner and Cooke (1984) discussed a number of ethical dilemmas that surround the formal appraisal process in organizational settings. They concluded that an organization can morally justify the use of performance appraisal in spite of the fact that it involves judging another human being using a rather subjective process. This justification can be based on a number of economic and behavioural perspectives that suggest that the appraisal process can have positive outcomes for both the organization and the recipient of the appraisal. In their article they also identified a number of specific ethical dilemmas that commonly arise in the appraisal process:

- The problematic use of trait oriented and subjective evaluation criteria
- Problems in the writing of performance standards and measurement indicators
- The use of different performance appraisal systems within the same organization
- How the results of the performance appraisal will be used
- Who determines the objective standards to measure performance.

While Banner and Cooke (1984) do an excellent job of focusing on and responding to the ethical dilemmas surrounding the *procedural* aspect of the appraisal process, we believe that they have overlooked the primary ethical dilemma of the *entire* formal appraisal process. They conclude their article stating:

> As long as the performance appraisal *procedure* is fair, is consistent, and is evenly applied to all, the performance appraisal is a just device that can be morally justified. (p. 332)

Their closing remarks tacitly assume that a well designed and implemented appraisal procedure can be morally justified because the organization has attempted to address each of the key procedural ethical dilemmas identified. Yet current research shows that a procedurally sound system alone will not necessarily produce effective, accurate, ethical performance ratings (Longenecker *et al.*, 1988).

We are clearly learning that 'even application' of the performance appraisal process does not simply depend on the appraisal procedure itself but rather on the person doing the actual rating. In most cases this is the employee's immediate supervisor or manager. Is accuracy and honesty the primary concern of managers when evaluating their subordinates? Recent research says *no*. Thus, the *key* ethical issue in performance appraisal moves well beyond the rather myopic concern with the procedural aspects of the appraisal process.

Motives behind deliberate inaccuracy in performance appraisal

In theory, then, employee appraisal is an objective, rational, and systematic attempt on the part of the manager to accurately describe subordinate performance (Sherman *et al.*, 1988). In reality, however, managers have a variety of concerns that are clearly more pressing than simply generating brutally accurate and honest ratings (Longenecker, 1989). Managers operate in organizational environments that place a high priority on getting results, on minimizing conflict and ultimately, on survival (Peters and Austin, 1983). This environment has a tendency to cause managers to focus on their self-interests in their efforts to manage their subordinates (Buchholz, 1989).

Self-interest, defined in either a narrow or broad sense, can easily find its way into the appraisal process as evidenced in the findings of a recent research project on rater accuracy. Longenecker *et al.* (1987) found in an in-depth study of sixty upper level managers that factors other than the subordinate's actual performance *frequently* influenced the ratings subordinates received. Managers stated that factors other than the subordinate's actual performance were almost always part of their evaluative process. In this research, it was generally *not* that managers had not been trained to do accurate evaluations or that the procedures were not sound. Rather, managers were choosing to play by their own rules instead of those created by 'the system'. Managers placed a higher priority on personal discretion in their attempts to manage their employees than on the organization's edict that accuracy be their primary concern.

The main outcome of this tendency involved managers intentionally inflating or deflating the subordinate's overall rating. Managers identified a number of compelling reasons for this deliberate manipulation. Over 70% of the managers in this research identified the following reasons for intentionally inflating ratings:

- The belief that accurate ratings would have a damaging effect on the subordinate's motivation and performance
- The desire to improve an employee's eligibility for merit raises
- The desire to avoid airing the department's dirty laundry, especially if the written appraisal will be reviewed by others
- The wish to avoid creating a negative permanent record of poor performance that might hound the employee in the future
- The need to protect good performers whose performance was suffering because of personal problems
- The wish to reward employees displaying great effort even when results are relatively low
- The need to avoid confrontation with certain hard-to-manage employees
- The desire to promote a poor or disliked employee up and out of the department.

Though negative distortions do not occur as frequently, they do occur. Managers report that they were very hesitant to deflate subordinates' ratings because of the legal, ethical, and motivational consequences of such behavior. Again, over 70% of managers cited the following reasons for intentionally lowering subordinate ratings:

- To scare better performance out of an employee
- To punish a difficult or rebellious employee
- To encourage a problem employee to quit
- To create a strong record to justify a planned firing
- To minimize the amount of the merit increase a subordinate receives
- To comply with an organizational edict that discourages managers from giving high ratings.

Clearly, many managers deliberately provide inaccurate ratings in the belief that they are serving some higher purpose. Indeed, many managers who engage in deliberate inaccuracy feel morally superior to other managers who provide 'brutally' accurate ratings despite the negative effects that these ratings may have on subordinates or organizational performance. It is therefore doubtful that exhortation to greater ethical integrity would increase the accuracy of these managers' rating behavior.

If we accept Banner and Cooke's (1984) conclusion, and also accept these findings that point to widespread unwillingness to engage in accurate ratings, we would be hard pressed to say that organizations are morally justified in their continued use of performance appraisal systems.

While the moral justification of performance appraisal is an interesting topic for debate, it may be distracting our energies from a more critical level of analysis. The moral justification analysis paralleled the historical concern of academics and practitioners for finding an instrument which would provide ratings of optimal accuracy; moral justification was defined in terms of the accuracy and fairness of the instrument and procedure. Concern has shifted away from instruments and procedures, and has begun to focus on the person doing the rating. Likewise, we believe the ethical concern must shift to this level of analysis. We believe the key ethical issues in performance appraisal revolve around the manager's *willingness* to provide the employee with accurate and honest ratings. *Should* accuracy and honesty be the manager's primary concern in performance appraisal? Is intentional inaccuracy in performance appraisal unethical? We will try to address these issues in the remainder of this article.

Ethical perspectives on inaccuracy in performance appraisal

We believe the issue of managers willfully submitting performance appraisal ratings which are false or inaccurate falls under the ethical debate dealing with the *right to lie or 'bluff'* in business. We ultimately believe that there is a 'Janus-Headed' dimension to this issue (Brady, 1985) because of the dual function of performance appraisal within the organization. Performance appraisal systems must be seen as both a tool for the manager's use to improve employee and unit performance and as a set of data to be used by the Human Resource department in the management of a whole host of HR functions. To the manager, performance appraisal is a means; to the Human Resource department performance appraisal data is an end in itself. We will examine intentional inaccuracy from three different ethical perspectives: formalist, utilitarian, and bluffing. A balancing and mixing of these perspectives will be needed in examining the ethics of intentionally inaccurate rating in performance appraisal. First, however, we will examine individual perspectives.

Formalist perspective

In an attempt to find universalizable principles, formalists would generally reject all forms of lying and deception as ultimately destructive even if there were some potential 'goods' coming from the lie. Most are familiar with the stereotypical portrayal of Kant's position on lying: that it is wrong to lie even if doing so is necessary to protect the lives of innocent people. The formalist approach is reflective of the position taken by Human Resource departments over the years. To the Human Resource department, performance appraisal represents a set of data that they employ to make a whole host of HR decisions. If the data is not accurate, they feel their decisions will be poor – garbage in, garbage out (Cascio, 1987). Indeed, without the universalizable principle of accuracy, Human Resource departments feel that their activities will collapse under the weight of favoritism and paternalism. While the individual manager may see performance appraisal as a *means* to encourage performance, the Human Resource department sees it primarily as an *end* – a set of data to be used in other decisions. Neither perspective is complete or sensitive to the other's needs and/or concerns.

It is important to point out to those who would quickly assimilate a formalist analysis of inaccuracy in performance appraisal, that this perspective is more flexible and sensitive than has been stereotypically portrayed. Kant, for instance, is very nuanced when the *judgement of people* is concerned and struggles with the concept of accuracy. Three observations from Kant's writings on truthfulness seem pertinent to a discussion of performance appraisal (Kant, 1930):

(1) Kant does not advocate thoughtless, complete, public disclosure of honest self-evaluation:

> Many of our propensities and peculiarities are objectionable to others, and if they became patent we should be foolish and hateful in their eyes. ... Therefore we arrange our conduct either to conceal our faults or to appear other than we are. We process the art of simulation. ... No man in his true senses, therefore, is candid.

(2) Kant *appreciates* the problem with what we have earlier in the paper referred to as 'brutal' accuracy and how 'brutally' accurate information might ultimately be used:

> If we were at all times punctiliously truthful we might often become victims of the wickedness of others who were ready to abuse our truthfulness. If all men were well-intentioned it would not only be a duty not to lie, but no one would do so because there would be no point in it. But as men are malicious, it cannot be denied that to be punctiliously truthful is often dangerous. This has given rise to the conception of a white lie, the lie enforced upon us by necessity – a difficult point for moral philosophers.

(3) Kant realizes that if appraisal is to lead to improvement, the truth cannot be 'brutally' applied (please overlook Kant's 18th century male perspective):

> Only if placed in positions of authority over others should we point out to them their defects. Thus a husband is entitled to teach and correct his wife, but his corrections must be well-intentioned and kindly and must be dominated by respect, for if they be prompted only by displeasure they result in mere blame and bitterness. If we blame, we must temper the blame with a sweetening of love, good-will, and respect. Nothing else will avail to bring about *improvement.*

While Kant ultimately rejects lying as ethically unacceptable, his writing is nuanced as to what constitutes a lie. Behrman (1987) similarly nuances 'differences in degree' between different acts. He notes that there are 'significant differences between secrecy and deception, between deception and lying, between lying and mere nondisclosure, between not disclosing some information and providing all relevant information and between providing relevant information and telling "the whole truth"' (p. 93).

It is not our point in this discussion to leave the reader with the impression that inaccuracy in performance appraisal may be ethically justified from a formalist perspective. Rather, we hope to reveal that this perspective is not as rigid as it is often portrayed and tries to acknowledge and accommodate the nuances of conflicting duties. Kant acknowledges the need for flexibility and sensitivity when the judgement of others is involved because he realizes both the dynamics and difficulties associated with subjective, interpersonal judgments and evaluations. Yet, Kant always returns to the point that accuracy and honesty must be a driving force to maintain trust and integrity.

Utilitarian perspective

A utilitarian perspective weighs the good and bad consequences produced for everyone affected by an action or decision – in this case, the decision for or against accuracy. Making an ethical decision entails (1) determining what alternative actions are available regarding any specific decision, (2) estimating the cost and benefits that a given action would produce for each and every person affected by the action, and (3) choosing the alternative that produces the greatest sum of utility or least amount of disutility (Velasquez, 1982).

Most managers perform some variation of this analysis when deciding to give intentionally inaccurate ratings. It is a useful perspective for managers who are used to weighing the benefits of alternative courses of action. Managers inflate and deflate ratings for a variety of reasons. Some have clearly weighed alternative courses of action and tried to choose that course which would do the most overall good. Many believe that the motive behind their intentional inaccuracy is positive; that is, their intent is to help either the employee or the organization by their manipulative rating behavior. Other motives could be classified as being negative or deviant in nature, focusing on trying to avoid personal hardship or enhancing their personal self-interests. In Figure 1 we have attempted to classify these tendencies to inflate and deflate by rater motive. Research shows that most intentional inaccuracy in performance appraisal falls into the cateory of 'inflated rating with positive motivation' (Longenecker *et al.*, 1987; Longenecker, 1989). A critical question is whether this sort of behavior can be justified using a utilitarian analysis.

Many managers find nothing morally wrong with the sort of positively motivated inaccuracy found in the top half of Figure 1. Yet we believe most managers fail in the utilitarian decision process in two ways. First, many managers do not clearly determine the array of alternatives before them. Many do not think about the appraisal process until it is on top of them and then have to make an expedient or convenient decision. Planning and ongoing concern about appraisal may have allowed them to be both accurate and sensitive to employee motivation. Second, many managers have a too narrow and short-sighted perspective and may fail to consider all of the parties (outcomes) affected by their performance appraisal decision. The very individuals that managers think they are helping through deliberate inaccuracy may in the long run be victims of the inaccuracy through poor decisions by the Human Resource department or a false sense of their actual contributions to the organization.

Utilitarian analysis of inaccuracy in performance appraisal, like formalist analysis, seems incomplete when taken alone. First, it assumes that the performance appraisal process is simply a tool – a mean, if you will – for the manager to use in enhancing the performance of his or her department. It ignores the fact that performance appraisal has a broader function within the organization. Second, it tends to focus on short-term, primary consequences and ignores longer-term secondary consequences that are less apparent to the manager. The ongoing,

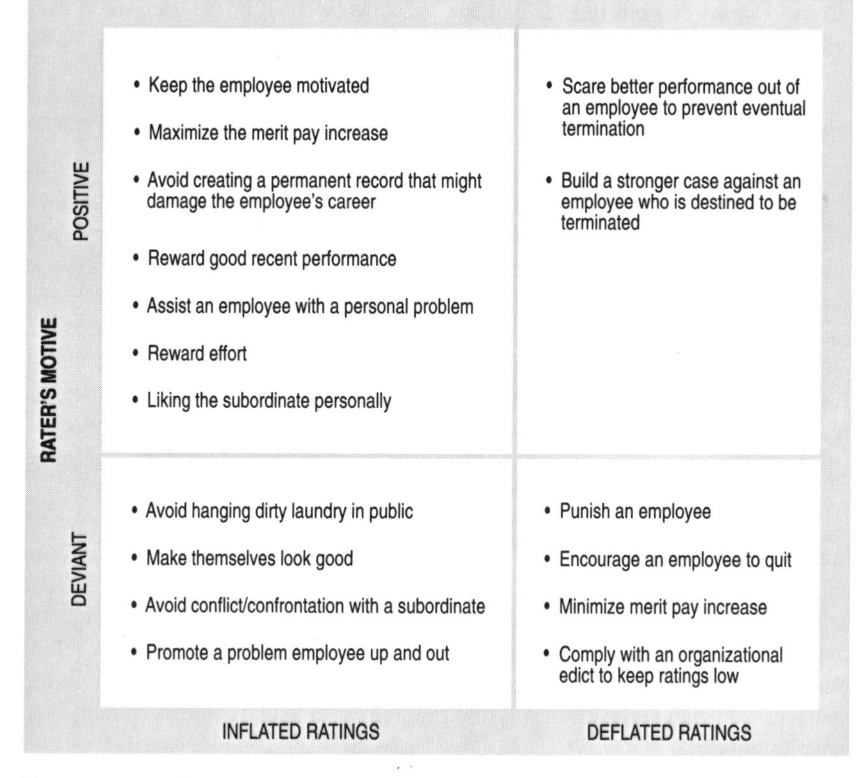

Figure 1 *A typology of rater motives and manipulative rating behavior*

widespread use of intentionally inaccurate ratings can have a variety of long-term negative effects such as cynicism building up around the appraisal process, pay-for-performance programs becoming meaningless, and data for promotion and training decisions becoming inaccurate and suspect (Longenecker, 1989). Ultimately, the notion of using such a process to enhance performance and productivity will be lost.

'Business bluffing' perspective

Albert Carr (1968) compares most instances of intentional inaccuracy in business to 'bluffing' in poker, which he argues is simply part of the rules of that game and does not reflect on the morality of the poker player. His perspective is most often used to describe negotiating behavior, but we believe it is worth discussing in this article since many managers (and subordinates) broadly construe the performance appraisal process as a negotiation. The manager negotiates for enhanced performance, and subordinates, from a less powerful position, negotiate for enhanced rewards. Intentional inaccuracy, according to the 'business bluffing' perspective, is an appropriate tool to be used by the manager to leverage broader objectives. Inaccuracy is appropriate because it is expected and useful. The pervasiveness of inaccuracy in actual practice makes us suspect that many managers view performance appraisal in this light. Carr (1968) argues that the individual manager would be foolish not to at times exercise this expediency:

> Most executives from time to time are almost compelled, in the interests of their companies or themselves, to practice some form of deception when negotiating. … By conscious misstatements, concealment of pertinent facts, or exaggeration – in short, by bluffing – they seek to persuade others to agree with them. I think it is fair to say that if the individual executive refuses to bluff … he is ignoring opportunities permitted under the rules and is at a heavy disadvantage…

Performance appraisal does have a legitimate function as a tool to achieve broader motivation and performance objectives, but this dimension can be easily abused. The 'business bluffing' perspective can easily lead the manager to believe that performance appraisal is one more tool to be used to their advantage in the game of business – that the ethics of appraisal need not be raised or discussed. While inaccuracy in performance appraisal appears to be so widespread that it might seem to be part of the rules of business, this perspective clearly ignores the heavy expenditures by Human Resource departments saying that inaccuracy is not and cannot be a rule of the game; that it will, in the long run, destroy the game if this sort of foul is permitted to continue.

The 'business bluffing' perspective has of course been attacked for creating 'moral sanctuaries' for managers, where they can play by rules other than those obeyed by the rest of society (Konrad, 1982). In general, we feel that the game strategy perspective fails to take into account some of the longer-term detrimental consequences of many of the practices of lying, inaccuracy, deception, non-disclosure, bluffing (or whatever you may want to call it) and their effect on the manager–subordinate relationship of Human Resource departments' attempts to make quality HR decisions.

'Janus-Headed' evaluation of inaccuracy in performance appraisal

None of the ethical perspectives presented in the previous section when taken alone seem complete or satisfactory. We believe that this is partly because of the dual nature of performance appraisal systems within the organization. Performance appraisal is both a means and an end. In the manager's hand it is a means to prompt, encourage, reward, and motivate. It is a managerial tool that can be used to enhance individual, unit, and organizational performance. For the Human Resource department, however, it is an end in itself. It represents a set of data which are used in the determination of a variety of critical human resource decisions such as compensation, promotion, training, and employee development. As an end, performance appraisal data must be accurate to be useful and of value to an organization.

Brady (1985) proposed a 'Janus-Headed' model of ethical theory, Janus being the Roman god of passageways who had two faces – one facing forward and the other backward. This model suggests that most ethical analysis must have both a formalist (retrospective) dimension as well as a utilitarian (prospective) dimension. On the one hand, Brady (1990) suggests that 'most formalistic positions in the business-society area look more like conceptual arguments, since the formalists inquire into the features of a given case that enable them to generalize their findings to similar cases.' But without the 'universalizability' requirement suggested by the formalist, 'ethics explodes into countless fragments of unshared intuitions regarding isolated personal experiences.' On the other hand, utilitarianism ignores general principles and culture heritage in order to focus on concrete cases and results. Again, Brady (1990) suggests that utilitarians 'remind us that although ethics seeks consistency and coherence, it may sacrifice them in order to pursue the best results.'

When we apply this analysis to performance appraisal, we must agree that accuracy should be a general principle guiding the process at both the managerial and organizational level. Without this general principle, the performance appraisal process will indeed explode into countless fragments. Managers must continually be reminded that inaccuracy violates the integrity of a system which demands integrity, and all departures from accuracy must in some sense be held suspect.

On the other hand, we have noted that accuracy can sometimes be 'brutal' or counter-productive. This 'brutal' accuracy violates the performance enhancing function of appraisal. Managers must act with a certain flexibility and sensitivity when the subjective, interpersonal judgments and evaluations of others are involved. While doing so, however, it is their obligation to minimize the possible loss of integrity to the system.

Thus, the 'Janus-Headed' model suggests that both accuracy and flexibility and sensitivity are prerequisites of ethical performance appraisal. Is this impossible? Can both of these lofty objectives be achieved? We suggest that both the organization and the manager have certain 'rights' and 'obligations' in the execution of performance appraisal.

The *organization* has the *right* to demand accuracy in performance appraisal. We suggest four *obligations* which accompany this right:

- As Banner and Cooke (1984) suggest, the organization must provide a sound procedure for managers to use in the execution of performance appraisal.
- Training in performance appraisal must be provided for managers. This training should formally address the issue of intentional inaccuracy, and should deal not only with manager's ability, but willingness and motivation to execute accurate ratings (Longenecker, 1989).
- Organizations must provide leadership from above. Middle and lower level managers cannot be expected to provide accurate ratings if intentional inaccuracy is practiced higher in the organization (Arthur, 1987).
- Like any procedure, the performance appraisal process must be audited to ensure the accuracy of the data generated and the overall integrity of the process (Bernardin and Beatty, 1984).

On the other hand, *managers* have the *right* to demand discretion and latitude in the execution of their performance appraisal responsibilities. Along with this right, we suggest that managers have certain *obligations* in the execution of performance appraisal responsibilities:

- Managers must develop and communicate clear standards with which they judge subordinate performance prior to the actual performance appraisal period.

- Managers must provide ongoing feedback, making performance appraisal an ongoing process and not a once or twice per year bureaucratic event.
- Managers must prepare for performance appraisal as they would for any negotiation, seriously examining alternatives, strategies, and long and short-run implications. Both written and face-to-face reviews must be carefully planned for and executed.
- Managers who believe that higher, strategic outcomes are so compelling that they warrant intentional inaccuracy should be willing to subject their thinking to review by their superiors or by the Human Resource department.

[...] Careful, ongoing planning can avoid much of the 'need' managers feel to engage in intentional inaccuracy.

Conclusions

We know that organizations spend millions of dollars annually designing and implementing performance appraisal systems that are state of the art. We know human resource decisions are based on the assumption of accuracy. We also know that managers that operate in these systems have a strong tendency to manipulate performance ratings in the perceived best interest of the management of their employees.

Future research must attempt to better understand (1) the cognitive process of manipulating ratings, (2) what, if any, ethical struggles managers face in the use of manipulative rating behavior, (3) what effect an organization's ethical culture has on the manager's willingness to play rating games, (4) what steps organizations can take to increase the manager's *willingness* to provide accurate and honest ratings, and (5) the long-term effects of inaccurate ratings on individual and organizational performance.

To the practitioner we concede that personal discretion should always be part and parcel of the appraisal process because managers need autonomy in the performance of their jobs. Yet we unequivocally believe that the short-term manipulation of employee ratings can lead to long-term motivational, behavioral, and even legal difficulties for all parties concerned. It is a well worn organizational axiom that 'trust is always the basis of the manager/subordinate relationship'. Any activity that tampers with this trust factor must be viewed as a threat to long-term managerial effectiveness and employee performance. Any short-term benefits derived from questionable rater discretion, can in the long-run damage the manager's ability to effectively lead and manage his/her subordinates. It may very well be that honesty is the best policy regardless of the procedure or setting involved.

References

Arthur, E.F. (1987) 'The ethics of corporate governance', *Journal of Business Ethics*, Vol. 6, pp. 59–70.

Banner, D.K. and Cooke, R.A. (1984) 'Ethical dilemmas in performance appraisal', *Journal of Business Ethics*, Vol. 3, pp. 327–333.

Beach, J. (1985) 'Bluffing: its demise as a subject unto itself', *Journal of Business Ethics*, Vol. 4, pp. 191–196.

Behrman, J.N. (1988) *Essays on Ethics in Business and the Professions*. Prentice Hall, Englewood Cliffs, NJ.

Bernardin, H.J. and Beatty, R.W. (1984) *Performance Appraisal: assessing human behavior at work*. Kent Publishing Co., Boston.

Bok, S. (1978) *Lying: moral choice in public and private life*. Pantheon Books, New York.

Brady, F.N. (1985) 'A Janus-headed model of ethical theory: looking two ways at business/society issues', *The Academy of Management Review*, Vol. 10, pp. 568–576.

Brady, F.N. (1990) *Ethical Managing: rules and results*, Macmillan, New York.

Carr, A. (1968) 'Is business bluffing ethical?', *Harvard Business Review*, January/February.

Cascio, W.J. (1987) *Applied Psychology in Personnel Management*. Reston Publishing, Reston, Va.

Feldman, J. (1981) 'Beyond attribution theory: cognitive processes in performance evaluation', *Journal of Applied Psychology*, Vol. 66, pp. 127–148.

Kant, E. (1930) 'Ethical duties toward others: truthfulness', in *Lectures on Ethics*, translated by Louis Infield. Methuen & Co. Ltd, London.

Konard, A.R. (1982) 'Business managers and moral sanctuaries', *Journal of Business Ethics*, Vol. 1, pp. 195–200.

Landy, F.J. and Farr, J.L. (1983) *The Measurement of Work Performance*. Academic Press, New York.

Landy, F.J., Farr, J.L. and Jacobs, R.R. (1982) 'Utility concepts in performance appraisal measurement', *Organization Behavior and Human Performance*, Vol. 30, pp. 15–40.

Latham, G.P. and Wexley, K.N. (1981) *Increasing Productivity through Performance Appraisal*. Addison-Wesley Publishing Co., Reading, MA.

Locher, A.H. and Teel, K.S. (1988) 'Appraisal trends', *Personnel Journal*, September, pp. 139–145.

Longenecker, C.O. (1989) 'Truth or consequences: politics and performance appraisals', *Business Horizons*, November/December, pp. 1–7.

Longenecker, C.O., Gioia, D.A. and Sims, H.P. (1987) 'Behind the mask: the politics of employee appraisal', *The Academy of Management Executive*, August, Vol. 1, No. 3, pp. 183–193.

Longenecker, C.O., Liverpool, P.R. and Wilson, K.A. (1988) 'An assessment of managerial/subordinate perceptions of performance appraisal effectiveness', *Journal of Business and Psychology*, Summer, Vol. 2, No. 4, pp. 311–320.

Peters, T.J. and Austin, M. (1983) 'A passion for excellence', *Fortune*, May 13, pp. 20–33.

Sherman, A.W., Bohlander, G.W. and Chruden, H.J. (1988) *Managing Human Resources*. South-Western Publishing Co., Cincinnati, OH.

5
Industrialization and the environment – a changing relationship

John Blunden

Introduction

This article sets out to show how the impact of industry on the environment has changed from the quite minimal levels of the period before the Industrial Revolution in the UK, through the significant but localized micro-scale effects of the early nineteenth century and the emerging regional or meso-scale consequences of much of the later nineteenth century and early twentieth century, to the more recent macro aspects where the results of industrial activities can have transnational, if not global, implications. Integral to this discussion of the changing spatial nature of the environmental impact of industry is the acceptance of the increasing size and complexity of productive processes. However, this is tempered by a growing range of legal constraints aimed at negotiating a reasonable balance between industrial needs and the well-being of the individual citizen, and the technological know-how available to achieve such ends. The legal framework itself is seen to develop from a restricted range of controls largely exercised at local level, through the emergence of national and, following initiatives from the European Union, supranational standards, to attempts to arrive at wider international agreements.

Early industrialization

Before the mid-eighteenth century most forms of industrial enterprise that existed in the UK were small and widely distributed, largely in rural locations. Frequently, where little more than human effort was required, they were cottage-based and organized by merchant businessmen who distributed raw materials and collected finished goods. Even where manufacturing operations required power, and were located close by sources of renewable energy such as running water, they remained very modest undertakings. Manufacturing, wherever it was to be found, had little or no environmental impact.

It was the discovery of the steam engine, which could power machines *en masse,* and of the large coalfields, which could provide their fuel, that transformed the location of industrial activity to fast-growing urban centres on those coalfields. New sources of power also resulted in the reorganization of industry and the emergence of the factory system as the means of production. By the late eighteenth century Thomas Newcomen's original steam engine had been improved by James Watt. But it was the application of rotary motion to the steam engine in 1781 that greatly increased the kinds of machine to which steam power could be harnessed. By 1800, Watt, in collaboration with Matthew Bolton, was supplying engines to textile factories, ironworks, breweries, flour mills, potteries, waterworks and a wide range of other industrial premises.

However, as important sectors of British industry became organized into very much larger operations, so particular locations became increasingly specialized, with profound implications for local environments. It was this situation which stimulated the beginnings of concern about industrial pollution. Towns like Manchester, with their combination of cotton spinning and weaving, cloth-finishing factories and engineering, formed vast industrial complexes. As a result, the clouds of smoke which 'vomited forth from the numerous chimneys' were of such magnitude that, in the 1840s, one French traveller, Leon Faucher, compared Manchester to an active volcano (Faucher, 1844).

The application of steam power to the production of pottery, which had formerly been a handcraft activity, made the concentration of the industry in North Staffordshire even more pronounced. If conditions were poor inside the factories, outside, according to the contemporary observer J.T. Arlidge (1892), people were exposed to 'an abundant share of coal dust and coal smoke' which was disgorged from the ovens 'in the shape of dense black smoke, intermingled with the gases of combustion'.

The glass industry was similar to pottery manufacture in its reliance on minerals as raw materials, including sand, lime and sodium carbonate (soda ash), along with coal for firing its furnaces. Here, too, the industry became more mechanized and concentrated in the factories of a few large concerns. One of these, Pilkington, employed about 300 workers at St Helens in Lancashire in 1900 and was the largest glass manufacturing plant in the world. But as an industrial complex of factories and associated collieries it was a major source of air pollutants.

However, of even greater significance for the environment in the nineteenth century was the development of an industry already closely associated with glass making – heavy chemicals. Originally, the chemicals needed for manufacturing glass, together with those for textiles and soap (that is, detergents, bleaches and alkalis) were supplied from natural products such as sour milk and urine. But the processes were slow and supplies obviously rather limited, so that substantial and ultimately highly successful efforts were made to provide the necessary acids and alkalis from chemical sources. By 1862 the alkali industry, as it was called, was already employing 1,900 workers and producing goods worth £2.5 million.

Because the manufacture of soda, sulphuric acid and bleaching powder needed ready access to their basic raw materials such as coal and salt, production of these chemicals became concentrated on Tyneside, Clydeside and Merseyside. This in turn brought severe problems for the environment of these districts, primarily through air pollution. Efforts were made to disperse the waste products of such enterprises – hydrochloric acid gas, sulphuric acid and hydrogen sulphide – through tall chimneys. But the combined environmental impact of these noxious and destructive effluents was merely exported to the surrounding regions. Moreover, landowners in the areas beyond such industrial complexes, whose land was now damaged by their emissions, found it difficult if not impossible to attribute them to any particular individual source. They therefore had little success in seeking redress through the courts and, although the first attempt to apply statutory controls to individual chemical works came in 1863 through the Alkali Act, this related only to emissions of hydrogen chloride gas from soda and potash works.

The beginnings of air pollution control

Undoubtedly, many parts of the British countryside, especially in the North West, had been transformed by the middle of the last century into a 'drab lifeless grey of industrial wasteland' from industrial activities. Indeed, according to a witness who appeared before the Royal Commission on Injury from Noxious Vapours of 1878, in the fields around places like St Helens 'spring never comes thither ... the foul gases have killed every tree and blade of grass for miles around'. Even in light winds emissions from the alkali works could carry over distances of up to nine miles, damaging farms. Their appearance was such that it looked 'just as if a fire had gone over them', killing trees and hedges, stunting wheat and putting cattle off their feed. All the same, it could not be denied that such industry had brought in its wake unprecedented economic progress.

Thus, faced with the dire warnings of manufacturers about the financial damage that would be caused by restricting production, legislators were cautious. Yet it was clear that the environment could no longer be looked upon as a freely available dump for industry to use at will. At municipal authority level, where efforts might have been made to control air pollution using by-laws, any controls that did exist were largely ineffective. In Leeds, for example, industries which were most detrimental to air quality were excluded, whilst in Liverpool all industries that had 'done their best' to prevent the escape of smoke, were exempted from control! At national level, even the major Public Health Act of 1875, which required the abatement of smoke from furnaces to levels which could be deemed harmless or inoffensive, stated that this was to be achieved only 'as far as practicable, having regard to the nature of the manufacture or trade'. Indeed, several industries that had the worst pollution records were exempted from this 'best practicable means' approach, notably the manufacturers of coke from coal, brick-makers and iron-ore smelters, on the grounds that a proven control technology did not exist.

Whatever their shortcomings, the responsibility for smoke controls, including dust and grit, remained with local authorities well into this century. Their activities in this field were eventually modified under the Clean Air Acts of 1956 and 1968 and the Control of Pollution Act 1974. This was in contrast to the control system applied to emissions from the heavy chemicals industry which, by the original legislation of 1863, was vested in a national body, the Alkali Inspectorate. Unlike smoke, accurate chemical measurement of hydrogen chloride gas was always feasible, thus making the possibility of prosecution by the Inspectorate much simpler.

Although viewed with suspicion by industry, this body was able to establish itself and eventually press, not merely for more effective controls, but for jurisdiction over a wider range of polluting industries. As early as 1874 amendments to the original Act provided emission limits on hydrogen chloride and called for the use of the 'best practicable means' to minimize the discharge of other noxious gases. In 1881, 12 further types of chemical works came within its authority, with a subsequent consolidation of all piecemeal legislative amendments in the Alkali etc. Works Regulation Act 1906. This remained in force until 1974 when the work of the Inspectorate was enshrined in Section 5 of the Health and Safety at Work, etc. Act. A more recent statutory instrument, the Health and Safety (Emissions into the Atmosphere) Regulations of 1983, listed some 58 different categories of works liable to release any one of a whole range of offensive substances. Under these regulations the Alkali Inspectorate, renamed the Industrial Air Pollution Inspectorate, became responsible for the control and supervision of the discharge into the atmosphere of noxious or offensive substances from all the enterprises categorized, each one of which had to be re-registered every year.

In its utilization of the 'best practicable means' approach to restricting emissions, the Inspectorate, throughout its existence, considered not only the current state of technical knowledge regarding control but also the financial implications of control systems for the process operator, as well as the local environmental conditions and circumstances. Where problems of discharge to the atmosphere existed, the methods of restraint that it used were those of gentle persuasion, rejecting any kind of militant approach and largely avoiding legal prosecutions. Whilst its object was to attempt to reconcile the conflicting interests of the public, who suffered the effects of pollution, with those of manufacturers who were concerned to operate efficiently and profitably, and the nation as a whole which also demanded economic growth, the Inspectorate was frequently accused of being too sympathetic to industrial interests. Box 1 summarizes the current ways of reducing air pollution.

Box 1 Ways of reducing air pollution

In the context of current knowledge, environmental damage can be reduced in three ways:

Control at source

1 By altering the chemistry of the process which produces the harmful emission. This enables either the total amount of effluent to be reduced or its composition to be altered so that it is potentially less harmful.

2 By adding some effluent-cleaning process to the discharging plant so that the damaging constituents of the waste gases are removed or changed into some less harmful substance before discharge to the atmosphere.

Control between source and receiver

3 By discharging the waste gases from a high chimney, thus inducing them to travel further and become diluted to an acceptable level before reaching the ground. This method may also be used in conjunction with 1 or 2, but it is not always effective (see pp. 88 to 91).

Recent approaches to water pollution control

The impact of the discharge of industrial liquids to water bodies, usually rivers, has always remained much more localized and less of a health hazard than air pollution, although water pollution can have a regional or even an international dimension as will be demonstrated below. The control of water quality in England and Wales was, until the passing of the Water Act (1989) and the setting up of the National Rivers Authority, administered by the ten Water Authorities, and in Scotland by the seven River Purification Boards. Legislation (including the Control of Pollution Act 1974) has favoured a level of discharge for liquid effluents compatible with that of the receiving medium – in other words, by the uses to which the river, or a stretch of the river, is put. Only when this has been determined can maximum permitted emissions be established. In the years since the accession of the UK to the Treaty of Rome, this approach, which is known as an environmental quality objective (EQO), has given rise to problems over harmonizing UK legislation with that of other European Union countries. Instead of using EQO, the majority of member states have advocated a regulatory regime based on uniform emission limits (EL) in the determination of individual emissions of a given pollutant to the medium in question.

Clearly, the two approaches are not unrelated and represent two means to the same end; that is, ensuring that the concentration of a pollutant does not exceed a level at which damage to ecosystems or to human health arises. In terms of water pollution the different approach of the UK is easy to explain since it is a country of short, fast-flowing rivers which are not used for drinking water. For many years, these advantages, plus what has been regarded as the absorptive capacity of tidal estuaries and coastal waters, fostered an adherence to EQO.

However, EQO has been viewed with suspicion in other European Union countries since the uniform limits of the EL approach are much easier to administer. They do not depend on assumptions and complex mathematical models of pollution dispersion. Moreover, they are easier to enforce since measurement at the point of discharge (i.e. the end of a pipe) is far simpler than measurement of very low concentrations once diluted in the receiving medium. Where this receiving medium is a river which crosses national boundaries, such as the Rhine, the inherent merits of a system based on EL are even more obvious. Similar arguments are now seen to apply where there are discharges into a large body of relatively enclosed water whose shores form the boundaries of several nations, for example the North Sea or the Mediterranean.

Having argued the EQO case for water pollution, the UK's unenthusiastic acceptance of it for air pollution seems surprising. However, the UK government was prepared to endorse the European Union concept of non-mandatory air quality objectives against which the progress of pollution control might be measured, with these objectives being expressed in terms of target bands rather than a single figure and with different bands applicable to urban and rural areas. The final version of the Directive prepared by the European Commission contained both 'guide' values, which set long-term objectives for concentrations of smoke and sulphur dioxide, and 'limit' values to be attained throughout the European Union by 1993 at the latest. The Directive places a binding obligation on each member state to maintain and improve the quality of its atmosphere; this requirement represents a major shift in the UK approach which had hitherto been largely concerned with the technology of controls at source.

The UK and the European Union

By the mid-1980s British environmental controls had become intimately connected with European Community standards, even though the policing of the system remained firmly in the hands of local, regional or national bodies working within the UK. Thus, at this time, the European Commission was urging the UK to accept the idea that its separate legislative controls over air and water pollution were the outcome of historical inertia and were inappropriate in a period when problems were frequently of a multi-media type and therefore demanded the application of an integrated pollution control system. Moreover, a pollution problem could often be resolved in several ways. For example, toxic wastes could be incinerated, possibly creating a problem because of the discharge of the resulting gases to the atmosphere. Alternatively, they might be disposed of in a landfill site with the possibility of causing ground water pollution. Deciding the best practicable environmental option for the disposal of wastes demanded a co-ordinated approach to the problem, as the Commission made clear in its Framework Directive of 1984.

The UK somewhat belatedly adopted this approach and eventually demonstrated its commitment in two ways. First, in 1987, the Air Pollution Inspectorate was brought together with three specialized agencies within the Department of the Environment – the Hazardous Wastes Inspectorate, the Radiochemical Inspectorate and the Water Inspectorate – to form Her Majesty's Inspectorate of Pollution (HMIP).

Then in 1990, the Environmental Protection Act recognized the concept of Integrated Pollution Control (IPC) by requiring operators of scheduled industrial processes to use the 'best available techniques' for pollution control 'not entailing excessive cost' (BATNEEC) and to minimize pollution having regard to the environment 'taken as a whole'. Some 5,000 companies, including those in the fuel and power industries, oil refining, iron and steel manufacture, cement and asbestos production, chemicals, paper and pulp and fertilizer production, and those engaged in waste disposal, will be affected under a five-year plan which runs from 1991 to 1996. Each plant that is capable of polluting and uses a distinctive process, no matter how many there may be inside a single company, will be subject to separate authorization under IPC and subject to policing by HMIP.

However, this Act also has other implications in that some 25,000 other factories, which have never been subject to controls exercised by the Air Pollution Inspectorate or the other control agencies, and previously could only have been brought to account for pollution under public health legislation, now have to obtain authorizations for their activities from local authorities whether they have been in existence for some time or are new.

As for a manufacturer whose activities produce waste materials, other than those that might be discharged to the air or to water bodies, this Act lays at its door a 'duty of care' to ensure that any third party which disposes of such toxic materials on its behalf does so legally and, of course, in line with the appropriate EU Directive on the subject. In other words, it would have to be certain that these materials were taken to an appropriate disposal facility licensed under the 1974 Control of Pollution Act, such as a landfill site, a waste-processing plant, or an incinerator, and dealt with in a way that does not harm human health or the environment.

The increasing sophistication and comprehensiveness of controls on environmental pollution of the 1980s were also matched by a growing determination to ensure not only that industry should be responsible for environmental damage – the 'polluter must pay principle' – but also that every effort should be made to ensure that, from the outset, industry had a minimal impact on the general ecology of its surroundings. Emerging first in the USA in the late 1960s and early 1970s from the growing environmental debate of the period, a new concept was embodied in the Federal National Environmental Policy Act which became law in 1969. This attempts to address the issues of resource conservation and pollution together whenever a new major official land-use development is proposed, an objective which is achieved by undertaking an Environmental Impact Assessment (EIA). An Environmental Impact Statement (EIS) generally follows, documenting the EIA findings.

In setting out the ways in which the proposed development can affect the environment, the EIA usually incorporates a cost-benefit analysis of that development. EIA therefore offers the opportunity to supplement existing legislation, whether its aim is land-use control or the maintenance of public health, and to provide a means of analysing all the factors for and against a proposal. It is also a means of judging the compatibility of the proposal with the broader objectives of strategic planning at regional, national or supranational levels. If the concept requires the full disclosure of the likely environmental impact of the project by the developer, it also rests upon full consultation with both the public and a range of public authorities. It is an approach that has since been widely copied by other countries and is now mandatory within the European Union for all major industrial projects.

Case Study: Keeping ahead of environmental legislation – environmental impact assessment

Some companies have preferred to keep ahead of environmental legislation in whatever shape or form it may be. When the Aluminium Company of America (ACA), a bauxite mining and smelting business with world-wide interests, witnessed the development of EIA in the USA as an environmental tool, it decided to introduce it as a standard procedure for all new operations, whatever their location.

In 1980, for example, ACA joined Royal Dutch Shell in a consortium – Alumar – to construct a mining and processing plant. The EIA study began three years ahead of the proposed start-up date of 1984. It consisted of a complete characterization of the site, and then dealt with the probable environmental effects of the operation upon it, and the proposed control measures that might be used to minimize its impact. Both impacts and control measures were considered for all the stages of the life of the plant, from site preparation to construction and operation.

The studies at the location covered not only the physical and biological environment, including impacts on the terrestrial and aquatic systems, but also the people of the area. Monitoring station networks were planned to measure the impact of plant activities on vegetation, soils, surface and ground water, emissions (liquid, gaseous and solid wastes) and ambient air quality. But the monitoring programme began before construction started in order to collect and follow up the largest amounts of environmental data possible.

Alumar's EIA checklist

Physical, socio-economic, environmental

- Soils – geomorphology and characteristics
- Atmospheric resources – weather, meteorological conditions and air quality
- Water resources – surface and ground water; water use and quality
- Ecosystems – terrestrial and aquatic flora and fauna
- People – demography; land use; occupations; quality of life

Project characteristics

- Industrial process – lay-out; equipment; transport; raw materials storage; products
- Sources of emissions – air; water; solid wastes
- Environmental control technologies – processes; equipment for air, water, solid wastes treatment; disposal facilities

Environmental effects on soil, water resources, atmosphere, ecosystems, people

- Site preparation and implementation
- Operation
- Surface water quality
- Geology – ground water quality
- Spill prevention and counter-measure plans
- Air dispersion and modelling – climatology/air quality
- Air emissions; effluent discharge to receiving waters; solid waste disposal
- Monitoring programmes – air; water; vegetation; soils
- People – local and regional health hazards; socio-economic impacts

(Source: Vianna, 1991)

Also in the mid-1980s, the Control of Industrial Major Accident Hazards Regulations came into force in the UK after an EC Directive of 1982 which appeared in the wake of a series of devastating accidents at chemical works in the Community. As a result of the experiences at Beek in the Netherlands (1978) and at Manfredonia and Seveso in Italy (1976), the Directive is designed to highlight those sites which present the greatest risk to local populations and to limit the consequences of any incidents should they occur. In the UK a programme of risk analysis at the stage when such a plant is seeking consent under planning law might prove conclusive in its rejection or acceptance under that legislation. Therefore it may be considered to be an important element in the decision-making process. Where permission to build is given, or where the plant already exists, it is graded according to risk and policed accordingly. At all such sites regular safety reports are mandatory, together with full disclosure of the risks to the public and the action to be taken by the plant owners and the public should an accident occur.

Case Study – Estimating risk

A new water treatment works in an urban area has, as part of the complex, facilities to store chlorine in 30-tonne pressure tanks. The chemical, in liquid form, arrives aboard 20-tonne rail wagons and a network of pipes feed into and out of the storage tanks. This enables the liquid to be pumped from the supply vehicles and the gas given off by it to be used in the purification treatment of drinking water. Although chlorine performs a valuable role in this situation, it is, in fact, a highly toxic chemical which in concentrated doses could kill or seriously damage human health if released into the atmosphere by accident. Risk analysis of such a situation is established by producing a fault tree to which values can be attached which indicate probabilities of failure for each element in the fabric of the plant (Figure 1).

Data for this part of the risk analysis are drawn from reliability data banks which record details of different types of failure for pumps, valves, container vessels, etc. and their frequency. For the most catastrophic failure, that of a storage tank, the rate could be between 5×10^{-6} and 4×10^{-6} per vessel per year with each failure instantaneously releasing 1 tonne of chlorine.

In an attempt to establish risk, this procedure would be followed for all possible release cases and the resultant data input to a complex computer program. This would generate the probabilities and the likely consequences of a chlorine release from the site. Further calculations would indicate the probability of deaths at different distances from the site, allowing for the density of population around it. On the basis of these computer inputs, decisions can be made about the advisability of permitting such a development or the steps that would need to be undertaken to ensure its maximum safety.

The approach taken here is similar in many respects to the failure method used by systems theorists. The key features of the method include representing the situation in which failure occurs as a system and comparing it with other models based on typical failures. Although the problem of chlorine release from the storage facility can be recognized as a failure of the system, defects in any component part of that system leading to failure could be considered as a quality problem within its narrow definition of 'conformance to specification'.

(Sources: Blunden and Reddish, 1991; Systems Analysis of Failures as a Quality Management Tool, 1992)

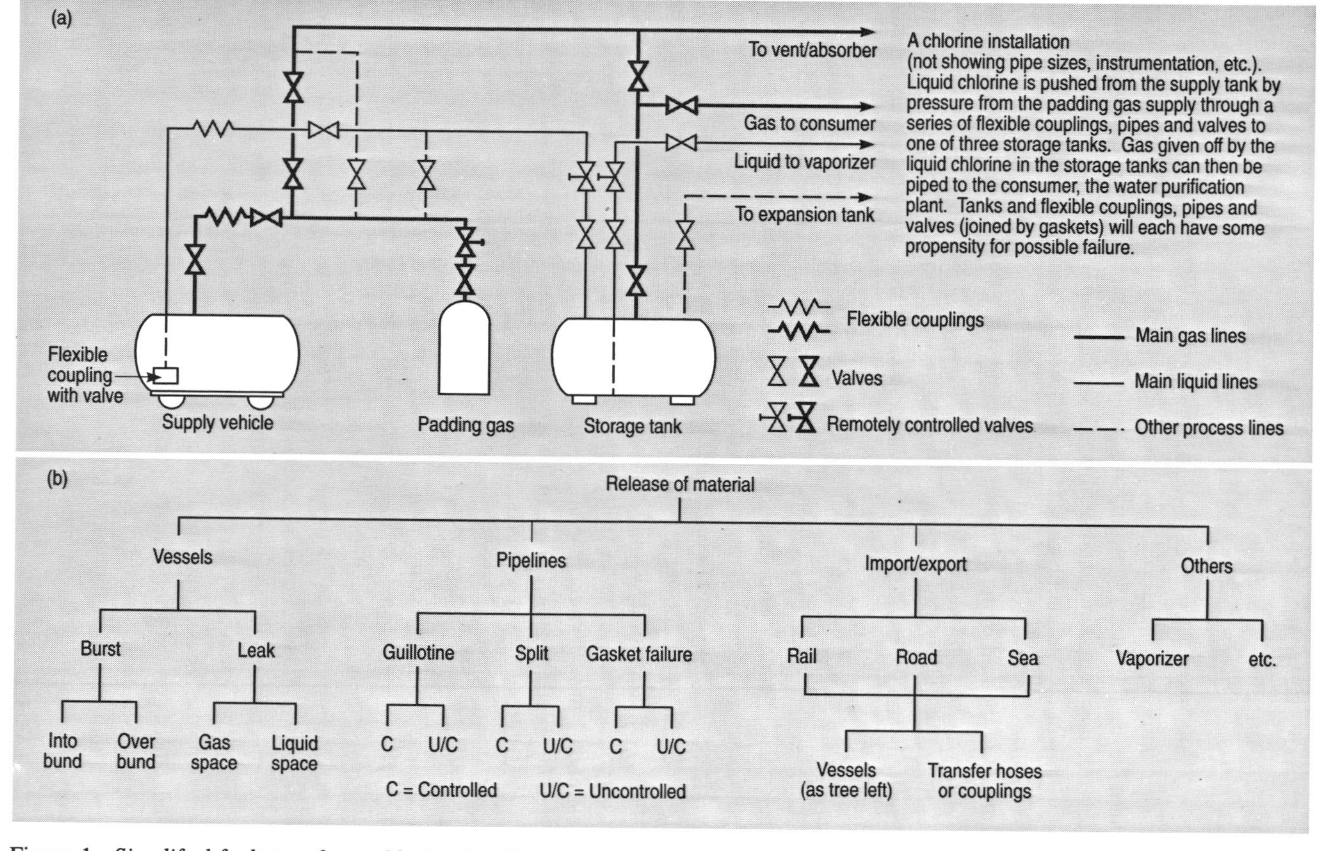

Figure 1 *Simplified fault tree for a chlorine installation*

The UK, the European Union and the wider environment

Until the 1980s, first the government of the UK and then the European Community had formulated regulations to control industrial and manufacturing activities in the interests of human health and the maintenance to an acceptable level of local environmental quality. In spite of rapid increases in the size and diversity of production processes, especially in the years after the Second World War, such an approach was all that was deemed necessary. However, by the middle of the 1980s, the emphasis had changed amongst legislators to a concern for the wider environmental problems operating at national, international and even global levels. This resulted from the recognition that the release of waste materials into the environment could become a hazard which transcends national boundaries.

The first of the problem emissions to be recognized as demanding positive action at this level involved the discharge to the atmosphere of acid gases, particularly sulphur and nitrogen oxides. These gases, emitted from numerous point sources such as large power stations, heavy industrial plant and motor vehicles, had long been recognized as possible pollutants, especially at a local level. Damage caused by the dry deposition of sulphur dioxide close to point sources of emission was not unknown. However, the rapid expansion of electricity generation to fuel a wide range of new industrial processes, as well as a significant growth in the use of household equipment, both of which characterized the 1960s and 1970s, led to the recognition that rising levels of discharges such as sulphur dioxide could build up in the atmosphere. Moreover, as part of the general movement of air masses, they can travel substantial distances across frontiers before rain washes out the sulphur dioxide as a form of weak sulphuric acid. The levels of acidity in this rain are measured on a logarithmic pH scale. Small downward changes in values below the norm for ordinary rain (5.6) have a significant effect on biochemical processes.

Thus acid rain poses a threat both to forests, causing the dieback of trees, especially conifers, and to lakes through the propensity of acid rain to alter the water chemistry and thus threaten aquatic bio-systems. Although initially recognized as a problem in North America and Sweden, acid rain was soon found to be affecting the Black Forest and the Bavarian Alps. These are environments where the soil is derived from granitic rocks and contains little or no calcium which might act to counter acidity. They are all downwind of major areas of industrial and commercial development. However, it should not be assumed that there is universal and precise agreement about the problems posed by acid rain, as Box 2 makes clear.

Recent industrial restructuring, increased use of low sulphur fuels such as natural gas instead of coal and oil, the more effective use of energy, and the introduction of equipment to remove sulphur from flue gases – they all seem to have played a part in containing the acid rain problem in spite of an expanding industrial economy. At the same time European Union countries are now bound by the Large Combustion Plant Directive which requires phased cuts, through the 1990s, in sulphur dioxide and nitrogen oxide emissions from power stations and

Box 2 Acid rain – the record in perspective

1. Acid rain is not a new phenomenon. Initially it was recognized by R.A. Smith, the first Alkali Inspector, who showed that sulphur compounds and hydrochloric acid could produce acid rain. However, in his day it was of a much higher acid content than that found today and the damage caused by it was largely local.
2. Claims about damage to trees from acid rain have sometimes been exaggerated. Tree foliage can naturally vary for a wide range of reasons, but loss of more than 25% is now an accepted threshold for damage.
3. Projections of increasing damage from acid rain made in the early 1980s have not been realized. Some forest areas, as well as lakes, which initially became acidified and unable to support marine life, have begun to show signs of recovery.
4. Forest damage, although it can be caused by acid rain, may be the result of a combination of phenomena even if it is triggered by a common factor. Magnesium deficiency, excess nitrogen and climatic stress may all play a part. Scientists from the UK's former Central Electricity Generating Board have argued that ozone derived from photochemical effects on vehicle exhausts is the main cause of forest damage.
5. Acid rain can damage buildings, eroding the surface of those constructed of limestone.

other large combustion plants. Another EU Directive also aims to limit emissions of nitrogen oxides (and hydrocarbons) from motor vehicles and is now being phased in according to engine size.

Global warming is yet another phenomenon that by definition has significance for all nations and is now receiving considerable attention. Normally, gases in the atmosphere, notably water vapour, carbon dioxide, methane and nitrous oxide, form an insulating blanket around the earth. This allows the rays of the sun through but stops some of the heat radiating back into space – like the role of glass in a greenhouse. Without such a phenomenon the world would be frozen.

Whilst the growth in industrial and commercial activities has generally been looked upon as desirable in recent years because it has offered higher living standards, it has also caused escalating levels of fossil fuel consumption (and therefore carbon dioxide release) and raised atmospheric levels of chlorofluorocarbons (CFCs). At the same time, vast tracts of tropical forest, which transform carbon dioxide into oxygen as part of the mechanism of plant growth (photosynthesis), continue to be felled and the wood frequently burnt, adding to the amount of carbon dioxide in the atmosphere. Logging, 'slash-and-burn' agriculture and development projects such as roads, mines and dams will have probably reduced forest cover, in the 50 years up to the end of this century, from one-quarter of the earth's surface to about one-sixth. Simultaneously, society at large generates more and more methane as a result of dumping organic materials into landfill sites.

Although there is some element of uncertainty (see Box 3), all of these practices appear to be feeding the greenhouse effect, which in turn appears to be adversely influencing weather patterns around the world and may lead to catastrophic

Box 3 Global warming – the record in perspective

1 The world's temperature has been rising gradually since 1850.

2 Although there is a widespread agreement that carbon dioxide levels are also rising (by 30% over a period of 150 years), and that concentrations of methane have doubled since 1800, their impact remains uncertain.

3 One prediction suggests that, if greenhouse gas emissions continue to increase at current rates, average world temperatures could rise by 0.3 degrees centigrade every decade, a change greater than any that has occurred since the last Ice Age, 10,000 years ago.

4 However, global warming may yet prove to be part of a minor cycle of temperature fluctuations that occurs between Ice Ages, as evidence from the past seems to suggest.

5 Nevertheless, there is a consensus view that the world should try to meet uncertainty with action on a 'just in case' basis by: reducing the consumption of fossil fuels; developing alternative renewable energy sources; engaging in the conservation of tropical and other forms of forest; and eliminating the disposal of organic wastes in landfill sites.

increases in sea levels as the ice caps at the poles of the earth melt. Attempts to ameliorate global warming seem to be one of the more positive results of the Rio UNCED conference of June 1992, even though the emergent treaty to curb emissions of greenhouse gases was weakened by the desire of governments not to prejudice economic growth. However, following the signing of the Climate Convention in Rio, the European Commission proposes to consider a range of measures to improve energy efficiency and reduce carbon dioxide emission, possibly via taxation, in order to stabilize or reduce carbon dioxide emissions unilaterally by the turn of the century or soon after.

Of the issues of global environmental significance, the third concerns ozone. This has nothing to do with the ozone which forms at ground level as a result of the action of sunlight on nitrous oxides and unburnt and partially burnt exhaust gases from cars – an environmental problem of some significance for people living in cities such as Los Angeles. The ozone of global significance exists naturally as a layer at about 25 kilometres above the surface of the earth and is present only in very small amounts at around three parts per million. However, this is enough to block the passage of a substantial amount of the sun's ultraviolet radiation which would otherwise be harmful to living organisms, causing skin cancer in humans and decreased rates of growth in plants.

Although fears about the reasons for the depletion of ozone in this layer may well have several explanations, the one which many people take very seriously derives from the manufacture and commercial use of CFCs. These extremely stable chemicals have been used by industry in fire extinguishers, as coolants in home refrigerators, in the foam technology used to produce their insulating panels, and as a propellant in aerosol spray cans. However, they have two dangerous properties. First, their stability means that they remain in the atmosphere for long periods, possibly between 40 and 80 years. This gives them plenty of time to reach the ozone layer. Second, when exposed to ultraviolet light they release chlorine which is what destroys ozone in a complex chain reaction.

A so-called 'hole' in the ozone layer has been detected in Antarctica, but in truth it is really a dent. It appears with the arrival of the sun, persists through the spring, and covers an area the si?e of the USA. Fears have been created by the increasing temporal persistence of the 'hole' and the worry that, although only minor thinnings of the ozone layer have been detected elsewhere, the situation may worsen globally. Consequently, there have been international attempts by the most developed nations to restrict and eventually ban the use of CFC compounds, even though there is uncertainty concerning the impact of such measures (see Box 4). Thus, signatories to the Montreal Protocol in 1990 accepted, on behalf of their governments, the need to eliminate CFCs totally by the year 2000 although the European Union expect to achieve the same end by 1997. Recognizing the problems for developing countries in joining in any ban on the use of CFCs, an international attempt has been made to establish a fund to help them use the more expensive substitutes that have been developed by the two major CFC producers, Du Pont and ICI.

Box 4 Ozone layer depletion – the record in perspective

1. It is uncertain what a ban on CFCs will do since there are other natural sources of atmospheric chlorine (e.g. methyl chloride and chloromethane) that can damage the ozone layer. These have been produced over long periods of time in amounts far in excess of CFCs.
2. In 1895 the eruption of Krakatoa destroyed about one-third of the ozone layer and a violent solar storm in August 1972 produced a shower of protons that destroyed 16% of the ozone layer without harmful results.
3. The Antarctic ozone 'hole' is disturbing, but there is no evidence to suggest that it will affect the whole globe.
4. If the ozone layer did disappear completely over the UK, ultraviolet radiation levels would increase only to those levels present in the tropics. This would lead to a need for people to use only the simplest protection measures against the sun. In the tropics, however, exposure to direct sunlight would need to be avoided.
5. Phasing out CFCs may avoid unnecessary risk to the ozone layer, but it is probably more important in reducing the greenhouse effect.

Conclusion – towards the level playing-field

Whatever the global implications of environmental pollution for the population at large may be, the fact remains that, for industry and for business in the European Union, its internal policies remain of greatest significance. The removal of internal trade barriers between EU countries can be effective only if a level playing-field truly exists. Among other things, this must embrace common environmental constraints and costs across the 12 member states, as opposed to a plethora of national standards that perhaps could easily become exacerbated by differences between the richer countries of northern Europe and those of the poorer south. Apart from the overall popularity of environmental policies amongst the populations in all EU countries – a rare enough aspect of EU affairs in itself – it is this that has driven EU strategy for the environment, now encompassed in a total programme for the 1990s called 'Towards Sustainability'.

Some environmentalists thought that the derailment of the Maastricht Treaty by Denmark in 1992 and the emergence of the idea of subsidiarity might seriously prejudice the unified environmental approach. Subsidiarity – with its implication that action should be taken at Union level only where it would be more appropriate than action at national or local levels – seemed for the President of the European Commission and its Competition Commissioner to call into question the need for some existing EU environmental rules. However, events since then do not indicate a radically diminished role for the EU, and legislation with transboundary aspects seems in the event least exposed to any post-Maastricht cull. Preparations for the Directive on integrated pollution prevention and control right across the EU remain on course because of the overwhelming logic of harmonizing industrial environmental protection costs. Moreover, several states, such as the UK, have no intention of letting the subsidiarity debate get in the way of a campaign for the stricter enforcement of EU environmental rules, or to permit any backing away from proposals for a Community Inspectorate to assure national enforcement of common standards. Indeed, the notion of a European Environmental Agency seems to have broad consent among member states and to be favoured as the ultimate means of providing and maintaining the level playing-field for business enterprise.

References

Arlidge, J.T. (1892) *The Hygiene, Diseases and Mortality of Occupations*. Percival and Co., London.

Blunden, J. and Reddish, A. (eds) (1991) *Energy, Resources and Environment*. Hodder and Stoughton, London.

Faucher, L. (1844) *Manchester in 1844: its present conditions and future prospects*. Manchester Athenaeum, London.

Vianna, Marcelo Drugg Barreto (1991) 'Alumar – environmental impact analysis study', in *Tools of Environmental Management*, Session V. Second World Industry Conference in Environmental Management, International Chamber of Commerce in co-operation with UNEP and UNCED, Rotterdam.

PART 2

THE BUILDING BLOCKS OF PERFORMANCE MEASUREMENT

Introduction

Jacky Holloway

Some of the articles in Part 2 have an operational focus, but they all have relevance to strategic performance, too. They draw the reader's attention to the dimensions of efficiency and effectiveness in particular. Within this Part we meet approaches that reflect national differences as well as industry sector specialities, but each of the six articles contains some generic lessons.

While the articles by Claes Fornell and Roger Dence could be linked together under a 'customer satisfaction' heading, this would be to oversimplify the scope of both of them. Fornell's description of the Swedish national Customer Satisfaction Barometer (CSB) shows this to be far more ambitious than simply large-scale market research. The CSB is sponsored by the Swedish post office. It measures the level of customer satisfaction – quality of output as experienced by the buyer – annually, in 100 organizations in 30 industry sectors. As well as describing the survey, Fornell presents research findings linking customer satisfaction with the firm's overall strategy, from which parallels can be drawn with the work of Porter. Of crucial importance is the match between the degree of homogeneity of the market and of the product or service.

Still keeping the customer and market very much in mind, Dence provides an accessible overview of the nature and scope of 'best practices' or 'competitive' benchmarking, which also has significant implications for strategic success. At the core is the notion of identifying key stages in the value chain and making comparisons between one's own practices and those of exemplars elsewhere. The comparator may be internal or external, a competitor or an unrelated business; the essential point is to identify and gain information about the best ways to undertake key activities. Although benchmarking had its origins in production and operations management, after reading Dence's article it should be apparent that the concept has potentially universal relevance.

Staying within the paradigm of 'excellence', we turn back to the field of operations management with the articles by Hayes *et al.* and Oliver *et al.* Underlying both articles is a desire to explain differences in efficiency or productivity between ostensibly similar organizations. Thus each reports empirical findings from comparative studies of progress towards 'best practices' which could contribute to their more realistic adoption, as well as shedding light on some of the contingency factors that are pertinent to innovation in performance management. *Dynamic Manufacturing*, the source of the Hayes article, includes a more detailed yet relatively accessible explanation of the calculation of Total Factor Productivity (TFP) at plant level. The article we have selected locates the development of this approach within the context of extremely pertinent questions about factors linking operations to strategic success. While the emphasis is on manufacturing, there are many lessons here for service operations, too. The ideas may be directly applicable and, if they are not, the identification of limits to their relevance may illuminate distinctive service characteristics which deserve their own forms of productivity analysis. Oliver *et al.* focus on the factors which may make 'lean production' (where unnecessary inputs are eliminated) achievable in some contexts and not others. Their research methodology is itself of interest as an example of the complexities of designing comparative management research.

On the face of it, the remaining two articles in Part 2 have little in common. The performance of health services has become an increasingly newsworthy topic in developed countries as economic recessions throw health care costs into sharp relief. Much effort has gone into the measurement of efficiency, relatively less into effectiveness analysis and the measurement of health care outcomes which, it could reasonably be argued, tell us more about the real value of such services. Peter Smith explores the reasons behind this imbalance, develops a typology of problems, and applies it to the use of one particular outcome indicator. Technical complexity, individual behaviour, organizational cultures and politics are all implicated.

One could be left with the impression that the measurement of performance on dimensions which are of vital importance is far from becoming routine practice. A lack of confidence is engendered in 'the figures' as well as in human behaviour. These doubts will not be reduced by the views of Andy Simmonds and Olivier Azières, unfortunately. Again our attempts to obtain an 'objective' view of organizational performance are thwarted, this time by historically-derived accounting practices. However, it is probably fair to say that there is usually a high degree of consistency within countries, and accordingly the challenge is to make valid and reliable international comparisons. While this is primarily a 'technical' matter, the successful implementation of the other approaches advocated in the articles in Part 2 depends above all on understanding and accommodating the 'human element' in performance measurement.

6
A national Customer Satisfaction Barometer: the Swedish experience*

Claes Fornell

Claes Fornell is the Donald C. Cook Professor of Business Administration and Director of the Office for Customer Satisfaction Research, School of Business Administration, University of Michigan. *The Swedish Post Office sponsors the Customer Satisfaction Barometer. Its financial support is gratefully acknowledged. The author thanks Gene Anderson, Rajeev Batra, Fred Bookstein, Jaesung Cha, Rabikar Chatterjee, Mike Guolla, Dan Horne, Lenard Huff, Mike Johnson, Don Lehmann, Paul McCracken, Bill Robinson, Mike Ryan, Karl-Erik Wärneryd, Claes-Robert Julander, and Youjae Yi for their input and comments.*

Abstract

Many individual companies and some industries monitor customer satisfaction on a continual basis, but Sweden is the first country to do so on a national level. The annual Customer Satisfaction Barometer (CSB) measures customer satisfaction in more than 30 industries and for more than 100 corporations. The new index is intended to be complementary to productivity measures. Whereas productivity basically reflects quantity of output, CSB measures quality of output (as experienced by the buyer). The author reports the results of a large-scale Swedish effort to measure quality of the total consumption process as customer satisfaction. The significance of customer satisfaction and its place within the overall strategy of the firm are discussed. An implication from examining the relationship between market share and customer satisfaction by a location model is that satisfaction should be lower in industries where supply is homogeneous and demand heterogeneous. Satisfaction should be higher when the heterogeneity/homogeneity of demand is matched by the supply. Empirical support is found for that proposition in monopolies as well as in competitive market structures. Likewise, industries in general are found to have a high level of customer satisfaction if they are highly dependent on satisfaction for repeat business. The opposite is found for industries in which companies have more captive markets. For Sweden, the 1991 results show a slight increase in CSB, which should have a positive effect on the general economic climate.

* This article was first published in *Journal of Marketing* (1992), Vol. 56, pp. 6–21.

Introduction

In an effort to promote quality and make its industry more competitive and market oriented, Sweden has become the first country to establish a national economic indicator reflecting customer satisfaction. The extent to which the business firm is able to satisfy its customers is an indication of its general health and prospects for the future. The Customer Satisfaction Barometer (CSB) is an index based on annual survey data from customers of about 100 leading companies in some 30 industries. It is a weighted composite that rates the level of customer satisfaction in the included industries and companies. In addition, the relationship of CSB to customer loyalty as well as product (service) performance is estimated.

Because customer satisfaction has a direct impact on the primary source of *future* revenue streams for most companies, the new index is expected to be an important complement to traditional measures of economic performance, providing useful information not only to the firms themselves, but also to shareholders and investors, government regulators, and buyers. Not surprisingly, efforts to measure customer satisfaction on a nationwide basis are now under way in several other countries. For example, the United States is establishing a national quality index very similar to the Swedish model. Efforts are also under way in Japan, Singapore, and the EC countries.[1]

This article reports the CSB development and industry results from the first three years in Sweden. Background and a brief description of some of the macroeconomic issues involved are followed by a discussion of how customer satisfaction relates to the overall strategy of the firm. That is the context within which the validity of CSB is examined.

Though the notion is controversial, substantial literature suggests that market share leads to profitability (see Buzzell and Gale, 1987 for a review). Customer satisfaction also is believed to lead to profitability (Business International, 1990). However, it is far from certain that market share and customer satisfaction themselves are positively correlated. In fact, the opposite could well be the case. The circumstances under which there is a *negative* relationship between the two is discussed as the basis for a proposition about the levels of CSB in different industries.

The impact of customer satisfaction for repeat business and customer loyalty is not the same for all industries. Loyal customers are not necessarily satisfied customers, but satisfied customers tend to be loyal customers. Aside from satisfaction, there are other means of customer retention. Customer switching barriers comprise a host of factors that also bring about retention. Hence, all companies are not equally affected by customer satisfaction, but virtually all companies depend on repeat business.

To understand the meaning of CSB as an economic indicator and its significance for the individual business firm, let us first examine the macro concerns, the relationship between satisfaction and market share, and the impact of customer switching barriers. After a discussion of those issues, the objectives, method, and results of CSB are presented.

Background

The macro level

As in other Western economies, many industries in Sweden face the combined difficulties of increasing international competition, slower growth rates, and mature markets. As a result, fewer new customers are being pursued by an increasing number of suppliers. Under those circumstances, a large share of the firm's resources must be devoted to the present customer base. How can that base be maintained? How can it be protected from (foreign and domestic) competition? Another effect of an increasingly competitive environment is rising pressure on price. The cost structure in most Swedish industries is such that price is not the most effective competitive weapon. Means of competition that *reduce* price elasticities among *repeat* buyers are therefore becoming increasingly important. A high level of customer satisfaction may be such a means.

The annual CSB is a nationwide gauge of how well companies (and industries as a whole) satisfy their customers. Similar to a productivity index, it measures economic performance. The difference is that productivity refers to quantity (output per factor), whereas CSB refers to quality (from the customer perspective). Obviously, any nation would like increases in both. However, if quality is costly (say, in terms of the manpower factor), a gain in one may imply a loss in the other. It is too early to speculate on the nature of that trade off, but it seems reasonable to assume that a weak growth in productivity is not necessarily detrimental if it is offset by increases in quality. According to the OECD Productivity Index, both Japan and (West) Germany are below the average productivity level for developed countries. Nevertheless, they are countries with a positive balance of trade, strong economy, and reputation for quality products. High quality leads to high levels of customer retention (for a review, see Steenkamp, 1989), which in turn are strongly related to profitability (Reichheld and Sasser, 1990).

Consider the effects of changes in the currency exchange rates as an example. Increases in the yen do not seem to have as strong a negative effect for Japanese products as an equivalent price increase for, say, American products. A nation whose industry generates high levels of customer satisfaction is probably better protected against cost increases as well as foreign competition.

The micro level

Figure 1 (overleaf) is an overview of the micro context of CSB in terms of the sources of revenue. Here, overall business strategy is composed of two parts, the offense and the defense. Virtually all firms employ some combination of offensive and defensive strategy – the offense for customer acquisition and the defense to protect the present customer base (Fornell and Wernerfelt, 1987, 1988). Traditionally, much more effort is devoted to acquiring customers than to their retention. The annual expenditure on advertising and sales promotion in the US alone is well over one trillion dollars. Though much of the advertising portion is directed to present customers, most such expenditures are for the offense. In the face of slow growth and highly competitive markets, however, a good defense is

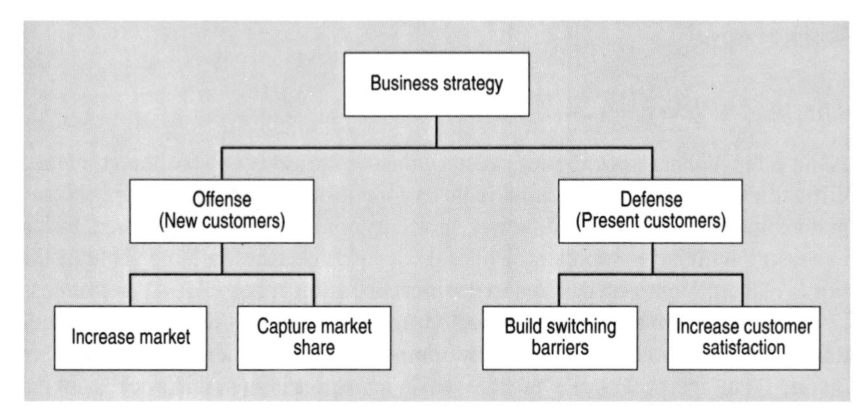

Figure 1 *Sources of revenue*

critical. When company growth is accomplished at the expense of competing firms (i.e. by capturing market share), firms with weak defenses are the first to suffer. In many cases the attention paid to the defense has been too slow or insufficient. The result is typically an erosion of the customer base. Witness what has happened in banking and the steel industry, and to companies that make automobiles, cameras, television sets, food products, machine tools, radial tires, computer chips, and medical equipment.

Defensive strategy involves *reducing* customer exit and switching. The objective of defensive strategy is to minimize customer turnover (maximize customer retention), given certain cost constraints (see Fornell and Wernerfelt, 1987, 1988 for an analytical treatment), by protecting products and markets from competitive inroads. One way of accomplishing that objective is to have highly satisfied customers. To understand CSB in a micro context, let us return to Figure 1 to examine a major approach of the offense – building market share – and discuss how it relates to a major approach for the defense – customer satisfaction.

Market share and customer satisfaction

Beginning in the 1970s and spurred by two very influential publications (one by the Boston Consulting Group, 1972; the other by Buzzell, Gale and Sultan, 1975), the pursuit of market share became a key part of management strategy. In popular simplifications, the maximization of market share was held to be a way to maximize profits. So widespread was the practice that a majority of the leading US firms employed some form of market share strategy in the belief that it would lead to greater profitability (Haspeslagh, 1982). Market share maximization was claimed not only to serve the individual firm, but also to improve a country's economy in terms of productive efficiency (Henderson, 1979).

In Table 1, the fundamentals of a market share strategy are outlined in relation to a customer satisfaction strategy. Both strategies often are used under the same market conditions, low growth or saturated markets – that is, when there is little prospect for company growth without taking business away from competitors.

Table 1 *Market share versus customer satisfaction*

	Market share	Customer satisfaction
Typically employed in	Low growth or saturated markets	Low growth or saturated markets
Strategy type	Offense	Defense
Focal point	Competition	Customers
Measure of success	Share of market relative to competition	Customer retention rate
Behavioral objective	Buyer switching	Buyer loyalty

Capturing market share is an offensive strategy; creating customer satisfaction is defensive. Success and failure in market share are evaluated in relation to competitors. For customer satisfaction, success and failure are evaluated primarily by changes in customer retention. In other words, the behavioral objective for the offense is patronage switching; for the defense it is loyalty. Costs, as a result, are typically higher for the offense, because more effort is necessary to create change (switching) than to maintain status quo. Clearly, a successful defense makes competitors' offense even more costly.

Several of the major consulting firms that prescribed some form of market share strategy a few years ago are now promoting strategies for customer satisfaction (*Business Week,* 1990). The argument is that customer satisfaction leads to profitability – the same argument that was used for market share. However, as indicated in Table 1, the two strategies are drastically different. If they both lead to increased profitability, what is the relationship between market share and customer satisfaction? Understanding that relationship is critical for firms that now change their overall strategy, as well as for understanding the role of CSB as an index.

Paradoxically, one can show that the relationship between market share and customer satisfaction can be negative. That will be the case when market demand is heterogeneous and supply homogeneous (standardized). Theoretically the relationship can be demonstrated with a location (address, ideal-point) model. That type of model commonly is used in analyses of utility and choice. It also brings new insights into the study of customer satisfaction.

Consider a distribution of customers with different tastes. For simplicity, let us assume that the tastes are normally distributed, there are two competitors, and taste can be represented on a single scale. That scenario is illustrated in Figure 2, where the taste dimension is a combination of price and quality. Some customers are willing to pay a high price for high quality; others prefer a lower price and are less concerned about quality.

For the purposes of the illustration, it is not necessary to explore the equilibrium positions of the firms (that aspect is analyzed by Rhee *et al.*, 1991) or to go beyond the duopoly. According to Figure 2, firm 1 offers a high quality product at a high price. It is thus positioned toward the right tail of the taste distribution. Firm 2 is positioned slightly to the left of firm 1.

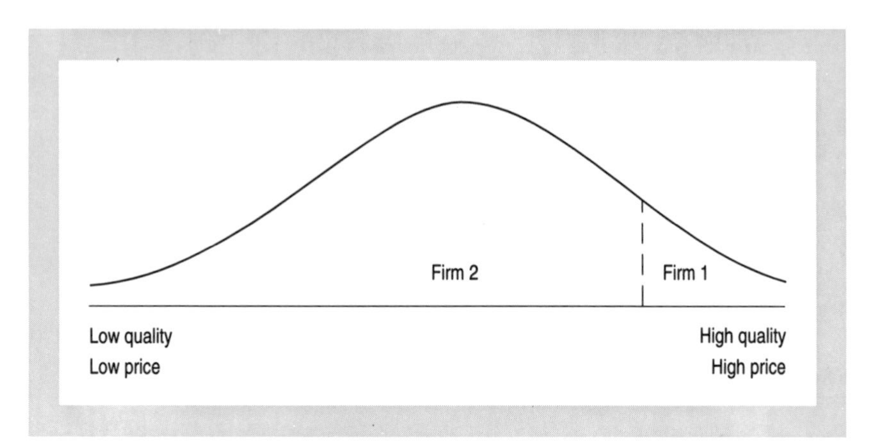

Figure 2 *Heterogeneous customer preferences*

The implications in terms of market share and customer satisfaction are as follows. Buyers on the left of the dotted vertical line will buy from firm 2 because it offers the product closest to their desires. That area represents about 80% of the distribution. Consequently, firm 1 has a market share of about 20%; firm 2 has a share of 80%.

On average, however, firm 1 has higher levels of customer satisfaction. The distance between a customer's 'ideal' (in terms of a certain price/quality combination) and the firm's offering represents a facet of that customer's 'dissatisfaction'. Firm 2 has many more customers that are far from their ideal than does firm 1. That is, the mean distance between customer ideal and product offering is much greater for firm 2. Accordingly, customers of firm 2 are less satisfied than customers of firm 1 (on average).

That reasoning does not mean the pursuit of customer satisfaction *leads* to lower market share. In fact, high levels of customer satisfaction should produce favorable word of mouth, which in turn has a positive effect on market share. However, market share gains that imply an increase in the heterogeneity of the customer base and/or are not commensurate with an increase in resources for servicing a larger number of customers could lead to problems with customer dissatisfaction. It is more *difficult* for a firm with a large market share to also have a high average level of customer satisfaction, especially if customer tastes are heterogeneous. Consider the market share leaders and the customer satisfaction leaders in the US automobile market. They are not the same companies. It is also obvious from Figure 2 that the large-market-share firm is more vulnerable to new entry under such circumstances.

The ideal-point conceptualisation as one (but not the only) aspect of customer satisfaction suggests a new hypothesis about market structure and customer satisfaction. The contention is that the monopoly will have a lower score on CSB than competing firms *if* it faces a heterogeneous demand. Low customer satisfaction is not only a result of insulation from competition (and thereby also from customer switching) and its possible manifestations in higher prices and lower quality, but also a reflection of the difficulty in serving a heterogeneous market with a limited variety of offerings.

However, all monopolies need not have lower satisfaction scores. Satisfaction will be low when customer preferences are heterogeneous and the supply standardized. That notion is the logical consequence of interpreting satisfaction/dissatisfaction in terms of an ideal-point model. It is not an empirical issue. The extent to which such a situation exists is an empirical question, however. Industries in Sweden that are characterized by a high level of heterogeneity that might not be matched by an equivalent diversity in supply include television broadcasting, the police force, telephone services, postal services, and the alcoholic beverage distribution outlets, as well as the retailers of furniture and clothing because they cater primarily to mass markets. Another industry in that category is the insurance industry, in which competition has been restricted and regulated. To a lesser extent, the degree of variety in supply is probably lower than buyer heterogeneity calls for in supermarkets, oil companies (gas stations), and department stores, although there is some differentiation due to variances in local customer tastes. A better match is found in the automobile market, where both demand and supply are heterogeneous. Food processing also has a better match – sometimes, as in the case of staples (milk, sugar, yeast), not because of greater heterogeneity in supply but because of a high degree of homogeneity in demand.

From the preceding discussion, we would expect industries characterized by a good fit between the levels of demand and supply heterogeneity (homogeneity) to have higher CSB values than those with a poor fit. Industries, including monopoly organizations that supply a high quality homogeneous product to a homogeneous market should have high satisfaction. That notion might be somewhat contradictory to traditional economic theory and the Structural Antitrust Doctrine (Thorelli, 1955), but is in line with previous empirical findings showing no relationship between seller concentration and customer satisfaction (Fornell and Robinson, 1983) and recent work in welfare economics (Daughety, 1990).

Customer satisfaction and switching barriers

As suggested in Figure 1, offense has two basic forms: (1) gaining new customers from market expansion and (2) increasing market share at the expense of competing firms. In principle, defensive strategy also has two basic forms: (1) switching barriers and (2) customer satisfaction. To understand the differential impact of CSB in different industries, let us now introduce the role of switching barriers.

Switching barriers make it *costly for the customer* to switch to another supplier (vendor, store, etc.). Customer satisfaction, in contrast, makes it *costly for a competitor* to take away another firm's customers. That is, in the first case, the firm makes it difficult, expensive, or even illegal for customers to switch. The monopoly is one example, but a firm can erect switching barriers in many ways without becoming a monopoly.

Search costs, transaction costs, learning costs, loyal customer discounts, customer habit, emotional cost, and cognitive effort, coupled with financial, social, and psychological risks on the part of the buyer, all add up to switching barriers. Others are costs of retraining personnel, capital requirements for change-over and costs of acquiring new ancillary equipment (Porter, 1980). Those barriers tend to be more formidable in business-to-business markets, but they can play an important role in consumer markets as well. Basically, any pursuit by the firm to limit the scope of comparable buyer alternatives for repeat purchase is equivalent to a strategy of erecting customer switching barriers.

Even within a single industry, it is not unusual to find competing firms with different combinations of barriers and satisfaction. An example is the airline industry. American airlines (domestic and international) discourage passenger switching by raising barriers. Frequent flier programs are designed to enhance repeat business, not through superior service or passenger satisfaction, but by providing an economic incentive for the customer to remain loyal. European and Oriental airlines, in contrast, rely more on customer satisfaction to secure repeat business. If they have a frequent flier program at all, it is usually not emphasized or is a result of a joint effort with an American partner.

At a general level, it may not be possible to determine whether satisfaction is more effective than barriers to switching, but two immediate problems with barriers are not present in the satisfaction approach.

The first is obvious. If the customer is aware of the barriers at the time of purchase, the barriers will be an impediment to the offense strategy. The presence of barriers makes the initial sales task more difficult. The opposite is true for customer satisfaction. Highly satisfied customers are an asset for the offense.

The second problem with barriers is that they might be eliminated by external forces. Frequent flier programs are easily imitated and monopolies can be broken. When that happens, the competitive weapon of the barrier can quickly become a liability. As illustrated in the airline industry, first-mover advantages (in the case of frequent flier programs) have dissipated (Kearney, 1990). Previously insulated organizations become vulnerable, for they are seldom well prepared and have not made the investments in quality and customer satisfaction necessary to prevent customer exit.

Low barriers and weak customer satisfaction force the company to compete on price. Compare the use of sales promotions by US and Japanese automobile manufacturers. American firms have come to rely on promotions. The Japanese employ such devices somewhat more sparingly. After all, sales promotions are (temporary) price cuts with a corresponding negative effect on gross margins. With high satisfaction, the effect on margins is the opposite, and there is less need for price promotions.

CSB: purpose and method

To recapitulate, the propositions that evolve from the ideal-point model and the switching-barrier effect suggest that customer satisfaction should be lower in industries where repeat buyers face high switching costs and where the industry offers a homogeneous product to a heterogeneous market.

If customer satisfaction is an indicator of a healthy company, CSB is a measure of performance that is oriented toward the future. Some writers (e.g. Kotler, 1988) even consider customer satisfaction to be the best indicator of a company's future profits. Accordingly, CSB can be seen as a future-oriented complement to traditional measures of performance such as return on investment, market share, and profits. In comparison with many of the traditional performance measures, customer satisfaction is probably less sensitive to seasonal fluctuations, changes in costs, or changes in accounting practices (Kotler, 1988). Consistent with the American effort (see NERA, 1991), the Swedish CSB should help focus public attention on improving quality and customer satisfaction as a source of a higher standard of living. It also should complement the national accounting measures, which do not (other than through prices) take quality or customer satisfaction into account. In addition, CSB is designed to provide the following information.

1 *Industry comparisons.* The government typically assembles customer complaint data for information about quality problems in various industries. A satisfaction index complements that information. It also complements traditional economic output measures such as productivity. However, the possibility of making industry comparisons is an issue of some controversy. Despite several thousand studies on the related, but even broader, topic of 'subjective well-being' (Andrews and Robinson, 1988) in which people and (sometimes) nations are compared, comparisons of customer satisfaction among different industries are not without difficulty. Johnson and Fornell (1991) give a detailed account of the foundations for making those types of comparisons.

Though the comparison of industries may be the most important objective for CSB (and what is reported here), there are other objectives as well.

2 *Comparisons of individual firms with the industry average.* In general, one would expect higher margins and more repeat customers for firms with high satisfaction scores. Overall, one would also predict a brighter future for firms with higher levels of customer satisfaction.

3 *Comparisons over time.* CSB is dynamic and continual. It provides information about firm (industry) improvement (decline) as well as general trends. Over time, it will be interesting to see whether there is a relationship to productivity indices. If consumers *at large* can anticipate changes in the macro economy, as evidenced by the Index of Consumer Expectations from the University of Michigan (which shows very good predictive power), a satisfaction index based on *customer* consumption experience ought to be a useful indicator of repeat business at the micro level.

4 *Predictions of long-term performance.* Though empirical evidence is limited, increases in customer satisfaction are generally believed to (1) shift the demand curve upward and/or make the slope of the curve steeper (i.e., lower price elasticity, higher margins), (2) reduce marketing costs (customer acquisition requires more effort), (3) increase marketing costs for competitors (satisfied customers are more difficult for competitors to take away), (4) lower transaction costs (contract negotiations, order processing, bargaining, etc.), (5) reduce customer turnover (fewer lost customers to replace), (6) increase cross-selling (more products, larger accounts), (7) lower employee turnover (satisfied customers affect the satisfaction of front-line personnel), (8) enhance reputation (positive customer word of mouth), and (9) reduce failure costs (reduction in downtime, rework, warranty claims, etc.). As a result, satisfied customers can be viewed as an investment. Some accounting

firms are now suggesting that the customer asset be included on the balanced sheet and in annual reports (Konrad, 1989).

5 *Answers to specific questions* such as the sensitivity of various industries (and firms) to customer satisfaction, the effects of overall quality and price, the impact of customer expectations, the quality increase necessary to retain dissatisfied customers, price sensitivity, switching patterns, customer complaints, and effects of word of mouth.

Measures

The literature on customer satisfaction/dissatisfaction suggests that satisfaction is an overall post-purchase evaluation. There is no consensus on how to measure it, however. Hausknecht (1990) identifies more than 30 different measures that have been used in previous research. Among them, three different facets of satisfaction can be identified – CSB attempts to capture the degree of (1) general satisfaction (as in the studies by Moore and Shuptrine, 1984; Oliver and Bearden, 1983; Oliver and Westbrook, 1982; Westbrook, 1980, 1981), (2) confirmation of expectations (as in the studies by Oliver, 1977; Swan, Trawick and Carroll, 1981), and (3) the distance from the customer's hypothetical ideal product (similar to the work of Tse and Wilton, 1988; Sirgy, 1984). In other words, customer satisfaction is *defined* as a function of three indicators that are allowed to be measured with error. An advantage over traditional approaches to satisfaction measurement is that causes of satisfaction are not confounded with the phenomenon itself. Other advantages are that the fallibility of measures is acknowledged and taken into account, and that the indicators defining customer satisfaction can be weighted such that their composite (i.e., CSB) has maximal impact on loyalty and customer retention (the estimation is discussed shortly).

Loyalty is measured by repurchase intention and price tolerance (for satisfied customers). The latter measure is similar to the 'dollar-metric of loyalty' introduced by Pessemier (1959) – the price differential needed to make loyal customers switch. Dollar-metric measures have shown acceptable levels of reliability and validity in previous research (Olson and Jacoby, 1971), and are often used in studies of brand loyalty (e.g., Raju, Srinivasan and Lal, 1990).

Presumably, customers take both price and quality into account as they form an overall evaluation about a product's performance. To avoid a confounding of the two, each was measured in light of the other – perceived performance is thus measured by price (given quality) and quality (given price).

A direct measure of switching barriers is very difficult to obtain. All costs (financial, psychological, learning, etc.) associated with deserting one supplier in favour of another constitute switching barriers. The nature of those barriers can be very different in different industries. Any attempt to measure all of them would be an overwhelming task. Instead, the assumption is made that causes of loyalty *other* than customer satisfaction, complaint management, and switching barriers are negligible. Accordingly, the effect of switching barriers can be represented by the intercept term in the loyalty equation, which would constitute the firm-specific switching barrier. In addition, there is a customer-specific barrier due to individual factors such as previous consumption experience, learning, propensity for risk taking, and so on. Some recent findings on switching barriers (with this database) are reported by Anderson and Sullivan (1990).

Model

Three fundamental principles guide the modeling effort. First, it is recognized that variables take on meaning depending on the context in which they are applied (Blalock, 1982; Fornell, 1982, 1989; Fornell and Yi, 1992). Second, all survey variables are measured with some degree of error (Andrew, 1984). Third, the construct 'customer satisfaction' is not directly observable (Howard and Sheth, 1969; Oliver, 1981; Westbrook and Riley, 1983).

The task is thus to specify a reasonably comprehensive system of post-purchase outcomes in which customer satisfaction is part. Accordingly, the index is specified as a composite latent variable in a system represented by multiple equations, where measurement error (i.e., noise) is accounted for. Each individual company is estimated separately in order to capture differences in relationships with respect to how the latent variables relate both to their indicators and to each other. A major difference between CSB and other customer satisfaction indices is that CSB is measured (and estimated) in the context of other interrelated variables (as represented in a model of structural equations). That approach leads not only to better reliability and validity (Fornell and Yi, 1992), but also to improved ability to translate customer satisfaction changes into repurchase behavior. The typical approach, used by most companies today, is to measure satisfaction in isolation of the context in which it is to be applied (causes and consequences) and then retrospectively estimate the relationship to some criterion (such as loyalty, sales, or profit). The result is likely to show low reliability and strong bias in the estimated coefficients (because of misspecification). As a consequence, many firms fail to find a strong relationship between their satisfaction measures and economic performance. The approach described here should reduce bias and increase the quality of measurement. The full set of equations is given in Appendix A. The most important specifications follow.

In accord with the findings of Churchill and Surprenant (1982), Tse and Wilton (1988), and Oliver and DeSarbo (1988) and as discussed by Yi (1990) and Johnson and Fornell (1991), customer satisfaction is expressed as a function of prepurchase expectations and postpurchase perceived performance (of the respective product/service), both of which, in line with Rational Expectations Theory, are expected to have a positive effect:

Customer satisfaction = f (expectations, perceived performance).

Tse and Wilton (1988) provide theoretical and empirical support for including the direct effect of perceived performance on satisfaction and suggest that it may actually have a stronger influence than expectations in determining satisfaction. That does not mean the traditional view of satisfaction/dissatisfaction as the discrepancy between expectations and perceived performance is dismissed *a priori* in CSB. Recall that the discrepancy is a part of the definition of the latent satisfaction variable and is reflected in one of its indicators. However, the preceding specification allows for the possibility of *dissatisfaction* even when expectations are confirmed. For example, if low quality is expected but the product is purchased nevertheless (because of supply restrictions or price) and delivered, the expectations are confirmed. Clearly, the fact that expectations are confirmed is not sufficient for satisfaction.

The final endogenous variable is loyalty. As discussed previously, loyalty is caused by a combination of satisfaction and switching barriers. Hirschman (1970) identifies three basic consequences of changes in satisfaction/dissatisfaction – exit, voice (i.e. complaints), and loyalty. To capture the possibility that the firm's complaint handling might be able to turn a complaining customer into a loyal customer (a finding reported by TARP, 1979), loyalty is also specified to be a function of voice:

Loyalty = f (customer satisfaction, switching barriers, voice).

If the relationship between voice and loyalty is positive, the firm's complaint handling is functional and purposeful; it turns complainants into loyal customers. If it is negative, an increasing number of complaints makes the firm more resistant to customer grievances and complainants are more likely to seek other suppliers.

Data

In 1989, customers (in Sweden) of the largest companies in 28 industries were selected as the target population. In 1990, the number of industries was increased to 32. The objective was to include a sufficient number of companies in each industry that their combined sales would represent at least 70% of the market. For firms selling multiple products, the product with the highest sales (in Kronor) was chosen to represent the company. Annually, some 100,000 respondents are contacted on a random basis. After screening questions to determine whether the respondent is a customer of any of the selected companies, the total sample size amounts to about 25,000 respondents per year who are subjected to an eight-minute telephone interview.[2] Except for a few industries (food and television broadcasting), each respondent was asked about a single company only. With a yearly sample size ranging from 250 for some monopolies to more than 4000 for industries in fragmented markets, the sampling error for CSB ranges from 1.5% to .6% at the 95% level.

Scales and estimation

Virtually all customer satisfaction research is hampered by highly skewed distributions for the indicators of the satisfaction construct (see Hunt, 1977; Michalos, 1986; Oliver, 1981; Westbrook, 1980). For example, in studies of products ranging from shoes (Westbrook and Cote, 1980), to medical care (Ware, Davies-Avery and Stewart, 1978) to department stores (Fitzgerald, 1990) and clothing (Hughes, 1977), more than 80% of the customers were satisfied.

Those findings are not particularly surprising. Even in less than perfect markets, as long as there are available alternatives and/or some elasticity of demand, the distribution of satisfaction scores should be negatively skewed. Only in captive markets might repeat buyers be dissatisfied in general.

Skewness is a problem, but it is a statistical one. Highly skewed variable distributions do not lend themselves to conventional tests of significance and, what is equally serious, lead to downward biases in correlational analysis, low reliability, and sometimes misleading arithmetic means. The implications are that it is very difficult to account properly for the variation in satisfaction ratings by use of other variables and that the results are unstable.

In CSB, the problem of skewness was handled by (1) extending the typical number (usually 5 or 7) of scale points to 10 (to allow respondents to make finer discriminations), (2) using a multiple-indicator approach (to achieve greater accuracy), and (3) estimating via a version of partial least squares (PLS).[3]

Though all the specified relationships might not be linear and PLS uses a nonlinear operator, the resulting relationships are linear. Nonlinear relationships could be estimated but require specific knowledge about exact functional forms. In the absence of such knowledge, linear approximations are assumed to be good enough within reasonable ranges. Over time, however, it should be possible to examine differences in slopes and perhaps find the appropriate nonlinear expressions.

Results

The index results for 1989–1991 are reported in Table 2 (overleaf). A more detailed account is provided in Appendix B, where the highest scoring firm in each industry is also identified. Mean customer satisfaction scores (on a scale from 0 to 100) are shown for 28 industries in 1989 and an additional four industries (shipping of light goods, newspapers, pharmacy, mail order) in 1990 and 1991. Both consumer and business markets are represented. In some cases (postal services, telecommunication, banking, insurance), the industry serves both business buyers and consumers. Only business customers were surveyed for computer mainframes and personal computers. For business buyers, the respondents were individuals responsible for purchasing the product/service in question.

The statistics in Table 2 are the nonweighted means of 19 firms producing nondurable goods, 16 firms producing durable goods, 19 retailers, 5 monopolies (including postal and telephone services for both business buyers and the general public), and 34 service providers (including banks and insurance companies for both business buyers and the general public). Obviously, the categorization of industries is not without ambiguity, because some of the entries are overlapping. For example, all the monopolies in Table 2 are also service providers. Basic foods (among the nondurable goods) are local monopolies (supplying milk, yeast, and sugar).[4]

According to the reasoning presented previously, CSB should be higher (1) in differentiated industries if customer tastes are heterogeneous *and* (2) for standardized (undifferentiated) products if customer tastes are homogeneous. In contrast, CSB should be lower where customer tastes are heterogeneous and industry offerings undifferentiated. That is, if the heterogeneity in tastes is not met by differentiated supply, some customers would give their chosen products low marks on satisfaction. The extreme category here would be the type of state monopoly for which the public at large is the customer and in which there is little variation in the supply despite a heterogeneous demand.

The results seem to fit that reasoning. Overall, CSB scores are significantly higher in industries where heterogeneity/homogeneity in demand is matched by

Table 2 *CSB Results 1989–1991*

	1989	1990	1991
Nondurable Goods			
Basic foods[a]	77	79	78
Candy, coffee	75	79	80
Dairy, bread	68	69	69
Beer	66	67	68
Meat products	63	65	65
Canned/frozen foods	64	70	70
Group mean	**69**	**72**	**72**
Durable Goods			
Autos	77	76	78
PCs	70	66	67
Mainframes	68	64	64
Group mean	**72**	**69**	**70**
Retailers			
Supermarkets	66	68	65
Oil (gas stations)	67	68	70
Furniture	64	63	65
Department stores	62	63	61
Clothing	63	62	63
Group mean	**64**	**65**	**65**
Monopolies			
Pharmacy	na	76	73
Postal, business	59	62	65
Postal, public	65	61	67
Alcoholic beverages	59	59	65
Telecom–public	55	59	61
Telecom–business	54	57	57
Police	56	55	58
Group mean	**58**	**61**	**64**

Table 2 *CSB Results 1989–1991 - Continued*

	1989	1990	1991
Services			
Banks, public	69	69	67
Banks, business	70	66	64
Charter travel	68	67	68
Life insurance	65	65	63
Property insurance	65	63	66
Insurance, business	64	62	64
Mail order	na	64	63
Transportation[b]	59	63	63
TV broadcasting	44	43	48
Shipping[c]	na	65	69
Newspapers	na	60	64
Group mean	**63**	**62**	**64**

[a]*Milk, yeast, sugar.*
[b]*Airlines and long distance railroads.*
[c]*Excluding the parcel service of the post office.*

the supply. The mean score for basic foods, candy/coffee, dairy products, beer, and automobiles is 74 for all three years. The grand mean for all industries is 64 in 1989 and 1990 and 65 in 1991.

Staple foods and automobiles score at the top of CSB; the railroad, the police force, and television broadcasting are at the bottom. Though the staples (yeast, milk, sugar) have no direct competition, they also face a homogeneous demand. Hence, there is no need for differentiation. That situation is in contrast to the market structure for automobiles – automobile makes are differentiated, as is their demand.

For television broadcasting, viewer tastes vary considerably and most people in Sweden did not (until very recently) have access to more than two state-owned channels. As a result, the program alternatives are very limited (at any given time). Achieving higher levels of customer satisfaction would probably necessitate offering more narrow and specialized programming to distinct segments of the viewer population. With the advent of cable television and more channels in Sweden, that now seems possible and should lead to higher CSB scores for the broadcasting industry and to a narrowing gap in scores across the broadcasting companies.

Overall, it is noteworthy that services score lower than products, both among monopolies and among competing firms. One monopoly that does not seem to fit the general pattern is the Pharmacy Organization – a state-owned enterprise that distributes pharmaceuticals and information to the general public. It has a very high CSB value. Apparently, the organization either adapts well to different customer needs or faces a relatively homogeneous type of demand.

Among the service providers, consumer banking and charter travel companies were a notch above the rest in 1989–1990. That finding should give concern to the insurance industry, as the Swedish government is about to eliminate the barriers between the banking and insurance businesses. However, business banking had a significant decline in CSB for 1991, whereas the insurance industry edged upward.

The changes from 1989 to 1990 were mainly negative, with more industries showing a decline than an improvement in CSB. That pattern has been reversed for 1991, suggesting that the prospects for more repeat business (with a resulting improved economic performance) for Swedish companies are somewhat better now than they were a year ago. Yet, the grand mean (65) does not seem overwhelmingly high. Obviously, giving a precise interpretation to that statistic is difficult in the absence of a longer data series or comparable data from other nations, but one should keep in mind that the respondents are all *customers* (not the general public or consumers in general) of the firm they evaluate. In other words, it is the preferred choices (given prices, incomes, etc.) of the respondents that are rated. The unweighted grand mean CSB is probably a fairly crude indicator[5] of how well a nation's industry is satisfying its customers and, in the case of Sweden, that mean is pulled down by a few state monopolies and by the television broadcasting industry. For 1990, it is (slightly) 'biased' upward because of the addition of some high scoring companies and industries. The most significant overall pattern is the improvement of most of the monopolies and the decline of the banks.

Against the backdrop of recent developments in the European Community and Sweden's pending EC membership, firms with low levels of customer satisfaction will either have to improve or design new types of switching barriers (because the increased level of competition will probably eliminate many of the present ones). Certainly, markets with low levels of customer satisfaction will become tempting targets for foreign firms.

Reliability and validity

As mentioned previously, no measurement is without error. To what extent do the results reported have satisfactory levels of reliability and validity? Table 3 gives the measurement results for the latent variables.

The average variance extracted should (at least) be higher than 50% (Fornell and Larcker, 1981) to avoid a situation of more error in measurement than valid variance. All models meet that criterion – the loadings of the indicators are high and error variance is small. In other words, the correlation between the indicators and the construct they are supposed to measure is high.

Reliability over time appears solid. For the satisfaction construct (i.e., CSB), the slight decline for 1990 in average variance extracted is due to the addition of the ideal-point measurement scale.[6] The slight reduction in convergent validity is compensated for by the higher level of nomological validity (i.e., the 1990 model fits the data somewhat better).

A clearer picture of nomological validity is obtained by examining the coefficients in the structural equations, reported in Table 4 (overleaf).

Table 3 *Measurement results*

	Average variance extracted								
	Performance			Satisfaction (CSB)			Loyalty		
Industry	1989	1990	1991	1989	1990	1991	1989	1990	1991
Airlines	.63	.73	.54	.74	.63	.61	.67	.7	.67
Automobiles	.65	.6	.58	.79	.6	.59	.64	.65	.63
Banks, public	.66	.64	.67	.77	.67	.7	.6	.57	.57
Banks, business	.68	.63	.61	.82	.73	.71	.57	.54	.54
Charter travel	.74	.63	.68	.82	.7	.72	.7	.69	.68
Clothing, retail	.61	.63	.59	.75	.59	.63	.62	.62	.61
Computer mainframes	.68	.65	.64	.78	.65	.62	.63	.59	.67
Department stores	.66	.58	.61	.74	.6	.67	.62	.69	.67
Food processing	.65	.66	.65	.78	.68	.67	.61	.65	.64
Furniture	.63	.54	.64	.79	.61	.67	.66	.72	.7
Insurance, business	.63	.6	.63	.82	.72	.74	.65	.55	.63
Insurance, property	.62	.68	.66	.8	.72	.74	.64	.69	.67
Life insurance, public	.62	.6	.63	.8	.63	.7	.64	.64	.58
Mail order	na	.65	.61	na	.7	.66	na	.67	.67
Newspapers	na	.59	.6	na	.69	.68	na	.66	.64
Oil companies	.61	.54	.53	.74	.63	.62	.66	.58	.59
Personal computers	.7	.62	.58	.74	.62	.63	.76	.71	.7
Pharmacy	na	.59	.6	na	.65	.66	na	.7	.82
Police	.76	.67	.71	.72	61	.66	.69	.71	.59
Postal service, business	.67	.64	.6	.82	.59	.75	.68	.66	.72
Postal service, public	.61	.62	.67	.71	.65	.73	.78	.59	.65
Railroad	.61	.64	.61	.74	.66	.66	.71	.73	.76
Shipping	na	.62	.61	na	.71	.7	na	.61	.61
Supermarkets	.69	.69	.67	.76	.61	.67	.66	.61	.64
Telecommunications, business	.71	.68	.72	.82	.7	.73	.74	.73	.77
Telecommunications, public	.77	.63	.78	.76	.63	.73	.76	.64	.72
Television broadcasting	.67	.68	.63	.84	.74	.73	na	na	na

Table 4 *Parameter estimates*[a]

	P→S			E→S			S→L			V→L			SAT .R^2		
Industry	1989	1990	1991	1989	1990	1991	1989	1990	1991	1989	1990	1991	1989	1990	1991
Airlines	.67	.63	.51	.11	.18	.22	.23	.38	.28	.01	.1	.01	.49	.48	.39
Automobiles	.48	.51	.51	.23	.18	.19	.51	.47	.49	-.05	-.04	-.04	.36	.34	.36
Banks, business	.7	.76	.7	.1	.04	.1	.39	.41	.36	-.13	.09	-.06	.54	.59	.54
Banks, public	.68	.68	.69	.05	.08	.06	.53	.52	.59	-.05	-.04	-.01	.49	.5	.51
Charter travel	.75	.73	.76	.03	.09	.06	.54	.53	.52	.03	.03	-.002	.67	.58	.61
Clothing, retail	.59	.47	.58	.19	.28	.45	.45	.38	.42	-.02	.08	.06	.48	.42	.46
Computer mainframes	.51	.65	.57	.11	.07	.11	.37	.43	.37	.01	.14	.03	.31	.45	.37
Department stores	.5	.49	.59	.34	.22	.24	.17	.35	.36	.02	.02	.13	.48	.38	.53
Food processing	.72	.71	.68	na	na	na	.59	.57	.58	.03	.01	.02	.52	.5	.46
Furniture	.49	.56	.64	.26	.16	.18	.32	.5	.56	.01	.04	.04	.4	.42	.54
Gas companies	.43	.52	.49	.37	.24	.3	.38	.38	.29	.05	.06	.03	.45	.44	.43
Insurance, business	.72	.75	.72	.08	.08	.12	.37	.32	.4	-.1	-.19	-.08	.57	.61	.68
Insurance, property	.7	.79	.78	0	.03	.05	.42	.64	.45	.01	-.06	-.03	.49	.63	.62
Life insurance, public	.7	.68	.75	0	.13	.08	.42	.38	.35	.01	-.06	-.04	.49	.55	.61
Mail order	na	.66	.71	na	.09	.04	na	.53	.48	na	-.04	.06	na	.48	.52
Newspapers	na	.5	.55	na	.31	.26	na	.41	.28	na	-.01	.02	na	.52	.62
Personal computers	.64	.61	.55	.05	.12	.22	.48	.46	.46	.09	.12	.15	.42	.42	.43
Pharmacy	na	.62	.54	na	.22	.23	na	.3	.2	na	-.08	-.05	na	.57	.48
Police	.52	.67	.77	.3	.04	.03	.13	.15	.27	-.13	-.22	-.03	.45	.47	.61
Postal service, business	.64	.75	.69	.06	.07	.12	.32	.31	.4	-.1	-.13	.04	.43	.59	.55
Postal service, public	.59	.61	.72	.13	.19	.11	.2	.17	.19	-.17	-.05	-.29	.4	.53	.59
Railroad	.61	.7	.6	.02	.13	.19	.5	.42	.39	.02	.14	.16	.38	.56	.5
Shipping	na	.73	.69	na	.08	.13	na	.47	.37	na	-.03	-.01	na	.57	.55
Supermarkets	.57	.64	.57	.3	.19	.27	.38	.44	.52	.08	.07	.15	.53	.55	.52
Telecommunications, business	.74	.74	.72	.07	.09	.08	.32	.29	.37	-.17	-.01	-.03	.58	.61	.56
Telecommunications, public	.59	.64	.67	.14	.17	.2	.38	.27	.38	-.1	-.12	-.07	.41	.53	.59
Television broadcasting	.6	.74	.63	.31	.14	.21	.63	.66	.48	na	na	-.02	.65	.68	.55

[a] P = performance, S = satisfaction (i.e., CSB), E = expectations, L = loyalty, V = voice (i.e., complaints).

In view of the fact that CSB is expressed as a function of no more than two variables, the R^2s are high. The mean R^2 increases from .44 in 1989 to .52 in 1990 and 1991. Overall, the results are consistent in terms of the relative impact of performance and expectations. In no industry did expectations have a greater effect than performance on satisfaction. Thus, the arguments advanced by Tse and Wilton (1988) and Johnson and Fornell (1991) are supported.

Further evidence in favor of the validity of the index is found in the signs and magnitude of the estimated coefficients. All coefficients relating performance to satisfaction, expectation to satisfaction, and satisfaction to loyalty have the expected positive sign. All but a few are significant. Discriminant validity is also evidenced by the fact that the correlations between CSB and its indicators are higher than correlations between CSB and any other variable in the system.

A limitation of the model is the assumption that the same basic specification governs the process of customer satisfaction across very different industries. To some extent, that restriction is offset by allowing CSB to be reflected by several indicators to different degrees. Nevertheless, if the overriding objective had been to account for the variation in customer satisfaction for each firm (or industry), a less general model would have been preferable. That is most evident in categories where there are clear product-specific attributes. Automobiles, personal computers, and mainframe computers are examples. As shown in Table 4, those are also the industries in which the model accounts for less variance in CSB.

A note on customer complaints

The results in Table 3 also provide insights into how industries are able to handle customer complaints. An objective of complaint handling is to turn a dissatisfied customer into a loyal customer. That can be done in many ways (see Fornell and Wernerfelt, 1988), and some evidence indicates that it can be done (TARP, 1979, 1986). However, the parameter estimates relating voice (complaints) to loyalty are small and in many cases negative.

A negative coefficient implies that an increasing number of complaints makes customers more prone to desert the firm. Significant negative coefficients were obtained for automobiles, banks, the postal service, the police, and the pharmacies. That finding is consistent with 'the vicious circle of complaints' originally observed by Fornell and Westbrook (1984), whereby the more complaints a firm receives, the less responsive it becomes. Instead of making use of customer complaints, the firm behaves dysfunctionally.

Significant positive coefficients are found for personal computers, clothing, computer mainframes (1990), newspapers, department stores (1991), the railroad, and supermarkets. Hence, firms in those industries appear to be more successful in turning complainants into loyal customers.

The effect on loyalty

Just as price elasticity varies among firms and industries, so does 'customer satisfaction elasticity'. Clearly, it is very important to determine how sensitive the

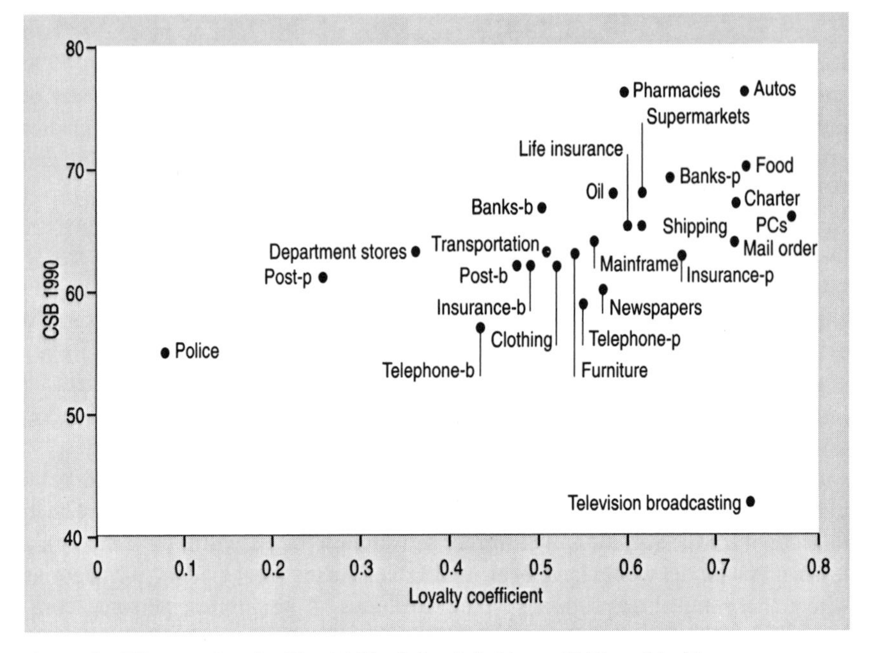

Figure 3 *Effect on loyalty [See Table 3 for definition of '-b' and '-p']*

present customer base is to satisfaction. In view of the current business emphasis on quality, one may well get the impression that quality and customer satisfaction are equally important for all firms. That is not the case. Customer satisfaction is more important (for loyalty) in some industries than in others.

Figure 3 depicts the effect of CSB on customer loyalty. The vertical axis measures CSB for 1990; the horizontal axis measures the unstandardized coefficient[7] that relates CSB to loyalty. With one exception (television broadcasting), the industries seem to be 'rationally structured' in the sense that those highly affected by customer satisfaction also have high CSB scores. Personal computers, food products, automobiles, charter travel, and mail order are all very sensitive to satisfaction. Not surprisingly, the police force is much less dependent on how it treats its 'customers' (citizens reporting a crime) to 'secure repeat business'. Most of the other monopolies are also less sensitive to customer satisfaction than industries in competitive market structures.

In view of the possibility of competition for the telephone company in the near future, respondents were asked about the hypothetical case of having alternatives available today. As a result, the coefficients for that industry are exaggerated if interpreted for the monopoly case. The same holds for the pharmacies, which also may face competition in the future.

Interestingly, the industries with low elasticities are those in which one would suspect switching costs to be high (police, postal services, telephone services, and business insurance). In contrast, switching barriers for automobiles, food, charter travel, and personal computers are probably less powerful. Companies in those industries are highly dependent on customer satisfaction for repeat business.

Summary

To sustain and improve the welfare of their citizens, all nations depend on international trade. For small countries, without an abundance of natural resources it is even more critical to do well in foreign markets and to defend domestic markets. Obviously, developed countries must increasingly rely on knowledge-intensive industry and cannot compete well on price or labor costs (Lindbeck, 1988). Nevertheless, most analysts agree that high levels of productivity are essential.

However, many industrial nations do not expect great improvements in productivity. Instead, they must concentrate more on quality production. When quality is recognized by the buyer, it is reflected in customer satisfaction. That is why a national index of customer satisfaction is not only a complement to productivity indices at the macro level, but also a complement to traditional measures of business performance at the micro level. Products and services that provide high customer satisfaction are less vulnerable to competition. They have a higher proportion of repeat business and higher gross margins.

After Japan, Sweden had the fastest GDP growth per capita in the world during 1870–1960. Since 1970, the country has slipped in relation to other nations. In an effort to promote quality and increase customer orientation within its industries, Sweden has developed a new economic indicator, the Customer Satisfaction Barometer. This article reports on the first three years of its application.

CSB estimates levels of customer satisfaction for about 100 firms in more than 30 industries from annual survey data that are used as input into a multiple-equation system. High levels of validity and reliability are demonstrated. In a micro context, the impact of (1) customer switching barriers and (2) the relationship between customer satisfaction and company market share leads to a proposition about the levels of CSB in different industries. Specifically, the contention is that heterogeneity/homogeneity of demand and supply is largely responsible for major differences in CSB across industries. The results indicate that industries selling homogeneous products to a homogeneous market or differentiated products (services) to a heterogeneous market typically had higher CSB than other industries.

With the caveat that absolute numbers are somewhat difficult to interpret in the absence of a longer data series and comparisons with other countries, the results suggest that customers in Sweden are not overly satisfied with many of their products and services. However, the recent trend appears to be slightly upward – especially for some of the state monopolies (which seem to gear up to meet possible deregulation).

To be competitive in world markets, a company must invest in productivity as well as in the quality of what is produced. Before quality can be improved, it must be measured. Measurement is a prerequisite for incorporating quality into the National Accounting Systems and thereby explicitly recognizing that the quality of what is delivered by the economy is an important source of improvement in the standard of living. At the micro level, there is a place for customer satisfaction measures in accounting as well. Satisfied customers are an asset to the firm. Changes in satisfaction are consequences of past decisions *and* predictors of future performance. The ultimate judgment of quality is with the customer. Quality improvements that are not recognized by the customer are questionable investments. Accordingly, the most meaningful measurement of quality is how it affects customer satisfaction. By taking the first step to systematically measure it, Swedish industry has, at the very least, a benchmark from which to improve.

Appendix A The CSB Equations

The systematic part of the predictor relationships is the conditional expectation of predictands for given values of predictors. The general equation is thus specified as stochastic:

$$E(\eta\eta,\xi) = \beta*\eta + \Gamma\xi$$

where $\eta = (\eta_1,\eta_2 \ldots \eta_m)$ and $\xi = (\xi_1,\xi_2 \ldots \xi_n)$ are vectors of unobserved endogenous and exogenous variables, respectively, $\beta*(m \times m)$ is a matrix of coefficient parameters for η, and Γ $(m \times n)$ is a matrix of coefficient parameters for ξ. This implies that $E(\eta\zeta') = E(\xi\zeta') = E(\zeta) = 0$, where $\zeta = \eta - E_{(\eta)}$.

The corresponding equation that relates the latent variables in CSB is:

$$\begin{bmatrix} \eta_1 \\ \eta_2 \\ \eta_3 \\ \eta_4 \end{bmatrix} = \begin{bmatrix} 0 & 0 & 0 & 0 \\ \beta_{2,1} & 0 & 0 & 0 \\ 0 & \beta_{3,2} & 0 & 0 \\ 0 & \beta_{4,2} & \beta_{4,3} & 0 \end{bmatrix} \begin{bmatrix} \eta_1 \\ \eta_2 \\ \eta_3 \\ \eta_4 \end{bmatrix} + \begin{bmatrix} \Upsilon_{1,1} \\ \Upsilon_{2,1} \\ 0 \\ 0 \end{bmatrix} [\xi] + \begin{bmatrix} \zeta_1 \\ \zeta_2 \\ \zeta_3 \\ \zeta_4 \end{bmatrix}$$

where:

η_1 = performance
η_2 = customer satisfaction (i.e., CSB)
η_3 = voice, and
η_4 = loyalty.

The general equations for relating the latent variables to empirical variables are:

$$y = \Lambda_y\eta + \varepsilon$$
$$x = \Lambda_x\xi + \delta$$

where $y = (y_1,y_2, \ldots y_p)$ and $x = (x_1,x_2, \ldots x_q)$ are the measured endogenous and exogenous variables, respectively. $\Lambda_y(p \times m)$ and $\Lambda_x(q \times n)$ are the corresponding regression matrices; ε and δ are residual vectors. By implication from PLS estimation: (Fornell and Bookstein, 1982), we have $E(\varepsilon) = E(\delta) = E(y\varepsilon') = E(x\delta') = 0$. The corresponding equation in CSB is:

$$\begin{bmatrix} y_1 \\ y_2 \\ y_3 \\ y_4 \\ y_5 \\ y_6 \\ y_7 \\ y_8 \\ y_9 \end{bmatrix} = \begin{bmatrix} \lambda_{1,1} & 0 & 0 & 0 \\ \lambda_{2,1} & 0 & 0 & 0 \\ 0 & \lambda_{3,2} & 0 & 0 \\ 0 & \lambda_{4,2} & 0 & 0 \\ 0 & \lambda_{5,2} & 0 & 0 \\ 0 & 0 & \lambda_{6,3} & 0 \\ 0 & 0 & \lambda_{7,3} & 0 \\ 0 & 0 & 0 & \lambda_{8,4} \\ 0 & 0 & 0 & \lambda_{9,4} \end{bmatrix} \begin{bmatrix} \eta_1 \\ \eta_2 \\ \eta_3 \\ \eta_4 \end{bmatrix} + \begin{bmatrix} \varepsilon \\ \varepsilon_2 \\ \varepsilon_3 \\ \varepsilon_4 \\ \varepsilon_5 \\ \varepsilon_6 \\ \varepsilon_7 \\ \varepsilon_8 \\ \varepsilon_9 \end{bmatrix}$$

where:

y_1 = quality (given price),
y_2 = price (given quality),
y_3 = overall satisfaction,
y_4 = confirmation of expectations,
y_5 = distance from ideal product (service),
y_6 = complaints to personnel,
y_7 = complaints to management,
y_8 = price increase tolerance, and
y_9 = repurchase intention,

and

$$x = \xi$$

where:

x = expectations.

Appendix B CSB Results 1989 to 1991

	CSB			Leading firms		
Industry	1989	1990	1991	1989	1990	1991
Automobiles	77	76	78	Toyota (87)	Mazda (81)	Mazda (85)
Basic foods	77	79	78	Jästbolaget (82)	Jästbolaget (83)	Jästbolaget (84)
Pharmacy	na	76	73	na		
Food processors	67	70	70	Marabou (78)	Marabou (79)	Marabou (80)
Oil (gas stations)	67	68	70	Statoil (70)	Statoil (70)	BP (71)
Shipping	na	64	69	na	JetPak (70)	JetPak (73)
Airlines	67	67	68	SAS (67)	SAS (69)	SAS (69)
Charter travel	68	67	68	Spies (69)	Ving (70)	Atlas (69)
Banking, public	69	69	67	SHB (75)	SHB (73)	SHB (72)
Postal service, public	65	61	67	Letter (69)	Letter (62)	Letter (68)
Personal computers, business	70	66	67	Apple (76)	Apple (69)	Apple (73)
Insurance, property	65	63	66	Trygg-Hansa (66)	Trygg-Hansa (64)	Länsfskr. (69)
Postal service, business	59	62	65	Letter (62)	Letter (63)	Letter (67)
Supermarkets	66	68	65	ICA (70)	Vivo (70)	ICA (70)
Furniture, retail	64	63	65	MIO (68)	MIO (66)	MIO (71)
Vin & SpritCentralen	59	59	65			
Banking, business	70	66	64	SHB (75)	SHB (72)	SHB (68)
Newspapers	na	60	64	na	SvD (67)	SvD (72)
Insurance, business	64	62	64	Skandia (66)	Trygg-Hansa (63)	Trygg-Hansa (67)
Mainframe computers	68	64	64	IBM (70)	HP (70)	HP (70)
Mail order	na	64	63	na	Halens (68)	HM&R (65)
Insurance, life	65	65	63	Trygg-Hansa (67)	Länsfskr. (69)	Länsfskr. (67)
Clothing, retail	63	62	62	Lindex (66)	Lindex (64)	Lindex (65)
Telecommunications, public	55	59	61			
Department stores	62	63	61	NK (68)	NK (68)	NK (64)
Police	56	55	58			
Telecommunications, business	54	57	57			
Railroad	45	55	54			
TV broadcasting	44	43	47	TV3 (57)	TV3 (52)	TV3 (53)
Mean, all industries	64	64	65			

References

Anderson, E.W. and Sullivan, M.W. (1990) *Customer Satisfaction and Retention across Firms*, Working Paper. University of Michigan, School of Business Administration.

Andrews, F.M. (1984) 'Construct validity and error components of survey measures,' *Public Opinion Quarterly*, Vol. 48, 409–42.

Andrews, F.M. and Robinson, J.P. (1988) *Measures of Subjective Well-Being*. Institute for Social Research, University of Michigan, Ann Arbor.

Blalock, H.M., Jr (1982) *Conceptualization and Measurement in the Social Sciences*. Sage Publications, Inc., Beverly Hills, CA.

Boston Consulting Group (1972) *Perspectives on Experience*. Boston Consulting Group, Boston.

Business International (1990) *Maximizing Customer Satisfaction: meeting the demands of the new global marketplace*, Research Report. Business International Corporation, New York.

Business Week (1990) 'King Customer', March 12, pp. 88–94.

Buzzell, R.D. and Gale, B.T. (1987) *The PIMS Principles*. The Free Press, New York.

Buzzell, R.D., Gale, B.T. and Sultan, R.G.M. (1975) 'Market share – key to profitability', *Harvard Business Review*, Vol. 53 (January–February), pp. 97–106.

Churchill, G.A., Jr and Surprenant, C. (1982) 'An investigation into the determinants of customer dissatisfaction', *Journal of Marketing Research*, Vol. 19 (November), pp. 491–504.

Daughety, A.F. (1990) 'Beneficial concentration,' *American Economic Review*, Vol. 80 (December), pp. 1231–7.

Fitzgerald, K. (1990) 'Sears' plan on the ropes,' *Advertising Age*, Vol. 61 (January 8), pp. 1–42.

Fornell, C. (ed.) (1982) *A Second Generation of Multi-variate Analysis*. Praeger Publishers, New York.

Fornell, C. (1989) 'The blending of theoretical and empirical knowledge in structural equations with unobservables,' in Wold, H. (ed.) *Theoretical Empiricism*, pp. 153–74. Paragon House, New York.

Fornell, C. and Bookstein, F.L. (1982) 'Two structural equation models: LISREL and PLS applied to consumer exit-voice theory,' *Journal of Marketing Research*, Vol. 19 (November), pp. 440–52.

Fornell, C. and Larcker, D.F. (1981) 'Evaluating structural equation models with unobservable variables and measurement error,' *Journal of Marketing Research*, Vol. 18 (February), pp. 39–50.

Fornell, C. and Robinson, W.T. (1983) 'Industrial organization and consumer satisfaction/dissatisfaction,' *Journal of Consumer Research*, Vol. 9 (March), pp. 403–12.

Fornell, C. and Wernerfelt, B. (1987) 'Defensive marketing strategy by customer complaint management: a theoretical analysis,' *Journal of Marketing Research*, Vol. 24 (November), pp. 337–46.

Fornell, C. and Wernerfelt, B. (1988) 'A model for customer complaint management,' *Marketing Science*, Vol. 7 (Summer), pp. 271–86.

Fornell, C. and Westbrook, R.A. (1984) 'The vicious circle of consumer complaints,' *Journal of Marketing*, Vol. 48 (Summer), pp. 68–78.

Fornell, C. and Yi, Y. (1992) 'Assumptions of the two-step approach to latent variable modeling,' *Sociological Methods and Research*, forthcoming.

Haspeslagh, P. (1982) 'Portfolio planning: uses and limits,' *Harvard Business Review*, Vol. 60, No. 1, pp. 59–75.

Hausknecht, D.R. (1990) 'Measurement scales in consumer satisfaction/dissatisfaction,' *Journal of Consumer Satisfaction, Dissatisfaction and Complaining Behaviour*, Vol. 3, pp. 1–11.

Helland, I.S. (1988) 'On the structure of partial least squares regression,' *Communication Statistics*, Vol. 2, pp. 581–607.

Henderson, B.D. (1979) *Henderson on Corporate Strategy*. Abt Books, Cambridge, MA.

Hirschman, A.O. (1970) *Exit, Voice, and Loyalty – Responses to Decline in Firms, Organizations and States.* Harvard University Press, Cambridge, MA.

Höskuldsson, A. (1988) 'PLS regression methods,' *Journal of Chemometrics,* Vol. 2, No. 2, pp. 211–20.

Howard, J.A. and Sheth, J.N. (1969) *The Theory of Buyer Behavior.* John Wiley & Sons, Inc., New York.

Hughes, D.A. (1977) 'An investigation of the relation of selected factors to consumer satisfaction,' in Hunt, H.K. (ed.) *Conceptualization and Measurement of Consumer Satisfaction and Dissatisfaction.* Marketing Science Institute, Cambridge, MA.

Hunt, H.K. (1977) 'CS/D – Overview and future research directions,' in Hunt, H.K. (ed.) *Conceptualization and Measurement of Consumer Satisfaction and Dissatisfaction.* Marketing Science Institute, Cambridge, MA.

Johnson, M.D. and Fornell, C. (1991) 'A framework for comparing customer satisfaction across individuals and product categories,' *Journal of Economic Psychology,* forthcoming.

Kearney, T. (1990) 'Frequent flyer programs: a failure in competitive strategy, with lessons for management,' *Journal of Consumer Marketing,* Vol. 7 (Winter), pp. 31–40.

Ketterlinus, R.D., Bookstein, F.L., Sampson, P.D. and Lamb, M.E. (1989) 'Partial least squares in developmental psychopathology', *Development and Psychopathology,* Vol. 1, pp. 351–71.

Konrad (1989) *Den Osynliga Balansräkningen.* Affärsvärlden Förlag AB, Visby, Sweden.

Kotler, P. (1988) *Marketing Management – Analysts, Planning and Control,* 6th edn. Prentice Hall, Inc., Englewood Cliffs, NJ.

Lindbeck, A. (1988) 'Swedish industry: in a national and an international perspective,' *Skandinaviska Enskilda Banken Quarterly Review,* Vol. 3, pp. 60–9.

Lohmöller, J.-B. (1989) *Latent Variable Path Modeling with Partial Least Squares.* Physica-Verlag, Heidelberg, Germany.

Martens, H. and Naes, T. (1987) 'Multivariate calibration by data compression,' in Williams, P. and Norris, K. (eds) *Near-Infrared Technology for the Agricultural and Food Industries.* American Association of Cereal Chemistry, St Paul, MN.

Michalos, A.C. (1986) 'An application of multiple discrepancies theory (MDT) to seniors,' *Social Indicators Research,* Vol. 18 (November), pp. 349–73.

Moore, E.M. and Shuptrine, F.K. (1984) 'Disconfirmation effects on consumer decision making processes,' in Kinnear, T.C. (ed.) *Advances in Consumer Research,* Vol. 11, pp. 299–304. Association for Consumer Research, Ann Arbor, MI.

NERA (1991) 'Developing a national quality index: a preliminary study of feasibility,' National Economic Research Associates, Inc., New York.

Oliver, R.L. (1977) 'Effect of expectation and disconfirmation on post-purchase product evaluations: an alternative interpretation,' *Journal of Applied Psychology,* Vol. 62, No. 4, pp. 480–6.

Oliver, R.L. (1981) 'Measurement and evaluation of satisfaction process in retail settings,' *Journal of Retailing,* Vol. 57 (Fall), pp. 25–48.

Oliver, R.L. and Bearden, W.O. (1983) 'The role of involvement in satisfaction processes,' in Bagozzi, R.P. and Tybout, A.M. (eds) *Advances in Consumer Research,* Vol. 10, pp. 250–5. Association for Consumer Research, Ann Arbor, MI.

Oliver, R.L. and DeSarbo, W.S. (1988) 'Response determinants in satisfaction judgments,' *Journal of Consumer Research,* Vol. 14 (March), pp. 495–507.

Oliver, R.L. and Westbrook, R.A. (1982) 'The factor structure of satisfaction and related postpurchase behaviour,' in Day, R.L. and Hunt, H.K. (eds) *New Findings in Consumer Satisfaction and Complaining,* pp. 11–14. Indiana University, Bloomington.

Olson, J.C. and Jacoby, J. (1971) 'A construct validation study of brand loyalty,' *Proceedings of the American Psychology Association,* Vol. 6, pp. 657–8.

Pessemier, E.A. (1959) 'A new way to determine buying decisions,' *Journal of Marketing,* Vol. 24 (October), pp. 41–6.

Porter, M.J. (1980) *Competitive Strategy – Techniques for Analyzing Industries and Competitors.* The Free Press, New York.

Jagmohan, R., Srinivasan, S.V. and Lal, R. (1990) 'The effects of brand loyalty on competitive price promotional strategies,' *Management Science,* Vol. 36, No. 3, pp. 276–304.

Reichheld, F.F. and Sasser, W.E., Jr (1990) 'Zero defections: quality comes to services,' *Harvard Business Review,* Vol. 68 (September–October), pp. 105–11.

Rhee, B.-D., DePalma, A., Fornell, C. and Thisse, J.-F. (1991) *Restoring the Principle of Minimum Differentiation in Product Positioning,* Working Paper. Washington University, John Olin School of Business.

Sirgy, J.M. (1984) 'A social cognition model of consumer satisfaction/dissatisfaction,' *Psychology and Marketing,* Vol. 1, No. 2, pp. 27–43.

Steenkamp, J.-B.E.M. (1989) *Product Quality.* Van Gorcum, Assen/Maastricht, The Netherlands.

Stone, M. and Brooks, R.J. (1990) 'Continuum regression: cross-validated sequentially constructed prediction embracing ordinary least squares, partial least squares and principal component regression (with discussion)', *Journal of the Royal Statistical Society,* Series B, Vol. 52, No. 2, pp. 237–69.

Swan, J.E., Trawick, F. and Carroll, M.G. (1981) 'Effect of participation in marketing research on consumer attitudes toward research and satisfaction with service,' *Journal of Marketing Research,* Vol. 18 (August), pp. 356–63.

TARP (1979) *Consumer Complaint Handling in America: summary of findings and recommendations.* Technical Assistance Research Programs, US Office of Consumer Affairs, Washington, DC.

TARP (1986) *Consumer Complaint Handling in America: an update study.* Contract HHS-100-84-0065. Technical Assistance Research Programs, US Office of Consumer Affairs, Washington, DC.

Thorelli, H.B. (1955) *The Federal Antitrust Policy – Origins of an American Tradition.* The Johns Hopkins Press, Baltimore.

Tse, D.K. and Wilton, P.C. (1988) 'Models of consumer satisfaction formation: an extension, *Journal of Marketing Research,* Vol. 25 (May), pp. 204–12.

Ware, J.E., Davies-Avery, A.R. and Stewart, A.L. (1978) 'The measurement and meaning of patient satisfaction,' *Health and Medical Care Services Review,* Vol. 1 (January–February), pp. 1–115.

Westbrook, R.A. (1980) 'A rating scale for measuring product/service satisfaction,' *Journal of Marketing,* Vol. 44 (Fall), pp. 68–72.

Westbrook, R.A. (1981) 'Sources of consumer satisfaction with retail outlets', *Journal of Retailing,* Vol. 57 (Fall), pp. 68–75.

Westbrook, R.A. and Cote, J.A., Jr (1980) 'An exploratory study of non-product-related influences upon consumer satisfaction,' in Olson, J.C. (ed.) *Advances in Consumer Research,* Vol. 7, pp. 577–81. Association for Consumer Research, Ann Arbor, MI.

Westbrook, R.A. and Reilly, M.D. (1983) 'Value-percept disparity: an alternative to the disconfirmation of expectations theory of consumer satisfaction,' in Bagozzi, R.P. and Tybout, A.M. (eds) *Advances in Consumer Research,* Vol. 10, pp. 256–61. Association for Consumer Research, Ann Arbor, MI.

Wold, H. (1973) 'Nonlinear iterative partial least squares (NIPALS) modelling: some current developments,' in Krishnaiah, P.R. (ed.) *Multivariate Analysis,* pp. 383–407. Academic Press, Inc., New York.

Yi, Y. (1990) 'A critical review of consumer satisfaction', in Zeithaml, V.A. (ed.) *Review of Marketing,* pp. 68–123. American Marketing Association, Chicago.

Notes

[1] The US index is the result of a joint venture between the American Quality Foundation and the University of Michigan Business School. In Japan, preliminary work is under way. Again, the Swedish model is the prototype. The Norwegian project is co-ordinated by the Norwegian School of Management with Johan Roos and Fred Selnes as program directors. For a feasibility study that reviews various approaches to developing a national index, see NERA (1991). Business International (1990) also includes a description of the Swedish model.

[2] For most industries surveyed, sample frames were not used unless they could be obtained from a neutral and independent source (e.g., the car registry). In no case were company customer lists used as sample frames. Hence data were costly but presumably more objective. Respondents were drawn via random digit dialing and screened about customer status. The average response rate was 95%.

[3] PLS is a family of estimation techniques originally developed by Wold (1973) and documented by Fornell (1982), Lohmöller (1989), and Helland (1988). Skewness was reduced from an average of -2.5 for the measured variables to an average of -.46 for the CSB index. There are other reasons for using PLS. It has proven effective in coping with noisy data (Stone and Brooks, 1990), and robust under conditions of non-normality and collinearity (Höskuldsson, 1988). It has also been very successful as a predictive method (Ketterlinus *et al.*, 1990; Martens and Naes, 1987). Among the drawbacks is the somewhat incomplete knowledge about the properties of its parameters. The implication is that empirically based methods (jack-knifing and blindfolding) are used for significance testing.

[4] To make the results comparable across industries and time, the criterion for fitting the CSB function is the same for each company: the maximization of CSB impact on loyalty (subject to the constraint that CSB is a linear combination of the three indicators mentioned previously). The implication is that the composition (the pattern of loadings) of CSB may vary across firms and over time, but the following property of CSB is uniform: no other linear combination of the indicators will produce an index that has greater impact on customer loyalty.

[5] Research is now under way to determine an appropriate weighting scheme in order to develop a single index that better reflects the level of economic activity.

[6] An examination of the covariance structure of the errors in measurement indicates that we are still working with a one-dimensional construct.

[7] As in covariance structure analysis, the metric of the latent variable is indeterminate. PLS standardizes to a mean of zero and a variance of one. To make comparisons across industries and time, unstandardized coefficients were obtained by multiplying the structural coefficient (for the combined sample 1989 and 1990) by the ratio of the mean standard deviations for the relevant variables.

7
Best practices benchmarking

Roger Dence

Abstract

Best practices benchmarking has become recognized in recent years as a valuable performance measurement and evaluation technique, which can make important contributions in many different areas of business endeavour.

It has its roots in the drive to seek enhanced competitive advantage by learning from comparative performance viewpoints on an internal or external basis, at a strategic, operational or business management level.

These comparisons are based typically on cost, time and quality considerations, viewed from either an internal, a functional, a competitive (or industry), or a generic business perspective.

In this article, the rationale for best practices benchmarking is highlighted and placed in a business strategy context. Approaches to different types of best practices and benchmarking issues are outlined, and implementation issues considered.

These aspects are illustrated with relevant examples. A profile is given of how one company, Xerox, has gained significant business benefits from the use of best practices benchmarking.

The article reflects the author's main professional interest, and thus concentrates primarily on corporate manufacturing and service organizations. However, best practices benchmarking is relevant to all organizations, whether involved in the private or the public sector, and whether large, medium or small in scale. It is limited only by the imagination, creativity and resourcefulness of the management of the organization, and the will to succeed in improving performance.

1 Introduction

For many organizations, the most critical challenges of a strategic nature are found in the improvement of competitive business performance, and in the management of change in order to achieve and sustain such improvements.

Best practices benchmarking (also known as best demonstrated practice) is now recognized as a valuable technique which can make significant contributions in these and other key business areas.

In the 1990s benchmarking has become something of a management watchword, with increasing numbers of seminars devoted to the subject and an increase in the published literature.

First used in the USA in the late 1970s and early 1980s, best practices benchmarking has only recently become more widespread as a management technique in Europe.

Benchmarking has its roots in the drive to seek enhanced competitive advantage by learning from comparative cost, time and quality viewpoints. Much impetus has been given by cost reduction programmes and total quality management concepts, benchmarking being one of several key analytical tools in both areas in identifying performance improvement targets.

However, there is more to benchmarking than cost performance or quality management issues alone. It should be seen in a wider business context as a means of enhancing competitive behaviour and of searching for ways of doing business more effectively.

Thus, benchmarking can be seen essentially as a learning process. In a competitive context, the well-known management thinker Tom Peters has observed that organizational learning is the most fundamental source of competitive advantage.

Benchmarking is seen also as being about much more than performance improvement by many leading commentators. The strategy consultants McKinsey & Co. view benchmarking as '... a skill, an attitude, and a practice that ensures an organisation always has its sights set on excellence, not merely on improvement'.[1]

Insights into the underlying reasons for the relative performance of an organization can be provided through the comparison – or benchmarking – of its best practices and its key business parameters with those of other relevant organizations. It can also provide the means to develop a greater understanding of the underlying business drivers that make an organization successful.

Such comparisons can often be made most readily with closely related operations or business units within the same corporate organization. They are made more usefully with competitors or with peer group organizations in the same or closely related business sectors.

However, the most valuable comparisons are those made with leading 'out of sector' organizations which are recognized leaders in their field, having achieved 'best-in-class' status or 'best demonstrated practice' in directly comparable processes in their operations.

Examples quoted by PA Consultants, which highlight the performance gaps between companies and their benchmark partners on different business process parameters, include:

- a multi-million turnover company with a debtor days figure of 76 days when the best practice was 49, representing an annual failure cost of some £5 million
- labour productivity differences of 50% between different building materials manufacturers
- best practices for order to despatch five times faster and for despatch to delivery twice as fast as those of an engineering spares supplier
- a 200% productivity differential for the same processes in different plants in a commercial foods company.[2]

Many well known companies have used best practices benchmarking successfully for a number of years. It is now a well established technique in strategic business research, analysis and planning and in change management and continuous performance improvement programmes.

2 Background

Business viewpoints

In recent years, best practices benchmarking has attracted many converts and a professional following of its own, and made new contributions to the management vocabulary. However, other concepts also relate closely to the basic aims of benchmarking. These complementary approaches come from various functional backgrounds, including finance/accounting, strategic planning, quality, technical, production, and organizational development. They include:

- relative cost analysis
- reverse engineering
- continuous improvement programmes
- statistical process control (SPC)
- total quality management (TQM)
- culture change/change management
- competitor analysis.

Notwithstanding the particular starting point for best practices benchmarking, there are several fundamental issues to consider. These are:

- the approach to be taken
- the effectiveness of the process used
- how the information and insights gained will be used to improve overall business performance.

At one level, benchmarking can be seen as a simple, but effective, management tool, because it provides clear comparators as the basis for planning improvements and closing performance gaps. Or, as one benchmarking exponent has expressed it, it is '.... another name for how to run your business properly'.

However, many major manufacturing and service companies that are active as practitioners, and consultants involved in best practices benchmarking, have developed individual definitions. Some other definitions are considered in subsequent sections.

What is benchmarking?

The origins of benchmarking are generally credited to the Xerox Corporation in the United States. It stems from the recovery programme implemented by Xerox in the face of severe competition from Japanese photocopier companies, which threatened its core US business in the mid-1970s.

This situation, together with aspects of the Xerox response and benchmark approach and results, and subsequent further developments, are outlined in more detail in the case profile at the end of this article.

In the early days of benchmarking, the emphasis was primarily on measurement *per se*, and on relatively straightforward (but not necessarily simple) comparisons of suitable performance parameters within and between companies.

Such parameters were usually basic productivity and efficiency measures, whether in a manufacturing or a service environment.

This was followed by a gradual shift in attention on to business processes within a more diverse range of business functions which had a key influence on overall performance. Subsequently, competitive benchmarking became more prominent, with comparisons against companies within the same industry.

Today, the main focus of benchmarking activity is on best practices, information on which is obtained by active collaboration with best-in-class companies having comparable business processes, wherever and in whichever industry they may be situated.

In contrast, the benchmarking of performance, both within and across industries, can not only identify and quantify performance gaps, but also can provide a comparison of the fundamental operational and management processes that provide competitive advantage. Thus, benchmarking can establish how much a company needs to improve to be at the highest possible levels of functional performance, and helps to ensure continuing sustainable competitive advantage at all management levels.

A question of definition

As noted already, various definitions exist of what constitutes best practices benchmarking. These depend on the starting point for the benchmarking activities and on the interest of the parties involved.

For example, a group of leading US high technology corporations comprising Boeing, Digital, Motorola and Xerox sees a *benchmark* as 'the best-in-class achievement which becomes a recognised standard of excellence against which similar things are compared' (see, for example, Soderstrom, 1992[3]). *Benchmarking* as a *process* is then expressed separately as 'a systematic, continuous approach to identify the benchmark, compare yourself to the benchmark, and identify practices that enable you to become the new best-in-class.'

According to these companies, which are involved in both manufacturing and service activities, the key objective in benchmarking is ' ... to make changes that lead to quantum and continuous improvements in products, processes and services that result in total customer satisfaction and competitive advantage'.

In the services sector, a leading UK exponent of benchmarking is Royal Mail Quadrant, the in-house catering arm of the Post Office. It sees benchmarking as '... a structured process for learning from the practice of others, internally and externally, who are leaders in a field or with whom legitimate comparison can be made'.[4]

From a consultancy viewpoint, PA Consultants regards benchmarking (from the client's outlook) as ' ... the ongoing task at all levels of our business, of finding and implementing world best practice in the key things we do that deliver customer satisfaction'.[5]

Thus, from these different perspectives, the overall purpose and intent of best practices benchmarking can be summarized as the:

- development of an understanding of the fundamentals that create business success, based on an objective measurement of relative performance (both real and perceived) against relevant companies, in areas involving critical business processes
- focus on continuous improvement efforts, based on an ongoing analysis of the essential differences between similar processes in comparable businesses, and of the underlying reasons for these differences
- management of the overall change process and of the individual changes involved in achieving the improvements, based on the development and implementation of action programmes to close the gap between a company and the 'best-in-class' companies with the most relevant key performance variables.

3 Rationale

Why do benchmarking?

Today most organizations operate in a business climate in which uncertainty, risk and complexity in the external environment are fundamental facts of life. These factors can have economic, political, social and technological origins.

Increasing market globalization and the pressures of international competition mean that organizations intending to become or remain among the leaders in their respective fields should aim to be the 'best-in-class' in the key areas that sustain competitive advantage.

In addition, customers are becoming more informed and more demanding of their suppliers. Issues of quality of service and customer satisfaction are now much more critical than just a few years ago.

All of these diverse conditions relate closely to the longer-term strategic issues facing companies and their survival. This is highlighted by the fact that only some one in five companies of the Top 100 US corporations in the 1970s were in the same business in the same form at the start of the 1990s.

In the automotive industry, the major US manufacturers made strenuous efforts to catch up with the Japanese competitors, which had moved ahead dramatically in the early 1980s. Yet, despite heroic improvements in productivity, many remained behind. They had failed to recognize that the nature of the playing field had changed, and that the performance target at which they had been aiming had either moved further ahead or on to a different issue.

Whatever a company's mission and the vision and values it espouses, and whichever strategy options are followed, the role of benchmarking must be to direct the actions and organizational changes necessary for the achievement of competitive advantage.

In these terms, it is helpful to consider benchmarking in the context of a company's value chain[6] and the different processes which constitute primary and secondary activities. Each stage of the value chain should be examined to assess its importance and contribution as a key business driver.

So, the scene for best practices benchmarking can be set, at each stage, by posing four fundamental performance questions:

- Are we performing better than we ever have?
- Are we performing better than other plants or business units in the company?
- Are we performing better than our competitors?
- Are there any other industries that are performing well and from whom we can learn?

The value chain concentrates primarily on hard-edged issues, such as process, cost, quality, profitability, etc. However, benchmarking the key elements of the value chain can also help to address other softer management issues, such as employee communications and motivation, setting shared or common goals, and workforce commitment and performance.

Business performance is clearly important not only in absolute terms, but also relative to the 'competition'. This applies whether the 'competition' is external in the market-place or internal in a closely related company or operation. By identifying and analysing the best practices involved, an improved understanding of the underlying business drivers can be made know within, as well as between, companies.

The internal sharing and transferring of best practices is used by many leading companies to promote self-improvement and to encourage healthy internal competition or rivalry. Developing individual improvement programmes and actions is seen to result in a stronger sense of ownership and a commitment to achieving results.

And there is also the notion, prevalent in many corporate cultures, that 'what gets measured, gets done!' If something cannot be measured, then it cannot be managed effectively.

According to the leading distribution company TNT Express, strategic benchmarking leads to better business performance for four main reasons, namely by:

- gaining a fuller understanding of the processes and costs involved
- understanding the company's relative position in the market
- leading to a cost-effective operation
- having a highly motivated and well organized workforce committed to improved and improving standards.[7]

Other organizations see performance measurement through benchmarking in more broad terms, as being part of the overall process of change and concerned with changing behaviour to achieve the desired results.

What to benchmark

There are four types of benchmarking activity which are recognized generally within business today. They are internal, functional, competitive, and generic benchmarking.[8]

Internal benchmarking is done within an organization and typically between closely related divisions, similar plants or operations, or equivalent business units, using common or shared performance parameters as a basis for comparison.

Because of the relative ease of starting a new activity internally, the lower resource implications, and the higher assurance of gaining co-operation, this is the area in which many organizations choose to start benchmarking activities. This is valuable in gaining initial knowledge, experience and commitment, but is limited to internal criteria only.

Functional benchmarking is a comparison of performance and procedures between similar business functions, but in different organizations and industries.

It represents a more positive approach than internal benchmarking by being externally focused. However, in relating only to specific functions, it may not be of wider benefit in other areas of the organizations concerned.

Competitive benchmarking generally focuses on direct competitors within the same industry and with specific comparable business operations, or on indirect competitors in related industries (perhaps key customers or suppliers) having complementary business operations. There are often practical difficulties with sourcing information, and activities may be limited to arm's-length product comparisons, possibly using reverse engineering techniques.

Comparisons based on softer functions such as quality of service, and facilitated by consultants or academics operating a round table or a benchmarking club to preserve the confidentiality of individual company data, may also be relevant in this context. However, these approaches may not indicate best practice.

Generic benchmarking is undertaken with external companies in different industries which represent the 'best-in-class' for particular aspects of the selected business operations.

Benchmarking can be undertaken in almost any area of business and organizational endeavour. The basic requirement is that key performance variables can be identified, measured, analysed and compared to provide a basis for planned performance improvement.

In many companies, such performance variables are found initially in operational areas, such as production, logistics and distribution, installation and field services. However, all functions can provide candidates for benchmarking activities, where these are a key to business success in the context of the value chain concept. The key is to be clear about the needs and what it is important to improve.

Comparing benchmarking with other activities

As outlined at the start of this section, other business activities also have a close affinity with the aims and objectives of benchmarking. Having provided a background to benchmarking, covering its evolution and rationale, it is useful to make a brief comparison with other techniques.

Of all the various business analysis techniques available, competitor analysis is arguably the most relevant in strategic terms, market research in commercial terms, and reverse engineering in a technical or an operational sense.

Table 1 (opposite) shows a matrix comparing these three techniques with benchmarking, and covering issues of the technique's intent or purpose; the usual focus employed in the activity; the application of the technique; its perceived limitations; and the information sources which generally are most relevant.

Table 1 *Comparing benchmarking with other types of analysis*

	Benchmarking	Competitior analysis	Market research	Reverse engineering
Purpose	Analyse operational characteristics of best practices for the key drivers of the business	Analyse competitive strategies; influence business decisions	Identify/assess/analyse market response to products, services, etc.	Comparison with similar products; understand competitor products and processes
Common focus	The key business practices that drive customer needs and satisfaction	Competitive strategies and tactics within own industry	Customer needs, attitudes, expectations and demand	Product characteristics and functionality
Application	Business practices and own and best practice attributes, wherever they are found	Attitudes of own and competitor strategies, organization, markets, products and services	Products and services within own industry and markets	Mainly manufactured products
Limitations	Internal procedures in own firm and best practice partners; covering people, work practices, equipment, management, etc.	Focus on market performance, industry structure and high-level alternatives; tends to parity or incremental advantage in industry	Usually limited to market response, customer and channel needs	May highlight product differences, but not underlying business process rationale
Information sources	Customers/ competitors, industry leaders, analysts, consultants; any industry where relevant best-in-class practice is found	Analysts, researchers, consultants and competitors within the same industry	Customers and business partners in own industry	Competitors in own industry

(Source: Media articles and conference papers by Motorola, PA Consultants and McKinsey)

Some further consideration of these issues is given in the following section on the approach to benchmarking.

4 Approach

The general process

A variety of methodologies have been proposed in recent years for the most effective way to undertake best practices benchmarking, as either a practical user framework, a theoretical rationale or a proprietary approach from an academic or a consultancy viewpoint.

Whichever formal methodology is adopted, and whether a 6-, an 8- or a 10-step approach is used, arguably matters less than spending sufficient time planning the approach before starting out. Having the necessary system in place, together with an initial knowledge base and awareness of the issues to be addressed, are vital factors in helping to ensure eventual success.

For example, NCR has adopted a 6-step approach to its benchmarking activities. In contrast, Xerox has adopted a 10-step approach, which gives a broader structure to the different activities involved, and thus more visibility and flexibility to monitor and review ongoing progress (see section 6).

The Xerox approach, which is outlined in the case profile later in this article, is regarded widely by other practitioners as one of the leading models for benchmarking.

Whichever approach is taken to suit internal company needs, the process of benchmarking can be expressed generally as covering the following activities:

- determine the key performance areas
- set the key standards and variables to measure
- identify the most relevant competitors and 'best-in-class' companies
- measure regularly and objectively (quantitative)
- analyse the best-in-class performance (qualitative)
- specify programmes and actions to close the gap, and implement
- monitor ongoing performance.

The essence of effective best practices benchmarking is that it should involve a 'clean sheet of paper' approach, without current thinking or preconceived ideas influencing the outcomes and, most importantly, using the benefits of third-party assistance to stretch the horizons of the existing outlook and practices.

Benchmark parameters

The key initial task in benchmarking is to consider the areas of a business in which it would be most beneficial and practical to attempt to benchmark and the specific parameters to use.

The relevance of this is demonstrated once again by the example of the US and European auto industry, compared with its Japanese counterparts. Based on dramatic success in world automotive markets by Japanese companies, Western companies visited auto plants in Japan and focused on the technology used. Plants in the US and Western Europe were subsequently reconfigured and heavy investments made in production automation. However, the actual approach of their Japanese competitors was to use the smart automation of simplified processes, coupled with a very productive labour force.

The differences in labour productivity were assessed by Western companies as being due to cultural factors and were thus not transferable. The response was to build new car plants in areas with low labour costs, such as Central and South America. However, the next step of the Japanese companies was to build new world-class production plants in the Western countries themselves, providing a new edge to the intense competition which had developed in car markets across the world during the 1980s.[9]

Therefore, in seeking to establish priorities for benchmarking, a critical approach to the selection of key performance parameters should be taken. This assessment should be based on the value chain, covering (as appropriate) the major business functions and cross-functional considerations, such as logistics management and make/buy economies.

The selection criteria should take into account the strategic importance of the benchmark parameters; their potential impact on company performance once the improvements identified have been implemented; and the readiness of the organization to self-improve in these areas. They should cover: the significant cost, time and quality measures that affect the key customer deliverables; the existing and potential competitive pressure points; anticipated trends in new technology; the critical business process involved; and the identification of possible new areas of competitive advantage.

A structured approach for evaluating these key parameter issues has been developed by the strategy consultancy McKinsey & Co. This considers the input practices and measures involved in benchmarking, based on a '5Ps' approach covering the partners (i.e. suppliers and customers); people; procedures and systems; product and process design; and physical configuration (Figure 1).

This approach enables the key process to achieve performance to be characterized fully, and the candidate improvement programmes to be matched closely to the company's skill base. Consideration of the appropriate areas to benchmark also demands an assessment of the benefits and risks involved, and of the investments necessary in implementing change.

Another structured approach to the issue of where and what in an organisation should be benchmarked is advocated by the consulting group KPMG, with the framework provided by a concept termed the 'balanced scorecard', first developed by Nolan Norton & Co.

This is based on the view that benchmark parameters must focus on the customer, measure how business processes create value (i.e. quality, service and cost effectiveness), and provide benefits in terms of encouraging internal innovation and learning.

In the 'balanced scorecard' approach, the aim is to look at processes across the business overall, rather than at the organizational hierarchies which make up the business. Four separate domains – covering financial, customer, business process and organizational learning perspectives – focus on fundamental questions and provide pointers towards those areas in which it would be most effective to concentrate the search for viable benchmark parameters.

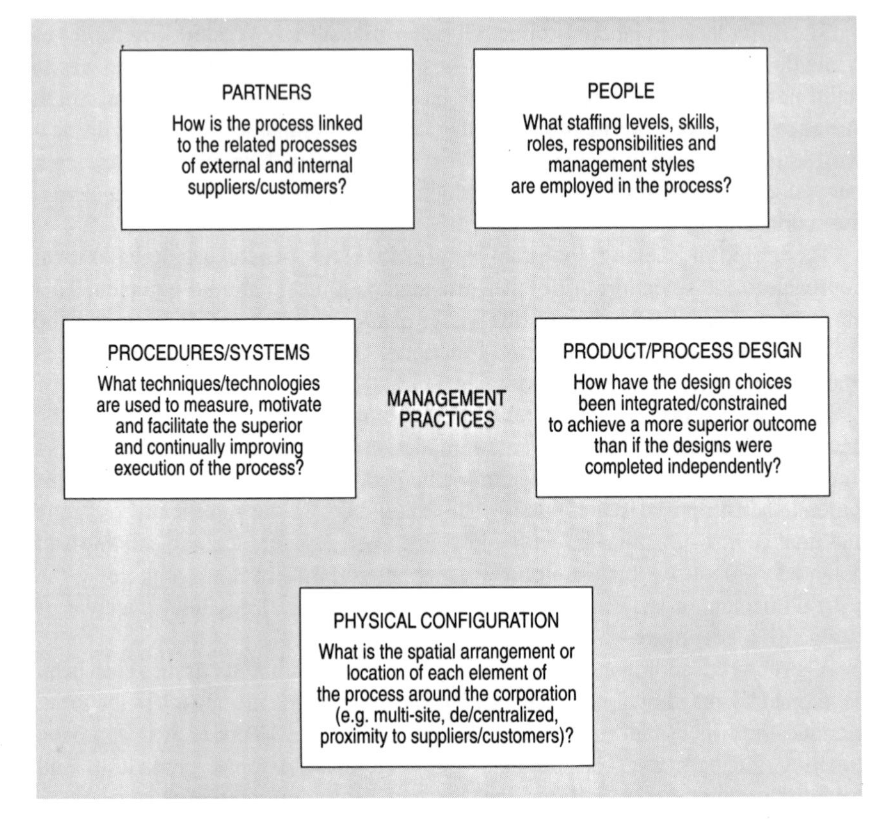

Figure 1 *Input practices and measures*

The 'ideal' benchmark

Such varied approaches to determining which parameters should become benchmark priorities are designed to overcome a basic problem: the 'ideal benchmark' as such may not exist in practice.

Just as the ideal example of the ideal plant, system or process does not exist, so the search for the ideal or perfect benchmark may prove elusive and ultimately fruitless. In reality, any best practices approach will be founded on a collection of best practices gleaned from a range of different sources, wherever the best-in-class or best-of-breed company for a particular business process can be found.

However, an 'optimum' benchmark can be characterized as follows:

- clearly, it should be measurable in terms of cost, time, value, head-count or some other quantitative parameter
- it should be meaningful, worthwhile and relevant
- simple productivity measures are often the best and often the most easily accessible
- it should be potentially available in external and competitive environments
- if an actual external measure cannot be obtained, a well founded estimate should be used as a substitute, providing that a strong and defensible rationale for the estimate can be developed.

The key to successful benchmarking is to develop a selection of performance variables where access to information can be reasonably assured. The general aim should be to 'keep it simple' by concentrating on a few well chosen measures in the first instance, and then getting into the details of why.

The aim of benchmarking is to search for significant differences in parameters, not necessarily for high accuracy *per se*. However, a sufficient degree of accuracy will usually be necessary for subsequent analysis, for gaining an understanding of the performance gap and for developing the improvement actions to be taken.

The numbers should be relatively accessible, but bear in mind that they are incidental to getting into the process and understanding the underlying issues. While the numbers are a means to an end, the soft business issues are more challenging and difficult but much more important.

Overall, the best practices benchmarking process can be seen as one of encouraging people to stand back from established practices, to 'look above the fence'. The aim is to take a critical look outside the company, and to learn from what others are doing in comparable business activities.

Internal considerations

Performance improvement, as with culture and organizational change, is often about addressing behavioural matters and developing relationships.

Internal issues are important, therefore, to the long-term success of benchmarking endeavours. It is necessary to identify the internal stakeholders and to involve them from the outset, taking steps to understand their culture and concerns. A team approach should be encouraged by seeking ideas, suggestions and co-operation through a process of internal consultation.

To create the right perception of the aims of best practices benchmarking is an essential first step in building and maintaining communications. Because of this, it may be politic, at least in the early stages, to avoid using existing formal reporting and control procedures, so that the potential threat of corporate or peer group pressure is removed.

The aim is to enable people to learn from each other, so that the process becomes one of habit and trust, and to create an environment in which self-assessment and self-improvement can be encouraged more readily.

Care should also be taken with target setting. The initial targets should not only be clear, achievable and realistic, but equally demanding and providing tangible benefits to the company, together with a sense of achievement for the participants.

Once the benchmarking habit has been seen to provide benefits, it can then be institutionalized on a gradual basis, either as part of a routine reporting system or as part of a broader continuing improvement process.

Benchmarking is inherently a team activity, even if individuals may act as sponsors or facilitators for the process. In some companies benchmarking is seen as being part of every individual manager's mandate, based on his or her specialist knowledge and expertise, and with no special resources being dedicated to benchmarking.

Sources of information

A wide range of potential sources of information is available for best practices benchmarking purposes. In practice, benchmarking activities are likely to draw on information from a variety of sources in the same way as, for example, a competitor analysis exercise or an ongoing competitor monitoring programme.

All information obtained in business requires careful evaluation before it can be classified as 'intelligence', which can then be acted on. Information acquired for benchmarking purposes is no different, given that a clear set of objectives should be in force before the proactive search for possible sources, potential partners and specific information subjects begins.

The list below indicates the types of information sources which may be relevant to best practices benchmarking activities:

- employees (sales and marketing personnel, technical representatives, former employees of competitors)
- media information (professional and trade press)
- analyst reports (public companies), financial data and credit rating reports
- published market research reports and consultant studies
- industry and trade associations
- professional networks within the firm or industry
- competitors (site visits, products, corporate and product literature, public affairs activities)
- customers and suppliers (including those of competitors)
- consultancy or academic bodies operating benchmarking databases, clubs or round tables
- industry information exchanges and clearing houses
- inter-company data-sharing arrangements (subject to any legal, anti-trust, anti-competitive or other regulatory constraints)
- benchmarking partners.

Although some useful information may well be obtained from searches of public domain sources, the most valuable information for the purposes of best practices benchmarking is probably that obtained from partners on an agreed sharing basis.

The insights to be gained from exploring issues via discussion with other interested and co-operative parties will result in a better understanding of the business processes and the underlying practices and procedures involved.

The benefits of a benchmarking partner as an information source are that the other company is also learning 'with you' at the same time as learning 'from you', and gaining recognition for the performance improvements and superior business practices that have already been achieved.

A diverse range of external relationships has been forged in seeking to benchmark with organizations in different industries which have the most relevant and comparable business processes. A selection of these companies, the business process of interest to them, and the choice of best practices benchmarking partner is included to demonstrate this point in Table 2.

Table 2 *Comparisons of external best practice*

Benchmarking originator	Business process to be benchmarked	Benchmarking target
Oil company	Retail shop operations	Fast food/drug stores
Electronics company	Time to market	Fashion house
Electronics company	Time to finalize accounts	Bank
Office systems vendor	Order processing	Mail order clothes
Office systems vendor	New production layout	Car manufacturer
Computer manufacturer	Distribution system	Leading retailer
Retail bank	Process flow efficiency	Car manufacturer
Telephone company	Billing system	Credit card company
Telephone company	Staff suggestion scheme	Airline

(Source: Media articles, private communications, Bain & Co.)

Legal and ethical issues

Consideration of best practices benchmarking opportunities may also raise some legal and ethical issues, which should be addressed at the outset.

The most fundamental of these is probably that concerning questions of confidentiality. This embraces the protection of information which is shared or exchanged between two or more parties, and more general discussions aimed at developing an understanding of one another's processes and procedures.

The issue is particularly relevant, given that the focus of benchmarking is on actions that can help to improve business efficiency and thus competitive performance.

Issues of confidentiality can arise at all levels where a third party is involved. Typically, this may be a potential benchmarking partner, and both parties need to have confidence that future collaboration between them can be undertaken with the potential benefits primarily in mind, rather than the possible risks.

If necessary, a confidentiality agreement can be put in place, but it is important for the relationship that a basis for sharing and using potentially sensitive information is agreed clearly in advance.

In other contexts, where benchmarking clubs or round tables are run on behalf of the participants by industry bodies, academic institutions or external consultants, the issue may be even more important. This is to protect not only the professional reputations of the organizers of such forums but also the fact that the members may be in closer competition with one another than in more generic benchmarking. The issue then becomes one of 'client' confidentiality being protected.

In some situations, clearance may have to be obtained from official or regulatory bodies, so that the mutual co-operation which is at the heart of benchmarking is not judged to be anti-competitive and against the public interest. Such approval may place limitations on the type of information which can be shared or on the means by which such sharing can be made.

5 Benchmarking in action

The power of benchmarking can best be demonstrated by citing examples of practical approaches in a variety of industrial, manufacturing, service or functional situations, either as a general illustration or in a specific company context.

The examples quoted already illustrate the range of processes which can be addressed, and the extent of some of the gaps in achievable performance which can be revealed by taking an external best practices benchmarking approach.

Further examples of performance gaps are given in the case profile on the Xerox experience (see section 6).

Industry level benchmarks

As an illustration of industry-level benchmarks obtained on a global basis, the auto industry once again provides suitable examples by reference to Japanese, US and European companies.

A comparison of productivity trends between three leading Japanese companies, namely Mazda, Nissan and Toyota, with a Western car manufacturer, showed that all three Japanese firms achieved consistently higher unit production levels per head and work-in-process turns per year over the period from the early/mid-1970s to the early 1980s.

It is evident from these figures that, even though the Western company was making significant improvements in its performance, its Japanese counterparts were making even better progress in enhancing their competitive positions in world markets.

An analysis of unit assembly costs between another Western car manufacturer in the early 1980s and four Japanese companies producing a comparable small family car showed that the Japanese companies enjoyed significantly lower unit costs. However, the best performing company had an equivalent unit assembly cost of less than half that of its Western counterpart.

The 1989 performance of volume car plants also shows useful comparisons between Japan, the USA and Europe. Comparing assembly hours, inventory days, defects per 100 hours and rework area as a percentage of the plant showed the Japanese companies to be clear leaders in all areas. The US plants were in second place, with the exception of the inventory management performance, where Europe came second to Japan (Figure 2).

In the mid-1980s, the Japanese car companies took the battle for market share into the USA, with Honda building a car assembly plant on a greenfield site. Although enjoying significant productivity advantages from the outset over its now local competitors, the philosophy of continuous performance improvement was maintained. A rolling five-year analysis of the time taken to change a die showed an overall 50% reduction, together with a manpower saving.

Other benchmark comparisons on new model developments, between Japanese companies having adopted a 'lean producer' approach and US car manufac- turers still using a mass production philosophy, also showed significant time differences.

Engineering time for new model development by the US mass producer company was 75% more than the Japanese lean producer at three million hours,

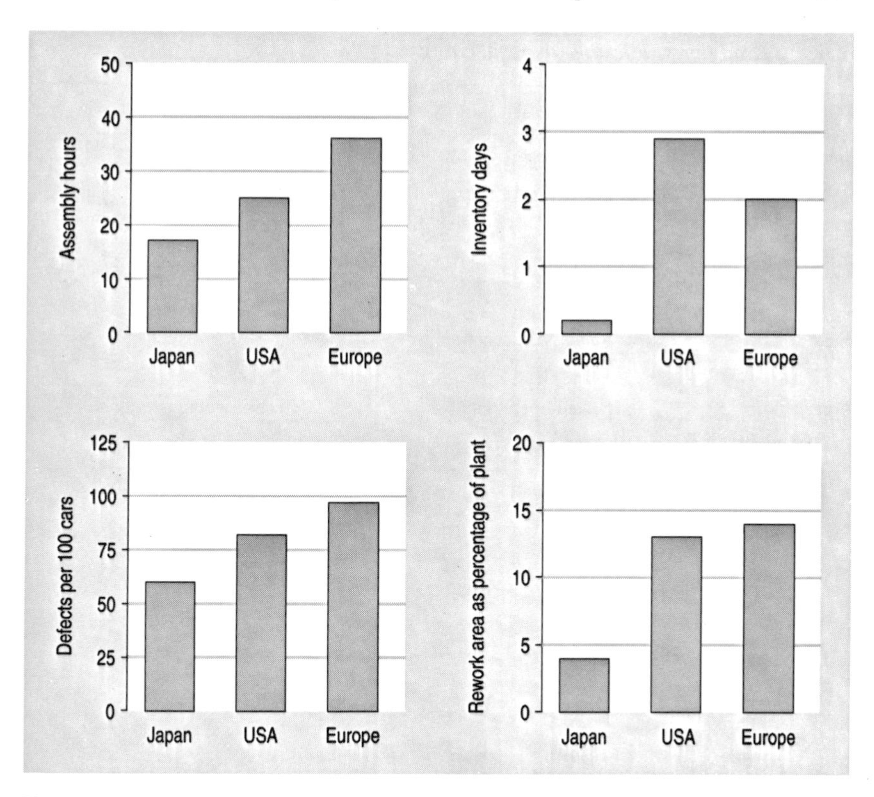

Figure 2 *Performance of volume car plants*

and the time to complete development was 60 months compared with only 46 months for the Japanese company. In 1990, the average age of model lines in Ford and General Motors was five years, while the figure for equivalent Toyota cars was two years.

Manufacturing benchmarks

In other manufacturing contexts, examples from various industries show the application of benchmark comparisons between one company and its benchmark partner (or partners).

In the textiles industry, a study of lead times showed significant benchmark differences in the time taken to complete orders, and in the use of technology in the ordering process and in production working practices (Table 3 overleaf).

A further textile industry example showed significant time-based gaps in the performance in the changeover from one product to another in two key processes compared between several plants.

Comparison of process costs between a number of plants shows the different best practices in the processes involved. A best practices model based on the best performances will identify the potential cost improvement gap to be bridged for each site.

A comparison of manufacturing costs between plants and a competitor based on the different stages involved also enables a best practices model to be

Table 3 *Lead times in textiles manufacturing*

Business process	Company X	Benchmarking target
Order to delivery	35 days	3 days
Ordering process	Manual, with weekly stocktake	Electronic point of sale with nightly dump
Cutting	Cookie cutter	Numerically controlled machine, vacuum assisted
Work practice 1	Single skill function groups	Multi-skill work cells, self-inspection, self-pack
Work practice 2	Seated operators	Mobile, standing operators
Work practice 3	Individual piece work rates	Flat rate plus profit share

(Source: PA Consultants/ATI Conference, 1992)

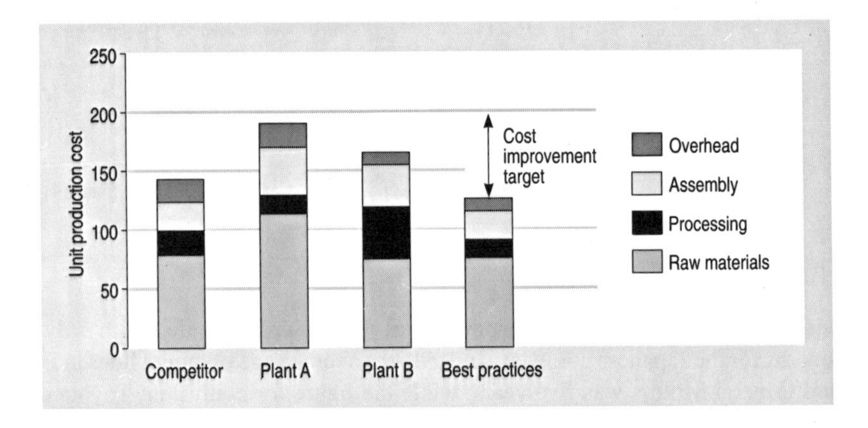

Figure 3 *Manufacturing costs*

developed with an external element included. The model thus provides a more challenging target for performance improvement (Figure 3).

Service industry benchmarks

In a services industry environment, there can be distinctive characteristics which may not be shared by product-based businesses. These can include:

- *intangibility* – a service is intangible, and although it may not be possible to 'sample' services beforehand, opinions and attitudes towards the service provider (i.e. customer satisfaction) can be important in purchase decisions
- *inseparability* – services often cannot be separated from the 'person' of the seller, being sold and then produced and consumed (unlike products which are produced and consumed) – this inseparability of creation and performance is especially relevant in personal and professional services

- *heterogeneity* – it can be difficult to achieve standardization of output, depending on who provides the service and when – different units of service produced by a standard system are provided to meet individual needs at different times
- *perishability* – services not sold cannot be stored or kept in inventory and, conversely, demand which cannot be met may represent lost business or result in dissatisfied customers.[10]

Key operational issues which have been identified in services are: productivity improvement; standardization versus customization; batch versus unit processing; facilities layout and design; job design; capacity management; and managing queues.[11]

Thus, critical business processes in a services environment are similar and capable of being benchmarked in the same way as in manufacturing environments.

For example, in a company from the retail sector, the value chain was used to identify the activities that were critical to achieving superior competitive performance. Primary activities were product sourcing, warehousing/distribution, operations, sales, and customer service, while the support activities were procurement (of equipment and sites), technology, human resources and infrastructure.

Targeting the operations area, a comparison was made of store operations costs, covering such areas as staffing, stockholding, direct labour, theft and loss (shrinkage), and miscellaneous overheads. Several branches were selected and compared with a collaborator company and a strategic peer organization.

Building on the previous analysis, the drivers contributing to the performance differences in the collaborator and peer companies were then examined to establish the significant forces at work. A further comparison, this time of staff productivity within the overall store costs, showed significant differences between the stores and the collaborator and peer companies.

Functional benchmarks

In the area of functional benchmarking, a diverse range of issues can be addressed, including, for example, human resources, finance, research and development.

In a comparison of the financial management functions in 16 leading US corporations, undertaken by a consultancy firm, the data enabled the high, median and low figures for the number of staff per billion of revenue, the staff as a percentage of total employment and the cost as a percentage of revenue to be obtained. These figures were then compared by organizations with their own figures, as a basis for identifying areas for improvements. They revealed major differences in each of the figures.

In a process-based industry company, the staffing ratios at different levels between one major site and its related sites in the same company were analysed, and the same information was then obtained for selected competitors. Further best practices analysis showed the functional areas in which the site was 'strong in class' and 'weak in class', as the basis for planning corrective actions.

In an analysis of two leading consumer electronics companies in the US market, both were found to have financial results well above the industry average, but to derive their competitive success from distinctively different functional strategies. While one company invested heavily in product R&D, the other adopted a 'me too' approach. One company did its own manufacturing, while the other used offshore sub-contract facilities. In distribution and promotion, different strategic approaches were also used (Table 4).

Table 4 *Functional strategies*

(a) Comparative profitability of US consumer electronics companies, 1983–1986

	Average operating margin (%)	Average return on assets (%)
Sony	10	8
Emerson	7	15
Industry average	3	5

(b) Summary of functional strategy benchmarks

	Sony	Emerson
Price point	High end $1000 VCR	Low end $250 VCR
Research and development	Pioneer	Copy others
Manufacturing	In-house	Sub-contract to Taiwan
Distribution	Mass market and speciality stores	Mass market stores only
Advertising	Significant	None

(Source: Kaiser Associates, Inc.)

Also in a product development context, the issue of 'time to market' is important in industries other than the car industry example quoted above. Research has shown that, in manufacturing industry, leading companies typically generate new products up to 2.5 times faster than the industry average and at half the cost.

In one leading electronics company, the time to market performance was compared not only with the industry average, but also with a leading fashion house compared to the fashion industry average, emphasizing the scope for significantly shorter time to market.

Benchmarking results

More examples of the results of benchmarking in action are now beginning to become available as public information, either as case studies, as articles in the professional media or as conference papers.

This is due to the sensitivity which characterized many such performance improvements in the past being overtaken by the continuous nature of the process, and, more significantly, by the growing awareness of the potential of best practices benchmarking.

To illustrate the benefits, reference can be made once again to the significant successes of Xerox, with some of the performance improvements achieved through best practices benchmarking and other quality initiatives over a period of years being cited in the case profile in section 6.

Other results include a US-based printer manufacturer which succeeded in cutting the average design lead time for its new products from 4.5 years to set a new best practice of 22 months, a dramatic performance improvement of almost 60%.

A pan-European example of best practice quoted by Bain & Co. identified potential cost savings of £19 million out of a cost base of £120 million by examining the composition of total revenue (including profit) across the various international operations. The actions taken included establishing partnership sourcing arrangements with key suppliers, introducing standardized computer technology in processing, and reducing space per employee to save overhead costs. The net result was that costs were reduced by a total of £16 million after two years, some 84% of the potential identified.[12]

In the UK, Lucas has cited a variety of improvements achieved in its aerospace operations by focusing clearly on customer requirements and on more effective supplier management (including make/buy decisions).[13]

These include:

- a reduction in the number of changes of ownership in its order administration procedures from 20 to 8
- the time to answer customer enquires reduced from 30 to 5 days
- stock levels reduced by 15% in one year
- the number of suppliers reduced by 50%
- the number of stores locations reduced from 14 to 2
- the ratio of support staff reduced from 2:1 to 0.9:1
- sales per employee increased from less than £26K to £60K.

Such examples of results achieved show the power of best practices benchmarking as an agent for far-reaching organizational change when coupled with the adoption of a quality-based culture, and for very significant improvements in performance to be achieved.

6 Case profile – The Xerox experience

6.1 Introduction

The Xerox Corporation in the USA, together with international affiliates such as Rank Xerox in the UK, is regarded as being among the leaders in the development and implementation of programmes of best practices benchmarking.

Not only has Xerox been practising benchmarking for longer than most other companies, but also there is a clear track record of success in significant performance improvements based on these and other quality initiatives. These have enabled the company to recapture, develop and maintain leadership positions in its various market-places, reflected in its achievement of major quality awards in the USA and Europe.

Also, the Xerox experience highlights the softer aspects of benchmarking in terms of engineering internal changes in culture, in communications and in employee commitment in order to improve its external market position.

The following case profile is presented as a list of points to provide a concise overview of how one major company has achieved success with, and through, best practices benchmarking.

6.2 The Xerox philosophy

'Competitive benchmarking is the continuous process of measuring our products, services and practices against our toughest competitors or those companies renowned as the leaders.'

'Our goal is superiority in all areas – quality, product reliability and cost.'

6.3 Some definitions

Benchmarking: A continuous, systematic process of evaluating companies recognized as industry leaders, to determine business and work processes that represent best practices and establish rational performance goals.

Best practices: The methods used in work processes that produce outputs which best meet customer requirements in a particular market-place.

Benchmarks: The conversion of best practices into measurements of best performance.

6.4 Historical evolution

1979	Benchmarking introduced as a competitive strategy
1981	US and Japanese manufacturing studies initiated
1982	Benchmarking began in non-manufacturing areas
1983	Benchmarking integrated into the 'Leadership Through Quality' strategy
1984	Corporate-wide benchmarking network formed
1984–89	Benchmarking application internalized
1990+	Benchmarking totally integrated at all levels

6.5 Xerox background

- Plain paper copier market share fell from 67% in 1976 to under 45% in 1982, as the market almost tripled in size.
- Profits fell from $1149 million in 1980 to $600 million in 1981, with the first-ever workforce lay-offs by the company.

- Strategic plan was based on annual productivity growth of 8%, versus a 3% industry average – however, an 18% growth was needed to catch the Japanese competitors within 5 years.
- A challenge of economic survival, rather than growth alone.
- Approach problem via a 'Leadership Through Quality' programme, with competitive benchmarking as a key tool.

6.6 The Xerox 10-step approach

Planning

1 Identify benchmark outputs
2 Identify best competitor
3 Determine data collection method

Analysis

4 Determine current competitive gap
5 Project future competitive performance levels

Integration

6 Communication of data; acceptance of 'analysis'
7 Develop new goals and functional actions plans

Action

8 Implement specific actions
9 Monitor results and report progress
10 Re-calibrate benchmarks

Maturity

- Leadership position obtained
- Process fully integrated into company practices

6.7 Establish benchmarks

A wide range of benchmarks was established initially, including:

- Functional costs as a percentage of revenue
- Labour overhead rates
- Cost per page of documentation
- Number of production machines free of problems
- Billing error rates
- Service response times.

Other areas added to give coverage of all areas including: quality, reliability, asset utilization, cost, delivery and customer service.

6.8 Off the benchmark – the competitive gap

- Indirect:direct ratio – 2 times that of the best practice
- Number of production suppliers – 9×
- Assembly line rejects (ppm) – 10×
- Product lead time – 2×
- Defects per 100 machines – 7×
- Unit *manufacturing* cost was equal to Japanese competitors' *selling* cost

6.9 Some results

- Product and operations quality – defects per 100 machines improved 10×, benchmark met
- Production suppliers (in US/EEC/Pacific regions) – reduced 10×, from 5000 to 500
- Production line defective parts (ppm) – reduced 13× (from 4000 to 300)
- Receiving inspection – reduced to 5% of incoming materials
- Goods inwards acceptance better than 99.5%
- Inventory reduced by two-thirds
- Service labour cost down by 30%
- Customer satisfaction increased 38% in five years

6.10 Benefits perceived

- Takes the focus out of the boardroom.
- The enemy is on the street, not across the table.
- Brings facts to the decision-making process.
- Removes the emotion.
- Effectively cures denial problems.
- Specifies what needs to be changed, and why.

6.11 Lessons learned

Benchmarking provides:

- Better awareness of yourself:
  - what you are doing
  - how you are doing it
  - how well you are doing it.
- Better awareness of the competition and/or the best:
  - what they are doing
  - how they are doing it
  - how well they are doing it.

6.12 Summary

The transformation of the business required a focus on:

- a culture based on total quality
- customer requirements
- establishing effective goals and objectives
- true measures of productivity
- developing best practices
- continuous and rigorous reassessment.

7 Implementation issues

The power of benchmarking has been emphasized widely. However, it is not all plain sailing, and there are many factors to take into account in implementing benchmarking programmes.

There are potentially significant pitfalls and problems to be avoided, and important considerations in terms of resources, information and partners.

Positive and negative factors

From the various experiences which have been reported, benchmarking can be seen to have many positive benefits over and above any improvements in performance.

New ways of working can be introduced which utilize the talents and abilities of employees more effectively. The active involvement of employees at all levels is to be encouraged, and most will be motivated by activities designed to enhance their own roles and thus their organization's position.

The internal teams used in obtaining and analysing benchmarking data will make recommendations to change, improve or remove processes, systems and practices which affect them directly. In many situations, they will have to implement these changes as well, thereby ensuring their continuing interest and commitment.

Thus, benchmarking is a powerful agent for change and motivation, provided that the initial consultation and ongoing feedback processes are handled properly. However, to counterbalance the forces for good that benchmarking can provide, there are some potentially negative factors which also need to be borne in mind.

One necessary characteristic of benchmarking is that it is intended specifically to disturb the status quo, and thus can create situations in which perceived changes may be unsettling and produce insecurity with possibly disruptive consequences. This emphasizes once again the importance of good consultation and communications.

The use of the word 'benchmarking' itself can be threatening in some company cultures and internal environments, with its connotations of job (rather than process) measurement. In these situations, the focus should be on sharing good practices and the individual benefits that will ensue as a result of improvements.

The senior management of an organization may be unsure of the concept or reluctant to admit that their competitors or other organizations may be more effective than their own.

Senior management has a natural tendency to look for quick results, but in best practices benchmarking there will almost certainly be disappointments and failures *en route*.

Pitfalls and problems

Compared with other analysis techniques, benchmarking does not have any predictive power to anticipate future performance, results or benefits. It is not a planning or a forecasting tool. Thus, the iterative nature of the benchmarking process should be emphasized, together with the habit of learning from one's own and others' experience and the continuing improvements to be made.

The level of resources and length of time involved, and the ongoing commitment required, should also not be underestimated. Benchmarking is not a 'one-shot' or 'quick-fix' process, but one which must be continuous and internalized formally as a fundamental way of doing business if any real long-term benefits are to be obtained.

One company with a few years of initial benchmarking experience to its credit estimated that it would be another two to three years before the benefits of improvements began to make a significant impact on the overall performance of the business. That said, major change programmes do take a matter of years to be implemented and for the anticipated benefits to be realized fully.

The use of dedicated resources for benchmarking activities can be costly, and brings the additional danger that the wide practical experience of individual business processes which is necessary for success may be lost. Thus, the most favoured approaches are those using teams which have strong business process knowledge, and with the benchmarking process itself being facilitated where necessary by internal or external resources with the necessary outlook and skills.

Ensuring relevance

In looking at benchmarking as a strategic information process, the stage of market evolution and maturity can have a major bearing on cost drivers and on the key business issues to address. At a lower level, the position on the product life cycle can have a bearing on the actual cost information obtained and on its correct interpretation.

Adjustments for variations in accounting definitions and treatments may be necessary when making comparisons between company operations located in different countries, or with benchmarking partners in different countries.

In the context of competitive benchmarking, gathering relevant data on direct competitors can be difficult. The use of industry clubs facilitated by consultants or academic bodies can provide a successful bridge in some situations, provided any confidentiality or anti-competitive issues can be overcome. Alternatively, consultancy or research studies may need to be commissioned.

In situations where an individual business unit may find it difficult to justify resources in the first instance, the use of central resources and seed corn funding can help to launch benchmarking programmes, and especially external comparisons with their greater demands for research effort.

External target organizations which have developed clear positions of leadership on key business processes may see approaches from intending best practices benchmarking partners as potential consultancy opportunities.

In selecting potential external partners, therefore, it is important to choose companies to which the benchmarking team can relate and to ensure that there is compatibility in size and scale. There are drawbacks in focusing the search for potential partners only on well known, and therefore probably the larger-scale, organizations. The business processes may not be directly comparable, the scale criteria may not be satisfied, and there may also be the problem of too much demand for their collaborative efforts.

To get the best from partnership arrangements there must be a focus on specific and predetermined issues. Reviews must be undertaken immediately, and conclusions shared so that the analysis can be challenged and the dialogue continued in a spirit of mutual learning from one another.

It is important to make every effort to understand one's own organisation before attempting to understand competitors or companies in other industries. Thus, initial efforts in benchmarking can usefully focus on sharing internally and between closely related business units in the first instance.

Benchmarking in context

To complete any assessment of what benchmarking 'is', some brief comments on what it 'is not' should be added.

Benchmarking is not about cost cutting *per se*, but about improving performance. If benchmark-based improvements do provide cost savings, these are the end result itself, rather than the means. Also, benchmarking should not be another means of gathering management information under the guise of a new organizational initiative or via a special task force.

It is not properly regarded as a control procedure or as a routine management reporting system. If benchmarking is perceived as such in the early stages of development and implementation, there is a real danger that internal motivation, goodwill and co-operation will be affected adversely.

However, in most responsible organizations, the proper reporting of benchmarking activities and results will be a necessity, if top management endorsement is to be won and continuing support retained.

Keys to success

Several general characteristics can be defined which will have a material effect on success in implementing benchmarking initiatives. These include:

- commitment to the aims and the process throughout the organization
- involving the people who will make the changes

- understanding customer needs and own internal business processes
- focusing on the processes first and the metrics second
- identification of the right performance variables to benchmark
- taking small steps at a time by focusing on a few key processes initially
- making the measurements objective and truly comparable
- being honest in assessment, in sharing information and in providing feedback.

Any successful approach to benchmarking will be pragmatic in outlook, and have as its primary task the creation of a climate for initial and then continuous improvement. This involves a clear focus on the business and the bottom line, and a continuing emphasis on being externally, rather than internally, orientated.

8 Summary and conclusions

The aim of this article was to provide an introduction to best practices benchmarking, and an overview of the issues involved in the context of improving performance in key business processes.

It has outlined the background to best practices benchmarking as a management technique, and explored factors concerned with developing benchmarking programmes. Examples of benchmarking activity in different business environments have been provided, together with some results, and implementation matters have been considered.

In addition to the organizations which have been cited already in this article, many other leading organizations have gained benefits from joining the ranks of benchmarking practitioners. These include multinational corporations, such as IBM, Ford, GE, Canon and NEC, as well as major UK companies such as ICL, British Airways and BP.

However, the interest in benchmarking is not confined to medium or large-scale organizations. Benchmarking is relevant to private and public sector concerns, of all sizes, and across a wide range of business processes.

There is growing interest in the public sector, in local government and in the health service, with the widespread introduction of performance indicators. Many of these initiatives are driven by changes in the political environment in terms of securing better value-for-money in public services, encouraging greater openness and accountability, and for service improvements in dealing with the general public as customers or consumers.

The publication of 'league tables' for hospital waiting lists, for the cost of surgical treatments in different regions, and per capita spending on essential services in different local authorities all provide evidence of this trend. Such examples create pressure for business process improvements, but more importantly provide an opportunity for best practices benchmarking to be undertaken.

With benchmarking, anticipated improvements in competitiveness or efficiency are based on an understanding of the true nature of the business and the use of proven practices. Without it, changes may be more evolutionary or incremental in nature (and thus less dramatic and with unrealised potential), and assessments suffer from having been internally, rather than externally, focused.

In helping to establish goals and objectives for performance improvements, benchmarking provides credible arguments for proactive change, rather than those which may be reactive or based on an inwards-looking viewpoint. Also, benchmarking provides the potential to solve the real problems by understanding outputs based on business best practices, rather than being based on an imperfect understanding of the processes which really matter.

Notes

[1] Walleck, A.S., O'Halloran, J.D. and Leader, C.A. (1991) 'Benchmarking world-class performance', *The McKinsey Quarterly*, No. 1.

[2] 'Benchmarking – A Driver of Change', by Martin Dada, PA Consultants. Paper presented at 'Best Practice Benchmarking' conference held in London in November 1992, organized by ATI.

[3] Various sources including: 'Successfully Managing the Benchmarking Process', by Rolf E. Soderstrom, Motorola University. Paper presented at 'Improving Efficiency Through Best Practice Benchmarking' conference held in London in September 1992, organized by IIR.

[4] Opening remarks by Lew Chamberlain, Royal Mail Quadrant and Chairman of the BQA Benchmarking Management Group at the 'Practical Benchmarking' conference held in London in May 1992, organized by ICM in association with KPMG.

[5] 'Benchmarking – A Driver of Change', by Martin Dada, PA Consultants. Paper presented at 'Best Practice Benchmarking' conference held in London in November 1992, organized by ATI.

[6] Porter, M.E. (1985) *Competitive Advantage*. Free Press, New York.

[7] 'Benchmarking for Best Practice', by Alan Jones, TNT Express (UK) Limited. Paper presented at the 'Practical Benchmarking' conference held in London in May 1992, organized by ICM in association with KPMG.

[8] Camp, R.C. (1989) *Benchmarking*. Quality Press, Milwaukee, Wisconsin.

[9] 'Why and How Benchmarking Can Be Used to Improve Manufacturing Operations', by Michael Graff, McKinsey & Co. Paper presented at 'Improving Efficiency Through Best Practice Benchmarking' conference held in London in September 1992, organized by IIR.

[10] Cowell, D.W. (1988) 'New service development', *Journal of Marketing Management*, Vol. 3, No. 3, pp. 296–312.

[11] Lovelock, C. (1992) 'Seeking synergy in service operations: seven things marketers need to know about service operations', *European Management Journal*, Vol. 10, No. 1, March.

[12] 'The Power of Best Demonstrated Practice', presentation prepared by Bain & Co., February 1991.

[13] 'Some Best Practices in Benchmarking' and 'Total Business Redesign', by Philip Barrington, Lucas Aerospace Limited. Papers presented at benchmarking conferences held in London in May and November 1992, organized by ICM in association with KPMG and ATI, respectively.

Acknowledgements

This article has drawn on desk and library research on best practices benchmarking, on reference material and on advice provided by various organizations and individuals, and on personal experience in consultancy and management education tutoring.

The following individuals and organizations are acknowledged with thanks:

Hilary Utley
Peter Pay
Jeremy Nutter
David Palmer
Niven Duncan
Lionel Dawson
Tony Stapleton.

Permission to use selected material from company publications, conference papers and other published sources is acknowledged with grateful thanks to the following organizations: Rank Xerox UK; Digital Equipment Company; TNT Express; NCR; Royal Mail; PA Consultants; Bain & Co.; McKinsey & Co.; Kaiser Associates; KPMG Management Consulting; and SRI.

8
Measuring manufacturing performance*

R.H. Hayes, S.C. Wheelwright and K.B. Clark

Introduction

Most of the assets of a typical industrial company are invested in its manufacturing organization. That is also where most of its people and managers are found, and most of its costs incurred. Its prosperity – even survival – lies in its ability to control those costs and use those assets effectively. Following Lord Kelvin's famous dictum: "When you can measure what you are speaking about, and express it in numbers, you know something about it; but when you cannot measure it ... your knowledge is of a meager and unsatisfactory kind', most companies develop elaborate and pervasive accounting systems to record costs, shipments, and revenues. These systems measure the performance of specific activities and managers and compare them with what had been anticipated. In the process they have a profound effect on human behavior, because people are more likely to do what you *inspect* than what you *expect*.

Such measurements can provide useful information to managers who are trying to identify the sources of their problems or the reasons for their success. But most measurement systems in place today do not provide the kind of information needed by companies that seek to create a competitive advantage through manufacturing. That information is of two kinds. The first is insight into the direction and rate of improvement in performance over time, answering such questions as, Are we getting better at the things that are most important to our manufacturing strategy? and What is our rate of improvement? The second kind of information has to do with competitors. Most systems compare performance against some form of internal budget or standard. But a competitive advantage in the marketplace is revealed only by how one measures up to one's competitors; in other words, the right 'standard' to apply in measuring performance must be an external one. A measurement system, therefore, must be outward looking, providing accurate information regarding how the capabilities that are key to a company's success compare to the best in the world.

Putting in place a measurement system that supports a manufacturing advantage involves more than minor adjustments to traditional accounting systems. To understand the nature of these differences, in both concept and practice, and to lay the foundation for our discussion of alternative approaches, we begin this article by reviewing some of the basic concepts behind traditional systems for measuring

* This article was first published in *Dynamic Manufacturing: creating the learning organization* (1988), pp. 130–160. Free Press, New York.

factory performance, including a bit of their history. We then describe an approach for measuring the rate of improvement in manufacturing performance that is based on the concept of 'total factor productivity'. Next we describe an approach for evaluating a manufacturing company's competitive position, focusing on the capabilities of its key competitors. We conclude with a brief discussion of the implications of this approach.

The measurement tangle

Modern manufacturing accounting systems have long historical roots. From the time of the earliest factories in medieval Europe, accounting systems have been evolving to meet an increasingly complex set of demands. When managers collect data from a manufacturing process, they have a variety of purposes in mind, falling into three basic groups:

1. *Process management*: How long will it take to produce and deliver a given order? How much material must be ordered and when? How many people and machines must be assigned to produce it? When should they begin? How much assistance will they need from supervisors and specialists?
2. *Business management*: What products should be developed? What price should be assigned to a given product? How should this price be affected by the volume ordered? Should a product be dropped from the line? What wages can be paid workers and managers? How much and which kind of equipment should be bought to assist them? How much factory space is required to house these people and equipment?
3. *External reporting*: How much profit was made during the most recent reporting period? What are the values of the various stocks of raw material, partly finished goods, and finished goods that are being held? What is the value of the buildings and equipment assigned to production?

These three sets of issues can be thought of as dealing with progressively longer time horizons. Process management is essentially concerned with scheduling and staffing decisions that generally are reviewed and changed rather frequently. The important costs are almost entirely variable, depending on the rate of production, and can be directly assigned to specific products, materials, machines, and people. Those costs that cannot be directly assigned are not particularly relevant to making the kinds of decisions that process managers are concerned about.

On the other hand, the time frame over which pricing, wage, and facilities decisions are expected to endure might cover several years. Costs that look fixed in the short run, like the supervisor's salary – or even 'sunk', like the cost of the plant and its equipment – become more and more variable (that is, subject to management influence) in the long run. The numbers that are relevant in making such decisions, therefore, include both the direct costs of production and the indirect 'overhead' costs associated with staff specialists, product designers, and top managers. These costs must somehow be assigned to specific products for pricing purposes, and to specific activities for the purpose of deciding whether to increase or reduce the investment in those activities.

Reporting is somewhat more difficult to classify. Even though one might be required to report on the performance of a given manufacturing unit quite frequently (monthly or even weekly), the rules that govern this reporting must not be allowed to change very often or the information reported will not be consistent – either across companies or over time. In addition, because all revenues and costs must be accounted for, including corporate overhead allocations, there is no place for the concept of 'fixed' costs. Reporting, therefore, can be considered to have the longest time frame of all.

This ordering also reflects the historical emphasis placed on these sets of issues. In the early days of the industrial revolution the concerns of process management and control dominated data collection; hence the title 'controller', which is today something of an historical residue. Questions relating to pricing and equipment purchase were made on the fly, and largely on the basis of intuition, by the managers most closely involved with the decision. And the basic reporting instrument – as it is in most small firms today – was the cash-box: if it held enough at the end of every week to meet the payroll, pay one's suppliers, and provide a comfortable living for the owner, the business was a success.

Later, as companies expanded in size, number of locations, breadth of product line, and the complexity of the production process – and as top management and its staff groups became separated from line personnel within a complex hierarchy – management decision making began to demand more and more data collection activity. Over the past fifty years or so, the increasing importance of public ownership, government taxation, and a variety of forms of regulation (together with the resulting emergence of a powerful accounting profession) have tilted the emphasis of most companies' accounting systems toward the external report of cost and revenues in periodic financial statements.[1]

It does not take much reflection to come to the conclusion that the three different types of issues just described are likely to require the collection of very different data and the preparation of entirely different reports. In fact, one might easily infer that, to do a really good job at all three, one really needs three entirely different data collection and accounting systems. If the needs of only one set dominate the accounting function of a company, as financial reporting dominates in most companies today, one might expect that the other needs would be poorly served – just as one might expect that the needs of financial reporting might be poorly served by a cost reporting system that is set up primarily to assist in short-term scheduling decisions.

Perhaps an analogy would be useful here. Consider the origins of modern accounting systems: voyage accounting as it was practiced 500 years ago. A ship owner would hire a captain and crew, buy merchandise and load it on the ship, and then send it on its way (accompanying it himself or sending a representative) to some foreign port. When – and if – it arrived the merchandise would be sold at whatever price could be obtained, new merchandise purchased (based on the price and availability of goods at that port at the time, a well as on the owner's sense of the demand at home), and the ship would return. If it arrived safely the new merchandise would be sold, the captain and crew paid, and whatever was left over was the 'surplus', or profit, from the voyage. Accounting was essentially confined to bookkeeping.

But suppose an emissary approached the ship's captain two months after leaving his home port, halfway to his destination – in front of him only open ocean and unseen dangers, the uncertainty of what prices might be obtained for his merchandise and what goods would be available for purchase, the perilous return trip, and the uncertainty as to the revenue that might be received for this new cargo – and said, "The owner is curious: how much money have we made so far?" How should he answer? On the one hand, no money has been made; only costs have been incurred. On the other, the ship and its cargo are closer to the completion of their voyage, and therefore must be worth more, than when they first left their home port.

That is the question that financial reporting requires be asked in today's business environment; one must estimate the profitability over an arbitrary time period, before all the results are in, of a complex web of voyages (i.e., equipment and products) that encompass a variety of destinations and are sometimes expected to last several years. Attempts to assign lumpy costs and revenues to any given short time period (as compared with the length of the average voyage) will almost inevitably lead to questionable estimates, because the expenditures that have been incurred and the revenues that emanate from them have to be arbitrarily assigned.

Moreover, the insistence on the use of standard approaches, based on generally accepted accounting principles (GAAP), in preparing such reports, although giving them the appearance of consistency and objectivity, robs them of their ability to measure the nuances of performance in ships that are carrying different cargoes and following very different courses to different destinations. If one is competing on the basis of delivery speed, it seems obvious that one would use different measures of performance than if competing on the basis of lowest delivered costs. Yet the influence of the highly conservative GAAP, policed by the accounting profession, together with limited information collecting and processing capabilities (which, until recently, made it both costly and confusing to keep multiple sets of accounts) has led most companies to adopt similar measurement and reporting systems no matter what their competitive strategy or approach to production.

Finally, whatever answer is given to the emissary's question, one can be sure of only one thing: it is of little use to the captain as he tries to stay on course, evaluate the performance of his ship and crew, or decide whether and how to react to the changing winds and currents. Our focus in this article is on the needs of that captain, today's business manager, as he or she attempts to deal with the problems of managing operations and making effective business decisions.

Cost accounting's increasing 'reality variance'

To price their products and evaluate the efficiency of their various operations, most manufacturing companies today employ a methodology called cost accounting. Initially developed in the late 1800s for the purpose of attributing the total costs of operating textile mills, railroads, steel mills, and retail stores to specific products, departments, and activities, the cost accounting systems now in place are increasingly showing their age.[2] Not only are they providing inadequate or misleading information to managers (and indirectly to investors); they are leading to bad decisions. In addition, because they communicate distorted information about performance, the rewards and punishments they give rise to affect motivation and morale at lower levels of the organization in dysfunctional ways. In this section we will explore why this is happening.

The basic cost accounting methodology is simple. The costs of operating a manufacturing facility are collected and divided into two categories: those that vary directly (variable costs) with the production of an identifiable part or product – such as direct labor, materials, and energy – and those that do not but are required in order for the production of any product to take place. These include the cost of the buildings and equipment used, the salaries of supervisors, managers, and support groups, and ancillary costs such as taxes and insurance. Because they do not vary directly with the production of any particular item, but instead tend to reflect commitments (such as salaries, interest and depreciation expenses) that cover specific time periods, these are typically called period, indirect, or (in order to juxtapose them more clearly with variable costs) fixed costs.[3]

One cannot properly evaluate management performance using these measures alone, of course, because it is difficult to say whether a given measure indicates good, bad, or average performance unless one can compare it with some appropriate reference value. This reference value may be an historical figure (making it possible to measure the trend in performance over time), a budgeted figure (permitting the evaluation of a manager's ability to forecast and control the operations under his or her control), or a 'standard' determined in some objective manner: time-and-motion studies, industry data, engineering calculations, or the concurrent performance of other plants within the same company.

Given such reference measures it then becomes possible to perform 'variance analyses': separating the total deviation of an aggregate performance measure from its reference value (between, say, a product's measured cost per unit and its standard cost) into its various components. Was an apparently above-standard performance due to a low usage or cost of materials? A higher-than-expected production rate? Higher machine efficiency (perhaps due to new equipment)? Or higher direct labor efficiency? The answer is, Probably some combination of the above. But the exact combination can give one better insight into how much of the outcome was due to good management rather than good fortune.[4]

Although this kind of analysis allows one to assess the efficiency of the various activities that take place in a factory, it does not help the manager establish the selling price for a given product, decide whether to retain it or replace it in the product line, or determine which managers, departments, or products are deserving of particular credit for the facility's overall profit. To answer these types of profit-dependent questions it is necessary to factor in *all* the costs of producing each product, including the so-called fixed costs.

The impact of changing cost structures

When cost accounting was in its infancy, factoring in fixed costs was not a particularly difficult problem, since the great bulk of the total costs of production were variable costs, primarily direct labor and materials. Therefore, elaborate systems were developed to measure and evaluate them. The fixed costs, which represented only 10 to 20 percent of the total, were then allocated to specific products and activities in some reasonable way. Usually this was done by identifying (or simply asserting) a strong relationship with one or more of the direct costs and then distributing the fixed cost on the basis of the amount of that direct cost. For example, if supervision and factory support costs were small compared with direct labor but there was a clear relationship between the two – for example, an operating policy that there should be one supervisor for every ten workers – then the cost of supervision could be attributed to a specific product by measuring the ratio between supervisory costs and direct labor hours *over all products* and multiplying that 'supervisory burden rate' by the number of direct labor hours consumed.

The fixed costs in different circumstances might be driven by a variety of direct costs, including the consumption of a critical material or the number of machine hours required. But because of the historical importance of direct labor, as well as the existence of systems for measuring it quite precisely, it became by far the most prevalent means for allocating most fixed costs.

Relatively few American companies base their overhead allocation on materials consumption, on the other hand, even though materials account for more than 50 percent of the total manufacturing cost in most companies. What they call 'materials consumed' is often, instead, an estimate derived by multiplying a product's standard material cost by the amount produced. Periodically, typically every few months, this estimated consumption is reconciled with actual material usage, based on a physical count. Even when actual (rather than standard) materials transactions are recorded, they are typically recorded in dollar, rather than in physical, terms.[5]

Returning to our history, as companies began substituting equipment for labor, investment costs became increasingly burdensome to the small, cash-poor company of the time – which still tended to finance itself out of its cashbox. This led to the development of another set of systems for evaluating capital investment – the capital budgeting system, and one for measuring the effectiveness with which existing capital equipment was being utilized. As a result, the internal accounting systems of most companies today are dominated by mechanisms for measuring direct labor and machine utilization. These measures, developed with great precision (but often too late to guide effective decision-making), then serve to drive their cost allocation schemes, capital budgeting systems, and, ultimately, management evaluation systems.

It is our position that this approach to cost accounting and capital budgeting is increasingly afflicted with a new and dangerous type of adverse variance: a 'reality variance'. This new variance owes its existence to a variety of causes but is essentially due to the application of a set of tools developed in an early twentieth-century context to today's very different technological and competitive environment. For example, the cost of direct labor in a typical high-technology company today seldom exceeds 10 percent of total costs; increasingly it is under 5 percent, as are depreciation charges. Indirect factory costs – particularly materials control, quality assurance, maintenance and process engineering, and software development – have been growing rapidly, on the other hand, and in many companies now add up to five to ten times direct labor costs. As a result, the cost accounting systems such companies are using to measure performance, and which influence their behavior, devote three-quarters or more of their energies to measuring costs that are likely to account for less than 15 percent of the total. By focusing attention on less important factors in today's production environment, they distract managers from other factors that are more critical to their success.

As the so-called fixed costs become a larger and larger component of total costs, as product life cycles shorten, and as shared activities become more and more critical to competitive success, one might expect that the traditional means for assigning them to products would start to break down. Indeed, it can lead to quite bizarre behavior if managers are deluded into thinking that costs constructed in this way actually bear some relationship to the true costs of making a product or operating a process. For example, if a company uses indirect workers for equipment changeovers and setups but it allocates indirect costs on the basis of direct labor hours, almost inevitably it will underestimate the cost of producing low-volume products while overstating the cost of high-volume products.[6]

We know one high-tech company whose overhead costs add up to almost ten times its direct labor costs, which come to roughly ten dollars per hour. Managers in this company are motivated to buy a part from an outside vendor, if at all possible, instead of making it internally because in so doing they reduce the costs for which they are responsible (which include the allocated costs) by $(1 + 10) \times$ \$10, or \$110, for each direct labor hour saved. Managing an increasing volume of subcontracting, however, requires additional overhead personnel. Therefore, this company finds that its direct labor costs are decreasing, while its overhead costs are increasing – which drives up its overhead allocation rate for the remaining products and motivates its managers to subcontract even more. While extreme, this company is not atypical of many today that are being driven in unanticipated directions by the apparently innocuous mandates of their accounting systems.

Not only are overhead costs increasing as a percentage of the total, but many companies today are finding that direct labor costs are not as variable as they used to be, and as their cost allocation schemes assume. Seniority rules, the fear of permanently losing especially good workers or particularly valuable skills in the event of a layoff, and the increase in worker motivation and worker-manager interaction that come from various forms of 'lifetime employment' have made labor costs almost as fixed as management costs in many companies today. Nor are the fixed costs quite as fixed as they were assumed to be. The increasing pressure of foreign competition has led a number of companies to make substantial reductions in their management and investment costs in the past several years. Just as all costs are variable in the long run, in today's sophisticated manufacturing environment they are increasingly fixed in the short run. And as companies discover how complicated the interplay is between reject levels and factory throughput time, between product design and manufacturing productivity, between purchasing and equipment maintenance and work-in-process, the notion that one can somehow separate all these interrelated costs into tidy packages on a monthly or even quarterly basis becomes somewhat ludicrous.

Moreover it is dangerous. Not only does it tend to blur what is really going on in a factory – while giving managers a false sense of accuracy and completeness – it may induce companies to pursue the mirage of increased profitability (as depicted in their financial reports, prepared according to GAAP) by avoiding actions and investments that are essential to their long-term survival. They become dependent on external suppliers for critical skills and parts, a process that has come to be called the 'hollowing out' of corporations, and then watch indignantly as these suppliers evolve into competitors. They choose to use an older machine to make a given part rather than a more modern machine, even though it produces higher quality and requires less setup, because the old machine is fully depreciated.

Almost as bad, they delay investing in advanced manufacturing technology because their traditional approach to measuring its costs and benefits suggests that it will not offer as high a return on investment as they are used to, since it does not take into account the profound changes that the new technology can make in their cost structure, flexibility, and relationship with customers. They overinvest in hardware and underinvest in the software development and worker training essential to extracting the full potential from that hardware, because hardware can be depreciated over several years but software and training expenses reduce profitability immediately. They avoid splitting up oversized, bureaucratic factories into small, entrepreneurial units with limited product lines and responsibilities because their traditional cost models suggest that this will lead to higher overhead costs without any effect on variable costs. Many companies that have carried out this kind of refocusing, however, have found both assumptions to be incorrect.

Today's accounting systems for measuring manufacturing performance thus have become an impediment to competitive advantage. Their preoccupation with variances from internal standards and annual budgets obscures the importance of continual improvement. And without clear ties to one's competitive environment or strategy, or references to comparative manufacturing capabilities, the numbers generated by them can lead to poor decisions and competitive weakness.

As a result, many companies (and even a small but increasing number of academics) have begun the search for other approaches to measuring and evaluating manufacturing performance. Some are experimenting with more satisfactory ways of allocating overhead costs, perhaps based on different 'cost drivers', such as machine hours, the number of customer orders or jobs scheduled, factory throughput times (or the amount of work-in-process inventory), and the number of parts produced. Others are exploiting the capabilities of new computerized manufacturing technologies to capture detailed data about a given job or process on a real-time basis, thereby allowing individual operations or transactions to be assigned to specific support activities. Still others are attempting to develop entirely new types of performance measures – such as customer perceptions of quality or service satisfaction, time to launch new products, or process throughput times – and new ways for combining them.[7]

Measuring improvement in manufacturing performance

If a firm thoroughly dominates its markets, controls the basic technologies in its products and processes, expects little change in the demands of its (satisfied) customers and has little actual or prospective competition, it may get along quite well doing what it always has done. For everybody else, long-term success depends on getting better and better: continually learning and applying new knowledge to improve performance. This requires a clear conception of where the organization has been and where it is going. Manufacturing therefore needs a measurement system that provides perspective on its direction and rate of improvement. Traditional accounting systems rarely do this.

The last thing most manufacturing managers need, however, is another new statistic or report added on to all the others they have to deal with. The typical factory, in fact, has too many measures and reports, generated over time for a variety of purposes: internal control, pricing of special customer requests, inventory valuation, capital budgeting requests or audits, governmental mandates, special studies, and on and on. Like the number of products in a product line, or the number of personnel in a staff group, measurements and reports seem to have an ability to grow of their own accord.

Many of the reports that routinely get produced in a company have been developed in response to the needs of the company's external reporting system and therefore reflect the concerns discussed in the preceding section. In the case of others, the original reason for developing the report may either have been forgotten or is no longer relevant. Many are likely to violate one or more of the three criteria every report should satisfy:

1 It should be tailored to the satisfaction of a specific, important need (and one not met by other reports), in a timely fashion.
2 It should be based on the most relevant and objective information available.
3 It should be simple enough to be widely understandable, credible, and usable within the organization.

By making report generation easier and faster, the advent of powerful computers, low-cost storage devices, and high-speed printers have tended to accelerate report proliferation. Moreover, rather than centralizing and standardizing their preparation, modern technology tends to encourage the development of different reporting and measuring systems for different plants within the same plant system, making it difficult for them to properly compare their performance or to learn from each other's experience. As a result, the complaint of factory managers in many companies is not that they do not have enough data but rather that they are inundated by a *blizzard* of reports – each conveying a somewhat different message depending upon the measures used and whether performance is compared against standards, last year's results, budgets, or industry (or sister plant) averages.

Rather than helping to bring blurry data into clearer focus, these reports often tend to obscure and distort the operating realities that managers have to understand. What they need are detailed, accurate data about the important activities that are going on in their plant and some way to combine those data together so that one can answer such questions as, "How effectively is the plant operating, overall?" "What activities within it are operating particularly well or poorly?" and "Are we getting better at the things that are really important to strengthening our competitive position?"

In this section we will describe an approach to answering these questions that a number of companies are beginning to experiment with. It requires the calculation of the efficiency (productivity) with which the plant converts key resources into outputs, an analysis of the behavior of these productivities over time, and then a procedure for tying them all together into an overall total factor productivity (TFP) measure of performance.

Single-factor productivity

In essence, productivity is a measure of the efficiency with which physical inputs are translated into physical outputs. This focus on *physical* transformations is in contrast to the usual *financial* measures of performance, which assess the effectiveness with which monetary inputs are translated into monetary outputs. In practice, however, as will be discussed, physical inputs and outputs are often difficult to deal with, so one is forced to use approximations based on monetary values.

If adequate physical measures (units, tons, gallons, etc.) are available, however, one can begin to estimate a company's overall productivity by calculating the single factor productivity (sfp) of each of the important resources (labor hours, material, management time, etc.) that are used in the production of its products:

$$sfp_{A,2} = \frac{\text{output of product A}}{\text{input of resource 2}}$$

Note that $sfp_{A,2}$ is *not* equal to the amount of resource 2 that is used in producing each unit of product A (which is the basis of most product cost analyses); instead it is the *inverse* of that number – the average amount of product A generated per unit of resource 2.

Unless the process is exactly specified by the design of the equipment it uses or by the physical or chemical laws that underlie it, there is seldom any way of determining whether the value of a partial productivity ratio is good or bad. That is, although it is usually possible to estimate how many worker hours were consumed in producing a given product, it is difficult to say how many *ought* to have been consumed. Industrial engineers can perform time-and-motion studies to estimate the number of hours that an 'average' person working at a 'normal' work pace using a given method and tools should need to produce a given amount of a certain product, but the industrial engineers at one company may arrive at a very different estimate than would those at another company which produces a similar product using a different process. Therefore, lacking any objective measure of what a given ratio ought to be, companies usually confine their attention to determining how it is changing over time.

Consider the following simple example. A company produces the same product, using the same raw materials, during two time periods. The specific inputs and outputs during these two periods are as in Table 1.

Table 1 *Resources utilized in producing product A*

	Period 1		Period 2	
Output	Amounts	sfp	Amounts	sfp
Units produced (thou.)	22.14		24.78	
Inputs				
Materials used				
material 1 (lbs)	25.99	0.852	29.08	0.852
material 2 (sq ft)	19.41	1.141	20.95	1.183
Energy (mill. of BTUs)	51.30	0.432	56.19	0.441
Labor (thou. of hrs)	4.73	4.681	5.31	4.667
Equipment (thou. of hrs)	3.22	6.876	3.60	6.876
Working capital (thou. of $)	68.75	0.322	78.64	0.315

If a single factor productivity has increased between period 1 and period 2, it indicates that more output has been produced per unit of that resource than in the earlier period; conversely, a smaller ratio indicates decreased productivity. The actual productivity changes are therefore as follows:

Table 2 *Productivity changes between period 1 and period 2*

	Single factor ratios			
Resources	Period 1	Period 2	Ratio	Productivity change (%)
Material 1	0.852	0.852	1.00	0
Material 2	1.141	1.183	1.0368	+ 3.68
Energy	0.432	0.441	1.0208	+ 2.08
Labor	4.681	4.667	0.9970	- 0.30
Equipment	6.876	6.876	1.00	0
Working capital	0.322	0.315	0.9780	- 2.2

Measuring productivity using value added

In the attempt to simplify the calculations required and reduce the impact of changes in material prices on their productivity measure, many companies prefer to base their productivity calculations on the concept of 'value added' rather than on sales output or revenues, where

Value added = Sales revenue – Cost of purchased materials and services

Some companies, in fact, define productivity as 'value added per employee'. The problem with this measure is that it does not take into account the effect of price changes on either value added or wage rates. Therefore, these companies can be lulled by ever-increasing values of value added per employee into thinking that their labor productivity is increasing when, in fact, it may be decreasing.

This approach has two additional drawbacks. First, it eliminates the possibility of determining how much of a company's total productivity improvement is due to more efficient use of purchased materials. Second, it takes the productivity improvement that *is* due to purchased materials and attributes it instead to more efficient use of energy and labor. For example, the 0.3 percent deterioration in labor productivity calculated in Table 2 might be converted into an apparent *increase* if output were measured in terms of value added rather than units produced and if materials comprised the bulk of total input costs.

Total factor productivity

Normally, as in the example in Table 2, single-factor productivities do not change at the same rate. The productivity of material 2, for example, has increased, while the productivity of labor hours has decreased. How can one determine whether this trade-off is favorable or unfavorable – that is, whether the *overall* process is operating better or worse than before? Managers generally have to rely on their informed judgment in evaluating such trade-offs, but some are so critical that specific procedures are mandated. The capital budgeting system in place in most companies is the usual means for making the trade-off between the productivity of capital and that of labor and other factors. Its function is to determine whether the increase in investment in a particular machine or project (which will cause capital productivity to decline, if output does not rise sufficiently) is justified by the reduction in the usage of other inputs (causing their productivity to increase).

Looking at just one or two productivities, as do companies whose accounting systems focus attention primarily on direct labor and machine utilization, can seriously bias management evaluations and lead to dysfunctional game playing within an organization. Consider the consequences of adopting total sales per employee as one's primary measure of productivity. If managers are being measured by the value of that ratio alone, they would be tempted to begin purchasing more and more parts and services from outside vendors. Or they might shift their emphasis to products whose costs are dominated by purchased parts or materials or require very little labor. They might even – if the manufacturing organization is given credit for everything produced, whether it is sold directly or goes into the finished-goods inventory of some downstream distribution organization – emphasize long runs of simple products rather than incur the time-consuming setups and additional process steps required for producing more sophisticated products in frequent, small batches.

To determine whether the overall productivity of the process that transforms all these resources into product A has increased or decreased, one has to find some way for combining the productivities of different resources (hours, pounds, BTUs, etc.) into an overall TFP. Similarly, if one wants to determine the overall productivity of the factory or department that produces several products, it is necessary to combine their individual TFPs in some way. The easiest way to do this is to take a weighted average of the different productivities of different resources or products, where the weights reflect the monetary value of each resource or product. Similarly, assuming that the price of a product reflects changes in its quality over time, weighting the number of units produced by their market price allows one to adjust for different quality (or product performance) levels from one year to the next.

If one introduces monetary values into one's calculations, however, at some point one will have to correct for the impact of whatever price changes have occurred between two periods. Otherwise, one's single factor productivity ratios will reflect the changes that have occurred in prices as well as in efficiency. For example, the conclusion (from Table 2) that the productivity of product A's working capital decreased between periods 1 and 2 rested on the assumption that a dollar of working capital in period 2 was equivalent to a dollar in period 1. If the value of a dollar in period 2 were only 95 percent of the value of a dollar in period 1, however, then only \$74,710 (= .95 × \$78,640) worth of period 1 dollars was used for working capital in period 2, implying that the productivity of working capital *increased* by 3 percent in period 2.

Using (inflation-adjusted) monetary values o reflect resource consumption makes it possible to estimate the aggregate change in TFP between periods 1 and 2. For example, again using the results of Table 2, if material 1 accounts for 40 percent of the total cost of product A, material 2 for 20 percent, energy for 5 percent, labor for 25 percent, and equipment for 10 percent,

$$\frac{TFP_2 - TFP_1}{TFP_1} = (.4)(0)+(.2)(3.68)+(.05)(2.08)+(.25)(-.30)+(.10)(0) = 0.77\%.$$ [8]

Using a measure like TFP to track factory performance gives managers an integrated perspective on performance. But it also lays the foundation for understanding the dynamics behind where the plant has been, and where it is going. Figure 1 graphs the behavior of TFP over a ten-year period in a plant that we have studied in some depth. Until 1982, this plant had tracked performance using cost variances and comparisons with annual budgets, focusing considerable attention on direct labor. According to these measures, the plant had performed quite well. But no one had ever looked at a measure that was as comprehensive as TFP, and no one had ever looked at any measure over the entire history of the plant.

Figure 1 shows that the plant has had an uneven history. The TFP data document a significant increase in performance over the period, but they also suggest that much of that improvement came in the early years of the plant's history. After strong improvement during a start-up phase that lasted into 1976, TFP went through a long up-and-down cycle; performance in 1982 was only

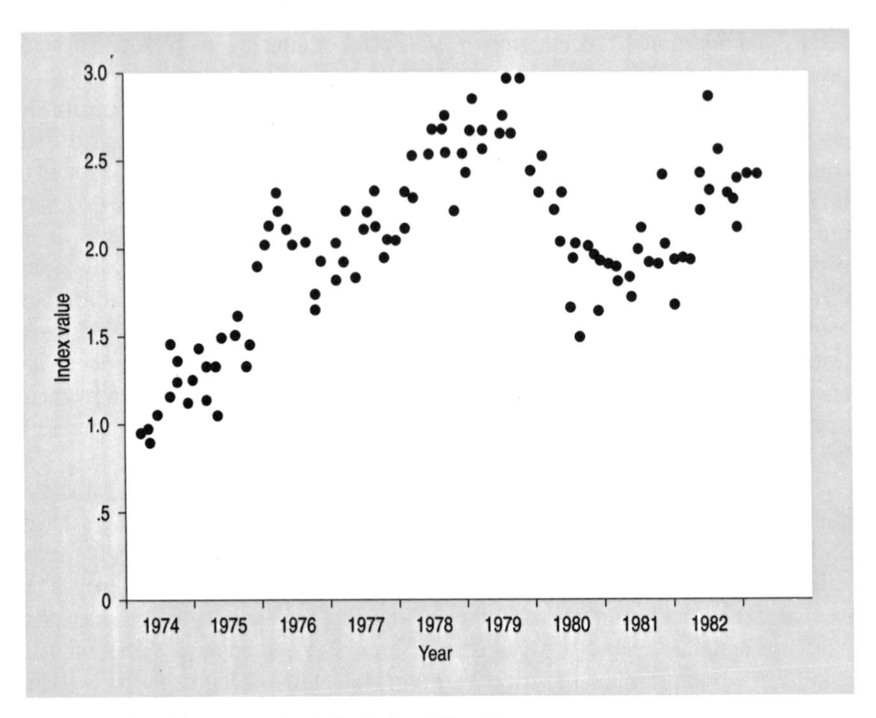

Figure 1 *Total factor productivity index: Plant B*

somewhat above that of 1976. Investigation showed that only part of this pattern could be explained by cyclical changes in demand. Much of it reflected changes in capital investment, and in particular, the way the plant managed equipment introductions. Given such a perspective, plant managers are in a much better position to gauge changes in performance, and to focus their efforts on improving TFP over time.

As this example suggests, TFP can be a useful way to measure factory performance. Most companies already collect the basic raw data required but need to develop a new way to process and report these data. This can be surprisingly difficult, since most companies find it much easier to build factories in remote locations, master new technologies, and enter new markets than to change the derivation and arrangement of the numbers in their accounting reports. But unless an organization finds some way of measuring productivity directly, rather than using existing surrogates (such as gross margin, machine utilization, and labor variances), the people in it will probably perceive any attempts to improve manufacturing performance to be simply the latest in a long history of cost-reduction programs. Such a perception can cause them to fall back on traditional approaches for reducing costs, as measured by their familiar accounting reports, in the short run.[9] In so doing, they may miss opportunities to uncover the real sources of superior performance and competitive advantage in their organization.

Conducting a manufacturing competitive analysis

The central question that any system of measurement must answer is, How are we doing? For captains of ships as for captains of industry, the necessary follow-on question is, Compared to what? We have already suggested that a look at a factory's (or a firm's) history is essential. But in creating a competitive advantage in manufacturing, the only standard of comparison that really matters is the performance of one's best competitors (actual or potential). Thus, an effective performance measurement system must provide insight into how a company compares with its best competitors with respect to the manufacturing capabilities upon which its manufacturing strategy is based.

Such a competitive analysis contains three elements. The first is an objective review of the company's fundamental decision patterns in manufacturing, to see whether and how they translate into manufacturing capabilities and competitive advantage. The second is an analysis of manufacturing's impact on overall sales, investment, and profitability. The third is a compilation of benchmark data for evaluating key manufacturing activities; this indicates the potential for improvement.

Decision patterns in manufacturing

Behind a firm's manufacturing capabilities and performance lies a pattern of structure and infrastructure decisions: capacity, facilities, technology, sourcing, work force, quality, production planning and control, and organization. A manufacturing analysis that does not include an understanding of these decision patterns and the forces that drive them is incomplete. Similarly, a competitor's decision patterns implicitly define its manufacturing strategy and provide a framework within which to analyze its behavior.

The first step in the approach we recommend for analyzing competitive manufacturing decision patterns (see Table 3) is to identify a relatively small number of competitors who are representative of the major modes of competition in the industry. Many pharmaceutical firms, for example, separate their competitors into two major groups – ethical and generic. The first do research on, and develop, proprietary drugs sold under a brand name. The second develop and produce drugs that are not protected by patents and are sold under a generic label.

Let us examine a representative company in each group: Merck (ethical) and Zenith (generic). These two companies are both successful, and good information about their manufacturing strategies is available.[10] The following brief comparison – based both on information about the policies each company has followed in each of the decision categories and on an assessment of the forces or attitudes that drive those decisions – suggests what one can do with publicly available information, examined within the framework of Table 3. This second step requires insight into each company's basic values (such as Merck's overriding commitment to customer service) or strategic objectives (Zenith's insistence on carrying a broad line), since its intent is to discover what the company's competitive capabilities are, and how those capabilities are likely to evolve in the future.

Table 3 *Competitive analysis of manufacturing decision patterns*

Step 1:	Establish Structure
A	identify major modes of competing
B	generate complete competitor list (actual and prospective)
C	select a representative subset for study
Step 2:	Data Analysis for Selected Competitors
A	manufacturing strategy by element: evidence, sources, drivers
B	insights from each element
Step 3:	Overall Competitive Assessment
A	comparison of firms
B	comparison of modes of competing
C	across firms and modes (self versus full range of competitors)
Step 4:	Manufacturing's Competitive Response
A	conclusions from above
B	implications for one's manufacturing strategy
C	plan of action

Table 4 presents a summary of our analysis of the decision patterns at Merck and Zenith. The dominant themes that run through Merck's manufacturing decisions are quality and customer service. The mission of manufacturing, which is integral to Merck's strategy, appears to be, Never fail to deliver a high-quality product to a customer whenever that customer demands it. Thus, Merck's efforts to become a leader in manufacturing technology, and its significant investment in internal processes and software, were driven more by a desire to create higher-quality products and faster response to customer demands than by a desire to cut costs.

In contrast to the coherence and integration found at Merck, Zenith's manufacturing decisions demonstrate some conflicting tendencies. It is influenced most strongly by the heavy cost pressure it faces in its markets. Decisions about capacity (pursue high utilization), technology (minimize R & D; invest for cost reduction), and work force (low wages) all seem to be driven by a desire to produce products of acceptable quality at low cost. However, Zenith also tries to produce a broad line of products and to introduce new products frequently. Thus, its main plants are not focused, it carries high inventories, and it has little control over its sources of supply. There is little evidence that Zenith has been able to develop a manufacturing strategy that will create the capabilities it needs to deliver a high variety of products at low cost. In the meantime, manufacturing's mission seems to be, Produce a broad line, but run as lean as possible.

Once information about representative competitors has been developed, a company needs to compare its decision patterns in manufacturing with theirs (step 3). Top management must ask itself: "How well does manufacturing support our business strategy?' and 'In what ways does manufacturing create a competitive advantage for us?'

Table 4 *Comparison of manufacturing strategy decision patterns in the pharmaceutical industry*

Decision category	Company: Merck	Zenith
Capacity	Maintain excess capacity; avoid stockouts; build new capacity ahead of market demand	Past: match demand; expand by working overtime or adding shifts Current: lead demand, but try to achieve high utilization
Facilities	Bulk (active ingredients): traditionally focused, now moving to multipurpose, modular Pharmaceutical: multiple products, strategically located near markets	Pharmaceutical: broad product lines produced in all facilities
Technology	Manufacturing technology leader; internal development of both software and hardware for automated processes; focus on improved quality and customer service	Follower in technology; standard off-the-shelf equipment; introduce automation only if justified by cost savings
Vertical integration	High level of vertical integration, from packaging to direct sales	Low level of integration; purchase packaging and active ingredients from many suppliers
Work force	'We hire the best.' Above average pensions, generous fringes; substantial in-house training and support for education; union relationships legalistic, adversarial	Hourly workers paid less than industry average; senior level executives have significant industry
Quality	Product quality is top priority; company quality standards set higher than regulatory requirements of *any* country	Exists at 'razor's edge' of FDA regs; 33 recalls in 1986 – but major effort to upgrade quality under way
Production planning	Centralized production scheduling using MRP II system; maintains high finished goods inventory: will meet any demand with 24-hour delivery	Short production runs, many changeovers, many products make scheduling a 'nightmare'; very high finished goods inventory, but very low work-in-process
New product development	Heavy R & D investment, focused on proprietary products and applications over a broad range of categories	Minimal investment in R & D, focused on generic versions of established products, and formulations that permit lower cost
Performance measurement	Tied to quality, dependability, and image of the firm	Focused primarily on manufacturing cost
Organization	Functional, process-focused organization; centralized control; technically oriented leadership; decision-making is cross-functional, and collaborative; strong communications system	Flat organization; decentralized decision-making fostering entrepreneurial spirit; reporting structures at operating level are a loose matrix

Given such an assessment of decision patterns, a manufacturing organization will have a more realistic sense of what is possible and where it stands. It will understand both its own tendencies and those of its competitors, and it will have a clearer sense of the threats and opportunities it faces. As interesting as such an analysis may be, however, it will have little impact if the organization does not act upon it.

The capstone of a competitive measurement system, therefore, is step 4: developing a competitive response for the manufacturing organization. For example, after looking at Merck and Zenith, one of their competitors might come to the conclusion that achieving production flexibility (defined as the ability to produce a wide variety of products at a competitive cost) is critical in their business. Such a comparison may also reveal that its own plants are poorly focused, its broad product line has been achieved only at the expense of very high overhead costs, and that failure to act will leave it vulnerable to competitors who are able to develop a more flexible, less overhead-intensive system. Such implications become the starting point for a plan of action.

Manufacturing's impact on business profitability

An analysis of comparative manufacturing decision patterns provides one type of insight into the nature of different competitors' manufacturing strategies. But an effective competitive measurement system also needs to provide information about how decisions in manufacturing combine to influence the performance of the business. The second element in our manufacturing competitive analysis, therefore, is a financial analysis of manufacturing's role in the profitability of the business as a whole.

There is a method for decomposing the profitability of a business unit (measured by return on assets) into four determinants: the profit margin on sales, the ratio of break-even sales to capacity, the capacity utilization rate, and the ratio of sales to assets. Breaking profitability down in this way enables one to learn something about manufacturing's financial impact on the business, since manufacturing decisions and capabilities principally affect costs, capacity, break-even sales, and asset intensity. With comparative information one can thus gain insight into how different approaches to manufacturing affect profitability.

For example, a manager who wants to improve the ROI of his or her business can follow one or more of the following approaches:

1. Increase one's production volume if this can be done without reducing selling prices to the point where the reduction in profit margin offsets the increase in capacity utilization.
2. Decrease the business's fixed costs (which serves to reemphasize that 'fixed' costs are not fixed in the long run), thereby reducing its break-even sales level.
3. Increase the profit margin by increasing selling prices, by reducing variable conversion costs, or by selectively culling low-contribution products from the product line; or
4. Reduce the asset intensity of the business by improving capital productivity and reducing work-in-process inventories.

By observing how a management group chooses to maneuver its way through this thicket of possibilities, one can learn much about manufacturing's role in the business.

The basic information needed to estimate these components of profitability can often be obtained through some creative digging into public documents (such as annual reports, prospectuses, government studies, and trade journals), and discussions with suppliers, customers, employees, and consultants. The following example demonstrates the kind of insight that can be provided by this approach. Three business units, all making similar products, generated comparative financial statistics over three two-year periods as are shown in Table 5.

Business B had historically been regarded as the industry's best, whereas business C was a 'dog' that had been acquired by a new management group in 1976 and appeared to have been 'turned around'. How good, in reality, is business B, and how good a job have the new managers of business C done?

An analysis based only on the data in Table 5 suggests that business C's major problem is its profit-to-sales ratio, while business B's profitability has been both strong and stable. More insight is provided in Table 6, where other measures are provided.

Table 5 *Performance measures for three manufacturing businesses*

Business	Year	PBT/Sales	PBT/Net assets
A	1983–84	.033	.11
	1981–82	.008	.02
	1979–80	.030	.08
B	1983–84	.034	.16
	1981–82	.032	.12
	1979–80	.036	.15
C	1983–84	.013	.05
	1981–82	(.010)	(.03)
	1979–80	.019	.10

Table 6 *Performance measures for three manufacturing businesses*

Business	Year	Contribution (%)	B-E Sales/capacity	Capacity utilization (%)	PBT /sales	Sales /assets	PBT /assets
A	1984–84	.23	.74	.86	.033	3.3	.11
	19818–2	.29	.69	.71	.008	2.5	.02
	1979–80	.26	.75	.85	.030	2.7	.08
B	1983–84	.25	.77	.89	.034	4.7	.16
	1981–82	.24	.78	.90	.032	3.8	.12
	1979–80	.27	.75	.87	.036	4.3	.15
C	1983–84	.25	.90	.95	.013	3.8	.05
	1981–82	.31	.81	.79	(.010)	3.1	(.03)
	1979–80	.35	.76	.81	.019	5.2	.10

What becomes clear, given this additional detail, is that all three businesses are achieving similar contribution levels (although business C's has actually *fallen* significantly under the new management). Business C's major problem, or at least the major difference between it and the other businesses, appears to be in its fixed costs, which have driven its B-E sales up to 90 percent of capacity. Interestingly enough, this figure has also deteriorated under the new managers. Their major accomplishment appears to have been that they increased substantially the volume of production. Upon investigation it was found that they achieved this largely by pulling back from subcontractors some small-volume, nonstandard products that formerly had been farmed out because they had been felt to interfere with the normal production flows in the business. The net effect was to increase the variable costs of the operation but spread its fixed costs over a substantially greater volume. As a result, the profit/sales ratio of the business increased.

This, together with a write-off of some apparently obsolete equipment, enabled the new management group to leverage a modest PBT/sales figure into a barely acceptable return on assets. The questions that arise out of this analysis are, Have business C's actions really constituted a 'turnaround', and have they enhanced or impaired its future profitability in the process? Our analysis suggests a quite different answer to these questions than the initial performance data indicated. Clearly their actions have caused a short-term improvement in the business's profitability. But the business is vulnerable. Unless real improvements in cost or differentiation occur, the situation in business C is likely to deteriorate.

Competitive benchmarking

For operating managers in factories, engineering departments, laboratories, and distribution centers, information about things like market share or the ratio of corporate sales to assets is interesting but not particularly helpful in creating the kind of operating capabilities that make a difference in the marketplace. What is needed are data on competitive performance in specific activities that are central to the operation's mission; this is the purpose of a technique called competitive benchmarking.

The experiences of two very different companies, Chaparral Steel and Xerox, illustrate how benchmarking can work. Chaparral started in 1975 as a mini-mill producing simple reinforcing bars. Today it manufactures a wide range of structural shapes and special quality bar steel; production in 1987 was 1.5 million tons. From the day that it opened its doors, Chaparral set out to be the best in its business. And that meant that it had to identify who were the best makers, rollers, and finishers of steel in the world and compare itself against them.

Chaparral therefore established relationships with steelmakers in Europe and Japan and began regular visits to observe and learn from them. Typical practice is to send a small team (an operator, a supervisor, an engineer, and a maintenance technician) to talk with their counterparts at the target site. The team gathers data on specific parameters like equipment cycle times, yields, and inventory levels. But they also examine practices and methods to get some understanding of what lies behind the performance observed. Similar visits are made to equipment manufacturers to learn about the latest developments in technology.

The data developed in these benchmarking trips are compared with existing practice at Chaparral and then translated into higher targets for the operating groups. These targets are credible to operating personnel because they have observed comparable performance in other companies and understand that if they don't achieve them, their business will suffer. As each target is reached, Chaparral people watch for new developments in key companies, and for the emergence of new leaders. Recently, for example, Pohang, the Korean steelmaker, has become the benchmark for landed cost in the United States. Gordon Forward, CEO of Chaparral, has therefore stated, "Our objective is to get our labor costs below the cost per ton of the ocean voyage from Korea. That way, they can pay their people zero and we can still meet them at the unloading docks with a cost advantage."

Benchmarking has also played an important role at Xerox.[11] Faced with declining market share and eroding profitability in its basic copier business, in 1979 Xerox began a searching examination of its methods and practices. Beginning with an engineering examination of competitive products, including a study of Fuji Xerox, its partly owned subsidiary in Japan, Xerox managers uncovered strong evidence of a sizable cost gap between it and its major Japanese competitors. The lower Japanese costs replaced the traditional annual budgets as targets for Xerox manufacturing.

Xerox soon found that even deeper insight could be achieved by looking at similar activities in companies with which it did not compete. A particularly interesting example is the benchmarking relationship that Xerox developed with a retailer and mail-order house for outdoor goods. Eager to improve its warehousing and distribution operations, the logistics and distribution organization at Xerox assigned a staff member to find a prime candidate for benchmarking. After searching in trade journals and discussing warehousing systems and performance with consultants and logistics professionals, he recommended L. L. Bean of Freeport, Maine. It had developed a strong reputation for customer service, and the distribution problems it faced were similar to Xerox's.

A visit to Freeport by a small group of Xerox managers uncovered both similarities and differences in practice and performance. Although Bean's operations were largely manual, it had achieved a high level of productivity. Table 7 (overleaf) compares 1982 labor productivity in L. L. Bean's warehouse operation with a proposed operation at Xerox. Much of Bean's superiority could be explained by differences in methods: arranging materials so that fast moving items were closer to stock pickers, choosing storage locations to minimize forklift travel distance, and batching orders to minimize travel distance.

Xerox incorporated these findings into the performance targets and systems being proposed for its modernized warehousing operations. This kind of benchmarking against similar activities in non-competitor companies has won widespread support at Xerox and has become standard practice in the operating groups responsible for implementing change. Xerox senior managers believe that it has been an important factor behind their significant improvements in performance over the last nine years.

Table 7 *Comparison of productivity in warehouse operations, 1982*

Productivity measure	L. L. Bean	Xerox (planned)
Orders per worker per day	550	117
Lines[a] per worker per day	1,440	497

[a] *A line is a standard measure of travel distance for one trip to a storage bin.*

(Source: Tucker *et al.*, 1987)

Table 8 *Methods for benchmarking*

	Step or objective	Source or method
1	Identify superior performance in critical activities (in both competitors and noncompetitors)	Trade journals; consultants; professional meetings; annual reports
2	Expand information through direct contact	Visits to selected firms by small multifunctional operating teams
3	Prepare reports and communicate findings	Summarize key findings; define benchmark levels of performance
4	Develop and implement action plan	Turn benchmarks into targets; change practices and procedures to achieve targets

Although Chaparral and Xerox do benchmarking somewhat differently, there are common themes in the methods they use and the philosophy that guides them. Table 8 briefly summarizes these commonalities and the way information is developed and used. Perhaps the most important element is the involvement of operating personnel in identifying target companies and collecting data. Members of the benchmarking team must be well trained; but if they do their job well, the data collected will be relevant and the changes suggested will be implemented successfully.

Summary and implications

For the ship's captain in the midst of a long and uncertain voyage, the central questions a measurement system must answer are not how much money was made during the previous month or quarter but whether the ship is being guided and operated properly: Is it on course? Are the crew and vessel performing well? A measurement system should also raise strategic issues: Is the destination that has been chosen still appropriate? Is the course correct? What winds and currents are likely to be encountered? Is the crew prepared for the emergencies that are most likely to occur?

Like ship captains, captains of industry need systems of measurement that give them information about how they are doing compared both with their own history and with their toughest competitors. The approach to measurement that we have outlined in this article using TFP to capture dynamic performance in the factory, breaking down an overall performance measure into its component parts, and conducting a competitive analysis to assess one's position relative to competitors – provides perspective and insight into capabilities, opportunities, and vulnerabilities. To be useful in supporting the creation of a competitive advantage in manufacturing, one's measures need to be both broad and integrated.

Too many managers try to steer their ships using accounting data that are narrow in focus and static in perspective. We suggest that a more dynamic perspective is necessary, and that the scope of the measurement system be broadened. Understanding output and input patterns over time is an important first element. But managers also need an external perspective – a comparison of competitive capabilities. An understanding of competitors not only can provide insight into one's own manufacturing strategy but it can also reveal relative strengths and weaknesses and how competitors are likely to react to various changes.

A dynamic and broadly based system of measurement will generate information that can be used at different levels in the organization for different purposes. Benchmarking, for example, can provide information that is useful both at the operating level, to improve the yields in a particular operation, say, and to top managers who want to assess their manufacturing organization's overall position. These dual requirements – relevance and timeliness at an operating level, and integration at a strategic level – have implications for the way the measurement system is organized and managed.

Any new measure (such as TFP), moreover, must provide information that is both accurate and credible. Operating groups should participate in defining and monitoring the system, because the information collected is more likely to be relevant and put to good use if the people who are going to use it are involved. This suggests that measuring manufacturing performance must be largely a line responsibility. Technical specialists may provide assistance, but the responsibility for defining the system, getting the right information, and putting it to use rests with the general manager.

Notes

1 See Thomas, H. Johnson and Robert S. Kaplan, *Relevance Lost: The Rise and Fall of Management Accounting* (Boston: Harvard Business School Press, 1987).

2 More complete descriptions of the development of the modern cost accounting system are contained in Johnson and Kaplan, *Relevance Lost*; Robert H. Parker, *Management Accounting: An Historical Perspective* (New York: Macmillan, 1969); and Alfred D. Chandler, Jr, *The Visible Hand* (Cambridge: Harvard University Press, 1977).

3 For example, see Charles Horngren, *Cost Accounting: A Managerial Emphasis* (Englewood Cliffs, NJ: Prentice-Hall, 1977); Robert N. Anthony and James S. Reece, *Management Accounting Principles* (Homewood, IL: Irwin, 1975); and Robert S. Kaplan, 'Accounting lag: the obsolescence of cost accounting systems,' in *The Uneasy Alliance: Managing the Productivity-Technology Dilemma*, eds Kim B. Clark, Robert H. Hayes and Christopher Lorenz (Boston: Harvard Business School Press, 1985).

4 A concise example of this approach is contained in Neil C. Churchill and John K. Shank, 'Managing against expectations (A): A note on profit variance analysis' (Boston: HBS Case Services, Harvard Business School), 9-176-182.

5 More detail is provided by Robert H. Hayes and Kim B. Clark, 'Exploring the sources of productivity differences at the factory level,' in *The Uneasy Alliance: Managing the Productivity-Technology Dilemma*, eds Kim B. Clark, Robert H. Hayes and Christopher Lorenz (Boston: Harvard Business School Press, 1985).

[6] For a more complete exploration of this issue, see Robin Cooper and Robert S. Kaplan, 'How cost accounting systematically distorts product costs,' in *Field Studies in Management Accounting and Control*, eds William J. Bruns, Jr, and Robert S. Kaplan (Boston: Harvard Business School Press, 1987).

[7] See Robert S. Kaplan, 'Measuring manufacturing performance: a new challenge for managerial accounting research,' *The Accounting Review*, Vol. 63, No. 4 (October 1983), pp. 686–705; and Kenneth A. Merchant and William J. Bruns, Jr, 'Measurements to cure management myopia,' *Business Horizons*, May–June 1986, pp. 56–64.

[8] There is a large and rapidly growing literature on various approaches to measuring productivity. For a representative sampling, see John W. Kendrick and Daniel Creamer, 'Measuring company productivity,' *The Conference Board Studies in Business Economics*, No. 89 (1965 ed.); *New Developments in Productivity Measurement and Analysis: Studies in Income and Wealth*, Vol. 44, eds John W. Kendrick and Beatrice N. Vacarra (Chicago: University of Chicago Press, 1975); C.E. Craig and C.R. Harris, 'Total productivity measurement at the firm level,' *Sloan Management Review*, Vol. 14, No. 3 (1973), pp. 13–29; and James Mammone, 'Productivity measurement: a conceptual overview,' *Management Accounting*, June 1980, pp. 36–42.

[9] We have left out the productivity of working capital because it must be treated differently. This analysis can also be extended to determine how much of the change in profits between period 1 and period 2 is due to price changes, how much is due to volume changes, and how much is due to productivity changes.

[10] This point is provocatively made by Wickham Skinner in 'The productivity paradox,' *Harvard Business Review*, July–August 1986, pp. 55–59.

[11] The information for this comparison was drawn from public sources and from interviews with managers and engineers in the industry conducted by a team of MBA students – Gary King, Mary Ng and Tom Saxe – under the direction of one of the authors.

[12] See Frances Tucker, Seymour Zivan and Robert Camp, 'How to measure yourself against the best,' *Harvard Business Review*, January–February 1987, p. 8.

Reference

Tucker, F., Zivan S. and Camp, R. (1987) 'How to measure yourself against the best,' *Harvard Business Revew*, January–February, pp. 8–10.

9
World class manufacturing: further evidence in the lean production debate*

Nick Oliver, Rick Delbridge, Dan Jones and Jim Lowe

Summary

This article reports the results of a study into the performance and management practices of 18 autocomponents plants, nine of which were located in the UK and nine in Japan. The study compared the performance of these plants and used quantitative measures to test the use of lean production techniques among the high performers. Five plants displayed high performance on measures of both productivity and quality. All of these were located in Japan. Several measures of management practice provided some support for the lean production model, particularly in the area of process discipline and control; measures of human resource management policy and work organization proved less significant. Contextual factors pointed to the conditions necessary to support lean production; higher performing plants had more stable demand and lower absenteeism.

Introduction

In the last two decades, Japan has come to be regarded as *the* model of best practice in manufacturing management. Japanese companies now dominate world markets in many sectors, particularly consumer electronics and vehicles. Western commentators have applied a variety of labels to these practices – just-in-time, total quality, theory-of-constraints, the systems engineering approach and world class manufacturing methods (Feigenbaum, 1983; Goldratt and Cox, 1984; Parnaby, 1987a, 1987b, 1987c; Schonberger, 1982, 1986). The last 3 years has seen the rise of the term *lean production* as an umbrella term to describe a set of practices, found in their purest form in Japan in the form of the Toyota Production System, which may explain the performance of Japanese manufacturers.

The lean production concept developed from the work of the International Motor Vehicle Programme (IMVP), the main findings of which were written up in *The Machine that Changed the World* (Womack *et al.*, 1990).

The IMVP was a 5-year research project into productivity and management practices in the world motor industry which involved 55 researchers worldwide.

* This article was first published in *British Journal of Management*, Vol. 5 Special Issue, pp. S53–S63, 1994.

The programme compared the performance of car assembly plants around the world. The main conclusion was that a model of production organization, for which the researchers coined the term 'lean production' was systematically related to superior productivity and quality. In terms of productivity and quality the IMVP showed Japanese vehicle assemblers to have almost a 2:1 superiority in performance over their European counterparts. Moreover, this was achieved whilst the Japanese assemblers were pursuing strategies of product proliferation, made possible by product development and life cycles that were much shorter than those of the Western car companies.

Although not reported in detail in *The Machine that Changed the World*, the IMVP empirically examined the relationship between management practices and manufacturing performance. This involved the construction of a series of management practice variables which were found to correlate with assembly plant performance, both in terms of productivity and quality (Krafcik and MacDuffie, 1989; MacDuffie, 1989, 1991).

Womack *et al.* (1990) argued that the performance superiority of Japanese producers was attributable to a system of practices covering the internal management practices of a factory, but also extending into design and development, retailing and supply chain management. The core characteristics of the lean model include:

- Team-based work organization. This involves flexible, multi-skilled operators taking a high degree of responsibility for work within their areas.
- Active shop floor problem-solving structures, central to *kaizen* or continuous improvement activities.
- Lean manufacturing operations, which force problems to be surfaced and corrected, manifested by: low inventories; the management of quality by prevention rather than detection and subsequent correction; small numbers of indirect workers and small batch, just-in-time production.
- High commitment human resource policies which encourage a sense of shared destiny within a factory.
- Close, shared destiny relations with suppliers, typically in the context of much smaller supply bases (Lamming, 1989; Nishiguchi, 1989; Sako, 1987).
- Cross-functional development teams.
- Retailing and distribution channels which provide close links to the customer and permit a make-to-order strategy to operate.

In the most widely cited account of the IMVP, Womack *et al.* (1990, p. 277) argue that:

> Lean production combines the best features of both craft production and mass production – the ability to reduce costs per unit and dramatically improve quality while at the same time providing an ever wider range of products and ever more challenging work.

The IMVP looked at approximately 80 vehicle assembly plants around the world, and the sample included a number of Japanese transplants in North America. The performance of the transplants was not far behind that of the

Japanese plants in Japan itself, which led the IMVP researchers to conclude that lean production represented a universal set of management principles which could be transferred anywhere, although the form these principles could take might vary from country to country.

> We've become convinced that the principles of lean production can be applied equally in every industry across the globe and that the conversion to lean production will have a profound effect on human society – it will truly change the world.
>
> (Womack *et al.*, 1990, p. 7)

This view has not gone unchallenged. Williams and Haslam (1992) produced a lengthy list of criticisms of *The Machine that Changed the World*, the main criticisms being that:

- The assembly plant productivity comparisons between the Japanese producers were exaggerated due to the exclusion of the variables of manufacturability and capacity utilization.
- Physical process comparisons of vehicle assembly (a relatively small part of the whole process of making cars) were overemphasized, giving an unrepresentative picture of the industry as a whole.
- Cause and effect relations were ambiguous, as was the weight assigned to individual variables.
- Companies were the units of analysis (and their management practices the explanatory factors) to the exclusion of wider context. Williams and Haslam argue that this means that the impact of features such as cyclicality of markets and capacity utilization were ignored.
- The wider social implications of the model were not fully explored (Fucini and Fucini, 1990; Kendall, 1984; Klein, 1989; Slaughter, 1987).
- Lean production is found in its purest form in the Toyota production system, and represents methods which are

> ... a historical response to Toyota's dominance of the Japanese car market which is uniquely non cyclical ...
>
> (Williams and Haslam, 1992, p. 352)

rather than a universal recipe for success.

This article presents evidence from a study into the performance of the Japanese and UK autocomponents industries. The purpose is to advance the debate about the determinants of manufacturing performance, particularly concerning the ability of lean production concepts to explain performance differentials. The data are used to address four main questions:

1. Is it possible to identify a group of 'world class' firms, which are able to simultaneously perform at high levels of productivity and quality?
2. If so, what is the magnitude of the gap between these firms and non-world class firms?
3. To what extent can any gap be explained by lean production concepts?
4. To what extent does the evidence support criticisms of the lean production model made by commentators such as Williams and Haslam?

Research design and methods

The first major decision concerned the choice of industrial sector. Two criteria guided this choice; there had to be at least three UK plants active in the sector to protect the anonymity of the participants, and the sector had to include plants which were likely to show a spread of performance. As an important objective of the study was to develop and validate measures of performance and management practice, the sample was constructed to include plants likely to show a spread of performance to test the discriminatory ability of the measures. The IMVP had demonstrated that the vehicle assemblers which showed high productivity and quality according to its measures of performance were located in Japan; it thus seemed reasonable to assume that Japanese autocomponents firms, by virtue of being within the same supply chains, could also be high performing.

Four autocomponents products were covered by the study – brake calipers, exhausts, seats and wire harnesses. These products spanned very labour intensive production processes, based largely on manual assembly (wire harnesses) to highly automated precision machining processes (brake calipers). An additional consideration in choice of products was the need for product areas in which there were at least three plants in each region – Japan and the UK. Applying this criterion to the UK autocomponents industry narrowed down the list of feasible product areas dramatically.

Methodology

The initial version of the benchmarking methodology drew on the IMVP assembly plant questionnaire, which was then refined (the document went through more than 20 drafts and progressively moved further and further away from the IMVP original). One of the major differences between this project and the IMVP was that the IMVP had looked at plants which not only *all* made cars, but which *only* made cars. Individual autocomponent plants in the same basic product area often make a multitude of products, and to complicate things further, the project spanned four products. This was tackled by developing a generic methodology, which was then customized for each product area. Throughout, the aim was to develop quantitative, objective measures that would allow precise comparisons between plants.

The choice of what to include in the methodology was partly informed by the aim of testing the lean production model, partly by other models of best practice and partly by the previous research activities of the members of the research team. The methodology was an extensive document, which covered the following areas:

Plant performance Productivity was measured at two levels: at the level of the plant, by looking at annual units of output divided by annual labour input; and at the level of the individual assembly line within the plant based on the output for a standard, non-overtime shift.

Measuring performance at the level of the individual line had the advantage of being relatively simple to do, with only adjustments for product complexity and automation being necessary. However, the performance of an individual line may clearly be unrepresentative of the performance of a whole plant. Plant level performance is a truer representation of manufacturing capability, but achieving a true like to like comparison is much more difficult as adjustments have to be made for factors such as product mix, subcontracting automation, overtime, absenteeism and holidays.

At both plant and line level, the principal measure was units of output divided by units of labour input. Labour input covered all those directly involved in the production process and their immediate line managers, namely production operators, team leaders, supervisors and materials handlers. Indirect support functions, such as maintenance, engineering and personnel, were excluded. At plant level, adjustments were made for subcontracting and product complexity. Quality was measured by the failure rate at final inspection and test.

Plant characteristics A series of features likely to impact on performance were measured, including annual volumes, value of sales and headcount.

Product characteristics Measures were taken of product variety (number of live part numbers), product age and product complexity, the last of these being assessed via a 'part count'.

Contextual measures Age and automation of equipment, capacity utilization and absenteeism were recorded.

Internal management practices Following Krafcik and MacDuffie's (1989) method, measures were taken in three areas *factory practice*, *work systems* and *human resource management*. The measures of *factory practice* were designed to capture production philosophy, by gauging how 'lean' or 'buffered' a factory was. This was gauged by the relative amount of effort going into rework and repaid vs. first-time production and also the inventory levels of specified parts. *Work systems* covered two areas; the extent to which responsibilities on the shop floor were focused within production teams, and the nature and intensity of shop floor problem-solving activity. *Human resource management* measured attributes such as training effort, the nature of problem solving, and reward schemes and employment practices.

Customer and supplier relations

The methodology gauged relationships between the components manufacturers and their customers – the car makers – and with their suppliers. Measurements were taken along a variety of dimensions, but around the core theme of the closeness of the relationships. This was measured *geographically* (travelling time between sites), *operationally* (size of buffers of parts between buyers and suppliers) and in the intensity of *communication* between the parties.

The data presented here are drawn from 18 plants, nine in the UK and nine in Japan.

The research process

An early version of the methodology was piloted at one UK plant. The research process consisted of an initial visit to each plant, usually of a half-day's duration, to explain the scope and purpose of the project, to gather background data and make an inspection of the plant. The methodology was then posted to the plants (translated into Japanese for the Japanese plants), after which members of the research team revisited each plant to collect the completed methodology and to go through the answers in detail with the respondents. The data were then analysed, and critical measures (for example performance indicators) were fed back to the plants for verification as a fair and accurate picture of plant performance. Any anomalies were corrected, the adjustment factors for subcontracting and complexity were applied, and each plant was given individual feedback against the top benchmarks for its product category.

Results

The first stage of the analysis identified the high-performing or world class plants in the sample. To qualify as world class a plant had to demonstrate outstanding performance on measures of both productivity *and* quality. Figure 1 clearly identifies a cluster of such plants. These were designated 'world class' plants. The characteristics of these plants were then compared with the others in terms of their performance, products and management practices, and examined in terms of their support (or otherwise) for the lean production model. Mini-tab's two sample t test routine was used to assess the significance of any differences between the two groups on each measure. Due to the small sample size and sometimes large variability in scores within the world class/non-world class categories, there are several instances where there are large differences between the two groups which we cannot be confident are statistically significant.

Plant performance

The performance differences between the world class and other plants in the study are shown in Table 1. The units per hour, units per m^2 and throughput time figures are standardized across product areas.

Across all the measures shown in Table 1 the world class plants showed consistently superior performance, though the differentials were greatest for the physical productivity ($p < 0.001$) and quality ($p < 0.05$) measures. The world class plants showed 43 per cent advantage on value of output per direct hour, a 38 per cent advantage on space utilization ($p < 0.05$) and an 82 per cent advantage on throughput time.

Plant and product characteristics

Table 2 shows the characteristics of the plants in terms of size, sales, product variety and a series of contextual measures such as automation, capacity utilization and age of equipment.

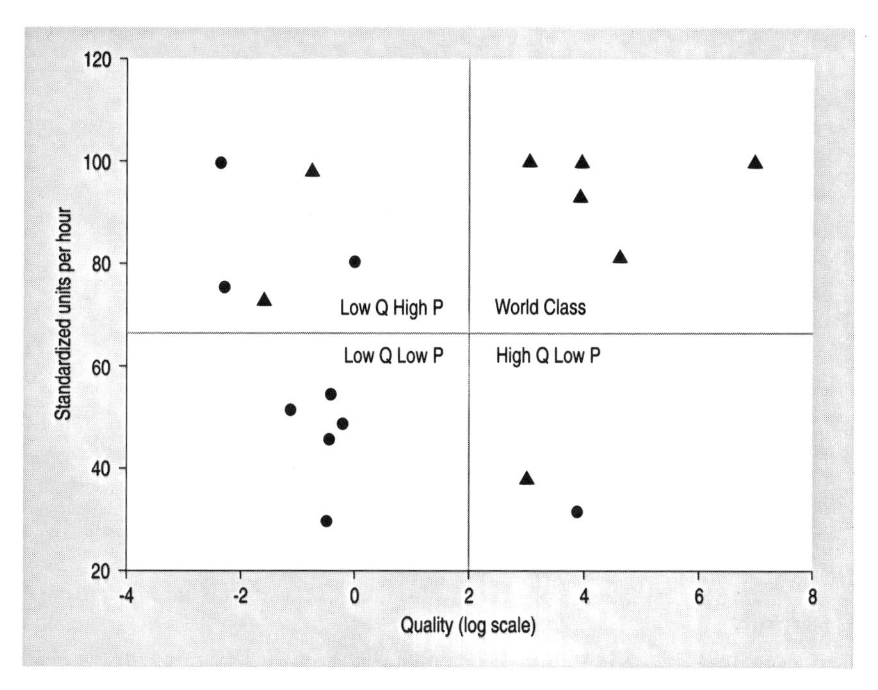

Figure 1 *Productivity vs quality*

Table 1 *Plant performance*

	World class plants	Other plants	*t* value
Units/labour hour (100 = best)	95.00	53.70	6.20**
Quality (% failures at final inspection and test)	0.03	2.50	2.60*
Value/labour hour (£)	£158.38	£111.13	2.06
Units per m^2 (100 = best)	89.40	64.40	2.68*
Throughput time (100 = best)	59.10	32.40	1.21

* = $p < 0.05$; ** = $p < 0.001$

The world class plants employ fewer people than the others (although they typically contract out a higher proportion of work than do the others), but their value of sales is double that of the other plants.

In terms of product variety, the world class plants carry more live part numbers, and are also introducing more new products – as measured by part numbers – than the lower performing plants. Of the current product ranges of the world class plants, 44 per cent had been introduced in the 12 months prior to the study,

Table 2 *Plant and product characteristics*

	World class plants	Other plants	*t* value
Number of employees	220	236	0.15
Volume of sales (in units)	2.8m	1.1m	1.24
Value of sales (in £)	£86.6m	£43.3m	1.68
Number of live part numbers	188	161	0.44
Number of products introduced in the last 12 months	82	28	1.97
Number of products introduced in the last 24 months	138	74	1.34
Percentage of operations automated	46	32	1.08
Absenteeism (%)	0.8	3.6	2.98*
Capacity utilization (%)	80	96	1.27
Age of equipment (years)	5.3	6.2	0.93

* = $p < 0.01$

and 73 per cent in the preceding 24 months. The equivalent figures for the other plants were 17 per cent and 46 per cent, respectively.

The world class plants show relatively higher levels of automation, with an average of 46 per cent of operations automated compared to 32 per cent, and age of equipment, a proxy measure for investment, is lower in the higher performing plants. Absenteeism is significantly lower in the world-class plants ($p < 0.01$).

Factory practice

The factory practice measures are important as they are indicative of the extent to which a lean or just-in-time production regime is being pursued. Table 3 shows the positions of the two groups of plants on the measures of factory practice.

Table 3 *Factory practice*

	World class plants	Other plants	*t* value
First time production (%)	98.48	95.92	1.50
In line rework and end of line rectification (%)	1.52	4.08	
Stock levels (specified parts, in hours)	10.2	76.6	4.81**
Stock turnover ratio (per annum)	93.6	34.4	3.29*

* = $p < 0.01$; ** = $p < 0.001$

The world class plants devote relatively fewer resources to rework and rectification, with rework levels just 37 per cent of those of the non-world class plants, though this difference is not statistically significant. The non-world class firms carry seven times the inventory across a range of specified parts, and show stock turnover ratios one-third of those of the world class plants; both of these differences are statistically significant at $p < 0.001$ and $p < 0.01$ respectively.

Work systems

Krafcik and MacDuffie's (1989) measures of work systems (covering issues of team-based organization, multi-skilling, flexibility, job rotation and operator's participation into problem-solving activities) discriminated significantly between the high and low performers, hence the importance given to these features in the lean production model.

The present study measured these attributes in a number of ways, including questions about the use of teams in the production areas, the concentration of responsibility for a series of specified activities within the teams, and the presence and activity rates of problem-solving structures such as suggestion schemes.

The use or non-use of teams in the production areas did not discriminate between the two groups of plants, as all plants bar one claimed to be using teams. A more sophisticated composite 'team index' also failed to discriminate between the two groups. However, measures of the dispersion of responsibility did produce some interesting patterns. These measures showed the concentrations of responsibility for 11 activities, ranging from routine maintenance to hiring decisions. Respondents were asked to indicate the relative input made by various groups – from production workers to staff specialists.

At the level of the production team the differences between the world class plants and the rest were not great; the production teams in the world class plants averaged 50 per cent of responsibility, compared to 44 per cent for those in the non-world class plants. What was striking, however, was the difference in the input of the production team leader between the two groups, which in the world class plants was double that of the rest. For most activities, the world class plants reported *less* input from the production workers than did the other plants.

This pattern, suggesting a pivotal role for the team leader, was found for most of the 11 activities – work allocation, routine maintenance (which was much more focused within the production teams in the world class plants), improvement activities, inspection and rework. The only exceptions were 'people' decisions – hiring, firing and grievance settling, which for both groups of plants were largely the prerogative of staff specialists.

Both groups of plants displayed similar formal shop floor problem-solving structures, with about the same number of problem-solving groups in each category. However, as Table 4 shows, there was more activity evident amongst the groups in the world class plants. The problem-solving groups in the world-class plants met more often, and covered a much greater proportion of the workforce – 80 per cent compared to 54 per cent.

Table 4 *Shop floor problem-solving structures*

	World class plants	Other plants	*t* value
Number of problem-solving groups	18	16.7	0.12
Number of meetings per month	3–4	2–3	0.29
Percentage of employees participating	80	54	1.52
Number of suggestions per employee	16.7	9.1	0.81
Percentage of suggestions accepted	83	52	1.97

Employee suggestions show a similar pattern. On average, the world class plants receive more employee suggestions and accept and implement a much higher proportion of these. The average reward per suggestion is lower in the world class plants; rewards for suggestions in these plants function as symbolic acknowledgements of contribution, rather than incentives in themselves. Indeed, in some plants there was an active policy of *not* rewarding suggestions, on the grounds that putting forward suggestions for improvement should be a normal part of an employee's job, and not something which was 'extra' and rewarded as such.

Human resource management

In their study of vehicle assembly plants, the IMVP researchers found that world class plants displayed 'high commitment' human resource management (HRM) practices, manifested by a high-training effort, 'progressive' employment practices and remuneration systems which, they argued, encouraged a sense of shared destiny between the employee and the organization.

The overall picture in this study was of less pronounced differences in HRM practices between the two groups than one might have expected. Training effort for production team members was almost the same for both groups of plants. In the area of reward systems, the world class plants used basic salaries and bonuses based on a combination of plant or company bonus and individual merit for production operators. Amongst the non-world class plants hourly pay based upon job classification predominated.

Customer relations

The comparisons between the world class plants and the others in terms of their customer relations are summarized in Table 5.

The conventional wisdom concerning best practice buyer–supplier relationships is of long-term relationships with relatively few 'preferred' suppliers, rather than competitive, short-term relations in which sourcing decisions are largely based on short-term price considerations.

In this study, the world class plants have about the same number of customer *companies* as the other plants, but supply to almost twice the number of customers *plants* as the non-world class plants. The dependency of the world class plants on their single biggest customer is a little higher, but the concentration of

Table 5 *Customer relations: selected comparisons*

	World class plants	Other plants	*t* value
Number of customers	3–4	3–4	–
Number of customer plants	10	6.8	0.54
Percentage of spend with major customer	81.8	74.3	0.48
Percentage of customers who run 'clubs' for their suppliers	100.0	30.0	–
Number of meetings per annum	24.0	14.7	0.75
Number of routine visits by the major customer last year	13	14	–
Hours of finished goods stock	6.2	23.1	2.02
Frequency of delivery to customers	every 2.6 hours	every 18.1 hours	1.61
Percentage variation from schedule (between delivery and one month out)	5.5	11.9	1.59

business with the major five customers is about the same. Plants in both groups have shares of their equity held by their main customer, but the levels of equity held were higher for the world class plants.

All the vehicle assemblers served by the world class plants operate clubs or associations for their suppliers. These function as forums for information sharing and exchange. In many cases these clubs had subcommittees which met independently to discuss particular issues – quality improvement, cost reduction and so on. In contrast, only 30 per cent of the customers of the non-world class plants operated supplier clubs. The clubs of which the world class plants are members are significantly more active than those of the others, meeting approximately 50 per cent more often.

The relative closeness to their customers on the part of the world class plants also extends to operational matters. The non-world class plants typically carry four times the stock of finished goods of the world class plants and deliver to their customers much less frequently – approximately once every two shifts compared to three to four times per shift. However, it is significant that the non-world class plants have to deal with almost double the variability in schedules from their customers compared to their world class counterparts – on average 12 per cent variation against schedule in the month leading up to delivery compared to 5–6 per cent. Such variability clearly makes planning difficult, and the holding of buffer stocks is one response to this problem. These figures suggest that one of the reasons for the higher performance of the world class plants may be that the *systems* within which they operate are much more in control than those of their lower performing counterparts.

Supplier relations

The findings on supplier relations are summarized in Table 6.

The world class plants have about the same number of suppliers as do the other plants, but the value of bought-in materials of the world class plants is almost double that of the others, indicating a much higher volume of business per supplier on average. The number of employees engaged in purchasing activities in both groups is almost the same; thus each member of purchasing staff looks after a much higher volume of business in the world class plants. Contrary to what one might have expected, the world class plants are relatively *less* dependent on their major suppliers than are the others.

Communication between the world class plants and their suppliers is relatively intense. All the world class plants operate clubs for their suppliers (compared to only a quarter of non-world class plants). Of those plants which do operate clubs, activity rates are much higher amongst the clubs of the world class plants.

As far as operational closeness is concerned, the pattern for supplier relationships is consistent with that of customer relationships. The world class plants experience fewer defective incoming parts (a 50:1 difference with the non-world class plants), and typically only carry one-fifth of the stock of incoming parts of the non-world class plants. The majority of the world class plants are linked to their suppliers via kanban and deliver seven times more frequently than the other plants.

Table 6 *Supplier relations: selected comparisons*

	World class plants	Other plants	*t* value
Average number of suppliers	45.0	42.2	0.23
Value of bought-in materials	£70.9m	£35.8m	1.08
Number of employees in purchasing	6.2	5.0	–
Percentage of spend with major supplier	12.8	29.7	3.16**
Percentage of plants with supplier 'clubs'	100.0	22.2	–
Percentage of suppliers who are members of the suppliers' 'club'	58.6	34.0	1.36
Number of meetings per annum	16.9	7.0	1.06
Defect levels of incoming parts (%)	0.015	0.757	2.23*
Percentage of suppliers on kanban links	56.40	7.33	2.44
Hours of normal stock of high-volume parts	14.2	66.9	4.11***
Frequency of delivery of high-volume parts	every 7 hours	every 47 hours	3.37**

* = $p < 0.05$; ** = $p < 0.01$; *** = $p < 0.001$

Discussion

The findings of this study have replicated the findings of the IMVP in some areas and produced different results in others. The discussion is structured around the four questions presented in the introduction.

First, the findings show that there are firms who can perform at high levels according to a range of performance measures, effectively challenging the idea of manufacturing trade offs (Skinner, 1974). Secondly, the results show that the 2:1 performance differential which the IMVP found between the Japanese and European car assemblies is mirrored in the relative performance of Japanese and UK autocomponents makers. This finding does not support the position of commentators such as Williams and Haslam (1992), who argue that the IMVP overestimated the performance differential between Japan and the West. It must, however, be pointed out that on closer examination the productivity comparisons of Womack *et al.* (1990) and Williams and Haslam (1992) are actually very close; using secondary data from the whole sector (including components manufacture) Williams and Haslam estimate that the Japanese producers have 41 per cent advantage over their US counterparts (132 compared to 186 hours per vehicle in 1988), whereas Womack *et al.* (1990, p. 85) estimate 16.8 and 24.9 *assembly* hours per vehicle for Japan and the US, respectively, a 48 per cent advantage.

Williams and Haslam argue that manufacturability and capacity utilization were important explanatory variables which were omitted from the IMVP analysis. The complexity adjustment used in the present study was based on a count of parts going into each unit, and so may be regarded as a reasonable, though not perfect, proxy for manufacturability. These adjustments were developed in conjunction with manufacturing people from the participating plants and were generally accepted as legitimate by those concerned. Indeed, during the plant feedback sessions, managers at one plant, which had its productivity figure reduced to compensate for its simple products, complained that their plant was being 'penalized' for its progress in design for manufacture.

The productivity figures shown in this article were corrected for product complexity, and therefore much of the 'manufacturability' effect should have been eliminated. Capacity utilization was measured, and showed that the plants designated as world class actually had, on average, *lower* levels of capacity utilization than did the lower performing plants. This does not of course refute the basic point that capacity utilization may be a major determinant of productivity, but it does not appear to be significant in this study.

The third major purpose of this article was to operationalize and test the 'lean production' model of manufacturing. By its very nature a cross-sectional study such as this cannot demonstrate cause and effect, but it does show that many of the elements of the lean model are found in conjunction with high performance according to a range of criteria. However, although most of the relationships are in the expected direction, relatively few attain statistical significance. Those that do are predominantly related to *process discipline and control*, such as inventory levels, defect rates and the like. Measures such as work organization and HRM policy do not, on the whole, significantly distinguish the high from the low performers.

Clearly a number of interpretations of this are possible. Western managers are regularly bombarded with the latest propaganda about progressive human resource policies, and current models of best practice in this area are well rehearsed. In this respect some of the UK – and a couple of the Japanese – plants who took part in the study and who appeared to be textbook plants on the basis of a visual inspection actually produced poor results according to the performance measures. Indeed, in some cases the research team were surprised at the discrepancy between this appearance and the actual hard performance measures. There are several plausible explanations for this.

The first explanation is that in the West the importance of these 'soft' factors has simply been blown out of all proportion to their real significance. Though there may be some truth in this, it is not of itself a convincing explanation, as there was no evidence that the high-performing plants did *not* use teams, or suggestion schemes or have 'progressive' HRM practices. It was simply that the lower performing plants *also* used teams and displayed rather similar HRM practices.

A second explanation is that the current findings represent a snapshot of a changing situation, in which Western companies have adopted some elements of the Japanese package, but not others. This explanation is also plausible, and suggests that UK firms have put in place Japanese-style work systems and HRM policies but that these have not yet translated into significant performance improvements, perhaps because they have not had time to do so. Alternatively, it may be that such arrangements are necessary but not sufficient conditions for high-performance manufacturing, and that there are further principles which must be adopted. The findings of this study suggest that process discipline and control figure highly amongst such principles.

A third explanation is that the quantitative measures used in this study were picking up *structures* which are relatively simple to measure (and probably to implement) but which say little about the underlying *processes* at work. Thus Japanese and UK plants may exhibit similar structures, but cultural differences may mean that the outcomes are quite different.

Finally, what of the factors which the critics claim have been overlooked in previous discussions of the lean production concept? The higher performing firms actually showed lower levels of capacity utilization than the others, a testament to the downturn in the Japanese economy which was occurring at the time the research was conducted. Despite this, the performance differential was substantial. Manufacturability has been discussed previously, and within the constraints of the method used, did not eliminate the gap between high and low performers. Demand stability, and environmental uncertainty more generally, may however be important as the most significant indicators of leanness – inventory levels – are heavily driven by *uncertainty* in one form or another.

References

Feigenbaum, A.V. (1983) *Total Quality Control*. McGraw Hill, New York.

Fucini, J.J. and Fucini, S. (1990) *Working for the Japanese*. Free Press, New York.

Goldratt and Cox (1984) [no other details given]

Kendall, W. (1984) 'Why Japanese factories work', *Management Today*, January, pp. 72–75.

Klein, J.A. (1989) 'The human costs of manufacturing reform', *Harvard Business Review*, March–April, pp. 60–66.

Krafcik, J.F. and MacDuffie, J.P. (1989) *Explaining High Performance Manufacturing: the International Automotive Assembly Plant Study*. Paper presented to the IMVP International Policy Forum, Pierre Marques, Acapulco, 7–10 May.

Lamming, R. (1989) *The International Automotive Components Industry: The Next 'Best Practice' for Suppliers*. Paper presented to the IMVP International Policy Forum, Pierre Marques, Acapulco, 7–10 May.

MacDuffie, J.P. (1989) *World Wide Trends in Production System Management: Work Systems, Factory Practice and Human Resource Management*. Paper presented to the IMVP International Policy Forum, Pierre Marques, Acapulco, 7–10 May.

MacDuffie, J.P. (1991) *Beyond Mass Production: Flexible Production Systems and Manufacturing Performance in the World Auto Industry*. PhD thesis, MIT.

Nishiguchi, T. (1989) *Is JIT Really JIT*? Paper presented to the IMVP International Policy Forum, Pierre Marques, Acapulco, 7–10 May.

Parnaby, J. (1987a) *A Systems Engineering Approach to Fundamental Change in Manufacturing*. Paper presented to the 9th Industrial Engineering Managers Conference, New Orleans, 9–11 March.

Parnaby, J. (1987b) 'Competitiveness via total quality of performance', *Progress in Rubber and Plastics Technology*, Vol. 3, pp. 42–50.

Parnaby, J. (1987c) *Practical Just-in-Time – Inside and Outside the Factory*. Paper presented to the Fifth Financial Times Manufacturing Forum, London, 6–7 May.

Sako, M. (1987) *Buyer-Supplier Relationships in Britain: A Case of Japanization*? Paper presented to the Conference on the Japanization of British Industry, Cardiff Business School, 17–18 September.

Schonberger, R. (1982) *Japanese Manufacturing Techniques*. Free Press, New York.

Schonberger, R. (1986) *World Class Manufacturing*. Free Press, New York.

Skinner, W. (1974) 'The focused factory', *Harvard Business Review*, May–June, pp. 113–121.

Slaughter, J. (1987) *The Team Concept in the US Auto Industry*. Paper presented to the Conference on the Japanization of British Industry, Cardiff Business School, 17–18 September.

Williams, K. and Haslam, C. (1992) 'Against lean production', *Economy and Society*, Vol. 21, pp. 321–354.

Womack, J.P., Jones, D.T. and Roos, D. (1990) *The Machine that Changed the World: The Triumph of Lean Production*. Rawson Macmillan, New York.

10
Outcome-related performance indicators and organizational control in the public sector*[1]

Peter Smith

Summary

There is increased interest in the widespread dissemination of outcome performance data to secure enhanced strategic control of public sector organizations. This article adumbrates the rationale for such schemes, and outlines the potential distortions induced by excessive reliance on outcome-related performance indicators, inferred from experience in the management control and Soviet literature. The article gives an outline of the performance review process in the United Kingdom National Health Service, and presents the results of a case study of the impact of the publication of outcome performance data in the maternity services. The research detected many of the expected distortions arising from reliance on performance indicator schemes, and concludes that they may have significant dysfunctional consequences. The article does not however advocate the abandonment of performance audit in the public sector. Instead, it warns that great attention should be given to the managerial incentives implicit in any strategic control scheme, and that the style with which the scheme is applied will have important bearings on its effectiveness.

Introduction

Public sector and not-for-profit[2] enterprises have always posed particular problems of organizational control not found in the private sector. Amongst the most resistant to solution are:

The difficulty of securing a consensus as to what the output and objectives of such organizations should be.

The difficulty of measuring such output and the eventual outcome of public sector intervention.

The difficulty of interpreting any output and outcome measures that can be developed.

The difficulty of persuading citizens to take any interest in performance measures or their interpretation.

*This article was first published in *British Journal of Management*, Vol. 4, pp. 135–151, 1993.

In spite of these difficulties, however, interest in the use of performance indicators in public sector management is becoming widespread throughout Europe (FEE, 1991). In particular, the measurement of the outcome of public sector activity is attracting increased political attention in the United Kingdom. In 1991, the three main political parties published 'Citizen's Charters' which proposed, in one form or another, a significant increase in the quantity of outcome-related performance data to be disseminated to citizens and their representatives (Labour Party, 1991; Liberal Democrats, 1991; UK Government, 1991). Although differing in underlying philosophy all three were put forward in the belief that increased provision of information about outcome will lead to improved public services. In the event, the Conservative Party won the 1992 election, and their proposals are therefore being implemented.

Performance indicator (PI) initiatives in the United Kingdom have had a variety of explicit objectives, most of which relate in one form or another [to] the enhancement of the control of the public sector organization (Smith, 1990). The purpose of this article is to set out the rationale for PI schemes in the public sector; to summarize the accumulated wisdom of the literature on outcome-related performance measurement in the private sector; and to assess its relevance to the public sector. The discussion is illustrated with the results of a field study which sought to identify the effects of a specific outcome-related performance indicator scheme on managers in the UK maternity services. The next section introduces the context within which public sector performance indicators have been developed; Section 2 describes the study of maternity service managers; Section 3 presents the results of the study in the light of predictions from the private sector literature; and the final section offers some concluding comments.

1 Public sector performance indicators

It is usual to consider control in two senses: internal to the organization; and external. The provision of increased information for the purposes of internal control in public sector services has been treated at length in the literature (see Ramanathan, 1982; Anthony and Young, 1984). In the UK, the original National Health Service (NHS) PI scheme was clearly seen as an internal control scheme, ostensibly aimed at managers within the NHS, to help them '... assess the efficiency of the service for which they are responsible' (Department of Health and Social Security, 1985). The scheme's emphasis was on measures of managerial process rather than outcome, and was therefore of limited interest to ordinary citizens. In practice, as Carter (1989) argues, the principal objective was to enable the central government to secure closer control of devolved management teams, and performance indicators have formed the cornerstone of the NHS system of performance review (Trumpington, 1987).

Rather less attention has been paid in the literature to the second, external use of PIs, as adumbrated in the Citizen's Charter (Pollitt, 1988). Such use is intended to enhance the accountability of devolved public sector organizations to external interested parties: what Stewart (1984) has termed programme accountability. It is for this purpose that outcome-related performance indicators (ORPIs) are most important. The external parties who might be interested in such data include service users, the electorate, taxpayers, the central government, and independent auditors acting on behalf of one or more of these constituencies. In this context, the role of the ORPIs is to furnish external users with information about the outcome of the organization's activities so that they can make informed judgements about the organisation's performance, and informed choices about future activity. This use of ORPIs is therefore servicing the top (political) level of organizational control in the hierarchy of public sector organizational control described by Hofstede (1981).

An early attempt in the UK to address the issue of external accountability was the first Thatcher Government's 'Comparative Statistics' initiative for local government (Department of the Environment, 1981). Under the terms of this initiative, each local government was required to publish in its annual report about 50 PIs. The local government was to compare its level of performance on these indicators with that of a number of other 'similar' local governments, selected by the local government itself. The stated objectives of the scheme were to 'give [local taxpayers] clear information about local government's activities; to make it easier for electors, [taxpayers] and other interested parties to make comparisons of and judgements on the performance of their authorities; and to help [elected representatives] form judgements about the performance of their own authority' (DOE, 1981). In practice, hardly any of the PIs related to outcome, and little notice was taken of the statistics (Butterworth *et al.*, 1989). However, under the terms of the Citizen's Charter, a greatly expanded scheme is envisaged for local government, and outcome issues will be addressed explicitly (Audit Commission, 1992).

The advocates of recent PI initiatives in the United Kingdom would argue that such ORPI schemes are addressing what Anthony and Young (1984, p. 649) consider to be the most important stimulus to improve management control in non-profit organizations: 'More active interest in the effective and efficient functioning of the organization by its governing board.' By improving citizens' awareness of the performance of local services, the ORPI schemes – it might be claimed – will increase the political pressure placed on elected and appointed representatives on governing boards, thereby enhancing both managerial and allocative efficiency in the public sector. The increased sensitivity of representatives to popular preferences will then permeate the organization, leading to many of the subsidiary stimuli to improved managerial control listed by Anthony and Young. In promoting accountability to stakeholders, therefore, ORPI schemes are envisaged as fulfilling the role adopted by financial reporting in the corporate sector. Moreover, it is likely that – as in the corporate sector – the design of any external reporting scheme will have a profound impact on internal control mechanisms, as managers are made sensitive to the indicators with which elected representatives are held to account.

However, as Smith (1990) argues, the analogy with corporate financial reporting is unsatisfactory, because public sector PI schemes have to service a considerably more complex pattern of accountability than the corporate financial statement. In discussing this problem, it is helpful to distinguish between output and input accountability. So far as outputs are concerned, in competitive (private sector) product markets, it is usually assumed that consumers can observe directly the merits of competing goods, or at least are prepared to pay for relevant information from informed intermediaries. Private sector accounting has therefore traditionally paid little attention to outputs (although the increased interest in social responsibility accounting may be signalling a change). In contrast, most public services are effective local monopolies, so citizens cannot directly experience services provided in different localities. In any case, many citizens may not directly experience the services within their own jurisdiction, even though they value such services. This is particularly true of pure public goods, such as police and fire services. One role of ORPIs is therefore to act as a proxy for direct experience of services provided by alternative jurisdictions. Baroness Trumpington (1987) claims that various notions of equity are the principal concern with this use of PIs.

In addition, through taxation, most citizens contribute to the finances of public services, and it can be presumed that they would therefore wish to see such finances used well. PI systems are one means of communicating the use being made of tax revenues and other inputs by public sector organizations. Clearly, in making such judgements, it is necessary to have access to measures of outcomes as well as measures of inputs. In this sense the analogy between PI schemes and the external financial reporting undertaken by private sector enterprises is more accurate, as the concern is more with efficiency and effectiveness than with equity. The use of PIs for input accountability is based on the familiar principal agent model of management (Baiman, 1990). However, although the management of the public sector organization is clearly the agent, identification of the principal is less straightforward. Unlike their counterparts in private sector corporations, public sector managers are responsible to varying degrees to a variety of constituencies, including elected representatives (local and national); the central government; taxpayers (local and national); and the users and potential users of their services. In addressing the external accountability of public sector organizations, therefore, it is important to note the potential complexity of lines of accountability.

Thus, by seeking to make principals more informed about the behaviour of their agents, PI initiatives are intended to secure a more efficient and equitable allocation of resources within the economy. For example, if a local government electorate is given more information about the activity of its local government, then it could be argued that it is able to make more informed decisions at the ballot box about the total level of activity to be adopted by the local government, and about the mix of activities provided. In addition, on the assumption that well-informed electors will not tolerate manifestly inefficient management teams, it can be argued that PI systems will also encourage managerial efficiency in the use of resources.

It is important to note, however, that most public sector organizations are subject to a very imperfect external control mechanism. In private sector product (or output) markets, the consumer has available the obvious and sensitive sanction of taking custom elsewhere. In financial (input) markets the investor has the sanction of selling securities if he or she is unhappy with managerial performance. In contrast, a system of (at best) annual elections gives the individual voter very little incentive to scrutinize public sector performance, or to pay others to do so on his or her behalf.

In any case, even if individual electors had an incentive to scrutinize performance data, they would be likely to encounter problems interpreting them. When comparing reported ORPI measures, the user may have to disentangle at least four cases of variability: different objectives being pursued by the organizations; different social and economic environments; different accounting methods; and different levels of managerial efficiency. When viewed in conjunction with the difficulties posed by the incompleteness of coverage and the bias towards measurable aspects of performance likely to be exhibited by most ORPI systems, it is clear that – even if the will exists – the user faces a formidable task if he or she is to develop a good understanding of the performance of the organization.

The external scrutiny of public sector performance therefore displays the characteristics of a prisoner's dilemma. The costs of scrutinizing the data vastly exceed the potential benefits for the individual voter, even though the community as a whole might benefit from such scrutiny. This analysis gives rise to the argument for an expert intermediary acting on behalf of the community. In the United Kingdom, two organizations fulfil this role. The National Audit Office scrutinizes the use of central government tax revenues, and reports to the national government. The Audit Commission was set up in 1982 to examine and promote the economy, efficiency and effectiveness of local government in England and Wales (United Kingdom Government, 1982). Its terms of reference have since been extended to include the National Health Service (UK Government, 1989).

The advocates of most ORPI systems appear implicitly (though rarely explicitly) to have in mind Hofstede's cybernetic model of organizational control, from which Figure 1 is taken (Hofstede, 1981). The first role of ORPIs is to service arrow a, and to shape individuals' perceptions of the outcome of public sector activity. Interpretation of performance measures (arrow b) helps those individuals to turn these perceptions into political actions, such as voting or other influential political activity. The political system (arrow c) translates individual actions into organizational choices (this process is of course highly complex and poorly understood). Note that, in informing the internal control mechanism, ORPIs will probably also play some direct part in forming organizational policies, as well as the indirect role of informing political choice. Finally – through its chosen programme – the organization changes the environment (arrow d) and the process continues. From a cybernetic perspective, therefore, an ORPI system should enhance the political control of the public sector by offering individual citizens timely and meaningful feedback on the effect of public sector activity, and should influence the design of the organization's internal control system. A more extensive description of the cybernetic view of the political process is given by Dunsire (1981).

However, as Hofstede and many others have pointed out, it is not at all clear that this simple cybernetic model is appropriate to high level, political control. We have already noted potential shortcomings in the ability of citizens to exercise sanctions in response to reported performance, and consequent difficulties in persuading citizens to take an interest in ORPIs. In addition, the management control literature is replete with reports of the distorting and potentially dysfunc-

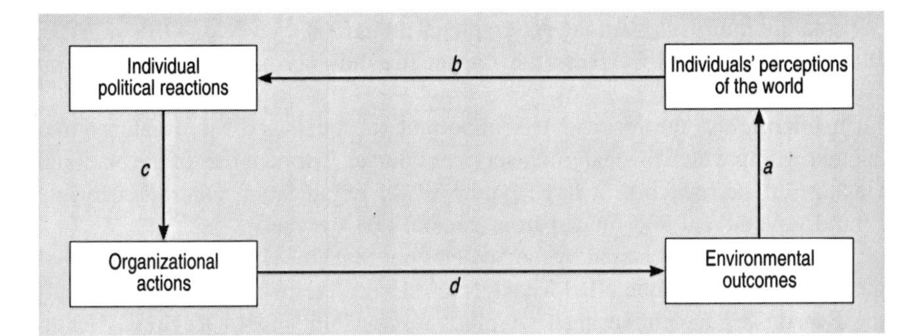

Figure 1 *The cybernetic model of organizational choice (Hofstede, 1981 after March and Olsen, 1976)*

tional consequences of excessive reliance on performance measures to secure organizational control (Merchant, 1990).

Underlying the critiques of performance measurement is the notion that performance data are not a neutral reporting device. To a greater or lesser extent, most of the data can be controlled by operational managers. Therefore, if personal rewards are dependent to any significant extent on reported performance, it is highly likely that any ORPI scheme will affect managers' behaviour. Of course, the architects of such schemes hope for just such an effect, in the sense that managers will be encouraged to increase efficiency and effectiveness. However, as we shall show, it is also plausible to suggest that unintended and possibly dysfunctional responses might be induced by excessive reliance on ORPIs to secure managerial control.

Moreover, to date most of the PI systems introduced in the United Kingdom have been imposed by central government with little consultation. As Jones (1986) notes, the predisposition amongst managers to indulge in dysfunctional behaviour is likely to be heightened if they perceive that a control mechanism is being imposed on them against their will. This increases the possibility that any private gains to be made from distorting behaviour will be exploited by at least some managers. Evidence from the private sector indicates that the style with which control schemes are implemented may have a profound impact on their effectiveness (Hopwood, 1972; Otley, 1978; Kenis, 1979.)

2 The maternity services study

The purpose of this study was to explore the managerial impact of a mature ORPI which enjoys widespread acceptance as a reasonable indicator of outcome. Few such indicators exist. However, almost uniquely in the health sector, there is a range of outcome measures in the maternity services relating to perinatal and neonatal mortality. These indicators have been published for many years, and even form the basis (albeit imperfect) for international comparison. Moreover, probably because of the availability of such outcome measures, the National Audit Office reported to Parliament in 1990 an assessment of the effectiveness of UK maternity services in which a high profile was given to large variations in perinatal mortality rates among geographical areas (National Audit Office, 1990). We therefore chose to explore the impact that this performance audit had on service managers.

In interpreting the results, it is important to understand the organizational context within which the maternity services operate. They are part of the National Health Service, which is a large public sector organization controlled by the central government and funded from general tax revenues.

A Policy Board is chaired by the Secretary of State for Health, and operational matters are vested in the NHS Management Executive, which is accountable to the Board. The Executive itself devolves responsibility to 14 Regional Health Authorities (RHAs), which in turn delegate operational matters to 190 District Health Authorities (DHAs). The DHAs are the enterprises primarily responsible for organizing the services – including maternity services – delivered to patients. Maternity services are either provided directly by DHAs, or are purchased from self-governing NHS Trusts. The maternity services manager is therefore responsible to the Chief Executive of the DHA, either through direct line of command, or through the terms of the contract negotiated between DHA and Trust (UK Government, 1989).

Thus the NHS is a highly centralized organization, posing considerable problems of control and accountability. There is some indirect local accountability brought about by local representation on DHA and RHA Boards, and by local Community Health Councils, which exert political pressure on behalf of patients. However, there is no direct democratic accountability at local level. The principal mechanism for securing control within the NHS is a system of performance review between the various tiers described above, with PIs playing an important role; and a system of contracts between purchasers and providers, in which PIs also play a prominent role.

The purpose of the National Audit Office document was to report to Parliament on the use being made of tax revenues by the NHS. The House of Commons Public Accounts Committee (PAC) received the report, and summoned the Chief Executive of the NHS to reply to the issues raised. The PAC then produced its own assessment of the effectiveness of the services (Committee of Public Accounts, 1990). Finally, the Government responded to the points raised by the PAC (Treasury, 1990). From the point of view of this study, the most interesting aspect of this process was that the National Audit Office report chose to focus on a single ORPI – the perinatal mortality rate (PMR) – as its principal analytic tool. Rates for England were compared with those of other European countries, and variations between DHAs within Great Britain were discussed. In particular, the report highlighted nine DHAs exhibiting particularly high perinatal mortality rates, and eight DHAs with particularly low rates. Thus some DHAs and their maternity services were exposed to exceptional public scrutiny by the report.

The perinatal mortality rate is defined as the ratio of stillbirths and neonatal deaths within seven days of birth to the total number of stillbirths and live births. It is usually multiplied by 1000. Because of small numbers, annual rates at the level of DHA are subject to considerable stochastic variability, so the National Audit Office presented three year averages. The local rates varied between 5.1 in

Huntingdon and 13.5 in Bradford. The determinants of a PMR are complex and only imperfectly understood (see Chalmers *et al.*, 1989, for a full discussion). One of the principal determinants of adverse outcome is the proportion of low weight births in an area. Low birth weight is in turn affected by socio-economic considerations, which also affect outcome independently of birth weight. Intervention by the health services moderates the impact of these considerations, albeit in a very poorly understood fashion. Thus there is considerable room for debate over the causes of a particular level of PMR. DHAs with high rates may nevertheless be providing effective care, given adverse social circumstances. Conversely, areas with a favourable socio-economic environment may achieve low rates in spite of poor services. There is therefore a need to examine with some care the context within which a particular PMR is achieved.

The evidence taken by the PAC from the NHS Chief Executive are produced verbatim in the PAC report, and shed considerable light on the pattern of accountability and control in the NHS. Throughout the evidence, the NHS Chief Executive makes it plain that the review process is principally concerned with pinpointing outlying performance, both in terms of PMR and other process indicators, such as resource provision. 'We do expect regions either through a formal process of annual review or routinely in the management process ... to use the information that is available. We have a very comprehensive list of nearly 60 indicators' (PAC, minutes of evidence, para 3203).

When asked what action would be taken if progress towards rectifying poor performance was inadequate, the Chief Executive replied that recalcitrant areas would be given 'a hard time' (para 3206), although when pressed he was unable to explain what this would amount to. Subsequently, however, his evidence suggests that individual managers are made accountable for poor performance (PAC, paras 3275 to 3281), with the implication that their remuneration and indeed job prospects were to some extent dependent on securing satisfactory PIs.

This study focuses on the impact that such exposure had on the behaviour of maternity units in some of the outliers identified by the National Audit Office. Accordingly, interviews were sought with the directors of maternity services in the five DHAs described as having the highest perinatal mortality rates, and in the five DHAs with the lowest rates. It proved possible to identify the relevant manager in all districts. However, in three (two with high PMR, one with low) the post was vacant, so meetings were arranged with acting managers. Of all the remaining seven, only three (two with high PMR, one with low) had been in post at the time of publication of the National Audit Office report, about two years before the interviews took place. (This high level of turnover amongst managerial staff is not uncommon in the NHS.) Thus the study reflects the perceptions of individual managers, all of whom work in organizations which have been singled out for comment by an ORPI scheme, but who will, as individuals, have been affected by the scheme in different ways. The work reported here therefore adopts a qualitative case study approach, supplemented by material from official documentation. The discussion is conducted at a general level as there is a need to preserve anonymity of respondents.

3 The impact of performance measurement

The management control and Soviet literature which documents the potentially distorting effects of control systems is extensive (Birnberg *et al.*, 1983; Briers and Hirst, 1990; Nove, 1980). It is however possible to infer at least seven ways in which excessive use of ORPIs might influence public sector managerial behaviour. In particular, it might encourage the following:

(a) Tunnel vision: Concentration on areas included in the ORPI scheme, to the exclusion of other important areas.

(b) Suboptimization: The pursuit by managers of their own narrow objectives, at the expense of strategic coordination.

(c) Myopia: Concentration on short-term issues, to the exclusion of long-term criteria, which may only show up in ORPIs in many years' time.

(d) Convergence: An emphasis on not being exposed as an outliner on any ORPI, rather than a desire to be outstanding.

(e) Ossification: A disinclination to experiment with new and innovative methods.

(f) Gaming: Altering behaviour so as to obtain strategic advantage.

(g) Misrepresentation: Including 'creative' accounting and fraud.

These distorting and potentially dysfunctional effects are now considered in turn within the context of the UK maternity services.

3.1 Tunnel vision

Clearly no package can comprehensively cover the entire domain of a public sector organization's activity. Indeed, even if such a package could be envisaged now, it might not be adequate in the future. It is in any case usually necessary to monitor unintended side-effects of new programmes. There is no guarantee that such side-effects will be noted by an existing PI system, and so there is a constant need to keep the domain covered by the PI system under review (Scriven, 1973).

In addition, it is intrinsic to the non-trading public sector that inputs and processes are more readily measured than outcomes. Thus most PI packages abound in cost data, resource provision data, measures of administrative processes, and intermediate measures of output, such as numbers of clients processed. Most notably lacking are many measures of the effectiveness of intervention, such as measures of quality of outcome in health services, or educational attainment in the education sector. There have of course been developed proxies for outcome, such as quality-adjusted life years – QALYs – in health care (Gudex and Kind, 1988) or examination attainment levels in education (Department of Education and Science, 1983, 1984). However, such proxies are usually the subject of ferocious debate, and rarely enjoy the universal acceptance given to input data, such as costs. As a consequence, many measures of outcome used in PI schemes are likely to be highly imperfect indicators of effectiveness, the relevance of which is easily challenged by public sector insiders. If managers are encouraged to pay excessive attention to PI schemes, they may be tempted to focus on the more easily managed aspects of activity, such as inputs and procedures, rather than the enhancement of effectiveness in terms of outcome, as measured by contentious ORPIs.

In this study it was generally accepted by all managers that the minimization of perinatal mortality, and its attendant trauma and grief, was one of the most important objectives of maternity services. In all units there was a regular meeting to review all perinatal deaths in some detail, and there was intense awareness of local performance. However, the managers also agreed that there were other legitimate objectives of maternity services in addition to the minimization of the PMR. The two most regularly cited related to the minimization of handicapped survival amongst infants, and the enhancement of the entire experience of pregnancy and childbirth for healthy mothers. Definition of these two objectives is very complex, no systematic attempt has been made to measure their achievement, and certainly no relevant PIs currently exist.

There were however differences in judgements as to the extent to which emphasis on PMRs distorted behaviour. Four of the managers (three from high PMR areas) appeared to take little notice of outcome, concentrating instead on what they considered to be an optimal process of service delivery. Such managers tended to make few references to the socio-economic context within which they were working, and saw their job principally as one of enabling professional doctors and midwives to deliver high standards of care to individual mothers and infants. When pressed, they appeared implicitly to take the view that the strategies required to minimize the PMR would also serve any other conceivable objectives of the maternity services.

Two managers, both from low PMR areas, agreed that there were multiple objectives, but claimed that they had adopted strategies that recognized all these objectives, even if this ran the risk of securing a slightly higher PMR than was technically feasible.

The remaining four managers argued that the emphasis on the PMR did indeed affect their services. They recognized that other objectives exist, but felt constrained by the performance review process to concentrate on strategies to minimize their PMR. The principal distortion cited was the provision of hospital resources at the expense of community ante-natal services. Three of these managers had been set explicit PMR targets.

Perinatal mortality caused by shortcomings in resources at the time of delivery is readily traced. It is much more difficult to trace a link between perinatal mortality and inadequate antenatal care, even if a strong such link exists, because of the much less clearly understood nature of the causal link.[3] As a result, some of the managers considered that excessive reliance on the ORPI will tend to distort resources provision towards services where the causal link with the ORPI was most direct and obvious, even if there were more effective ways of securing reductions in the PMR. The nature of this ORPI therefore tends to exacerbate the bias towards provision of hospital resources, particularly those devoted to perinatal care.

A noteworthy endorsement of the view that strategies to minimize PMR might be in conflict with strategies to secure other objectives can be found in an influential report on maternity health services produced by the House of

Commons Health Committee, which claims that 'the time has come for a shift of emphasis in the development of maternity services which gives due weight to other criteria for success additional to the reduction of perinatal mortality' (Health Committee, 1992). The report goes on to conclude that 'the majority of maternity care should be community based'.

3.2 Suboptimization

Most commentators consider that it is the multidimensional nature of organizational goals that most obviously distinguishes public sector enterprises from their private sector counterparts. The unifying concepts of financial returns and profit do not exist for most of the non-trading public sector. The problem of monitoring performance is therefore much more complex. In the profit-seeking firm, aggregation into one-dimensional measures of benefits (such as revenues) is commonplace. No such aggregation is possible in the public sector. Moreover, the boundaries of the organization's sphere of responsibility, and interactions with other public sector programmes, are far less clear than in most private sector enterprises. There is a potentially enormous environment to be monitored if all the consequences of public sector intervention are to be noted. An ORPI scheme may have to be correspondingly large if it is to note all the effects of an organization's intervention.

In addition, many of the programmes undertaken by public organizations yield benefits which contribute to a wide range of society's goals, and not just those being addressed by the programme manager. Outcome, as measured by ORPIs, may therefore be the result of an interaction between the activities of a number of diverse programmes. However, even if a comprehensive set of ORPIs could be developed, there is no guarantee that the individual managers will take account of the impact of their actions beyond the areas of their direct responsibility, as reflected in their performance targets. The lack of congruence between personal incentives and global objectives gives rise to the phenomenon which has become known as suboptimization. The United Kingdom public sector has operated hitherto with a remarkable shortage of explicit goals, and has relied for its efficiency on what is assumed to be a high degree of congruence between the implicit goals of the organization and those of its workers. Thus the model of control has traditionally been very loose. The management by numbers implicit in PI initiatives risks a divergence of the two sets of goals. Kerr (1975) gives a fuller discussion.

In the maternity services, there is a considerable professional concern, mentioned in the PAC report, that increased survival rates amongst very low birth weight babies may be resulting in an increase in the prevalence of adverse long-term outcomes, such as physical handicaps, learning difficulties and behavioural problems. As a result, there have been calls for comprehensive audit of the long-term morbidity patterns amongst surviving babies (Committee of Public Accounts, 1990, p. 26). This concern illustrates the danger of holding maternity service managers to account on a narrow measure of outcome, when the results of their policies may have profound implications for other parts of the NHS (as well as – more generally – society as a whole).

Many of the putative links between maternity service performance and eventual outcome are too speculative to have been cause for concern amongst the managers interviewed, although several mentioned the need for long-term research in this area. However, in three units the study did identify tensions between the maternity services and paediatric units, the services which encounter the most immediate consequences of adverse outcome amongst the newborn. The main source of friction was the extent to which paediatric services were being asked to devote resources to neonatal care which could be construed as being the responsibility of the maternity units. This type of demarcation problem is likely to become increasingly important as devolved budgeting becomes universal in the NHS.

It is difficult to judge the extent to which an emphasis on PMRs will tend to exacerbate this problem. Several managers mentioned that, in order to reduce the PMR, clinicians might choose to advise termination of high risk pregnancies, with implications for other parts of the NHS, such as gynaecological, fertility and counselling services. Alternatively, clinicians might seek to devote considerable resources to keeping very sick babies alive, even if there are only very slim prospects of good quality survival. The latter strategy might have serious consequences for paediatric services, as well as the wider public sector, perhaps responsible for caring for the infant, and supporting the parents.

None of the managers admitted that such practices might occur in their own units. However, the interviews indicated that there was an awareness of the potential for suboptimization, even when the performance indicator is not susceptible to substantial manipulation, and where there is a consensus that the ORPI is a good measure of at least part of the service's output.

3.3 Myopia

Most performance measurement schemes focus on short-term considerations, and therefore militate against investment which only brings rewards in the long run. The costs of long-term projects (such as research and development) are incurred immediately, while the benefits are uncertain, both in magnitude and timing. Admittedly there is a theoretical framework – discounted cash flow – which could be used to evaluate long-term projects for which financial benefits can be estimated. However, the data required for such computations are usually highly speculative, and investment in long-term projects must to some extent be an act of faith, the benefits of which no performance measurement scheme can capture.

It is in the nature of many public sector programmes, such as health and education services, that much activity yields returns only after many years, and that it is exceedingly difficult to quantify the benefits even after the event. The problem of incorporating long-term benefits of activity is therefore particularly acute, and it is likely to be very difficult to devise schemes that attach proper weight to projects with distant time horizons. In addition, there is no generally accepted framework such as discounted cash flow with which to evaluate deferred non-pecuniary benefits. Therefore, if managers' remuneration and employment prospects are materially influenced by defective ORPI schemes, either directly or indirectly, it will hardly be surprising if they give projects with long time horizons low priority.

Moreover, current ORPIs are almost certain to reflect investment in projects undertaken many years previously, and by previous management teams. Current ORPIs may therefore be giving a distorted picture of the effectiveness of current management. Indeed, given the short time for which many public sector managers remain in post relative to the time horizon of the investment programmes for which they are responsible, the problem of securing optimal commitment to such programmes would appear to be considerable, and certainly beyond the scope of any conceivable PI scheme. Hitherto, in order to secure long-term objectives, the UK public sector has usually relied on the measurement of *processes* relating to long-term issues (such as vaccination rates) and managers' personal commitment to the long-term effectiveness of their service.

Managerial myopia arises therefore because of lack of congruence between the time horizon of the manager and the time horizon of the projects for which he or she is responsible. Clearly no cross-sectional PI scheme can perfectly detect long-term effects of managerial choices. As a result, if long-term issues are considered important, then a PI scheme must focus on processes dedicated to long-term objectives rather than outcomes.

The discussion relating to handicapped survival of infants has already indicated the possibility of long-term objectives being compromised by over-zealous use of a limited set of ORPIs. There was clear evidence in four of the units visited that managers believed that ante-natal clinics and parentcraft classes, particularly at non-hospital sites, were being given inadequate priority, a shortcoming for which the emphasis on short-term perinatal mortality was partially to blame. In these areas, managers believed that the lack of attention to such community activity could lead to an increase in perinatal complications, and more general adverse development of children after birth. However, their inability to produce evidence of the effectiveness of such activity made it vulnerable in the budgetary process.

3.4 Convergence

There rarely exist objective 'engineering' benchmarks against which public service performance can be measured. Thus, in coming to an informed judgement on performance, the performance auditor is forced to compare the organization of interest with that of other organizations offering similar services and operating in the same sort of environment (see Smith, 1990 for a full discussion). The ORPIs of 'competing' organizations are therefore being used to form an idea about production functions in the service being studied. However there will inevitably be limited knowledge concerning the form of the production function or the variables or relevance to it. As a result, the performance auditor is likely to have to make some crude judgements. In particular, as Williams (1985) explains, it is unlikely that the auditor will seek to model the subtle relationships linking many ORPIs.

It is, for example, most instructive to examine the expert system developed by the UK Government to scrutinize the National Health Service PI set (Bowen and Payling, 1987). This system seeks to automate the performance review process amongst hospitals and health authorities, and in doing so concentrates on extreme performance. Only if an organization is exposed as an outlier on one of the 'first line' indicators is further analysis undertaken, entailing more detailed scrutiny of 'second line' indicators. This screening philosophy is a form of the management by exception. Its use has the effect of encouraging action to avoid extreme performance amongst organizations wishing to escape such detailed scrutiny. As a result, as ORPIs are given a higher profile, one would expect to see convergence in reported ORPI numbers. Such convergence could of course be secured either by real changes in behaviour, or by accounting changes, or by falsification. Salmon (1987) notes that the putative convergence process is the result of quasi-competition between jurisdictions.

The convergence phenomenon described above is likely to obtain in both profit-making and not-for-profit organizations. There is however a further incentive for convergence peculiar to the public sector. This derives from the desire to secure equity between jurisdictions. A for-profit organization that finds itself performing poorly on a particular profit-related PI has the option of ceasing operations in the relevant activity. A public sector organization has no such freedom. It must continue operations, and seek to overcome the obstacles to satisfactory performance.

Indeed, it is intrinsic to a high profile ORPI scheme that an apparently poorly performing public sector body should come under pressure from local politicians, media, user representatives and other parties to improve performance, even if local environmental circumstances militate against such improvement. Jurisdictions under pressure to improve may therefore seek to rectify matters by reorganizing or devoting extra resources to the service under scrutiny. To do so they may have to divert resources from programmes on which they are performing satisfactorily. This process is a form of negative feedback (Forrester, 1968), and because it is the result of a general (but poorly understood) political process, Smith (1992) has called it negative political feedback.[4]

The questioning of the NHS Chief Executive by the PAC indicates great concern at the variations in PMRs within the country, and the Committee Chair chose to focus on these wide variations. It never becomes clear whether his concern is with the inequity implied by the variations between areas or any inefficiency that might be implied. However, the questioning is strong evidence of the pressures that exist within the NHS to avoid especially poor performance (in terms of outcome) as a result of the review process. The architects of the control system presumably hope that the pseudo-competition implied by exposure of poor performers will lead to a general raising of standards as all managers strive to avoid the detailed scrutiny likely to arise if they report outlying performance. This phenomenon might be called the 'efficiency hypothesis'.

The interviews of maternity unit managers yielded considerable insight into the incentive operating on them, and brought to light a distinct asymmetry in the impact of performance audit. Managers in units with high PMRs used their poor performance to justify a number of strategies, such as reductions in the availability of general practitioner maternity beds, reorganization of community midwifery services, and reassessment of perinatal medical policy. Moreover, all five also gave the high PMR prominence in presenting their cases for additional resources in the budgetary process. They were, usually implicitly, suggesting that resources they currently controlled were inadequate to secure satisfactory results, given the adverse environmental context within which they were working. If objectives such as equality of outcome are important (which appears to be the case), it is very difficult for public sector governing boards to gainsay such arguments when the process of transforming inputs into outputs is poorly understood. As a result, managers stand a good chance of securing increased resources when they report poor performance.

In three of the five units with high PMRs, maternity services were considered a high priority service, and it was clear that the existence of a well-established outcome measure put maternity services at an advantage compared to other NHS services. Indeed, some of the managers in high PMR areas had considerable political skills, and had unashamedly used their apparently poor performance to secure additional resources from sources external to the NHS, such as charities and local government. From a managerial perspective, therefore, far from being unwelcome, an adverse ORPI may offer considerable opportunities for securing change and winning increased resources.

On the other hand, managers in low PMR units, although enjoying the favourable publicity, did not find ORPIs helpful when bidding for resources. They tended therefore to give a low profile to their PMRs in the budgetary process. Four of these managers indicated that they were a relatively low priority service.

Thus managers are prepared to give a high profile to adverse ORPIs when they are helpful in the budgetary process, and to ignore them otherwise. If this leads to a greater extent of managerial intervention in units with poorer performance – and if the intervention yields benefits in terms of outcome – then, rather than the general improvement in ORPIs suggested by the completion hypothesis, there might instead be a convergence in outcome measures, as the managerial pressure appears to be less intense in units with good outcome. Such convergence may not be economically efficient, in either an allocative or technical sense. Units with high PMRs may be devoting increased resources to maternity services even though they do not yield as many benefits as they would if directed at services with less well-developed outcome measures. And managers in managerially inefficient units may escape scrutiny because of favourable environmental circumstances. It therefore seems that the use of ORPIs might help more in the promotion of equity objectives than in the pursuit of narrower concepts of economic efficiency. The interviews suggest that this 'equity hypothesis' might be a more accurate description of the impact of PIs than the efficiency hypotheses adumbrated earlier.

3.5 Gaming

The phenomenon of convergence noted above derives from the use of performance in parallel organizations as benchmarks. The other principal source of managerial targets is the organization's own performance in previous time periods. In practice, a public sector organization is likely to set itself implicit or explicit targets based on the level of an ORPI achieved in previous years. This phenomenon was endemic as a means of setting production targets in the unreformed Soviet Union (Birman, 1978), and gives rise to potentially serious dysfunctional incentives. In particular, the organization operating under such a feedback process has a strong incentive to retain managerial slack in its performance. For if it reports exceptional performance in one year, that performance will form the basis for future expectations. Continued moderate performance on the other hand would enable the organization to sustain modest targets, with the excuse that external factors were inhibiting improvement. There is a considerable literature on budgetary slack in the private sector which relates to this problem (Lukka, 1988; Briers and Hirst, 1990).

The dynamic incentives implicit in a performance measurement scheme are potentially very important within the public sector for two reasons. First, most PIs are in practice intermediate measures of performance, measuring processes of service delivery rather than outcomes. As a result, the numbers reported are readily changed by the behaviour of managers (Flynn, 1986). Second, the impact of environment on performance is usually important, but very imperfectly understood. As a result there is little basis for challenging the assertion that poor performance is beyond the control of managers. The usual means of verifying such assertions is to compare with organizations in similar circumstances. However, perfect comparability is never possible, and there always exist sufficient idiosyncrasies in an organization's environment to offer managers ample scope for excuses. There is every opportunity and incentive, therefore, for public sector organizations to 'game' – or strategically manipulate – their PIs (Jaworski and Young, 1992), if these indicators are expected to be used as benchmarks for future targets.

Clearly perinatal mortality is one of the most serious adverse outcomes from the NHS, and there is no conceivable circumstance in which this indicator could be consciously 'gamed' without serious ethical and legal trangressions. None of the interviews brought to light the slightest hint of any such activity. However, in another context, Smith (1989) has indicated that potentially large gains in terms of resources available can accrue to the public sector manager prepared to game. Thus, if the ORPI were less easily audited, or the outcome being measured was less serious, or there was more scope for difference in interpreting the ORPI, then it is highly likely that some managers would manipulate their ORPI to secure strategic advantage. For example, one of the managers interviewed had been set the target of reducing the prevalence of maternal smoking. Clearly, unless the associated incentive scheme is devised carefully, there may be an incentive for this manager to do all she can to ensure that the baseline figure is high, and to secure only modest apparent reductions from year to year. Her superiors will find it difficult to judge whether the levels achieved are reasonable, and she will be able to claim that the environment precludes quicker improvements. As a result, her targets will be modest.

The opportunity for gaming in the public sector is therefore exaggerated by the poor understanding of most production functions, illustrating the importance of choosing ORPIs with great caution, and of ensuring that incentives are compatible with the organization's objectives.

3.6 Ossification

The Soviet literature offers many examples of the ways in which an excessively rigid performance measurement scheme can stifle innovation and suppress potentially healthy experimentation (Nove, 1980). Many of the factors inhibiting innovation have been noted above. If outcomes are enhanced by the innovation, there is no guarantee that the improvement will be captured by the current PI system, which will inevitably be to some extent incomplete (Section 3.1). Alternatively, the enhanced outcome may redound to the credit of the manager of a different programme (Section 3.2) or a successor manager (Section 3.3). Thus innovatory management may be exposed to exceptional scrutiny as outsiders seek to understand the reasons for apparently anomalous behaviour. In considering possible innovation, therefore, the public sector manager will have to resist the powerful incentive to 'run with the pack' noted in Section 3.4. Even if improvements arising from innovation can be measured, the gaming argument in Section 3.5 implies an alternative stimulus to ossification. Any organization delivering exceptional performance will raise expectations, and the manager looking for a quiet life may instead spurn the short-lived plaudits arising from the a beneficial innovation, and opt for chronic mediocrity.

However, as with most formal control systems, the most profound danger is that the system itself becomes ossified, and fails to react to new challenges and opportunities. Even if the problems of incompleteness noted in Section 3.1 could be overcome, there remains the problem of continuously scanning the infinite number of potential environmental factors on which the organization could conceivably have some impact. If managers have no incentive to look beyond the world encompassed in their ORPIs, the changing nature of the challenges confronting the public sector may be ignored.

For example, at the time of writing United Kingdom health policy is focusing on the time that patients wait for elective surgery, following a provision in the Citizen's Charter that no patient should wait longer than two years for such surgery (Department of Health, 1991). As a result any PI scheme devised now is likely to give great prominence to such waiting times. Because citizens, politicians and managers have bounded powers of comprehension, such attention to waiting times would almost certainly lead to the exclusion from a PI scheme of other potentially important criteria of health service performance which at present are not political priorities, such as the quality of post-operative care. With a well-developed and responsive political process, a switch in popular priorities would be noted and responded to rapidly. However, if the political process is constrained within a rigid PI straitjacket, there may be no incentive for managers to respond to new priorities lying outside the purview of the PI scheme, unless the PI scheme itself is changed.

Hofstede (1981) discusses the danger that a simple closed loop cybernetic system may lead to 'dynamic conservatism', and notes the need for a 'second-order loop ... which periodically adjusts the standards of the first-order cycle'. The difficulty in securing such second-order control is that the process by which such mechanisms are implemented must be predominantly political: almost by definition, there can be no systematic rules for adapting systems such as the PI schemes described above. Such a political process is likely to be arbitrary, slow to react to new circumstances, and completely antipathetic to the rationalistic philosophy underlying the primary PI scheme. In short, the need for such a messy and ill-defined second-order control must cast doubt on the validity of the relevance of the pellucid PI model to high order control of complex public sector organizations.

A wide range of managerial styles was detected in the maternity service interviews. The process-oriented managers, mentioned in Section 3.1, appeared to have rather rigid views about how the maternity services should be organized, while two of the managers in high PMR areas had initiated radical strategy changes in their units. The interviews revealed a spectrum of managerial styles, ranging from the passive to the active. Clearly, almost by definition, there is likely to be more evidence of ossification in areas managed in a passive style. However, there is no evidence that the ORPI scheme systematically encourages ossification. The interviews suggested that the attitudes of managers and their superiors are much more important, and identified two important qualities that helped to form responses: the style of intervention adopted by the unit; and the vision of the strategies described.

The concept of managerial style is indicated by the attitude towards intervention. Passive style implies an acceptance of current working practices, and reacting to rather than anticipating crises. Active style implies a more radical attitude towards methods of service delivery, and a more anticipatory attitude towards problems. Clearly measurement of the concept of style is fraught with difficulty, and could not be attempted within the context of this study. However, it was possible for the interviewer to gain an impression of where every unit stood on the spectrum by enquiring about changes that had been made, and observing the emphasis the manager placed on planning issues.

The concept of managerial vision is orthogonal to this concept of style. It reflects the extent to which managers perceive the problems they face to be strategic, reflecting concern with socio-economic circumstances and the design of services; or operational, reflecting a concern with the processes of care delivery. Clearly all managers would claim that they seek to address all these issues. However, there was a distinct range of emphases detectable in the interviews, often indicated by the concerns the managers chose to highlight.

Figure 2 (overleaf) presents a purely subjective indication of where the units visited lie along the two dimensions of style and vision. Some units were easier to place than others in the diagram. However, the impression gained is of a wide variety of circumstances. In 'high PMR' units, there is a tendency for active managers to adopt a strategic vision, instigating major upheavals in unit policy, and concentrating on organizational issues. The passive managers in such units tend to concentrate on pursuing excellence in the delivery of services. This too is a characteristic of active management in the 'low PMR' units, where there appears to be considerable emphasis in exploring new medical techniques. Passive managers in low PMR units tended to emphasize the system of delivery in place, and tended not to mention operational medical matters.

The pattern of causality between performance indicator, managerial style and managerial vision is clearly complex, and requires further clarification. However, a reasonable hypothesis would be that, in the short run, vision and performance measures should be considered exogenous. The style of intervention that emerges will depend on these two variables, so that an active style tends to emerge where the ORPI is poor and the managerial vision is strategic, and so on. However, in

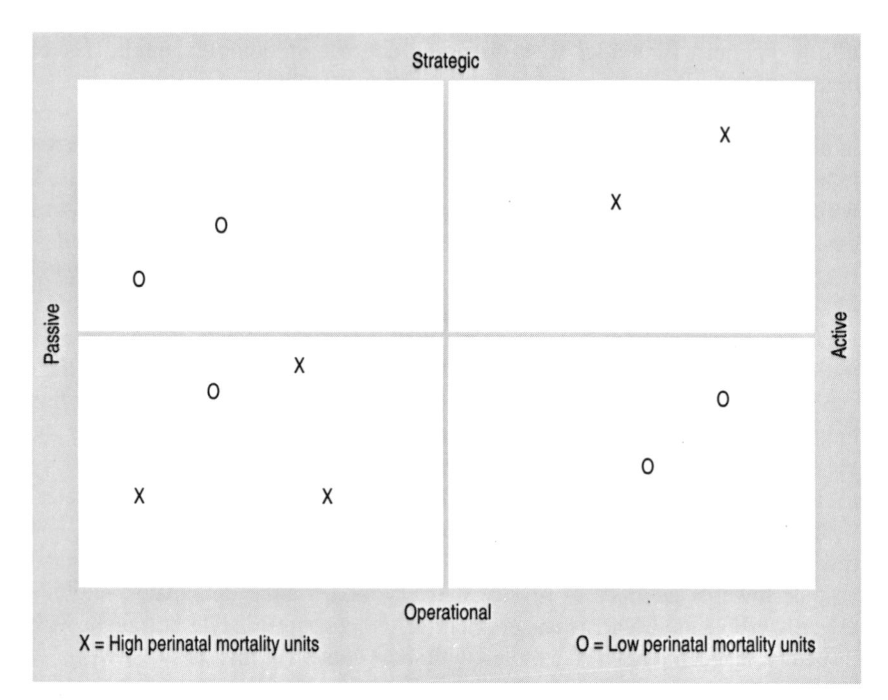

Figure 2 *Managerial style and vision amongst the 10 maternity units (X = high perinatal mortality units, O = low perinatal mortality units)*

the long run, all three variables might be endogenous. For example, areas with poor ORPIs may desire radical solutions to their problems, and therefore seek active managers. This is clearly an area for further research. The interviews in this study seem to suggest that ORPIs will if anything encourage innovation, at least in some units, and there appears to be little encouragement of ossification intrinsic to the scheme.

3.7 Misrepresentation

So far the discussion has considered the potentially distorting incentives implicit in ORPI schemes, without making a distinction between real changes in behaviour and changes in reported behaviour. Clearly both options are available to management. In this section we therefore focus on the ways in which it may be possible for management to distort ORPIs without necessarily changing behaviour. Such misrepresentation can take three general forms: smoothing, or dynamic misrepresentation; biasing, or cross-sectional misrepresentation; and fraud.

Smoothing in financial reporting is said to have two objectives (Ronen and Sadan, 1981). First, it seeks to dampen expectations about future performance; and second, it seeks to lessen the perceived riskiness of the enterprise. In a public sector context, for example, many indicators – such as a local education authority's examination results or a health authority's mortality rates – are presented as three rolling averages. The argument for this procedure is that the numbers involved are too variable over a one-year period to give reliable indications of performance. While such an argument may be perfectly valid for many purposes, there may nevertheless be good reasons for users to scrutinize data from a single year, particularly if a rapid response to new circumstances is required.

Biasing is endemic in external reporting. In preparing public sector financial accounts, for example, there is often a great deal of discretion concerning the extent to which general administrative overheads are allocated to specific services. So far as outputs are concerned, there may be considerable discretion as to how an activity is reported. Thus, for example, in the health services, a doctor may be able to allocate a patient to a number of diagnosis-related groups, and may have an incentive to choose the category which maximizes the apparent workload (Bardsley *et al.*, 1987). In this respect, it is noteworthy that doctors have an especially strong control over data relating to their activities, and that independent audit of medical judgements is difficult. As an ORPI scheme seeks to monitor more qualitative aspects of behaviour it will inevitably address matters of professional judgement which will offer potential for biased reporting.

Straightforward misreporting, or fraud, is of course always possible. In this respect public services are particularly vulnerable because, unlike the private sector – where outcome can be measured in terms of revenues, which are readily audited – the audit of public sector outputs would be a massive task, involving numerous techniques of verification. And, as we noted above, because there will always exist scope for differences in judgement in measures of activity and outcome, it seems likely that many audits would lead to fruitless debates about interpretation.

The distortions discussed above might therefore lead to reported performance being different from actual behaviour. This might be dysfunctional for a number of reasons, most notably because electors and politicians might be misled about the level and efficacy of public sector activity. The seriousness with which this possibility is viewed is indicated by the Audit Commission (1992) proposal that the data used in the Citizen's Charter PI scheme will be verified by external auditors.

In the maternity services, managers have very little direct control over the PMR reported for their area. Births and perinatal deaths are usually unambiguous events for which there is a well-established recording mechanism. As a result, there is little scope for misrepresentation. Instead, managers expended considerable energy in interpreting the data that emerged from their unit, and it is plausible that this might lead to interpretative misrepresentation. The potential for such misrepresentation is extensive in the public sector, because of the very ambiguous link between inputs and outputs, and because of the considerable scope for identifying plausible reasons beyond the control of management for poor performance.

Thus, for example, nine of the managers mentioned the need for caution in focusing on just one year's PMR. In a typical district, delivering perhaps 4000 babies per annum, there might be 40 perinatal deaths in a year. The standard error on a PMR of 10 deaths per 1000 deliveries is therefore quite large (of the order of 1.5), and so for most purposes an aggregation of several years' data is deemed necessary. Thus interpretative smoothing is endemic for this ORPI. Moreover, it was noticeable that there were differences in the use made of smoothing.

Managers at high PMR sites tended to place less emphasis on the need for smoothing, and two managers for whom recent data showed an improvement were happy to abandon the principle to focus on one favourable year. On the other hand, managers in low PMR areas were keen to emphasize the need to smooth, presumably as they felt vulnerable to adverse random fluctuations.

Another interpretative issue frequently raised was the need to consider the socio-economic circumstances prevailing in the district. All the high PMR areas mentioned issues beyond their control militating against a lower PMR, such as high proportions of ethnic minorities, high levels of maternal smoking, and high levels of poverty. In addition, three of the low PMR [areas] also acknowledged that context was an important determinant of their good results.

Two managers from high PMR units mentioned that the ORPIs misrepresented their performance because the reported figure referred to births to all mothers resident in their district, yet the managers only had control over births to mothers who chose to use their facilities. The managers pointed out that the PMRs at their hospitals were better than the published PMRs, and inferred that it was facilities elsewhere (presumably in neighbouring districts) that were giving rise to the high PMR in the area. This argument might of course ignore the possibility that high-risk mothers were being systematically referred to other districts, which perhaps ran specialist services, such as neonatal intensive care cots, and that therefore the local unit had a relatively high proportion of low-risk pregnancies. Several managers mentioned the potential for misrepresentation brought about by the arbitrary definition of the PMR. In particular, at the time of the study, any abortion occurring in the first 28 weeks of pregnancy was omitted from both numerator and denominator. There is some room for judgement in estimating the duration of pregnancy, so it was thought that some doctors might be encouraged to categorize borderline cases as late abortions rather than stillbirths. Two managers in high PMR units emphasized that their rates were 'genuine', with the implication that other units may not be so scrupulous.

Thus, because the ORPI is thought to require 'expert' interpretation, which tends to be provided by the responsible manager, there is considerable scope for interpretative misrepresentation. Whether such misrepresentation occurs to any great extent is of course a matter for conjecture. However, the interviews suggested an acute awareness that other units might indulge in creative interpretation, and so one must conclude that there is a strong possibility that it exists. The phenomenon is likely to be common in the public sector in general, where there is only a small number of expert intermediaries able to give dispassionate commentary on performance measures.

4 Conclusions

Much energy is being expended on the development of outcome-related performance measures in the public sector, although the behavioural impact of such measures has been the subject of surprisingly little research. The literature is nevertheless replete with studies of the impact on private sector enterprises of financial performance measures (Emmanuel *et al.*, 1990, chapter 9). It is not obvious that the accumulated private sector wisdom is necessarily transferable to public sector accountability (Pollitt, 1988). However it would appear prudent to consider the possibility that ORPI schemes might distort public sector activity.

To date most public sector PI schemes have been developed on the assumption that they are neutral reporting devices, and very little attention has been given to the organizational context in which they will be used. The management control literature suggests that such a cavalier attitude to context threatens the objectives of the scheme. Thus, Flamholtz (1983) notes that '... an accounting system cannot be viewed as a control system *per se*; rather [it] must be seen as a part of a carefully designed total system of organizational control'. The same must be true *a fortiori* of the sort of ORPI scheme described here, which has a far more ambitious objective – and which is operating within a far messier and less well-understood organizational context – than most corporate accounting systems.

Moreover, as Hofstede (1981) notes, 'the more formalized a control system, the greater the risk of obtaining pseudo-control rather than control'. This article has noted some of the possible distorting consequences arising from excessive reliance on ORPIs in the public sector. These distortions have potentially serious dysfunctional consequences, so it would appear that research is needed to discover the extent to which the phenomena described in Section 3 are relevant, and – if they are – whether it matters.

Ultimately, of course, it would be desirable to undertake a full analysis of the costs and benefits of any PI scheme. However, such an undertaking would probably only be possible with controlled experimentation, an approach which is unlikely to be adopted by political parties in the United Kingdom. We have therefore investigated the behavioural impact of a single mature outcome-related PI – the perinatal mortality rate – on operational managers in the UK National Health Service. Our findings suggest that, although presented as a strategic control instrument, the indicator is being given increased emphasis in performance review throughout the NHS, and that there are strong reasons to believe that some of the expected behavioural responses have started to occur. There is therefore a strong possibility that dysfunctional consequences will arise if excessive reliance is placed on an outcome PI in the control system, even if the PI exhibits the widespread acceptance enjoyed by the PMR.

In reaching this conclusion we should not be considered to be advocating abandonment of performance audit in the public sector. The collection, widespread dissemination and informed interpretation of performance data are almost certainly important prerequisites of any effective control mechanism. The study does warn, however, that great attention should be given to the managerial incentives implicit in any control scheme which uses such data, and that the style with which the scheme is applied and the attitude of managers will have important bearings on its effectiveness.

References

Anthony, R.N. and Young, D.W. (1984) *Management Control in Nonprofit Organizations* (3rd edition). Richard D. Irwin, Homewood.

Audit Commission (1992) *Local Authority Performance Indicators*. The Audit Commission, London.

Baiman, S. (1990) 'Agency research in managerial accounting: a second look', *Accounting, Organizations and Society*, Vol. 15, No. 4, pp. 341–371.

Bardsley, M., Coles, J. and Jenkins, L. (eds) (1987) *DRGs and Health Care: the management of case mix*. King Edward's Hospital Fund, London.

Birman, L. (1978) 'From the achieved level', *Soviet Studies*, Vol. 30, pp. 153–172.

Birnberg, J.G., Turopolec, L. and Young, S.M. (1983) 'The organizational context of accounting', *Accounting, Organizations and Society*, Vol. 8, No. 2/3, pp. 111–129.

Bowen, B. and Payling, L. (1987) 'Expert systems for performance review', *Journal of the Operational Research Society*, Vol. 38, pp. 929–934.

Briers, M. and Hirst, M. (1990) 'The role of budgetary information in performance evaluation', *Accounting, Organizations and Society*, Vol. 15, No. 4, pp. 373–398.

Butterworth, P., Gray, R.H. and Haslam, J. (1989) 'The local authority annual report: an exploratory study of accounting communication and democracy', *Financial Accountability and Management*, Vol. 5, No. 2, pp. 73–88.

Carter, N. (1989) 'Performance indicators: "backseat driving" or "hands off" control?', *Policy and Politics*, Vol. 17, pp. 131–138.

Chalmers, I., Enkin, M. and Keirse, M.H.N. (1989) *Effective Care in Pregnancy and Childbirth*. Oxford University Press, Oxford.

Committee of Public Accounts (1990) *Maternity Services, Thirty-fifth Report, Session 1989–90*. HMSO, London.

Department of Education and Science (1983) 'School standards and spending: a statistical analysis', *Statistical Bulletin*, Vol. 16, No. 83. DES, London.

Department of the Environment (1981) *Local Authority Annual Reports*. The Department, London.

Department of Health (1991) *The Patient's Charter*. DoH, London.

Department of Health and Social Security (1985) *Performance Indicators for the National Health Service, Guidance for Users*. DHSS, London.

Dunsire, A. (1981) 'Central control over local authorities: a cybernetic approach', *Public Administration*, Vol. 58, pp. 173–188.

Emmanuel, C., Otley, D. and Merchant, K. (1990) *Accounting for Management Control* (2nd edition). Chapman and Hall, London.

Fédération des Experts Comptables Européens (1991) *Performance Measurement in Public Sector Management*. Chartered Institute of Public Finance and Accountancy, London.

Flamholtz, E.G. (1983) 'Accounting, budgeting and control systems in their organizational context: theoretical and empirical perspectives', *Accounting, Organizations and Society*, Vol. 8, No. 2/3, pp. 153–169.

Flynn, N. (1986) 'Performance measurement in public sector services', *Policy and Politics*, Vol. 14, No. 3, pp. 389–404.

Forrester, J.W. (1968) *Principles of Systems: text and workbook*. MIT Press, Cambridge.

Gudex, C. and Kind, P. (1988) 'The QALY toolkit', *Discussion Paper 38*, Centre for Health Economics, University of York.

Health Committee (1992) *Maternity Services, Second Report, Session 1991–92*. HMSO, London.

Hofstede, G. (1981) 'Management control of public and not-for-profit activities', *Accounting, Organizations and Society*, Vol. 6, No. 3, pp. 193–211.

Hopwood, A.G. (1972) 'An empirical study of the role of accounting data in performance evaluation', *Empirical Research in Accounting*, Supplement to *Journal of Accounting Research*, pp. 156–182.

Jaworski, B.J. and Young, S.M. (1992) 'Dysfunctional behaviour and management control: an empirical study of marketing managers', *Accounting, Organizations and Society*, Vol. 17, No. 1, pp. 17–35.

Jones, C.S. (1986) 'Universities, on becoming what they are not', *Financial Accountability and Management*, Vol. 2, No. 2, pp. 107–119.

Kenis, I. (1979) 'Effects of goal characteristics on managerial attitudes and performance', *The Accounting Review*, Vol. 54, pp. 707–721.

Kerr, S. (1975) 'On the folly of rewarding A while hoping for B', *Academy of Management Journal*, pp. 769–783.

Labour Party (1991) *Citizens' Charter. Labour's Better Deal for Consumers and Citizens*. Labour Party, London.

Liberal Democrats (1991) *Citizens' Britain. Liberal Democrat Policies for a People's Charter*. Liberal Democrats, London

Lukka, K. (1988) 'Budgetary biasing in organizations: theoretical framework and empirical evidence', *Accounting, Organizations and Society*, Vol. 13, No. 3, pp. 281–301.

March, J.G. and Olsen, J.P. (1976) *Ambiguity and Choice in Organizations*. Universitetsforlaget, Bergen.

Merchant, K. (1990) 'The effects of management controls on data manipulation and management myopia', *Accounting, Organizations and Society*, Vol. 15, No. 4, pp. 297–313.

National Audit Office (1990) *Maternity Services*, HC297. HMSO, London.

Nove, A. (1980) *The Soviet Economic System*. Allen and Unwin, London.

Otley, D.T. (1978) 'Budget use and managerial performance', *Journal of Accounting Research*, Vol. 16, pp. 122–149.

Pollitt, D.T. (1988) 'Bringing consumers into performance measurement: concepts, consequences and constraints', *Policy and Politics*, Vol. 16, No. 2, pp. 77–87.

Ramanathan, K.V. (1982) *Management Control in Non-profit Organizations – Text and Cases*. John Wiley & Sons, New York.

Ronen, J. and Sadan, S. (1981) *Smoothing Income Numbers*. Addison Wesley, Reading.

Salmon, P. (1987) 'Decentralisation as an incentive scheme', *Oxford Review of Economic Policy*, Vol. 3, No. 2, pp. 24–43.

Scriven, M. (1973) 'Goal-free evaluation', in House, E.R. (ed.) *School Evaluation: the politics and process*. McCutchan, Berkeley.

Smith, P. (1988) 'Assessing competition among local authorities in England and Wales', *Financial Accountability and Management*, Vol. 4, pp. 235–251.

Smith, P. (1990) 'The use of performance indicators in the public sector', *Journal of the Royal Statistical Society, Series A*, Vol. 153, pp. 53–72.

Smith, P. (1991) 'Negative political feedback: an examination of the problem of modelling political responses in public sector effectiveness auditing', *Accounting, Auditing and Accountability Journal*, Vol. 5, No. 1, pp. 5–20.

Stewart, J.D. (1984) 'The role of information in public accountability', in Hopwood, A. and Tomkins, C. (eds) *Issues in Public Sector Accounting*. Phillip Allan, Oxford.

Treasury (1990) *Treasury Minute on the Thirty-Third to Thirty-Sixth Reports from the Committee of Public Accounts 1989–90*, Cm. 1323. HMSO, London.

Trumpington, Baroness (1987) 'OR in government', *Journal of the Operational Research Society*, Vol. 38, pp. 907–912.

United Kingdom Government (1982) *Local Government Finance Act*. HMSO, London.

United Kingdom Government (1989) *Working for Patients, CM555*. HMSO, London.

United Kingdom Government (1991) *The Citizen's Charter*. HMSO, London.

Williams, A. (1985) 'Performance measurement in the public sector: Paving the road to hell?' Arthur Young Lecture 7, Department of Accountancy, University of Glasgow.

Notes

1 This research was funded by the Nuffield Foundation. Thanks are due to the maternity service managers and their colleagues, who gave their time so generously. Additional help from Alison Macfarlane, Aileen Murphy, Andrew Pendleton, Eileen Robertson and Sally Stone is also gratefully acknowledged. An earlier version of this article was given at a seminar at the University of Maryland in April 1992, and to the Second European Management Control Symposium, Jouy-en-Josas, France in July 1992. Helpful comments were received from a number of participants.

2 In this article the two adjectives are used interchangeably. The key criterion in defining such organizations is that they do not have the pursuit of trading profits as an objective. Thus the definition excludes trading public sector organizations such as some nationalized industries.

3 In addition, the medical profession exercises a powerful hold on political processes within the NHS. It is very difficult for the advocates of community services – principally midwives and family doctors – to challenge the received wisdom promulgated by hospital consultants.

4 Smith (1988) undertook an exhaustive search for evidence of convergence amongst the local government comparative statistics, but could find no evidence for such a phenomenon. However, it may be that the time period studied was too short, or that insufficient importance was attached by local government to comparative statistics in the years studied, for an effect to be detected.

11 Accounting for Europe – success by 2000 AD?*

Andy Simmonds and Olivier Azières

1 Introduction

Accounting for harmony

While awareness of the coming European Single Market in 1992 is now widespread in the business community, the campaigns run by member state governments are still to be fully translated into action. For the accounting profession in the twelve European Community (EC) countries, a programme of change towards a comparable basis of reporting has already passed through several stages of action, and is now nearing completion. The process of change began in July 1978, when the Council of the European Communities adopted the Fourth Company Law Directive. Since then, EC companies and their statutory auditors have had to keep pace with the harmonisation process launched and directed from Brussels. By early 1990, the scheduled programme of legal harmonisation will be complete.

The general public, perhaps, have a limited awareness of what has been happening. As a result of its technical nature, changes in accounting law have not achieved a high coverage in the media in the way that, say, consumer issues attract attention. Nevertheless, at the current stage of development, it is interesting to consider some of the problems that face groups of companies operating across EC borders:

- an Italian group wishing to diversify into other European countries by making acquisitions will not be able to use published information to decide the price it should offer. In addition to variations in the legal structures of its chosen targets, it will find variations in the way published profits are calculated, and the way assets are valued for balance sheet purposes;
- Belgian and German companies wishing to establish a joint venture by contributing equal elements of their existing businesses will not be able to establish an 'EC company'. They will need to decide which country they will use for their joint venture's legal domicile. Beyond this, they will need to decide upon a common basis for equating their respective contributions, and reporting information to management;

* This article was originally published as a booklet by Touche Ross Europe (1989). Reprinted with

- a French company wishing to obtain a listing on the London and Frankfurt stock exchanges will not be able to rely only on meeting the requirements of the Paris Bourse. It will need to meet, and understand, the differing regulatory requirements of the markets in each country;
- a Dutch company wishing to prepare consolidated financial statements for its subsidiaries in other EC countries will not be able to use the local statutory accounts prepared by each subsidiary. It must first spend time, and incur cost, restating each subsidiary's accounts to eliminate the effects of adjustments made in each subsidiary's country, possibly to secure tax relief, or avoid tax charges.

These everyday issues suggest that while EC harmonisation has achieved a great deal for pan-European companies, such companies are not yet in the same position as a US company operating across US State borders, where the preparation of accounting information is to a common standard, tax is assessed principally on a federal basis, and stock exchanges are regulated by a single Commission. Outside the US, the quality of information published by US companies satisfies the needs of most analysts.

Europe, USA and Japan

The comparison made with the USA is heightened when we consider Europe within a global economic context.

Within the world economic groupings of the US, Japan and the EC, Figure 1.1 shows the European Community as a unit presents a fair comparison. In the area of accounting, comparison is more unbalanced.

At one extreme, the influence of US standards extends not only throughout US territory, but strongly influences the standards of Canada, Mexico and South America. The US system, popularly referred to as US GAAP, is comprehensive, and separate from the tax system.

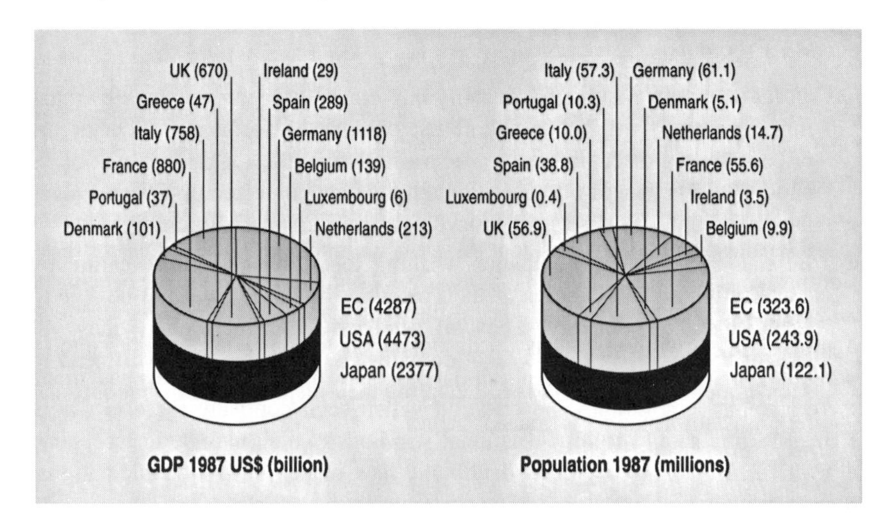

Figure 1.1 *Comparison of gross domestic product and population (Source: OECD)*

At the other extreme, the role played by Japan on the world accounting stage is not yet significant, and the accounting principles applied are still mainly based on the tax system. As a result, Japanese groups active on international markets generally base their accounting presentation on established US standards.

Between these two extremes lay a fragmented Europe. Historically, each nation has developed its own system. Prior to 1978, while a minority of countries had developed along US lines, the majority had developed a common system of tax assessment and published reporting similar to that found in Japan.

Harmonisation in the EC since 1978 has involved a series of two-stage processes: firstly a common directive (possibly containing a number of member state options) is agreed and translated into the various language versions; secondly each country enacts the directive's requirements by amending its own separate national laws. Negotiated options, difficulty of translating technical material, and national interpretations all contribute to the inherent risk of deviations in the directive system.

Over this same period, a separate group, the International Accounting Standards Committee (IASC) with representatives drawn from all the major accounting nations, has been developing accounting standards which provide a basis of international consensus but, at the current stage of development, include a number of options in each area and have yet to deal with some key issues.

The pressure towards global harmonisation

In the near future, the world market for financial and accounting information will undergo considerable upheaval in response to market forces. The recent emergence of a 'global' international capital market is already proving to be a driving force for standardisation of accounting doctrines at world level.

Looking outwards from Europe, EC companies are making significant investments in the US and, to a lesser extent, in Far Eastern markets. Their presence in these markets requires the publication of consolidated financial statements in accordance with recognised international standards.

Within Europe, the development of European stock markets is a sign of structural change in the means of raising corporate finance, even though the market capitalisation remains modest in comparison with the Japanese and US markets. [Figure 1.2 overleaf]

Within continental Europe, stock markets (with their higher inherent risks) are gradually replacing some elements of bank finance (with its more rigid guarantees). Japanese and US institutional investors are making increasing use of these European markets in order to tap the resources available, and enjoy the benefits of less tightly regulated regimes. The result of this increase in the use of stock markets is a growing emphasis on disclosure of financial information, and in particular, consolidated information. This demand is market driven and must, therefore, find a solution. The question which each company faces is whose standards they should follow – national standards (which may be unacceptable elsewhere), US GAAP (with its detail, and lack of flexibility), or International Standards?

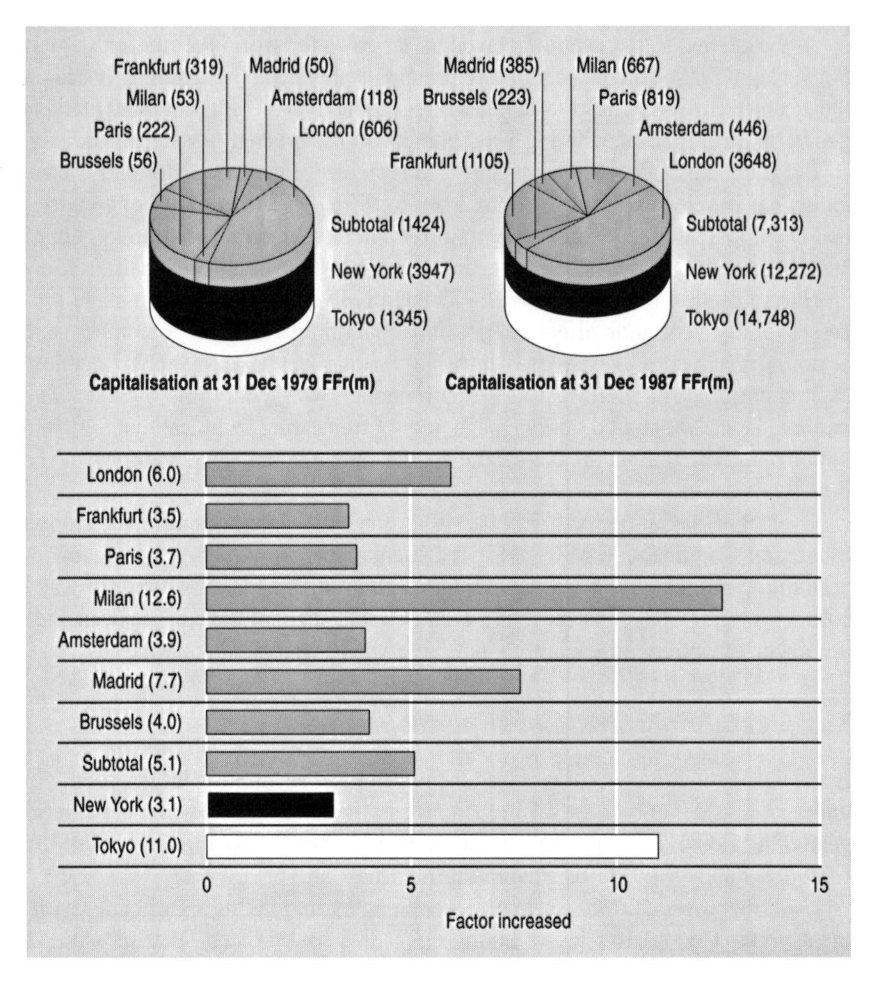

Figure 1.2 *Stock market capitalisation (Source: Rapport COB 87)*

The purpose of this article

Against a background of worldwide market forces, a rapid pace of change within Europe itself, and a need for EC companies to find an acceptable international standard, we considered it useful to take stock of accounting in Europe a few years before the date set for the creation of the European single market. In order to do so, this article aims to:

- summarise the current status of EC accounting regulations (see section 2)
- compare the practices followed by the seven largest EC countries (see section 3)
- illustrate by a case study the impact in value terms of the current discrepancies between the standards applied in these same countries (see section 4).

To conclude, section 5 attempts to give answers to the questions:

- what has been achieved?
- what obstacles inhibit further progress?

The section includes practical recommendations for the future.

2 Overview of accounting harmonisation in Europe

The process of EC harmonisation

The two major EC initiatives toward accounting harmonisation are the Fourth and Seventh Company Law Directives. Member states are required to have enacted the Fourth Directive into national law by 1 January 1984, and the Seventh Directive by 1 January 1990.

The Fourth Directive applies to individual company accounts. Its main objectives are:

- uniform presentation formats for profit and loss accounts and balance sheets;
- comparable valuation principles; and
- the presentation of standard minimum footnote disclosure in order to achieve a true and fair view.

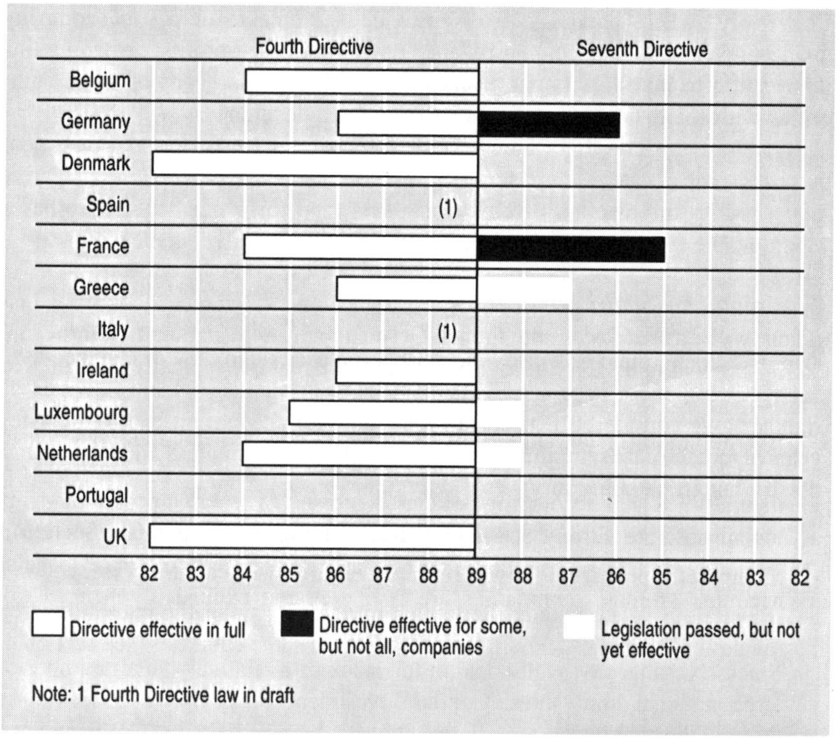

Figure 2.1 *Years of Directive implementation experience*

The Seventh Directive sets similar objectives for consolidated accounts and, in addition, establishes common definitions and methods of preparation. [Figure 2.1]

Current implementation status At the beginning of 1989, nine of the twelve member states have enacted the Fourth Directive (the exceptions being Italy, Portugal and Spain), and five (France, Germany, Greece, Luxembourg and the Netherlands) have enacted the Seventh Directive – although in all five cases, the national law will not be fully effective for all companies before 1990.

The influence of national factors

The development of accounting theory and practice in each EC country before 1978 [Figure 2.2] appears to have been dominantly influenced by one of the two following factors:

- a close relationship between published accounts and the taxation assessment system (the 'tax influence'); and
- the information needs of investors in developed capital markets (the 'capital market influence').

The two factors are, to an extent, related: in countries where the tax influence appears relatively strong, capital has traditionally been channelled through the banking sector, which is likely to be concerned more with security than with profits; accounts prepared for tax assessment purposes adequately meet this need. Conversely, where capital markets provide significant sources of company finance, investors place a higher reliance on the published profits; providing this information to investors is not easily reconciled with the needs of fiscal authorities with the result that separate systems have developed.

It naturally follows that where published accounts are used for tax assessment purposes, conservative choices often result; conversely, accounts preparers influenced by the reaction of capital markets tend to favour accounting bases which enable more flexible, and generally less conservative, choices.

Areas under tax influence In the geographical areas where accounting historians will attribute a strong French/German influence (national Commercial Codes, national mandatory accounting plans), the features typically encountered are:

1 It is common for tax authorities to allow only items which are charged in accounts and, conversely, to tax any profits which are taken. This approach naturally leads to accounting policies that result in reported profits being as low as possible. From being strong in Belgium and France, this influence in Germany and Italy can be described as very strong. In Spain, official accounts of many companies are still prepared exclusively from a tax perspective.

2 Stock Exchanges typically deal in the stock of a relatively small number of large national companies. Capital investment is otherwise concentrated through the banking system. In recent years, France, Italy and Germany have taken a lead in developing public offerings. In France and Italy particularly, large national groups have looked to international markets, and thus

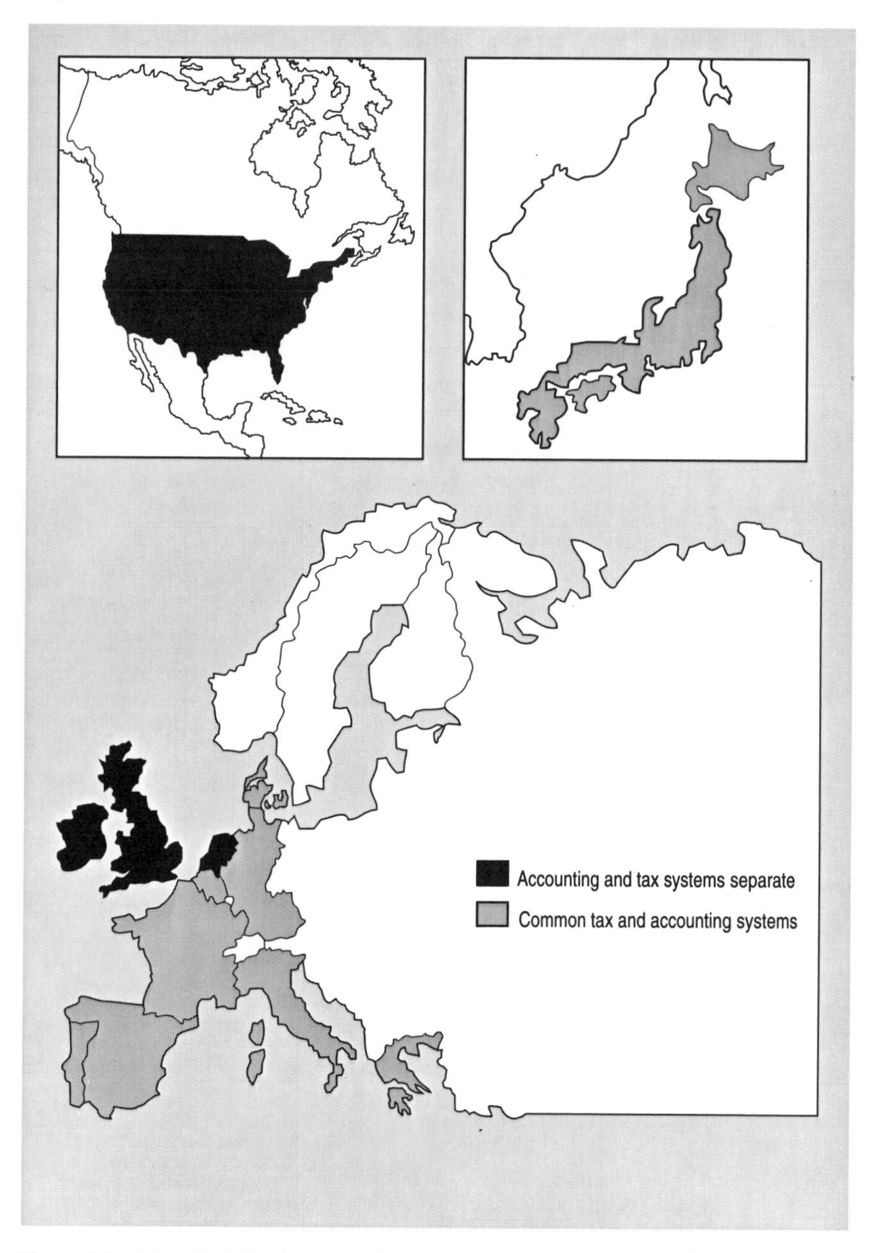

Figure 2.2 *Historical development of accounting systems prior to 1978*

presented accounting information in accordance with international standards, and not national rules. A similar trend is appearing in Germany and Belgium, with Spain likely to follow soon.

3 Since the majority of accounting rules are written within the law, they are difficult to change. Although new law is intended to reflect the views and requirements of a wide spread of interested parties, nevertheless the views of fiscal authorities remain influential.

4 Members of the main audit body are perceived as 'the profession'. The accounting profession is at least two tier, possibly with separate recognition of tax experts. It will be represented on committees advising government on new law, but will be but one voice among many. Published guidelines issued by professional bodies are generally recommendations only, and have no mandatory status.

5 Requirements for the preparation of consolidated accounts were not seen as a priority for many years. In Germany, the 1965 requirement currently relates only to domestic subsidiaries. In France and Italy, the stock exchange regulatory bodies (COB and CONSOB respectively) limited their requirements to listed companies issuing new shares. It is likely that the Seventh Directive will introduce major changes to this area.

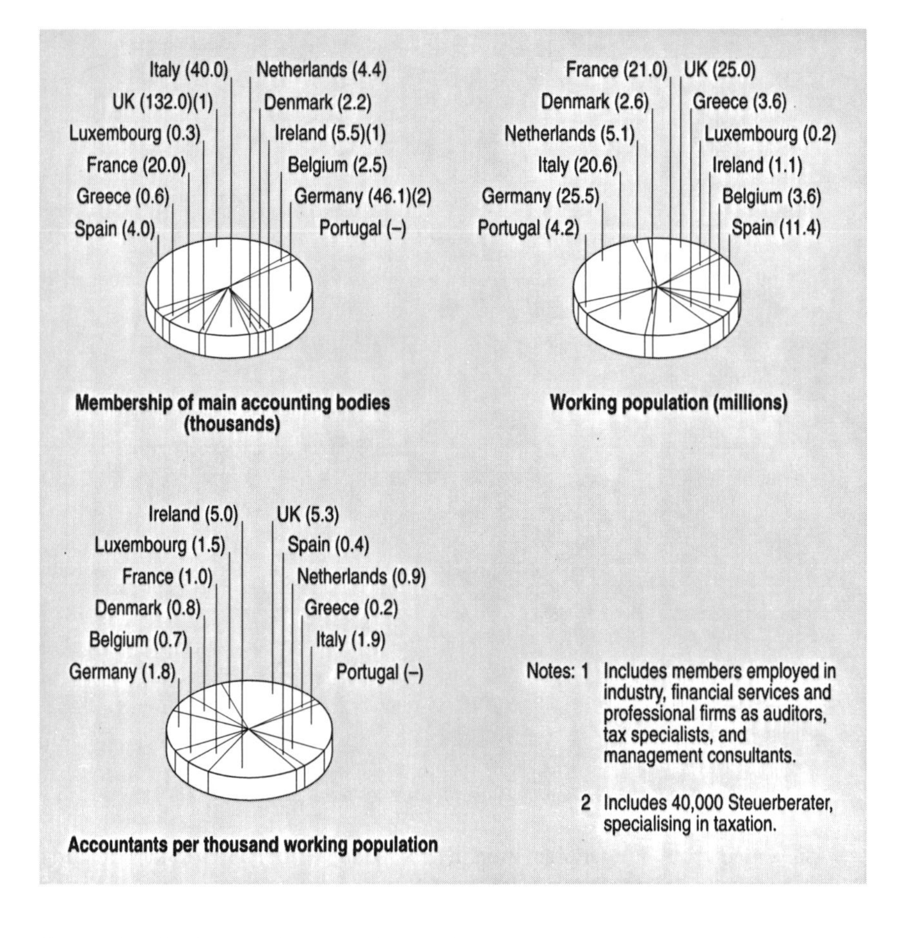

Figure 2.3 *Employment in accounting profession*
(Sources: OECD, Compagnie regionale des commissaires aux comptes de Paris)

Areas under the capital market influence In Ireland, the Netherlands and the United Kingdom, accounting practice has developed separately from tax law, giving rise to the following typical features:

1 Tax assessment is independent of accounts prepared for shareholders and public filing. The preparation of consolidated accounts, which are preferred by investors, is a long-standing tradition. Tax law has only a limited influence upon accounting practice.
2 Capital markets, and the advisory services that surround them, are highly developed. The market is sensitive to any piece of information released by a company, particular weight being put on the company's reported consolidated earnings per share, since this impacts directly upon the company's share price.
3 Accounting law has traditionally included only a framework of accounting principles.
4 The auditing and accounting professions are independent of Government, and are grouped within bodies including both auditors, preparers, and users of accounts. These self-regulated bodies represent a significant influence in the establishing and monitoring of detailed accounting regulations, and in advising Government on the framing of new law. In the Netherlands, such guidelines are non-mandatory, although closely followed. In Ireland and the UK, guidelines are mandatory, and heavily influenced by the pragmatic needs of accounts preparers.

Reconciling EC and national pressures

At the beginning of this section, we stated the main objectives of the Fourth Directive related to formats, valuation principles, and footnote disclosure.

In relation to formats, the Directive has, in theory, standardised the main accounting captions for balance sheets and profit and loss accounts. However, although each country had available to it a number of options for these formats (four profit and loss account options, and two balance sheet options), there has emerged a clear preference for one format in continental Europe (horizontal balance sheet, and profit and loss account analysed by type of costs – depreciation, staff costs, etc.) leaving the UK and Ireland with their traditional presentation (vertical balance sheet, and profit and loss account analysed by function of cost – costs of sales, administration, etc.) but with greater detail than previously.

In relation to footnotes, the most marked change has been (or will be) in Belgium, Denmark, Spain, France, Greece, Italy, Luxembourg and Portugal, where the Fourth Directive has resulted in a major restructuring of accounts layout. Since Germany had a strong influence in the Fourth Directive's presentation requirements, the main effect there has been to extend public company standards of reporting to all companies.

In relation to valuation rules, each country has been required to include a minimum of rules within law. There are few major changes, with Germany continuing to adhere closely to pure historical cost principles and, at the other extreme, the UK adopting the most flexible regime.

In each country where the tax influence has been described as the dominant influence, the Fourth Directive has not altered the use of individual company accounts for tax assessment purposes, although in France, the recognised effects of taxation are being separately disclosed. Italy may follow the French solution. The Belgian system is similar to France, but separate disclosure of tax effects occurs only within the balance sheet.

Potential impact of Seventh Directive With the exception of France, Germany, Greece, Luxembourg and the Netherlands, the Seventh Directive on consolidated accounts is at the draft stage of law only. With the exception of Spain and Portugal, the remaining countries already have some requirement for consolidated accounts, although the requirement may be for listed companies only. In enacting this Directive, countries will be able to adopt different principles from those used in individual company accounts. This is possible because consolidated accounts are not used by tax authorities to assess income to taxation.

Thus in France, where the Seventh Directive is already effective for quoted companies, consolidated accounts are adjusted to eliminate the effects of tax entries, and to reflect many adjustments favoured by international standards and not found in individual company accounts. Examples are the adjustment of depreciation charged to an economic basis, the provision of deferred taxation, and the capitalisation of leases. It is to be seen whether this opportunity will be taken up in other countries.

The changes required by the Seventh Directive can be viewed at two levels. At a surface level, countries will introduce requirements, within law, dealing with the size and status of companies that must prepare consolidated accounts, the definition of which companies are to be included in the consolidation, use of coterminous accounts, and adjustments to reflect consistency of accounting policies throughout the group. This latter requirement is likely to be a key point in countries like France, Belgium, Italy and Spain, where traditionally parent companies have not dictated precise accounting rules to their subsidiaries. In general we might expect these matters to be enacted on a comparable basis from country to country.

At a deeper level there is a need to consider detailed accounting practices such as the treatment of goodwill, provision of deferred taxation, valuation of stocks (inventories), provision for depreciation of fixed assets, recognition of exchange differences, and capitalisation of leases. Experience of implementing the Fourth Directive suggests that at this deeper level, different interpretation of accounting rules within Directives has led, in certain cases, to noticeable variations in the way member states have read, and enacted, the Directives. In addition, there are a number of areas which the Seventh Directive does not tackle, leaving member states, and their professional accounting standard bodies, free to make choices. In these cases, in the absence of a coordinating body of EC accounting standards, uniformity is unlikely to be achieved across the twelve EC countries.

3 Examination of significant issues

The close examination of significant accounting issues focuses upon the seven largest economies (see Figure 1.1). These countries are Germany, France, Italy, the UK, Spain, the Netherlands and Belgium.

The topics selected for the following survey concentrate on those accounting areas that generate material variations in reported profit, and net assets, within accounts prepared on those accounting bases that are in most common use within the seven selected countries.

Fixed asset policies

Fixed asset policies determine the basis for the amounts at which fixed assets are carried, and the resulting charges to the profit and loss account for depreciation.

Tangible fixed assets Figure 3.1 indicates that while revaluation of tangible fixed assets is permitted in most countries, it is practised in only three – the Netherlands, the UK and, to an extent, Belgium. In each case the tax effects are either neutral, or avoidable. The basis of revaluation in the Netherlands is replacement cost, and is practised by some 40%–45% of quoted companies. In the UK, freehold and long leasehold property is often revalued to open market value. In addition, the UK has a class of property called 'investment properties'.

These, broadly, are properties held for their investment potential, and not for occupation by the company's operating businesses. Such properties are required to be revalued annually without charging depreciation. Germany alone does not permit any revaluation.

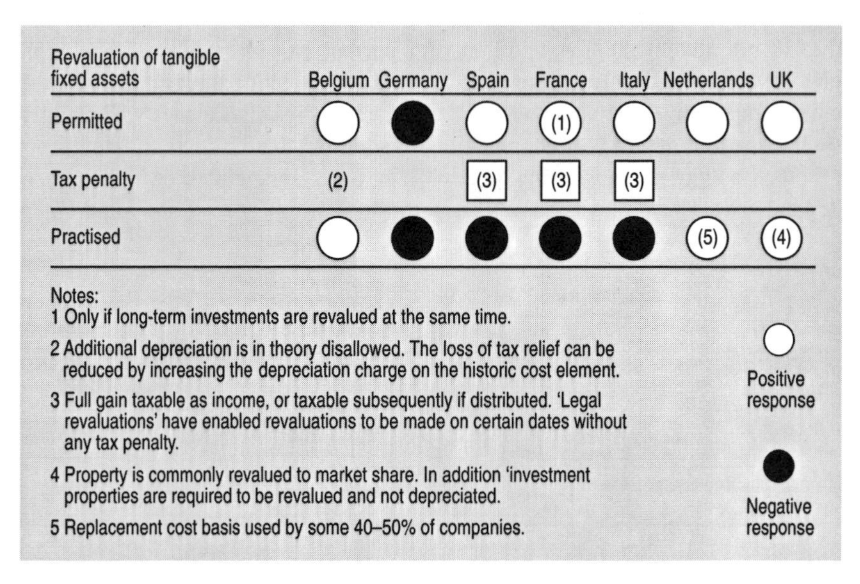

Figure 3.1 *Fixed asset policies*

'Legal revaluations' have been permitted in recent years in France (1976), Italy (last in 1983) and Spain (last in 1983). Such revaluations, which follow years of double figure inflation, permitted companies to perform revaluations with neither tax penalty, nor tax advantage.

Depreciation There is considerable diversity over the application of what is essentially the same principle, which is the allocation of the depreciable amount on a systematic basis to each accounting period during the useful life of the asset. Practice which meets this objective can be described as being on an economic basis.

Where the tax influence is strong (Belgium, Germany, France, Italy and Spain), the choice of asset life within individual company accounts is often dependent on the life allowed for tax purposes. In France and Belgium, the life for tax purposes is generally shorter than the asset's useful life. In Germany, tax and useful lives (that is, those adopted in commercial accounts) are generally comparable, but both are shortened by the effect of regional incentives which are expressed in terms of accelerated tax lives. In addition, the pattern of charges over the asset life in these countries may have more to do with tax regulations than with the asset's contribution to profits. In Italy and France, for example, charges in the earlier years may be higher (as a result of accelerated depreciation) than in the later years of the asset's life. In Spain, the tax life is expressed as a band within acceptable minimum and maximum limits; this allows the depreciation charge to be varied from year to year.

Within consolidated accounts, the opportunity is present to eliminate the tax influence. This opportunity is taken in France and Italy, and is expected in Belgium. Regional tax effects in German accounts are not generally adjusted.

Intangible fixed assets For intangible fixed assets other than goodwill, only the UK permits revaluation, and then on a current cost basis. Many UK companies are currently experimenting with methods of reflecting their intangible asset worth, for example the value of brand names, in their balance sheets. Generally, such valuations do not bear depreciation. In addition, there is increasing evidence of other countries transferring goodwill to other intangibles (which are not depreciated). This policy is possible as a result of the absence of any requirement to the contrary within EC directives.

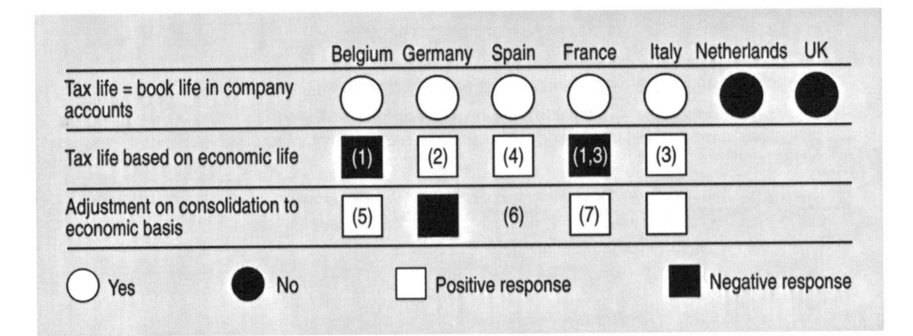

Figure 3.2 *Depreciation policies – relationship with tax basis*

Notes to Figure 3.2:

1 Tax life generally shorter.

2 Tax life generally comparable with economic life, but in certain regions, tax incentives result in shortened lives.

3 Rate of charge on certain classes of assets may be higher in the earlier years as a result of accelerated depreciation.

4 Tax lives expressed as minimum/maximum limits, allowing rate of charge to vary from year to year.

5 Adjustments expected, but not mandatory.

6 Consolidated accounts are not yet mandatory in Spain.

7 Adjustment is to replace the reducing balance with straight line based depreciation.

Capitalisation of leases All countries in the survey recognise the distinction between finance and operating leases. However, there is variation both in the legal definition of leases, and in the practice of capitalisation of finance leases within individual company accounts and consolidated accounts.

Within individual company accounts, practice varies from prohibition (France and Italy), through being permitted (Spain), to being required (Belgium, UK and Netherlands). In Germany, the definition of a finance lease is complex, with the result that few leases are capitalised.

Within consolidated accounts, the prohibition in France and Italy becomes an option, some French, but few Italian, companies taking the capitalisation option. Other countries retain the individual company accounts basis in consolidated accounts.

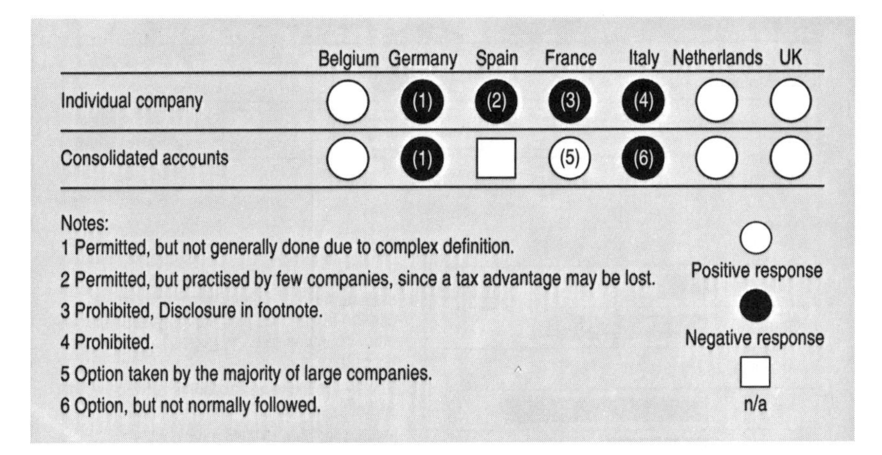

Figure 3.3 *Capitalisation of finance leases*

Goodwill and the fair value process The methods by which business combinations are achieved are largely determined by legal and taxation regulations, and by the business conventions found in each country. For example, the process of merging two companies in continental Europe is generally achieved by the two companies becoming a single company; in the Netherlands and the UK, it is more common for one to become a subsidiary of the other. Nevertheless, the question of goodwill and the accounting problems it generates are common in some measure to all countries.

In computing goodwill, it is normal practice for acquired net assets to be restated at their fair value to the acquiror. This procedure represents an application of the purchase cost to the underlying net assets. While each country either requires or expects fair value adjustments to be made, it is likely that there is significant flexibility in the precise methods employed by individual companies in all countries. In addition, there is generally little information provided on the level and amount of adjustments made.

Having determined the amount of goodwill in the light of the adjustments described above, the key questions are firstly whether goodwill should be capitalised or eliminated; and secondly, where the capitalisation route is followed, what rate of depreciation should be applied.

The ability to eliminate directly against reserves, an option within the Seventh Directive, appears to be theoretically possible in all countries – although in many cases it is limited to closely defined circumstances. However, the extent to which it is practised has much to do with the influence of capital markets, and the desire of accounts preparers to avoid charges for amortisation of goodwill being made in arriving at the published earnings per share figure. Thus in the UK generally, and for some companies in the Netherlands, elimination is the preferred method; in recent cases the ability to avoid charges for goodwill amortisation against earnings per share has given UK companies a competitive advantage over US

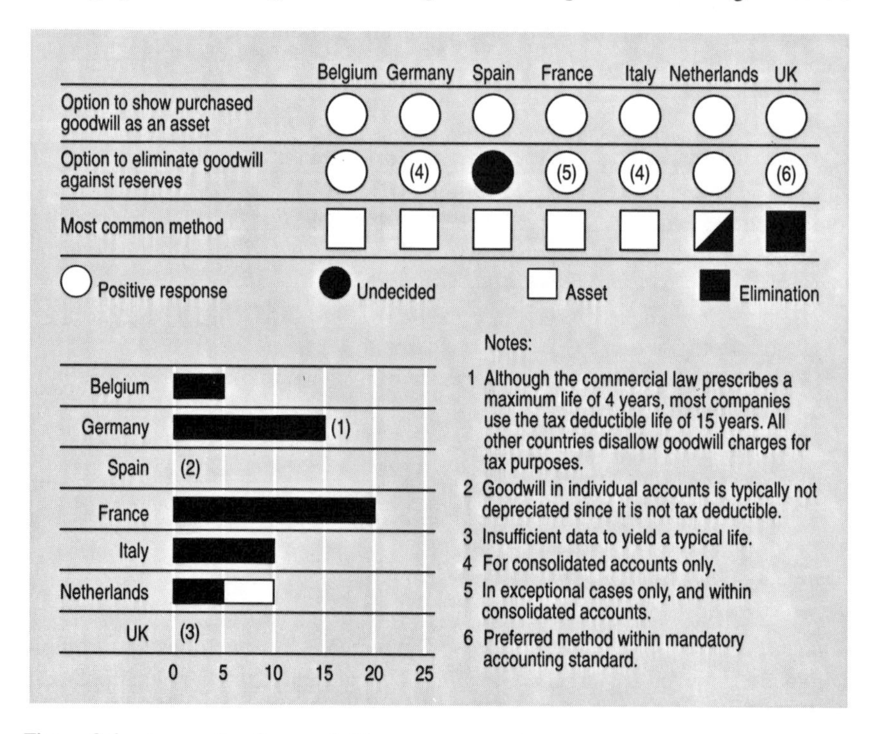

Figure 3.4 *Accounting for goodwill*

companies in determining the price each was able to pay in a takeover situation. There is evidence that this advantage has been noted in other EC countries, such as France, where the capital market influence is increasing, and that the practices of quoted companies in those countries are beginning to swing either towards a greater emphasis on the fair values of intangibles other than goodwill, or in special cases, the elimination method for goodwill.

In relation to useful life, while the Fourth Directive sets a maximum period of 5 years for write-off, most countries have taken the derogation option of allowing write-off over a longer useful economic life. A typical life can be observed within each country.

Fixed asset investments For fixed asset investments, Germany does not permit revaluation at all. Spain, France and Italy permit but rarely, or never, practise revaluation apart from legal revaluation. Belgium, the Netherlands and UK each permit and practise revaluation on a number of bases. In the Netherlands particularly, net asset based values are widely used for subsidiary and associate company investments within the investing company's balance sheet.

Stocks and work-in-progress

Use of replacement cost The valuation of stocks and work-in-progress (inventories) on a replacement cost basis, when that basis is higher than historical cost, is permitted in two countries only, the Netherlands and UK. In both cases the derogation was to allow companies to adopt replacement value methods of accounting. Within the Netherlands, such methods are practised by a minority of companies. Within the UK, the method is no longer used for commercial businesses, but is still in use by some State-owned industries.

Use of LIFO valuation method Use of the last-in-first-out (LIFO) method of cost identification results in a lower stock and profit result when compared with the first-in-first-out (FIFO) or average cost methods. It has thus proved more popular in the tax-influenced systems. However, in both Germany and Italy,

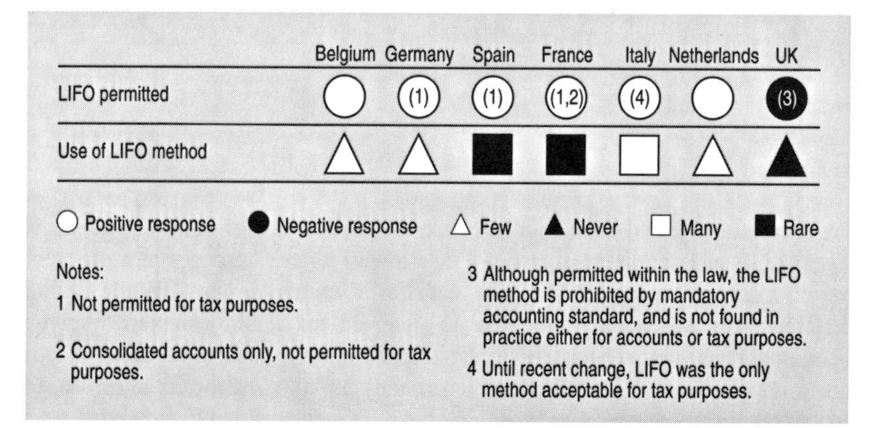

Figure 3.5 *Use of LIFO stock valuation method*

where its use has been most widespread, there have recently been moves away from LIFO, and towards FIFO. Thus in Germany the method is no longer acceptable for tax purposes since the assumptions implied by the method regarding physical movements of stock items is unlikely ever to be consistent with actual movements. In Italy it is no longer the only method acceptable for tax purposes.

Inclusion of overheads in cost With two exceptions, overheads attributable to production are required to be included in the cost of stocks and work-in-progress. The exceptions are Belgium and Germany. In Belgium, there is no mandatory requirement to include such overheads in cost, but the practice is generally followed. In Germany, inclusion for tax purposes is required; within commercial accounts there exists an option to include or exclude, and both bases are used.

Profit on long-term contracts Where the outcome of a contract has been assessed as profitable, the projected profit can be either spread over the duration of the contract, or taken as one amount on completion of the contract. In regimes where tax is charged on the reported profits, use of the completion basis is clearly beneficial since it delays the tax charge until the latest possible time. One result of using this method, however, is that the profit and loss account of any one period will not represent the activity of the business during that period.

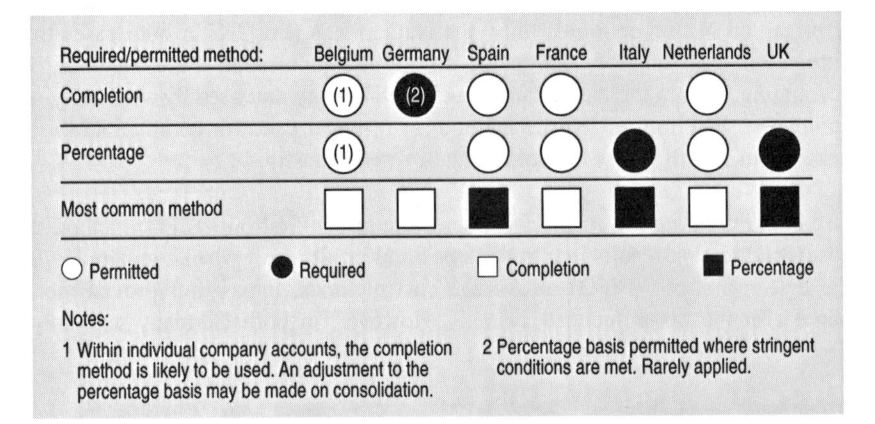

Figure 3.6 *Methods of taking profit on long-term contracts*

Deferred taxation

Provision for deferred taxation allows account to be taken of timing differences. These arise when an item is assessed or allowed for tax purposes in a different period from that in which it is dealt with for accounts purposes. While timing differences will generally give rise to deferred tax liabilities, there may be occasions when items, such as interest accrued but not paid, or certain types of provisions, are charged in accounts before they are allowed for tax purposes; in such circumstances the timing difference if recognised would give rise to a deferred tax asset which would be recovered by reduction of future tax charges.

In countries where individual company accounts are closely related to tax assessed accounts such as Belgium, France, Italy and Spain, there is either a limited need, or no need at all, for deferred taxation provisions at the individual company stage. However, where tax entries are reversed on consolidation, deferred taxation may become relevant at the consolidation stage. Within the Netherlands and UK, provision is necessary in both company and consolidated accounts to recognise the existence of timing differences. In Germany, while individual accounts are closely related to tax assessed accounts, a limited number of timing differences do arise, and provision is made accordingly.

In computing deferred taxation, three issues are relevant:

- The rate of taxation to be applied. Without exception, balance sheet provisions are computed by applying the current rate of tax to timing differences outstanding at the balance sheet date irrespective of the rate ruling when the difference arose. In the event of a change in the tax rate, the entire provision would be revised to the new rate. This method is called the liability method since it places more emphasis on the balance sheet liability than on the profit and loss account charge.
- Whether provision is made on all, or only some, timing differences. The most common practice is to provide on all timing differences; this basis is referred to as the full basis. An alternative basis, the partial basis, is found in the UK, Italy and to a lesser extent, the Netherlands. This basis recognises that a problem can arise where fixed assets attract high tax allowances in the early years of their life. Provided companies continue to purchase fixed assets, timing differences will continue to grow without any expectation of reversal. If deferred tax is provided in full, provisions would continually get larger, but rarely smaller. The partial deferred taxation basis requires companies to provide only for those timing differences that they expect to reverse in the future. The basis thus takes into account the future investment plans of a company's management. The partial deferred taxation method generally

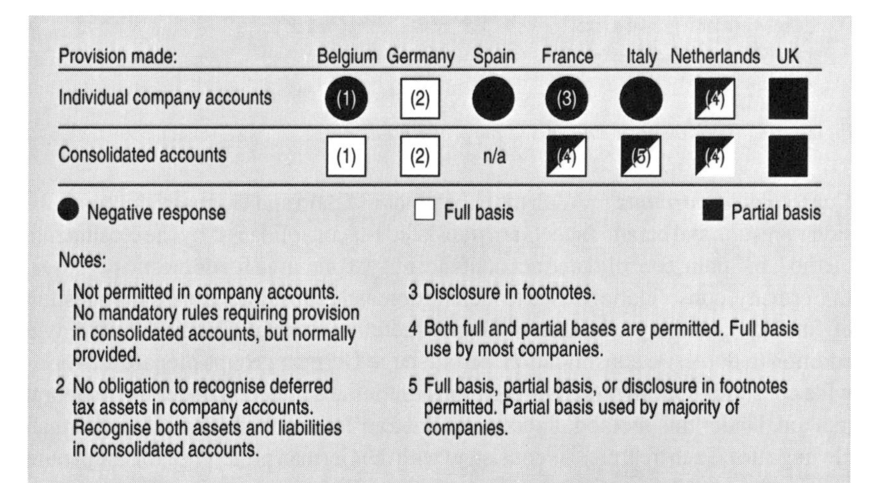

Figure 3.7 Deferred taxation provision

results in lower deferred taxation provisions, and higher reported profits and net assets than under the full basis.

- The extent to which deferred taxation assets may be recognised. This area is complex, and no general rules can be given.

Foreign currency translation

Individual company accounts Within individual company accounts, the major issue concerning foreign currency translation, and affecting reported profit, is the treatment of unrealised currency gains [Figure 3.8]. Unrealised differences arise, for example, on the retranslation to closing rate of loans held in foreign currencies. While all countries charge unrealised losses in their profit and loss account, there exists a choice of treatment in relation to unrealised gains between immediate recognition through the profit and loss account (UK and the Netherlands), or deferral until the time the gain is realised (Belgium, Spain, France, Germany and Italy); in the example of a loan, this would be at the time of repayment. Support for immediate recognition in the profit and loss account is that it results in the consistent treatment of both gains and losses. Support for the deferral treatment is the Fourth Directive requirement for the profit and loss account to reflect only realised gains.

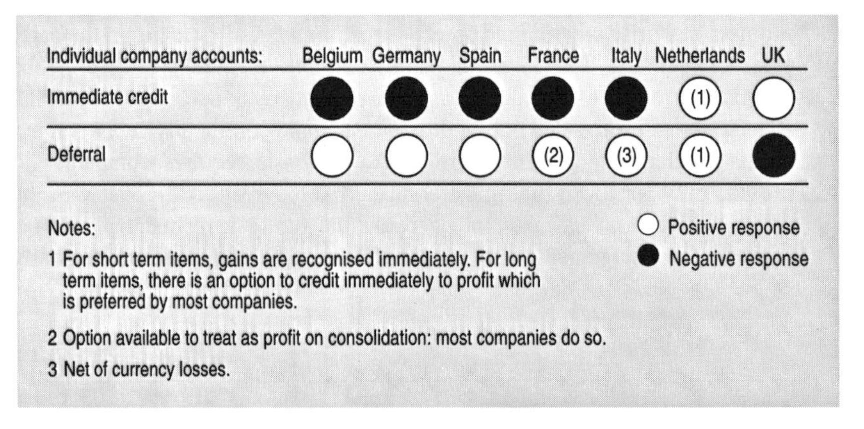

Figure 3.8 *Treatment of unrealised currency gains*

Consolidated accounts With the exceptions of Spain and Germany, foreign subsidiary results and balance sheets are translated for consolidation by the closing rate method. In Spain, consolidated accounts are not yet prepared for domestic purposes. In Germany, consolidations used to include domestic subsidiaries only; the question of foreign subsidiary translation did not therefore normally arise. However, in addition to domestic consolidation, certain large German groups prepare a 'worldwide consolidation' in which foreign subsidiaries are included under the temporal method. Under this method, fixed assets are translated at historic rates rather than closing rates. Such treatment is consistent with the German preference for use of pure historical cost techniques, and at a time of strong DM value, results in lower profits being reported for foreign subsidiaries.

To translate profits, Germany and Italy use the average rate exclusively. All other countries permit a choice of either the average or closing rate methods, and in each of those countries, both methods are in use.

Disclosure of unusual items

The Fourth Directive requires items arising outside the ordinary activities of the business (unusual items) to be disclosed separately from the results of ordinary activities. Since the terms used vary from country to country (for example: UK – extraordinary, France – exceptionnel), care should be exercised in determining the nature of any item under discussion. [Figure 3.9]

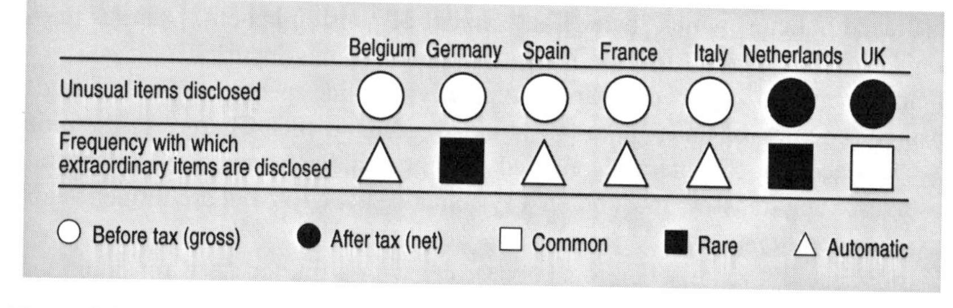

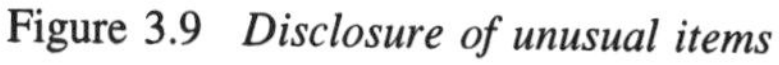
Figure 3.9 *Disclosure of unusual items*

In section 2, profit and loss account format options were discussed. As a result of a derogation possible under the vertical profit and loss account format, a further variation in format may arise relating to the way in which these unusual items, and related taxation, are presented. The original requirement of the Fourth Directive is for tax on ordinary activities, and tax on unusual items, to be separately disclosed. The derogation, taken by Belgium, Germany, Spain, France and Italy, permits the two items of taxation to be shown as a single item. If taken, this results in unusual items being disclosed gross (that is before tax), with total tax charges appearing as a single figure as the last item before net income.

Variations also arise both in the frequency with which companies in each country report unusual items, and in the nature of items included within the unusual category. For example, France uses this category to separate the elements of individual company accounts depreciation that are regularly charged for tax purposes only; Italy uses the category to allow the deferral of gains on certain fixed assets within individual company accounts which in turn defers the charge to taxation. Conversely, companies in the Netherlands and Germany apply a more restricted meaning, with the result that such items are reported less frequently in those countries.

Pension costs

The incidence of pension charges in company accounts is largely dependent upon the arrangements for paying pension benefits in each country. While all countries maintain state pension schemes, the level of benefits provided varies. As a result, it is common practice in some countries for employers to provide additional or substitute benefits, but again the level of benefit varies, as does the method of providing for the benefit.

The major factors are:

- whether resources are invested outside the company through insurance companies or in separate funds (externally funded pensions), whether reserves are set aside but the related funds are retained within the company (internally funded pensions), or whether pensions are charged to profit and loss account as they are paid to the employee (unfunded pensions);
- the basis of calculating charges to the profit and loss account;
- the basis of calculating payments, if any, to externally funded schemes, and the extent to which these may vary from the charge against profits.

In Belgium, it is common for large companies to operate comprehensive group insurance policies, which include an element of pension benefit. Charges to the profit and loss account will be the insurance premiums incurred.

In Germany, larger companies typically provide pension benefits under insured schemes, or under internally funded arrangements. Charges to the profit and loss account for internally funded arrangements are transferred to separate reserves. Such transfers must be on a systematic cost basis, but are influenced by tax considerations.

In France, the state scheme is very strong with a limited need for additional benefits to be provided. Employers are required, however, to provide employees with a lump sum on retirement, and are increasingly recognising the need to make provision for this liability, even though it is not allowable for tax purposes until paid.

In the UK, most employers provide pension benefits under externally funded schemes. A recently introduced accounting standard requires the charge to the profit and loss account to be a substantially level percentage of salary costs. As a result, this charge may be different to the contributions paid to a scheme.

In Italy, a growing number of companies provide pension benefits through externally funded schemes. Charges to the profit and loss account are the contribution payments to such schemes.

In the Netherlands, many employers provide pension benefits through externally funded schemes. Charges to the profit and loss account may be either contributions (the static method) or on an even trend (dynamic method). Under the dynamic method, contributions and accounting charges may differ.

In Spain, a recently introduced law enables employers to provide additional pension benefits. To date, most new schemes are internally funded.

4 Case study

Objectives

The case study was established to:

- illustrate the effects, on profit and net assets, of the differing accounting practices in use within each country;
- identify which of the acceptable accounting bases are in most common use within each participating country;
- test the variations in profit that can be achieved within each country.

In presenting the results, more weight is given to the reporting of profit than to the reporting of net assets. Similarly, more weight is given to consolidated results than to individual company results. The study does not attempt to quantify variations in tax regimes.

Conduct of the case study

The case study was conducted as follows:

- A simplified profit and loss account and balance sheet were drawn up from the recently published accounts of a multinational group. Figures were expressed in European Currency Units (ECUs).
- A series of transactions was designed, based where possible on actual data, to illustrate the areas of divergence.
- Practising accountants in each country prepared individual company, and consolidated, accounts on the alternative bases of:
  - the accounting assumptions most likely to be made by companies preparing accounts in their country (the 'most likely' result);
  - acceptable alternative assumptions that would result in net profit being as high as possible (the 'maximum achievable' result); and
  - acceptable alternative assumptions that would result in net profit being as low as possible (the 'minimum achievable' result).

The results presented are consolidated results. In the case of Spain, since there is currently no national requirement for consolidated accounts, the results presented are based on normal practice for consolidated financial statements prepared in Spain, but under external requirements, typically those of the UK and US.

Overall observations

The case study results demonstrate that:

- the highest 'most likely' consolidation net profit is achievable in the United Kingdom;
- the highest 'maximum achievable' consolidated net profit also occurs in the United Kingdom, but with Belgium, Spain and Italy close behind;
- the lowest 'most likely' consolidated net profit occurs in Spain, with Belgium and Germany close behind;
- the lowest 'minimum achievable' consolidated net profit occurs in Germany.

Comparison of consolidated net profit

Figure 4.1 presents the consolidated operating profit, and net profit, for each country on the basis of assumptions and policies most likely to be applied in each country. Operating profit represents profit before tax, and before finance items. Net profit is after all charges, but before dividends to shareholders are deducted.

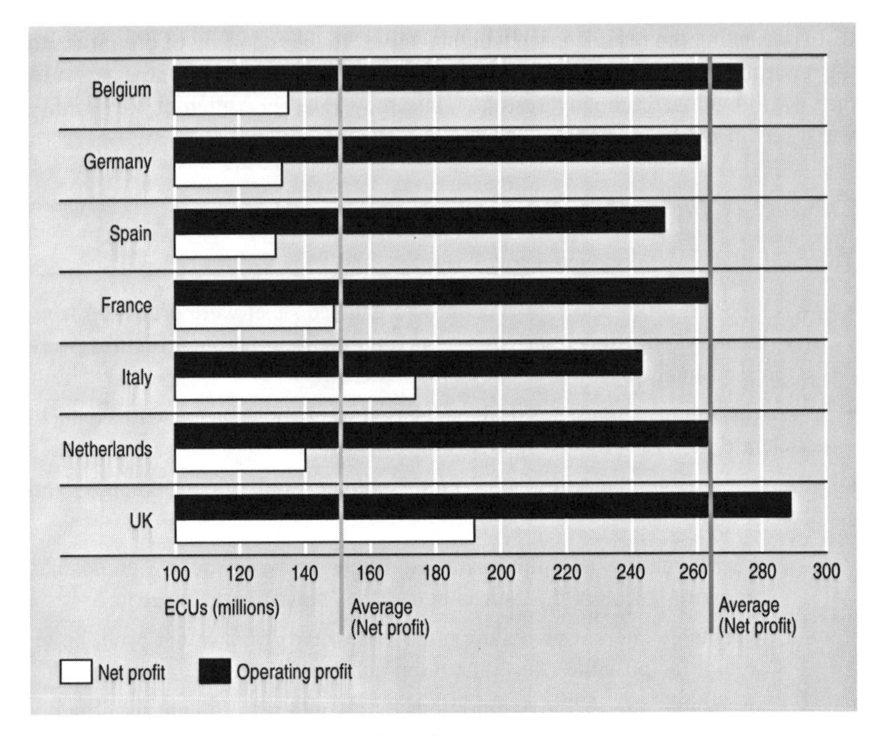

Figure 4.1 *Comparison of profit achieved*

Data used in Figure 4.1

Millions of ECUs	*Belgium*	*Germany*	*Spain*	*France*	*Italy*	*Netherlands*	*UK*
Operating profit (average 264)	274	261	250	264	243	264	289
Net profit (average 151)	135	133	131	149	174	140	192

The two most significant factors affecting the net profit are goodwill charges, and the basis of providing deferred taxation. The period over which goodwill is written off can have a very material effect – in the extreme case of the United Kingdom, this charge is avoided altogether by using the elimination method. The choice of the full or partial deferred tax method can also have potentially large effects on profit – although the precise effect will also depend on the way in which individual countries deal with tax depreciation allowances on capital assets.

The combination of no goodwill charges, and deferred tax on a partial basis, explains why the United Kingdom has both the highest operating profit and the highest net profit.

While Italy achieved the lowest operating profit – mainly from the use of the LIFO method of stock valuation – its net profit came second highest behind the United Kingdom. This is due to the use of the partial provision basis for calculating deferred taxation which affects net profit, but not operating profit.

Apart from Belgium, the remaining countries have a similar relationship between operating profit and net profit; in each case goodwill has been charged before operating profit. In the case of Belgium, the apparent variation results from the charging of goodwill as an unusual item which appears after operating profit. While this is not a required treatment in Belgium, the method was chosen as the preferred method.

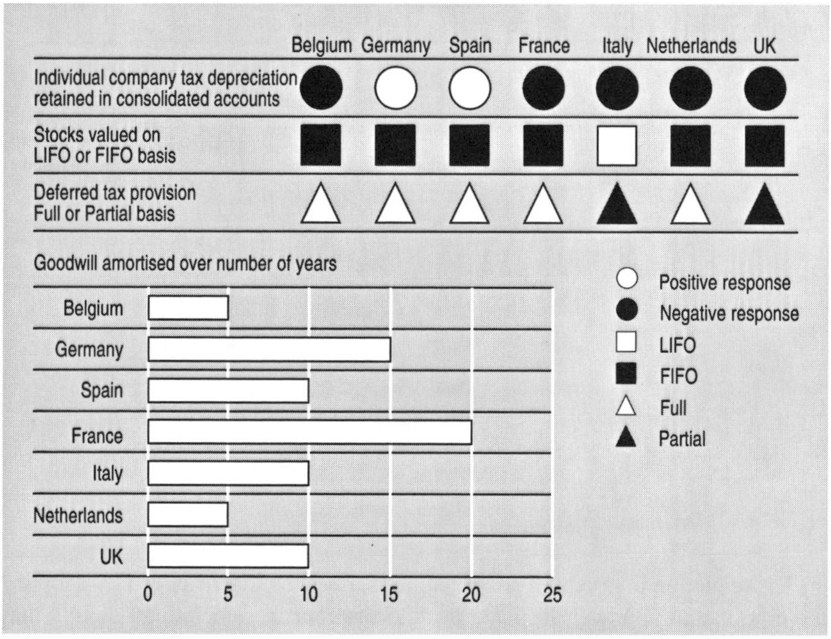

Figure 4.2 *Summary of net profit variations*

Variations of profit within countries

Taking the consolidated net profit from Figure 4.1 as a reference point, Figure 4.3 summarises the variations in this net profit that can be generated by applying alternative accounting policies that are at the limit of acceptability in each country.

Data used in Figure 4.3

Millions of ECUs	*Belgium*	*Germany*	*Spain*	*France*	*Italy*	*Netherlands*	*UK*
Maximum achievable	193	140	192	160	193	156	194
Most likely	135	133	131	149	174	140	192
Minimum achievable	90	27	121	121	167	76	171

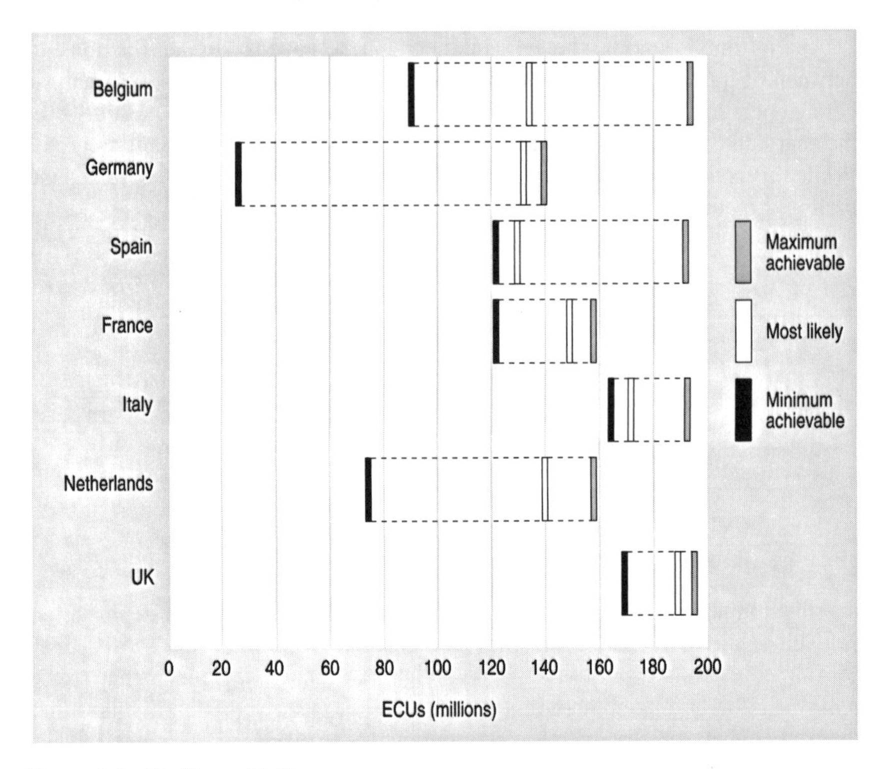

Figure 4.3 *Profit sensitivity*

The reduction in goodwill amortisation is, in each case, achieved by adopting the elimination approach in place of amortisation; in some countries this may only be possible in narrowly defined circumstances. Conversely, increases in the charge for goodwill are achieved either by increasing the rate of charge, effectively adopting a shorter life, or, in the case of the United Kingdom, by adopting the amortisation method (over an assumed five year life). The substantial reduction in profits possible in Germany and the Netherlands results from the ability in those countries to charge the cost of goodwill fully through the profit and loss account in the year of acquisition. [Figure 4.4]

An assumption has been made that stock values have increased over the year; this assumption affects the impact of the alternative uses of LIFO or FIFO stock valuation bases. On this assumption, Italian companies could increase their profit by using the FIFO, rather than the LIFO, basis of stock valuation, and companies in Belgium, Germany, France and the Netherlands could reduce their profit by using the LIFO, rather than the FIFO, basis. In the less likely event that stock values fell, the profit effects would be reversed.

The ability of a Belgian company to increase its profits by reducing its deferred tax charge assumes that it is possible to make no provision for deferred tax at all. While normal practice in Belgium is to make such provisions, there is no definitive requirement to do so.

The reduction in profits that can be achieved in Belgium by retaining individual company tax depreciation charges in consolidated accounts assumes that it is

	Belgium	Germany	Spain	France	Italy	Netherlands	UK
Profits maximised by	(1) (3)	(1)	(1) (3)	(1)	(1) (2)	(1)	
Profits minimised by	(5) (6) (7)	(4) (6) (7)	(4)	(4) (6)	(4)	(4) (6)	(4)

(1) Reducing the goodwill charge
(2) Valuing stocks on a FIFO basis
(3) Reducing the charge for deferred tax
(4) Increasing the goodwill charge
(5) Retaining individual company tax depreciation in the consolidated accounts
(6) Valuing stocks on a LIFO basis
(7) Removing certain overheads from stock valuation

Figure 4.4 *Maximum and minimum profit causes*

possible to make no adjustment on consolidation for the element of depreciation charged in the individual companies in a group to secure tax relief.

The reduction in profits which is possible in Belgium and Germany due to the removal of certain manufacturing overheads from stock valuation assumes that there would have been an increase in the amount of overhead in stock at the end of the accounting period. If there had been a decrease in this amount, profits would have been increased and not decreased.

Overall, it is interesting that the 'most likely' profit in the United Kingdom is near the 'maximum achievable' profit, while in Italy, it is near the 'minimum achievable' profit. If the effects of goodwill are excluded, the widest range of possible profits occurs in Belgium.

Comparison of net assets

The single largest component of balance sheet net assets is likely to be fixed assets. Figure 4.5 summarises the intangible and tangible fixed assets for each country.

A significant component of intangible fixed assets in the case study example was goodwill. The most significant variation between the intangible fixed assets of each country is the low intangible asset result for the United Kingdom. This is due to the use of the elimination basis of dealing with goodwill. Variations

Data used in Figure 4.5

Millions of ECUs	*Belgium*	*Germany*	*Spain*	*France*	*Italy*	*Netherlands*	*UK*
Intangibles	171	184	181	186	181	171	91
Tangibles	431	298	418	401	361	401	431
Total (average 558)	602	482	599	587	542	572	522

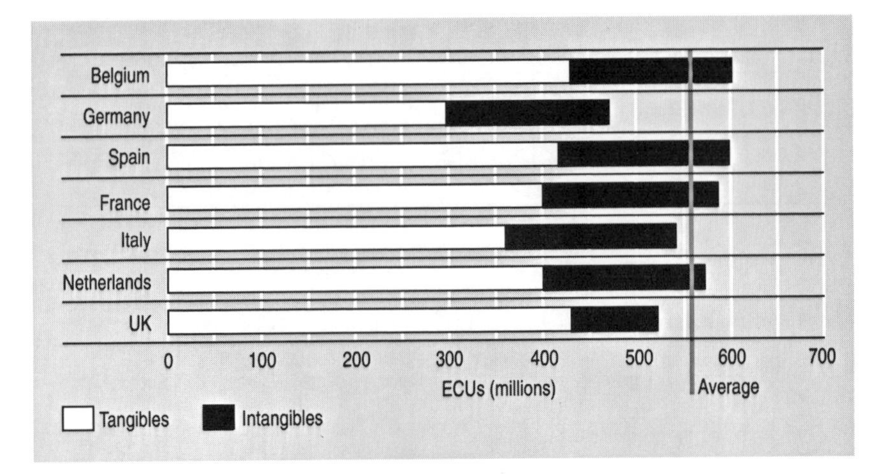

Figure 4.5 *Fixed assets*

between other countries are less significant, and result from the use of different lives for the amortisation of goodwill. This variation would result in larger differences in intangible fixed assets as time passes, and the variation in asset life takes effect.

The major factors affecting tangible fixed assets are summarised in Figure 4.6.

The adoption of a revaluation basis for the property assets in Belgium, Spain, and the United Kingdom suggests a flexible approach to revaluation in those countries. In Spain, such revaluation would not be contemplated in the individual company accounts. Revaluation in France and the Netherlands would only have been possible if a more wide ranging review of asset values had been made; the effect of such a review would have been to introduce revalued amounts for all classes of tangible fixed assets and investments. In the Netherlands, only the replacement cost basis would be acceptable.

The capitalisation of assets held under finance leases has the effect of increasing both tangible fixed assets and related liabilities. Capitalisation is possible in all countries, and is required in Belgium, the United Kingdom and the Netherlands. Capitalisation in the consolidated accounts of French companies reflects the most common treatment in that country, being a consolidation adjustment to reverse the prohibition on capitalisation in individual company accounts. The absence of capitalisation in Italy reflects the most common treatment there,

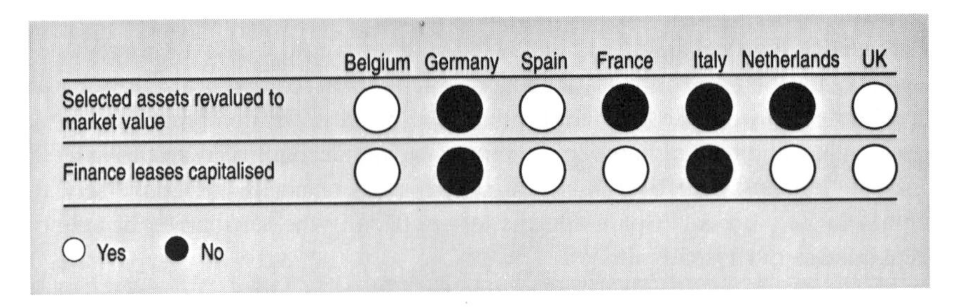

Figure 4.6 *Summary of tangible fixed asset variations*

while in Germany, it reflects complex conditions in the definition of a finance lease, which most leases do not meet.

Overall, the lowest tangible fixed assets were expected to occur, and actually did occur, in Germany as a result of the strict adherence in that country to historic cost principles, and to the retention of accelerated company tax depreciation, where available, within consolidated accounts. This has the effect of increasing the amount of accumulated depreciation, and hence of reducing the total net book value of tangible fixed assets.

Other variations within net assets

Other significant variations arose from:

- Use of the percentage-of-completion basis or completion basis for long-term contracts. Where profit is taken throughout the life of the contract, net assets will be increased by the cumulative amount of profit on uncompleted contracts included in work-in-progress. This will impact more upon companies in classes of business such as the construction industry than in others that have little or no involvement in long-term contracts. Variations were also noted in the methods by which progress payments are accounted for and disclosed. In some countries, progress payments are deducted from work-in-progress, while in others they are treated as a liability. Since this area is complex, and differing treatments may be adopted within the same country to reflect different circumstances, no general conclusions can be drawn.
- Use of differing deferred tax bases. The full basis of providing deferred tax results in a higher balance sheet provision for deferred tax than the partial basis. A higher balance sheet provision results in a lower total of net assets.
- Capitalisation of finance lease obligations. Where finance lease assets are capitalised and included within fixed assets, the related liability will be included within creditors. The effect on net assets is limited since the asset and the liability substantially cancel each other.

Return on net assets

The effects on net profit, and on net assets, can be combined into a single statistic, the return on net assets employed.

The explanation of differences lies with the separate explanations of profit variations and net asset variations already given. Certain factors are common between these: for example, where assets are exclusively carried at historic cost, the balance sheet net assets will be lower than they would if assets were revalued; against this, the profit and loss account charge for depreciation is also lower since it is computed from the balance sheet carrying values. The combination of lower asset value, and lower charge to the profit and loss account, may result, as in the case of Germany, in an overall increase in the return on net assets. Conversely, the return in Belgium and Spain appears low, reflecting the revaluation of tangible fixed assets in those countries.

Data used in Figure 4.7

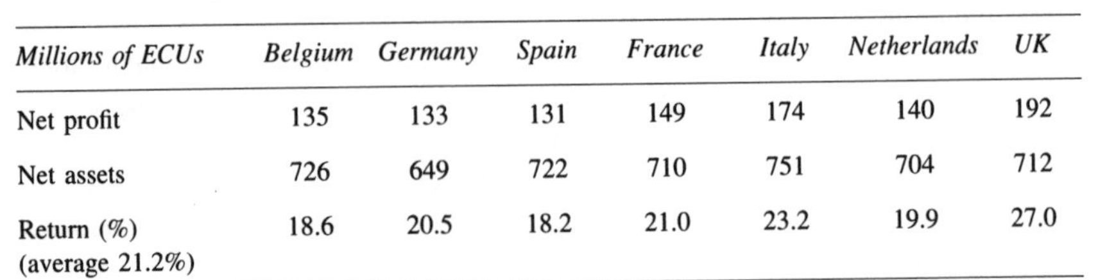

Millions of ECUs	*Belgium*	*Germany*	*Spain*	*France*	*Italy*	*Netherlands*	*UK*
Net profit	135	133	131	149	174	140	192
Net assets	726	649	722	710	751	704	712
Return (%) (average 21.2%)	18.6	20.5	18.2	21.0	23.2	19.9	27.0

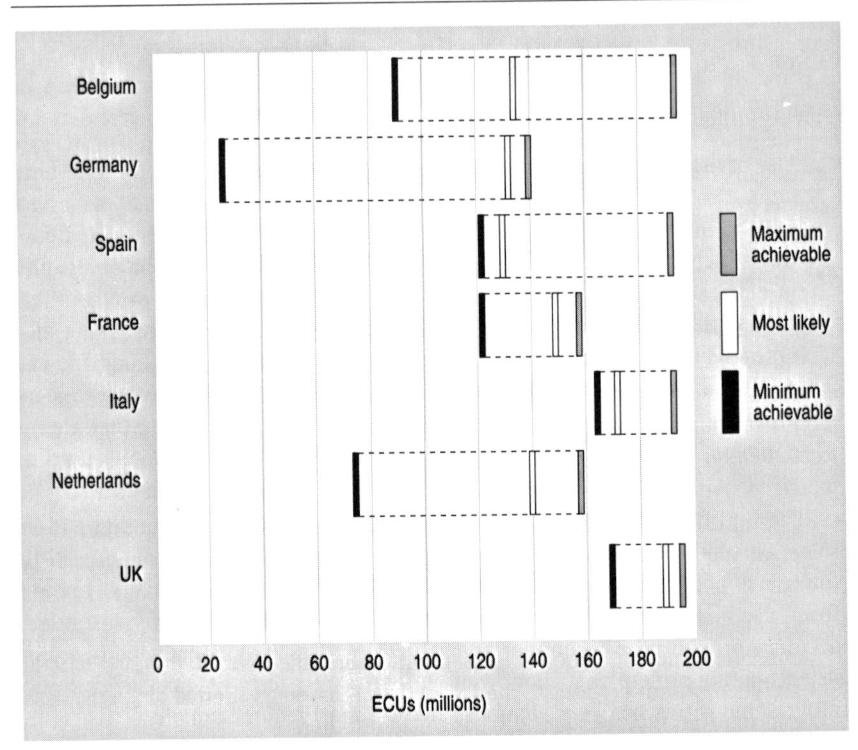

Figure 4.7 *Comparison of return on net assets*

The high return in the UK reflects the combination of the highest reported profits, and low intangible assets due to goodwill elimination [Figure 4.7].

5 Conclusion

Achievements

Accounting directives forged in Brussels have provided an overall framework for new European accounting law. From 1991, all interested parties will be able to obtain, for any medium or large company incorporated in any of the twelve member states:

- a directors' report;
- individual company (or consolidated) audited accounts; and
- notes to the accounts structured on a comparable basis.

European companies are, as a result, required to make more information available to the public than their American or Japanese counterparts. The process is irreversible, even if some Southern European countries take longer to adapt.

Even with this necessary legal framework, without which Europe would never have started on the long road to accounting harmonisation, many companies and financial market players may feel unsatisfied with the current practical outcome. Our survey has demonstrated, not only through comparative analysis of accounting principles, but also through a case study, that 'accounting Europe' currently remains compartmentalised when compared with American standardisation. On the positive side, there is now a high level of comparability in the form of accounting documentation; against this, there are still many differences in the detailed methods of computing profits, and the amounts at which assets and liabilities are stated. It is too soon yet to perform valid comparative analysis of earnings per share between London and Madrid, Frankfurt and Paris, Milan and Amsterdam, or Brussels and New York.

Obstacles to further progress

While the accounting profession in Europe are aware of this state of affairs, they would agree that the trend in business activity in Europe makes it essential that we continue to seek a common basis of accounting principles, even if the pursuit requires patience by all, and the sacrifice of some national positions. Realistically, in view of identified obstacles, the process of change can only be managed over a rather long period.

The first obstacle to future progress is the link between accounting and tax rules, presently too close in the majority of member states. Accounting in the future will not develop freely, or on sound technical principles, if it is not released from tax constraints. At the current time, the development of consolidated accounts provides the best opportunity for each country to independently rethink its accounting principles without waiting for the long-term EC tax harmonisation programme – this has been demonstrated by the French example.

The second obstacle lies in the text of the directives themselves. Drafted and discussed more than ten years ago, against a background of enormous divergence, and at a time when international understanding within Europe was less developed, the accounting methods that they incorporate are now somewhat out of date. This is particularly apparent in the area of valuation rules related to fixed assets and inventories, and the emerging issue of new financial instruments, which could not have been anticipated earlier. Certain options left open should now be removed; other areas require some amplification.

The third obstacle cannot be solved by Europe alone since it is a worldwide issue: a strong 'accounting Europe' is only conceivable and indeed worthwhile, if its standards are recognised by its main economic partners. This issue is especially relevant to countries seeking mutual acceptance of their reporting standards for international stock market listings. Discussions being conducted by the International Accounting Standards Committee, with a view to reducing options, are of key importance in this context. If this international organisation is to succeed in winning support from established accounting regimes, such as the United States, it is important that Europe is able to give strong support. Increased dialogue between the accounting profession, companies and rule setters, and an increase in the research budgets within Europe are preliminary conditions for success in the European voice being heard, and influencing the direction of worldwide accounting harmonisation.

Recommendations

Taking the inherent constraints of the EC structure into consideration, we consider the following recommendations are realistic.

EC harmonisation efforts should be concentrated on consolidated accounts
We have established that the Fourth Directive has failed to alter the use of individual company accounts for tax assessment purposes. Such accounts have little chance of achieving true comparability without the necessary separation of accounts and taxation. However, the implementation of the Seventh Directive is demonstrating that it is possible for consolidated accounts to break free from tax constraints, and be based on sound principles. It is this process that presents an opportunity. In practical terms, we are calling for:

- the EC Commission to concentrate their efforts on raising the standards of consolidated accounts. This will require careful monitoring of the Seventh Directive implementation, and action to ensure that emerging differences are resolved;
- in each member state, the preparation of consolidated accounts which have regard to international standards of presentation. At the heart of this recommendation are the adjustments made to company accounts at the time of consolidation. National governments, standard setters, accounting professions and accounts preparers may each contribute to achieving comparability.

Options should be reduced We have observed significant progress in many EC member states as a result of the company law directive programme. From a more mature starting point, it is now appropriate for the options written into Directives, particularly in relation to valuation rules, to be reviewed. At the same time, we consider that there is only a limited benefit in the development of European accounting practice if this is not linked to worldwide developments. In practical terms, we are calling for:

- accounts preparers and professionals at all levels to take advantage of the current opportunity to respond to the IASC options reduction initiative. Response is essential if Europe is to take its place in shaping the future;
- the EC Commission to review the Seventh Company Law Directive with a view to recognising the IASC programme of reducing options as it progresses;
- the IASC to respond quickly in developing standards on new and emerging issues where national standard setting bodies have not established written guidelines.

Comparative studies should be encouraged It is noticeable that the majority of comparative studies undertaken are limited to comparing laws and written regulations. Such studies do not take into account the way in which rules are interpreted, or the overall comparability of reported results. In practical terms, we are calling for:

- new detailed studies to monitor the progress of the Seventh Company Law Directive as it is implemented;
- an increase in the research budgets of private, national and international agencies to enable such studies to be undertaken.

Finally ... Achievement of accounting harmonisation in Europe before the end of 1992? The target is likely to be unrealistic in view of the unavoidable weight of traditions, and the complexity of present regulations.

If member states are willing to give their support, the plan will continue after January 1st 1993. As far as we are concerned, we will be satisfied if the main accounting differences listed in our survey are settled before January 1st 2000!

PART 3

STRATEGIC COMPARISONS

Introduction

Geoff Mallory

One crucial deficiency of conventional performance indicators as measures or indicators of strategic performance or corporate success is that they are invariably accounting-based measures which really reflect history and not future potential. Another view would be that they measure performance for a very specific group of stakeholders – the shareholders. This not only has implications for the ways in which such measures are designed but also puts important limitations on use. Few people would regard organizations' published, audited reports alone as sufficient data from which to produce comprehensive and meaningful measurements of strategic performance.

In the introduction to the article on measuring strategic performance, Balaji Chakravarthy argues that, while the topic has been discussed and written about, there really appears to be little agreement on how it should be measured and even whether it should be measured at all. However, the author does make the point 'that without a performance referent managers cannot objectively or consistently evaluate the quality of their strategic decisions' – the crucial decisions that they need to make to close the gaps between intent and actuality.

While the article is rather long and involved it does deal comprehensively with the topic. Chakravarthy develops several classes of performance indicators using a comparative methodology which seeks to account for strategic performance of 'excellent' as opposed to 'non-excellent' companies.

The first group of measures – identified as conventional – includes such indicators of profitability as Return on Total Capital (ROTC) and Return on Book Equity for Return on Investment (ROI) and Return on Sales (ROS). Chakravarthy concludes from his analysis that none of these are capable of distinguishing differences in the strategic performance of his sample in any consistent manner. In a similar way financial/market measures such as market to book value are explored and criticized and composite indicators such as the Z factor are discussed. However, the main contribution of the study is that it identifies slack variables as contributing to the strategic success of the various companies. It is the long-term rather than the short-term decisions that have the major impact on corporate success.

This idea and that of success being comparative is taken up by the next contribution which is a chapter from John Kay's book *The Foundations of Corporate Success* in which he further examines the strengths and weaknesses of performance measures, and argues from an analysis of British food retailing chains that the key measure of corporate success is added value.

Kay goes on to contrast the added value statement with the usual financial statements of companies and makes the point that success is really a relative concept and the best way to understand what it actually means is to compare the performance of different firms operating in the same domain. Corporate success is the ability of companies to add value to the inputs they use, that is labour, materials and capital costs. So, for example, a comparison of the value chains of the six UK retailing groups reveals two clear winners: Sainsbury's and Kwik Save. Kay goes on to compare a wide spread of companies across Europe using this measure and concludes that while size, market share, etc. are aspects of success it is the achievement of added value that underpins good performance.

This idea of added value is given an airing in a different sector (higher education) and tackled in a different way in the article on degree result differences between universities by Jill Johnes and Jim Taylor. They address the question of whether the quality of graduates (expressed in degree result) varies because of the quality of teaching – a degree being 'the most obvious outcome of teaching activity'. An alternative hypothesis is that any differences are due to the quality of the raw material input – the prior academic ability of the students. The authors find that the degree results for any one year vary more between universities than within them and investigate the causes by using multiple regression. The analysis reveals that a substantial proportion of this variation is explained by a set of variables which do not include a direct measure of teaching inputs. The main source of variance was the mean A-level scores of entrants. Thus the construction of a 'value added' statement is not straightforward in this case and any comparisons of performance must be mediated by a critical examination of the data.

Finally, Johnes and Taylor suggest that, indeed, the use of degree result as a performance indicator itself is problematic as it is within the control of the individual universities and thus there may become a temptation for universities to award more 'good' degrees if, for example, funding was granted based on such a measure.

In another approach to comparing performance Michael Schefczyk looks at the operational performance of airlines. This is a truly global industry with many international carriers exposed to different competitive pressures and regimes. Yet this article looks at operational performance and so how does it relate to strategic issues? After initially concentrating on operations the analysis shifts on to issues of profitability and utilization of resources, both indicators of the potential that underpins strategic success.

In the opening section, Schefczyk discusses at some length the issues surrounding performance measures in the industry and the problems of making valid comparisons. He then develops a model of performance based on data envelopment analysis and, while pointing out its limitations, concludes that it is a viable tool for benchmarking airline operational performance – the ability to produce given outputs with the minimum consumption of resources. In this industry, he argues again from a comparative perspective that high operational performance is a key factor in profitability.

The proposition that can be derived from this particular group of studies is that measuring strategic performance is a difficult but necessary undertaking. They indicate that making comparisons is an extremely common approach. Whether this is done by comparing excellent organizations with the not so good, by regression analysis or by other statistical techniques or across or within sectors, a significant problem remains with the indicators used for the comparison. How is excellence measured? How can differences due to accounting conventions and reporting requirements be controlled for? What is the impact of the measure used on behaviour?

It seems that discussions on measuring strategic or organizational performance raise rather more questions than answers. Is this such a bad thing?

12
Measuring strategic performance*

Balaji S. Chakravarthy

Summary

This article demonstrates the inadequacy of traditional measures, that are based on a firm's profitability, for evaluating its strategic performance. Two other measures, one that attempts to assess the quality of a firm's transformations (and not merely its outcomes) and the other that attempts to measure the satisfaction of all of the firm's stakeholders (and not merely its stockholders), are shown here to be important discriminators of strategic performance. The performances of seven 'excellent' firms from the computer industry, featured in the recent book by Peters and Waterman, are contrasted with that of seven 'non-excellent' firms from the same industry, to develop a framework for measuring strategic performance.

Strategic management is the process through which managers ensure the long-term adaptation of their firm to its environment (Chakravarthy, 1981; Miles, 1982; Miles and Snow, 1978; Sammuto, 1982). Useful measures of strategic performance are therefore those that help assess the quality of a firm's adaptation.

Organizational performance (Child, 1974, 1975; Lenz, 1981; Thorelli, 1977), and organizational effectiveness (Cameron and Whetten, 1983; Evan, 1976; Ghorpade, 1970; Goodman and Pennings, 1977; Spray, 1976; Steers, 1977) are but two of the labels under which aspects of strategic performance have been researched. Despite these attempts there is little agreement on how strategic performance should be measured (Cameron and Whetten, 1983). Some authors have even suggested that the construct be abandoned altogether (Goodman, 1979; Hannan and Freeman, 1977). It can be argued, however, that without a performance referent managers cannot objectively or consistently evaluate the quality of their strategic decisions.

This article seeks to identify useful measures of strategic performance that can help distinguish well-adapted firms from mal-adapted ones. It is divided into three sections. The first section discusses the research design used for the study. The next section evaluates some of the current perspectives on measuring strategic performance and points to their limitations. The third section analyzes alternate perspectives on measuring strategic performance that focus on the quality of the firm's 'slack' management and the satisfaction that a firm provides its various stakeholders. The paper concludes with a proposal for measuring strategic performance.

* This article was first published in *Strategic Management Journal* (1986), Vol. 7, pp. 437–458.

Research design

In search of a sample

The basic approach used in this study was to select a sample of well-adapted and mal-adapted firms from the same industry, and then to identify performance measures that best distinguished the two groups. A vexing problem was to assess the quality of a firm's adaptation without falling into the tautological trap of arbitrarily using a performance measure for that purpose.

In theory, the quality of a firm's adaptation can be evaluated on a number of dimensions. These include whether:

1 a firm's strategy is congruent with its industry structure (Porter, 1980) and competitive context (Buzzell, Gale and Sultan, 1975; Henderson, 1979)
2 its organization structure fits its environment (Lawrence and Lorsch, 1967) and strategy (Chandler, 1962; Rumelt, 1974)
3 its management systems fit its strategy and organizational structure (Miles and Snow, 1978; Vancil, 1979)

and

4 its management style is tailored to its strategic context (Mintzberg and Waters, 1983).

In short, a well-adapted firm must be able to match its strengths with the opportunities in its environment; and to align its various administrative systems to its chosen strategy, and efficient synchronization of its 7-Ss. Fashioned by McKinsey, the management consulting firm, the 7-Ss are the so-called hard Ss of strategy, structure and systems; and the soft Ss of style, shared values, staff and skill.

Appealing as the above framework is, it is difficult and time-consuming to classify the quality of adaptation of a firm based on whether it enjoys all of the above fits. The popular book on 'excellence' by Peters and Waterman (1982) was therefore very useful for this study. Both Peters and Waterman were consultants with McKinsey at that time and used the 7-S framework to guide their research. Given their privileged access as consultants, they were able to verify the fit between the 7-Ss in several of the 'excellent' firms cited by them. Firms that enjoyed superior fit between their 7-Ss were 'especially adroit at continually responding to change of any sort in their environments' (Peters and Waterman, 1982, p. 12). 'Excellent' firms were internally well fitted and externally well adapted.

Subjective and partial as Peters and Waterman's validation may be (Carroll, 1983), it still represents the only attempt at systematically examining the quality of adaptation in a large sample of companies. Moreover, each of the 62 firms short-listed by them was identified as well adapted by 'an informed group of observers of the business scene – businessmen, consultants, members of the business press, and business academics' (Peters and Waterman, 1982, p. 12). For [the] purposes of this article, therefore, 'excellence' as used by Peters and Waterman and quality of adaptation are treated synonymously. Performance attributes that discriminate 'excellence' also discriminate the quality of a firm's adaptation. They are reasonable measures of strategic performance.

It must be mentioned that Peters and Waterman subsequently applied two performance screens to further refine their sample. The first was financial performance. An 'excellent' firm had to be in the top half of its industry in at least four of the following six measures over a 20-year period, 1961 through 1980: compound asset growth, compound equity growth, ratio of market to book value, average return on total capital, average return on equity, and average return on sales. The second was a measure of innovativeness. Select industry experts were asked to rate the companies in their industry on their 20-year record of innovating bellwether products and services, and on their ability to adapt rapidly to changing industry conditions. As will be discussed later in the article, some of these measures are necessary conditions for 'excellence'. However, the financial criteria in particular were not sufficient to discriminate 'excellence' in the Peters and Waterman sample.

This article seeks to find a better definition of the performance profile of an 'excellent' firm. Such a profile can then form the basis for measuring strategic performance.

The sample

The structure of the industry in which a firm operates constrains its strategies and affects its performance (Porter, 1980). Given the difficulties in comparing performance across industries (Hirsch, 1975), only firms from a single industry, computers, were chosen for this study. The computer industry had the highest representation of 'excellent' firms (seven) among the industries studied by Peters and Waterman. The choice of this industry was also influenced in part by the difficulties in getting business-level performance statistics for diversified firms. Firms in the computer industry have been predominantly single-business firms, with very little diversification outside the industry. Their aggregate performance can therefore be used as a close surrogate for the performance of their computer business units.

The seven 'excellent' firms in the computer industry are IBM, Hewlett Packard (HP), Digital Equipment Corporation (DEC), National Cash Register (NCR), Amdahl, Wang, and Data General. The first three are among the handful of exemplar firms that were frequently cited by Peters and Waterman to illustrate various traits of 'excellence'.

The 'excellence' of the five larger firms chosen (excluding Data General and Amdahl) is also corroborated by the *Fortune* magazine survey of corporate reputations (Table 1 opposite). For the past 3 years, *Fortune* (1983, 1984, 1985) has been polling senior industry executives, outside directors and financial analysts knowledgeable about the computer industry (one of 20 industries surveyed), to score the reputation of its 10 biggest competitors on eight different performance attributes. The three exemplar companies in our sample ranked overall among the top four in their industry (Table 1). In fact, IBM and Hewlett Packard have been consistently placed among the top five in the entire sample of 200 companies surveyed by *Fortune*.

Table 1 *Ranking of corporate reputations (average score)*

		1982	1983	1984
1	IBM	8.26	8.53	8.44
2	Hewlett Packard	8.26	8.24	8.08
3	Digital Equipment	7.70	7.24	6.86
4	Wang	7.35	7.22	7.07
5	NCR	5.76	6.29	6.07
6	CDC	6.12	5.98	5.50
7	Honeywell	5.67	5.79	5.78
8	Burroughs	5.05	5.04	5.33
9	Sperry	4.93	5.16	5.00

(Sources: *Fortune*, 10 January, 1983, pp. 34–44; *Fortune*, 9 January, 1984, pp. 50–62; *Fortune*, 7 January, 1985, pp. 18–30.)

Table 2 *The sample*

SI no.	Company name	SIC code[a]	Evaluation by Peters and Waterman	1983 sales ($ billion)	1983 *Fortune* rank
1	IBM	3680	Exemplar	40.18	5
2	Hewlett Packard (HP)	3680	Exemplar	4.71	75
3	Digital Equipment (DEC)	3680	Exemplar	4.27	84
4	NCR	3680	Excellent	3.73	101
5	Wang	3681	Excellent	1.54	227
6	Data General	3682	Excellent	0.83	335
7	Amdahl	3682	Excellent	0.78	350
8	Honeywell	3680	–	5.75	60
9	Sperry	3680	–	4.91	66
10	Control Data	3680	–	4.58	76
11	Burroughs	3680	–	4.30	82
12	Commodore	3681	–	0.68[b]	–
13	Prime Computer	3682	–	0.52	451
14	Cray Research	3682	–	0.17	–

[a] 3680: Electronic computing equipment; 3681: Computers – mini and micro; 3682: Computers – mainframe.

[b] Unranked in *Fortune 500* because complete year's results were unavailable at the time of ranking.

The above sample of seven firms was then expanded to include seven other 'non-excellent' firms: Burroughs, Control Data Corporation (CDC), Sperry, Honeywell, Prime Computer, Cray, and Commodore. They were selected for three reasons:

1 Their omission from the short list of firms proposed by industry experts in the Peters and Waterman survey is construed here as evidence of their lack of 'excellence'. The corporate reputations of these 'non-excellent' firms, where available, was also lower than that of the 'excellent' firms (with the exception of NCR in 1983) in the *Fortune* survey (see Table 1).

2 Each of the selected 'non-excellent' firms has been held publicly since 1977, when Peters and Waterman first began their survey. Newer firms may not have been considered by industry experts in responding to that survey.

3 The selected firms belong to the same three SIC groups as the 'excellent' firms: electronic computing equipment (SIC 3680), mini and micro computers (SIC 3681), and mainframes (SIC 3682). The three groups are represented by eight, two, and four firms respectively, with equal numbers of 'excellent' and 'non-excellent' firms in each (Table 2).

The performance of the 14 firms, as reported in the Standard and Poor's Compustat data base, was analyzed on a variety of criteria. The more discriminating a performance criterion is in distinguishing 'excellence' from 'non-excellence', the more useful it is for measuring strategic performance.

Conventional measures of strategic performance

Measures of profitability

A recent survey of performance measures used in research on strategic management identified 14 distinct quantitative measures: Return on Investment, Return on Sales, Growth in Revenues, Cash Flow/Investment, Market Share, Market Share Gain, Product Quality Relative to Competitors, New Product Activities Relative to Competitors, Direct Cost Relative to Competitors, Product R&D, Process R&D, Variations in ROI, Percentage Point Change in ROI, and Percentage Point Change in Cash Flow/Investment (Woo and Willard, 1983). The authors factor-analyzed the 14 variables using the PIMS data base and isolated four factors which they named: profitability, relative market position, change in profitability and cash flow, and growth in sales and market share. Of these, again, the profitability factor demonstrated the highest factor magnitude. The primary variables that loaded on this factor were Return on Investment, Return on Sales, and Cash Flow to Investment, with the first and third variables being highly correlated.

Woo and Willard concluded that profitability measures such as Return on Investment (ROI) and Return on Sales (ROS), despite their many limitations (Dearden, 1969; McGuire and Schneeweis, 1983; Reece and Cool, 1978), were important measures of performance:

> Despite the problems inherent in ROI (Return on Investment), results from this study would support the continued use of this measure. The profitability factor demonstrated the highest factor magnitude (explaining 17.7 percent of the variance) and significantly exceeded the magnitude of the second factor, relative market position (which explained 10.7 percent of the variance) ... When properly complemented by other measures, this study shows that ROI is essential to the comprehensive representation of performance.
> (Woo and Willard, 1983, p. 13)

This was an encouraging conclusion given that data on two of the four factors, i.e. relative market position and growth in sales and market share, are not readily available for all businesses. The data are proprietary to the PIMS data base, limited therefore only to its members, and even then revealed not by company but only in aggregate form.

Return on Total Capital and Return on Book Equity are two popular variants of the ROI measure. Three variables associated with the profitability factor, Return on Sales, Return on Total Capital, and Return on Book Equity, were used to analyze the performance of the 14 computer companies in the sample (Table 3 overleaf). These incidentally were also the three profitability screens used by Peters and Waterman (1982).

The mean performance of each firm was compared on the three profitability measures with other firms in the sample. Tukey's (1953) standardized range test was used for the multiple comparison of means. Repeated *t*-tests were not used because with 91 different comparisons (14 companies paired two at a time), the chance of making at least one type 1 error approaches 1. The Tukey procedure controls MEER (maximum experimentwise error rate under any complete or partial null hypothesis) at specified α levels – 0.05 in this study. It also allows for an unequal number of observations, due to varying ages of the firms in the sample.

It must be noted, however, that the Tukey procedure is a conservative one. Its failure to reject the null hypothesis, that the means of the two companies compared are equal, does not imply that the population means are in fact equal. It only suggests that the difference between the two population means, if any, is not large enough to be detected with the given sample size.

None of the three measures of profitability was able to clearly distinguish 'excellent' firms from 'non-excellent' ones, despite their use as performance screens by Peters and Waterman (who incidentally must have merely looked at the means without examining the associated standard deviations). Table 4 (pp. 260–1) summarizes the results of the pairwise comparison of mean performances using the Tukey procedure. The table shows firms whose performance differed significantly from the focal firm on the three chosen measures:

1 The Return on Equity (ROE) measure did not show any significant difference between 'excellent' and 'non-excellent' firms. This came as a surprise given that ROE is a popular measure of performance.

2 Return on Total Capital (ROTC) was only marginally better as a discriminator. In fact the only conclusive finding using this measure of performance was that five of the seven 'excellent' companies (with the exception of NCR and Data General) outperformed Control Data.

Table 3 *Comparison of profitability (1964–83)*

Company	No. of years	Return on sales		Return on total capital		Return on book equity	
		mean	SD	mean	SD	mean	SD
Excellent companies							
IBM	20	13.43	0.93	34.06	3.75	19.02	2.28
HP	20	8.27	0.80	29.12	4.31	15.44	2.17
DEC	18	9.75	1.45	26.94	14.92	16.17	7.10
NCR	20	4.42	3.26	16.65	8.54	10.03	6.95
Wang	17	8.90	2.12	29.84	21.14	20.33	9.39
Data General	14	9.66	3.27	26.10	9.38	15.15	5.47
Amdahl	8	10.24	8.31	33.21	26.50	19.92	16.51
Non-excellent companies							
Honeywell	20	4.54	1.02	18.85	3.17	12.38	2.47
Sperry	20	4.17	1.06	19.16	4.70	10.49	2.57
Control Data	20	4.40	2.69	10.49	4.81	7.16	3.93
Burroughs	20	7.10	2.78	18.28	4.83	11.15	3.16
Commodore	19	5.92	8.91	26.55	36.00	14.22	47.80
Prime Computer	9	9.25	2.07	29.88	5.66	28.71	10.09
Cray Research	7	17.30	2.24	27.60	10.33	17.13	4.93

(Source: Compustat Data Base.)

3 While the performance of the 14 firms was more distinguishable on the Return on Sales (ROS) criterion, it did not help separate 'excellent' and 'non-excellent' firms in any consistent fashion. Several 'excellent' firms like Hewlett Packard, DEC, Wang, Data General and Amdahl were indistinguishable from 'non-excellent' firms like Burroughs, Commodore and Prime Computer. Cray Research, a 'non-excellent' company, outperformed six of the seven 'excellent' companies (with the exception of IBM) on this criterion; and NCR, an 'excellent' company, was surpassed on ROS by all other 'excellent' companies and two other 'non-excellent' companies, Prime Computer and Cray Research. Apart from demonstrating IBM's superiority, the ROS criterion was not very helpful in distinguishing the performance of other firms.

Conventionally profitability criteria are incapable, then, of distinguishing differences in the strategic performances of the computer firms in the sample.

Financial-market measures of performance

Measures of performance rooted in financial accounting, such as the ones described above, have come in for a lot of recent criticism (McGuire and Schneeweis, 1983). The problems that have been cited with this approach are: (1) scope for accounting manipulation; (2) undervaluation of assets; (3) distortions due to depreciation policies, inventory valuation and treatment of certain revenue and expenditure items; (4) differences in methods of consolidating accounts; and (5) differences due to lack of standardization in international accounting conventions.

Moreover, accounting-measures-of-performance record only the history of a firm. Monitoring a firm's strategy requires measures that can also capture its potential for performance in the future. The spread between the market and book values of the firm has been shown to be a measure of the perceived ability of the firm to return to its stockholders an amount in the future in excess of their expected return (Rappaport, 1981). M/B ratio is therefore a more appropriate measure of a firm's strategic performance. Peters and Waterman used this measure as a performance screen to evaluate the long-term wealth creation potential of a firm. However, the measure is not entirely free from accounting manipulations – the book value of a firm can be distorted.

The M/B ratios from 1964 to 1983 for the 14 firms in the sample are shown in Table 5 (see p. 262). Surprisingly, there was once again no statistically significant difference (at 0.05 level) on a pairwise comparison of the mean M/B ratios of the 14 companies over the period 1964–83. Digital Equipment (DEC) and Wang were the two major exceptions. They outperformed NCR and Sperry on this criterion (see Table 4).

It is interesting to observe, however, that the M/B ratios of all companies in the sample declined in the period 1964–83. Moreover, the spread between the M/B ratios of various computer companies was also much smaller in 1983 than it was in the 1960s. This may reflect either the financial market's scepticism about the industry's future prospects or its concerns over increasing competition in the industry. In the past two decades the financial market has only rewarded new entrants to the computer industry with a high premium over book value, and that too for the first few years after initial entry. This has been true both in the case of micro-computer manufacturers like Wang and Commodore, as well as mainframe manufacturers like Data General and Prime Computer.

Therefore the declining M/B ratio for a particular computer company is not so much an indictment of its strategy as it is a recognition of the increasingly tougher industry environment in which it operates. Instead of absolute M/B then, the M/B ratio relative to the industry is perhaps a more meaningful measure of a computer company's strategic performance. The M/B ratios of all companies in the sample were standardized using industry mean and standard deviation on M/B in a given year (assuming that the industry was represented by the 14 firms in the sample). Further, to neutralize the declining trend in M/B over the past 20 years, each year's industry mean was set to zero and its standard deviation set to 1. In other words, the standardized M/B value measures used in this study represent the number of standard deviations a firm's M/B ratio was from the industry average in a given year (Table 6, p. 263).

Table 4 *Companies in the sample significantly[a] different in their performance when compared with excellent firms*

	Return on sales		Return on total capital		Return on equity		Z factor		Market to book ratio	
Excellent firms	Other excellent firms	Non-excellent firms	Other excellent firms	Non-excellent firms	Other excellent firms	Non-excellent firms	Other excellent firms	Non-excellent firms	Other excellent firms	Non-excellent firms
1 IBM	HP NCR Wang	Honeywell Sperry Control Data Burroughs Commodore	NCR	Control Data Burroughs	None	None	None	None	None	None
2 HP	IBM[b] NCR	Sperry Control Data Cray Research[b]	None	Control Data	None	None	NCR	Sperry Control Data	None	None
3 DEC	NCR	Honeywell Sperry Control Data Cray Research[b]	None	Control Data	None	None	NCR	Honeywell Sperry Control Data Burroughs	NCR	Sperry
4 NCR	IBM[b] HP[b] DEC[b] Wang[b] Data General[b] Amdahl[b]	Prime Computer[b] Cray Research[b]	IBM[b]	None	None	None	DEC[b] HP[b] Data General[b]	None	DEC[b] Wang[b]	None

5 Wang	IBM[b] NCR	Honeywell Sperry Control Data Cray Research[b]	None	Control Data	None	None	None	None	NCR	Honeywell Sperry Control Data Burroughs
6 Data General	NCR	Honeywell Sperry Control Data Cray Research[b]	None	None	None	None	Amdahl NCR	Sperry Control Data Commodore Prime Computer Burroughs Honeywell	None	None
7 Amdahl	NCR	Honeywell Sperry Control Data Cray Research[b]	None	Control Data	None	None	Data General[b]	None	None	None

[a] Tukey's Standardized Range Test for unequal cell sizes. Confidence = 0.95.

[b] Indicates performance was significantly inferior when compared with these companies. Significantly superior otherwise. Level of significance = 0.05.

Table 5 *Market to book ratio (1964–83)*

Company	SIC code	1964	1967	1970	1973	1976	1979	1980	1981	1982	1983	Mean (1964–83)	SD (1964–83)
Excellent companies													
IBM	3680	6.41	9.18	6.12	4.11	3.30	2.51	2.40	1.85	2.90	3.21	4.72	2.21
HP	3680	4.40	7.68	3.87	6.25	3.62	2.83	3.48	2.52	3.90	3.74	4.86	1.91
DEC	3680	–	26.71	7.25	5.04	3.45	2.49	2.62	1.75	1.74	1.15	7.29	7.89
NCR	3680	2.38	3.03	1.39	1.14	1.10	1.33	1.27	0.67	1.27	1.76	1.54	0.74
Wang	3681	–	65.35	6.86	2.51	1.47	6.85	10.90	4.25	6.13	5.00	10.03	15.37
Data General	3682	–	–	9.38	8.35	3.75	2.18	2.12	1.47	1.01	1.80	4.27	3.15
Amdahl	3682	–	–	–	–	4.59	2.10	2.37	1.91	1.92	1.91	2.87	1.18
Non-excellent companies													
Honeywell	3680	3.27	4.54	2.63	1.48	0.94	1.19	1.40	0.81	0.96	1.39	2.18	1.40
Sperry	3680	1.13	3.69	1.13	1.56	1.14	0.99	1.12	0.63	0.64	0.91	1.39	0.72
Control Data	3680	6.24	12.24	1.18	0.63	0.50	0.78	0.92	0.83	0.81	0.95	2.26	2.99
Burroughs	3680	1.21	6.19	3.40	4.11	2.47	1.51	1.05	0.66	0.86	1.02	2.98	1.98
Commodore	3681	–	–	–	–	1.15	5.08	13.87	7.54	9.46	6.65	5.00	4.39
Prime Computer	3682	–	–	–	–	6.71	6.43	12.18	4.89	4.73	3.11	5.80	2.78
Cray Research	3682	–	–	–	–	–	5.90	8.68	5.24	3.87	4.70	5.46	1.91

(Source: Compustat Data Base.)

Table 6 shows some interesting patterns. Firstly, while 'excellent' companies did not always have the best M/B ratio, they consistently performed above the industry mean. IBM, Hewlett Packard, Wang and DEC exemplify this quality. Their standardized M/B ratio was negative very infrequently when compared to firms such as Honeywell, Sperry, and Control Data. However, the performance of NCR, an 'excellent' company, was generally indistinguishable from that of several 'non-excellent' companies, all showing M/B ratios below industry average in most years. In fact, *B*urroughs, Sperry-*U*nivac, *N*CR, *C*DC, and *H*oneywell, are unglamorously called the BUNCH by some industry analysts (Magnet, 1984).

Table 6 *Standardized market to book ratio*

Company	1965	1967	1969	1971	1973	1975	1977	1979	1981	1983
Excellent companies										
IBM	1.64	-0.28	-0.02	-0.70	0.32	0.51	0.68	-0.28	-0.39	0.26
HP	1.33	-0.36	-0.05	0.50	1.18	1.70	0.12	-0.13	-0.10	0.55
DEC	–	0.64	1.79	0.87	0.70	1.36	0.06	-0.29	-0.44	-0.91
NCR	-0.70	-0.60	-0.72	-1.30	-0.87	-1.04	-1.15	-0.82	-0.91	-0.56
Wang	–	2.66	1.84	1.58	-0.32	-0.80	-0.05	1.73	0.67	1.27
Data General	–	–	–	0.91	2.03	1.08	0.77	-0.43	-0.56	-0.54
Amdahl	–	–	–	–	–	–	1.17	-0.47	-0.36	-0.48
Non-excellent companies										
Honeywell	-0.04	-0.52	-0.51	-0.32	-0.73	-1.05	-1.36	-0.89	-0.85	-0.77
Sperry	-1.14	-0.57	-0.89	-1.21	-0.70	-0.73	-1.29	-0.98	-0.93	-1.04
CDC	-0.01	-0.012	-0.77	-1.33	-1.07	-1.28	-1.60	-1.08	-0.84	-1.02
Burroughs	-0.83	-0.44	-0.21	-0.03	0.33	0.24	-0.55	-0.74	-0.92	-0.98
Commodore	–	–	–	–	–	-0.68	0.25	0.91	2.12	2.20
Prime Computer	–	–	–	–	–	0.54	1.73	1.53	0.95	0.20
Cray Research	–	–	–	–	–	–	0.51	1.75	1.10	1.10

Standardized by year: mean = 0, SD = 1. (Source: Computstat Data Base.)

Summary

The empirical evidence from the computer industry suggests that conventional referents of performance, whether they be measures of profitability, like ROS, ROE and ROTC, or financial market measures, like the M/B ratio, are unsatisfactory discriminants of 'excellence'.

Perhaps this should not come as a surprise, since the above measures of performance have at lease three major limitations: (1) they assume that a single performance criterion can assess 'excellence', (2) they focus only on outcomes to the exclusion of transformation processes within the firm, and (3) they ignore the claims of other stakeholders besides the stockholder. Other perspectives on measuring strategic performance that overcome these limitations will be discussed in the next section.

Alternative perspectives on measuring strategic performance

Composite measures of performance

Several recent studies have pointed out that instead of searching for that single measure which most significantly determines performance, a multi-factor model of performance assessment should be used (Bagozzi and Phillips, 1982; Benson, 1974; Keats, 1983). Their argument is based on the fact that 'excellence' is a complex phenomenon requiring more than a single criterion to define it.

One of the better known multi-factor models of performance is the bankruptcy model (Altman, 1971; Argenti, 1976). These researchers found, through a careful study of several corporate bankruptcies, that a multiple discriminant function called the Z factor had very good predictive powers for determining corporate bankruptcies, especially close to the actual event. Z was defined as:

$$0.012\ X1 + 0.014\ X2 + 0.033\ X3 + 0.006\ X4 + 0.010\ X5$$

where

$X1$ is working capital/total assets,

$X2$ is the retained earnings/total assets,

$X3$ is the earnings before interest and taxes/total assets,

$X4$ is the market value of equity/book value of total debt, and

$X5$ is sales/total assets.

The prescription, offered by these studies based on an empirical analysis of bankrupt and healthy companies, is simple:

> You work out these five ratios for your company, multiply each by its own constant, add them up, and arrive at Z, the figure which shows if your company is going bust. If Z is less than 1.8 you are almost certain to go bust, if it is more than 3.0 you almost certainly will not. (Argenti, 1976, p. 57)

While the Z values were essentially constructed to predict bankruptcy (and even here, its success has been mixed), it can also be a valuable index of the company's overall well-being. The higher the Z value is beyond 3, the more healthy is the firm. By measuring distance from bankruptcy, Z factor could be a surrogate index of strategic performance. This measure is obviously flawed in that a well-managed firm does not focus all its energies only on staving off bankruptcy. Nevertheless, being the only multi-factor model of performance that has been extensively tested, the Z factor was included as one of the performance screens for this study. While very high Z scores may not account for much, scores lower than the threshold of 3 should be cause for concern.

The Z factors for the 14 companies (Table 7) do indeed show a more distinctive pattern than the profitability measures that were discussed earlier. The mean Z scores for 'excellent' companies like Data General, DEC, and Hewlett Packard were significantly higher (at 0.05 level of significance) than that for 'non-excellent' companies like Sperry, and Control Data (see Table 4). Four of the 'excellent' firms in the sample – IBM, Hewlett Packard, DEC, and Data General – did not experience a Z score of less than 3.0 even once in the 20-year period from

1964 to 1983. In contrast, Cray Research was the only 'non-excellent' firm to have such a clean record. In fact, four 'non-excellent' firms – Honeywell, Sperry, Control Data, and Burroughs, had *Z* scores of less than 3.0 in 7 or more years in the same 20-year period. However, the performance of NCR, an 'excellent' company, was equally disappointing on this performance measure – Z scores below 3.0 in 9 of the 20 years. Its *Z* scores were also significantly lower than that of three other 'excellent' companies – Hewlett Packard, Data General, and DEC.

Impressive as this criterion is in discriminating 'excellence' (NCR being the only exception), the linear discriminant function *Z* is more of an empirical artifact than a performance vector anchored in theory. An 'excellent' firm must not merely focus on short-term outputs to avoid bankruptcy, but it must also ensure its long-term survival. In other words a good *Z* score may be a necessary condition for 'excellence' but not a sufficient one.

Table 7 *Z factor (1964–83)*

											Number of years in which *Z* was	
Company	1964	1966	1970	1975	1977	1979	1980	1981	1982	1983	≤ 3.0 (unhealthy)	≤ 1.8 (bankrupt)
Excellent companies												
IBM	11.38	11.93	11.37	8.29	7.22	5.34	5.31	4.49	5.88	6.57	0	0
HP	12.18	10.44	10.13	11.65	7.14	6.44	7.65	7.14	9.13	9.46	0	0
DEC	–	8.58	11.62	8.56	6.07	5.04	5.35	6.66	6.93	5.14	0	0
NCR	3.93	3.94	2.25	2.19	2.87	3.34	3.19	2.91	3.61	4.12	8	1
Wang	–	–	14.95	2.96	3.67	5.26	5.70	5.21	6.04	6.33	2	0
Data General	–	–	23.82	10.35	5.05	4.39	4.12	3.82	3.27	3.80	0	0
Amdahl	–	–	–	–	6.00	3.47	5.13	4.13	2.82	3.70	1	0
Non-excellent companies												
Honeywell	5.31	3.90	2.42	2.17	2.89	3.26	3.44	2.89	2.97	3.19	8	0
Sperry	2.89	3.73	3.12	3.15	2.81	3.09	2.93	2.48	2.23	2.56	9	0
Control Data	5.04	1.94	1.74	1.59	2.06	2.60	3.04	2.94	1.41	1.19	7	7
Burroughs	2.08	3.65	2.93	3.67	4.17	3.97	2.52	2.18	2.56	2.96	7	0
Commodore	–	–	–	1.97	2.86	4.14	8.83	6.55	7.94	4.38	3	0
Prime Computer	–	–	–	3.08	4.88	4.65	9.36	6.12	9.69	7.08	0	1
Cray Research	–	–	–	–	8.21	12.55	18.64	11.18	7.56	7.87	0	0

(Source: Compustat Data Base.)

Satisfying multiple stakeholders

The performance measures discussed so far were solely focused on the welfare of the stockholder. A truly 'excellent' firm must also balance the competing claims of its various other stakeholders, in order to ensure their continuing cooperation (Barnard, 1938). The profit performance of a firm, and the strategies that it pursues, can often be interpreted differently by the firm's multiple stakeholders. Investors in a firm may welcome, for example, the firm's shift to robotics in its manufacturing plans, while the workers' union may find the option objectionable. The community at large may be apprehensive of the option's impact on the local economy. The increasing power of various stakeholder groups and their multiple, contradictory and often changing preferences (Freeman, 1984), confounds the problem of ensuring their satisfaction. As Kimberly, Norling and Weiss point out:

> Traditional perspectives on performance tend to ignore the fact that organizations also perform in other, less observable arenas. Their performance in these arenas may in some cases be more powerful shapers of future possibilities than how they measure up on traditional criteria. And, paradoxically competence in the less observable arenas may be interpreted as incompetence by those whose judgements are based solely on traditional criteria. Particularly in the case of organizations serving the interests of more than one group where power is not highly skewed and orientations diverge, the ability to develop and maintain a variety of relationships in the context of diverse and perhaps contradictory pressure is critical yet not necessarily visible to the external observer (1983, pp. 257, 258).

All the measures of performance discussed so far have to do directly or indirectly with maximizing stockholder wealth. Creating stockholder value need not always converge with the interests of other stakeholders. Top management goals, for example, can at times be at odds with such an objective (Donaldson and Lorsch, 1983). Getting the involvement of the firm's employees may detract from profit maximization but may be crucial to the long-term viability of the firm (Abernathy, Clark and Kantrow, 1983; Lawrence and Dyer, 1983). Maximizing stockholder wealth should not then be the sole guiding principle of 'excellent' companies. A necessary condition for excellence is the continued cooperation of the firm's multiple stakeholders. Minimizing their dissatisfaction should be a concurrent objective of 'excellent' companies.

In the *Fortune* survey of corporate reputations cited earlier (Table 1), the respondents were asked to rank the reputation of firms (other than their own) on a scale of 0 = poor to 10 = excellent on eight key attributes. These attributes covered the stakes of several stakeholders, including: (1) stockholder – financial soundness, use of corporate assets, quality of management and long-term investment value; (2) customers – quality of products or services and innovativeness; (3) employees – ability to attract, develop and keep talented people; (4) community – community and environmental responsibility. Firms that appealed to multiple stakeholders were the ones that had the highest reputation (Table 8).

Table 8 *Stakeholder satisfaction reputation scores (1983)*

	Stakeholders								
	Stockholders				Customers		Employees	Community	Overall
Company	Quality of management (1)	Value as a long-term investment (2)	Financial soundness (3)	Use of assets (4)	Quality of products (5)	Innovativeness (6)	Ability to attract and keep (7)	Social responsibility (8)	
Excellent companies									
IBM	9.16	8.88	9.45	8.47	8.40	7.51	8.39	7.95	8.53
HP	8.75	8.08	8.41	8.01	8.56	8.04	8.42	7.56	8.24
DEC	7.42	7.21	7.52	6.97	7.74	7.08	7.17	6.79	7.24
NCR	6.53	6.07	6.68	6.51	6.22	5.80	5.76	6.44	6.29
Wang	7.61	6.88	6.83	7.18	7.54	7.67	7.27	6.73	7.22
Non-excellent companies									
Honeywell	5.80	5.34	6.20	6.03	6.14	4.94	5.47	6.51	5.79
Sperry	5.22	4.68	5.15	5.08	5.63	4.78	4.90	5.91	5.16
Control Data	6.08	5.31	5.80	5.59	6.22	5.83	5.67	7.39	5.98
Burroughs	5.21	4.40	5.26	5.16	5.57	4.51	4.65	5.64	5.04

(Source: ***Fortune*** magazine survey records.)

IBM, for example, was rated highly for its appeal to stockholders, employees and various public interest groups. Hewlett Packard was rated highly for its appeal to stockholders and employees. Despite the poor financial performance of NCR, it had a better reputation than the other 'non-excellent' firms in the sample because of its superior ability to ensure the satisfaction of its customers, employees, and host communities. While more sophisticated surveys of stakeholder satisfaction are being attempted, the rudimentary survey done by *Fortune* points nevertheless to the need to look beyond performance measures that address only the concerns of stockholders.

Measuring the quality of a firm's transformation

While multi-factor measures of the firm's short-term viability, like the *Z* factor, or measures of satisfaction of the firm's stakeholders define the necessary conditions that an 'excellent' firm must fulfill, they ignore the ability of the firm to transform itself to meet future challenges. Performance measures that help evaluate the quality of a firm's transformations are the true discriminators of 'excellence' (Evan, 1976).

The transformation processes pursued by a firm can be classified into two broad categories: adaptive specialization and adaptive generalization (Chakravarthy, 1982). Adaptive specialization is the process of improving the goodness of fit in a given state of adaptation. In other words the emphasis is predominantly on profitably exploiting the firm's current environment, and generating a net surplus of contributions over the inducements paid to the various stakeholders of the firm for their cooperation (Barnard, 1938). The performance measures discussed in the earlier sections are useful for monitoring the quality of a firm's adaptive specialization. Adaptive generalization, on the other hand, is concerned with the investment of the firm's net surplus of 'slack' resources (Cyert and March, 1963) for improving its ability to adapt to uncertain or even unknown future environments.

While adaptive generalization is a must for the firm to ensure its long-term survival, its pursuit can detract from short-term profitability (Chakravarthy, 1981). For example, a firm investing heavily in R&D expenditures to avoid technological obsolescence may show a lower profitability than a rival not as committed to its R&D investment. The former's profitability is understated because a substantial portion of its 'current expenses' are in fact incurred to create 'future options' (Vancil, 1972). However, there are clear limits below which the firm's short-term profit performance cannot be allowed to slip. The *Z* factor discussed earlier defines one such threshold. While it may sometimes be necessary for a firm to keep bouncing off its long-term and short-term survival thresholds, a well-managed firm should be able to steer a middle course (Chakravarthy and Lorange, 1984). Such a firm makes steady investments of slack to generate future options, while replenishing the invested slack resources on a regular basis. It pursues adaptive generalization and specialization concurrently.

Generation of slack can often be quantified through financial measures; however, evaluating how well a firm invested its slack is more difficult. Slack can be invested, for example, in managerial or technical capabilities (Miles, 1982). It can also be used to expand the organizational capabilities of a firm (Christenson,

1973), or to reduce its resource dependencies (Lawrence and Dyer, 1983). The computation of option values in all of the above cases is problematic. Conventional financial techniques can miss them since options can often come 'dressed in non-financial clothes' (Myers, 1984).

Moreover, even where investment of slack has been measured it has typically been based on 'unobtrusive', publicly available data (Bourgeois, 1981). Managers are not only reluctant to disclose the true value of the options they hold for fear of hurting their firm's competitive posture, they are also not very effective in communicating this value to the public, even when they have tried (Bettis, 1983). The firm's strategic options may also be 'hidden' to avoid bringing the slack that is invested in them to the attention of the firm's stakeholders. Managers fear that an advertisement of the firm's surplus may lead to a bargaining for its disbursement with the firm's stakeholders. Consequently, an empirical assessment of the quality of a firm's adaptive generalization is difficult.

Despite the above limitations, this study uses a few of the publicly reported financial measures for evaluating the manner in which a firm has managed its slack resources. The purpose of such an analysis is to explore whether there is prima facie support for the hypothesis that 'excellent' firms manage their slack resources better than 'non-excellent' firms.

Profitability is an obvious determinant of a firm's slack resources. This study uses cashflow by investment ratio as a measure of profitability. The higher the ratio, the higher is the slack available to the firm in any given period. It is to be noted that other commonly used measures of profitability, for example, return on sales ($\rho = 0.67$), return on total capital ($\rho = 0.72$), return on book equity ($\rho = 0.63$), and net income by total assets ($\rho = 0.72$), were highly correlated in our sample with this measure.

Productivity is another important measure of a firm's ability to generate slack. Sales revenue per employee is a crude measure of the firm's labor productivity, and the firm's sales revenue per dollar of total assets is a measure of its capital productivity. Increases in these ratios indicate an increase in the slack resources generated by the firm. As will be shown later, profitability and productivity need not be correlated. The former is a surplus contribution (over inducements) received by the firm from its customers, the latter is a surplus it receives from its employees.

The ability of the firm to raise long-term capital resources is yet another measure of the slack available to it. Two popular measures of this ability are its market to book ratio and its debt to equity ratio (Bourgeois, 1981). As the former increases, the ability of the firm to venture into the stock market for additional equity capital improves. Conversely, as the firm's debt to equity ratio decreases, its ability to raise additional loan capital improves.

Profitability, productivity and the ability to raise long-term resources form the core measures in this study of the slack resources available to a firm. Three other measures that refer to the use of slack will be discussed next.

A popular measure of a firm's investment in its future is the percentage of its sales revenues that it allocates to R&D expenses (Old, 1982). Other uses of the firm's slack resources are abnormal increases in its fixed and working capital expenditures (Bourgeois, 1981), as measured by increases in the capital expenditure to sales ratio and working capital to sales ratio. Sales to total assets was used in this study in lieu of capital expenditures to sales. Not only are the two variables highly correlated (correlation coefficient = -0.68) in the current sample, sales to total assets also seems to be a better measure of abnormal increases in a firm's capital expenditures. The ratio of capital expenditures to sales may experience wilder swings than the ratio of sales to total assets because of the lumpiness in a firm's investments. Dividend payout ratio was used as a third measure of slack usage (Bourgeois, 1981). The higher this ratio, the lower are the earnings retained by the firm for investments in its future.

To summarize, the eight slack variables selected for the study were: Cashflow/Investment ratio (CFBYIN), Sales by Total Assets (SABYTA), R&D by Sales ratio (RDBYSA), Market to Book value (MBYB), Sales by Employee (SABYEM), Debt by Equity ratio (DTBYEQ), Working Capital by Sales ratio (WCBYSA), and Dividend Payout ratio (DIVPAY). The correlation in the sample between these variables was very low (see Table 9).

Since the norms for these ratios vary from industry to industry, the ratios were all standardized using the mean and variances in these ratios each year across the 14 companies in the sample (assumed to represent the entire industry). Furthermore, to allow for a comparison of slack measures from year to year, each year's mean was set to zero and standard deviation was scaled to 1. Thus, the standardized values for the eight slack variables represent the number of standard deviations from industry mean in any given year.

A cluster analysis was performed on the eight standardized variables to discern commonalities in them across the 215 usable sets of observations in the sample. Ideally, there should have been 14 (companies) × 20 (years) or 280 sets of observations. However, because some of the companies in the sample were less than 20 years old, and a few observation sets were incomplete (observations unavailable on all eight variables), only 215 sets of observation sets were available for analysis. Two clusters were obtained (Table 9). The first comprising Cashflow/Investment ratio, Sales per Employee, Sales by Total Assets, Market to Book value, and Debt by Equity ratio are variables that are *sources* of slack. Cashflow/Investment ratio is a measure of the firm's ability to generate cash in the short run. The next two measures, Sales by Employee and Sales by Total Assets, indicate the labour and capital productivity of the firm, respectively. Market to Book value reflects the firm's ability to raise equity capital, and Debt by Equity ratio measures the firm's ability to raise loan capital. While increases in the first four ratios beyond industry averages imply more slack generated by the focal firm, the Debt by Equity ratio must drop below industry average for it to represent a source of slack for the firm. The negative sign associated with the scoring coefficient for this variable (Table 9) was, therefore, reassuring.

The second cluster includes three variables all of which are *uses* of slack. R&D by Sales ratio measures the firm's investment in research and development. Working Capital by Sales ratio indicates the slack resources invested in working capital. Dividend Payout ratio is the percentage of earnings that the firm pays out as dividends. The negative coefficient associated with Dividend Payout ratio (Table 9) may be due to two reasons: (1) high working capital needs forces a firm to conserve its earnings, resulting in a low Dividend Payout ratio, and (2) high

Table 9 *Oblique principal component cluster analysis*

215 sets of observations: Proportion = 0,000000
8 variables: Maxeigen = 1000

	Correlations							
	CFBYIN	SA-BYTA	RD-BYSA	MBYB	SA-BYEM	DT-BYEQ	WC-BYSA	DIV-PAY
CFBYIN	1.00							
SABYTA	0.20	1.00						
RDBYSA	0.10	-0.03	1.00					
MBYB	0.41	0.14	0.41	1.00				
SABYEM	0.49	0.11	0.20	0.36				
DTBYEQ	-0.36	-0.29	-0.36	-0.22	-0.29	1.00		
WCBYSA	-0.21	-0.29	0.38	0.36	-1.00	0.01	1.00	
DIVPAY	0.22	-0.11	-0.24	-0.29	0.03	-0.05	-0.45	1.00

Cluster summary for two clusters

Cluster	Members	Cluster variation	Variation explained	Proportion explained	Second Eigenvalue
1	5	5.000000	2.193827	0.4388	0.995099
2	3	3.000000	1.717970	0.5727	0.764980

Total variation explained = 3.911797; Proportion = 0.488975

R-squared with

	Variable	Own cluster	Next highest	R^2 ratio	Standardized scoring coefficient
Cluster 1	CFBYIN	0.6287	0.0245	0.0389	0.36
	SABYTA	0.1894	0.0114	0.0602	0.36
	MBYB	0.4359	0.2169	0.4977	0.20
	SABYEM	0.5203	0.0003	0.0005	0.30
	DTBYEQ	0.4195	0.1430	0.0341	-0.30
Cluster 2	RDBYSA	0.4766	0.1054	0.2213	0.40
	WCBYSA	0.6881	0.0039	0.0057	0.48
	DIVPAY	0.5533	0.0000	0.0001	-0.43

R&D by Sales ratio may indicate that a firm is focusing on growth and reinvestment and therefore has a low Dividend Payout ratio. Table 10 compares the differences between 'excellent' and 'non-excellent' firms on the eight slack variables.

'Excellent' firms consistently generated more slack than 'non-excellent' firms as measured on four of the five ratios representing slack generation. On Sales by Total Assets, however, 'non-excellent' firms on an average scored higher than 'excellent' firms (though not statistically significant at a 0.95 confidence level). This is because of the high negative correlation (-0.68) that Sales by Total Assets has with the capital expenditure by sales ratio. A lower Sales by Total Assets for 'excellent' firms implies that on an average they invested more in their fixed assets when compared to 'non-excellent' firms. This is consistent with their commitment to future growth.

Interestingly, there was also no statistically significant (0.95 confidence level) difference between the productivities of the two classes of firms, as measured by their Sales by Employee ratio. This may in part be explained by the greater number of sales and service employees engaged by 'excellent' firms in the computer industry to maintain close links with their customers (Peters and Waterman, 1982).

On slack usage, 'excellent' firms showed significantly higher investments than 'non-excellent' firms in research and development, as expected. There was surprisingly no significant difference between the dividend policies of 'excellent'

Table 10 *Comparing excellent and non-excellent firms on multiple attributes*

	Excellent firms		Non-excellent firms	
Performance measure	Mean no. of SD above industry average [a]	SD	Mean no. of SD above industry average [a]	SD
Generation of slack				
1 CFBYIN[b]	0.18	0.91	-0.23	0.84
2 SABYEM	0.04	1.13	-0.09	0.78
3 SABYTA	-0.10	0.53	-0.40	0.90
4 MBYB[b]	0.23	0.91	-0.40	0.86
5 DTBYEQ[b]	-0.35	0.83	0.27	0.90
Investment of slack				
6 RDBYSA[b]	0.40	0.90	-0.04	0.74
7 WCBYSA[b]	0.24	0.91	-0.21	1.05
8 DIVPAY	0.14	1.06	0.12	0.89

[a] Data for each year were standardized setting industry mean = 0 and SD = 1. The observations for each company, therefore, represent number of standard deviations above (+) or below (-) the industry mean. The next column shows in turn the standard deviation of these.

[b] Mean values on these ratios were significantly different for excellent companies from those for non-excellent companies (0.95 confidence level using *t*-tests).

and 'non-excellent' firms (Table 11). In both categories there are firms that have paid no dividends from 1964 through 1983, and there are others that have paid over a third of their earnings as dividends. 'Excellent' firms also seem to have tied up more resources in working capital. It is difficult to evaluate the strategic significance of this finding without a more thorough analysis of each firm's strategy. For companies like IBM, Amdahl and Data General, this may solely be due to the higher cash reserves that they carry (Table 11). The low inventory turnover at IBM may also reflect its strategy of selling direct to its customers. As to why Honeywell, Sperry, Control Data, and Commodore turned their inventories faster than most of their 'excellent' competitors, there is no obvious explanation.

A discriminant function constructed with the eight variables discussed here successfully distinguished the companies in the sample in 73 per cent of the cases (see Table 12 overleaf). The discriminant function obtained was:

0.12 CFBYIN -0.19 SABYEM -0.10 SABYTA + 0.12 MBYB -0.28 DTBYEQ + 0.34 RDBYSA +0.19 WCBYSA +0.29 DIVPAY > = 0.14 for 'excellence'

Table 11 *Investment of slack: mean values of key ratios (1964–83, where available)*

	Working capital by sales	Accounts receivables by sales	Inventory by cost of goods sold	Cash by working capital	Earnings per share	Dividend payout (%)
Excellent companies						
IBM	0.23	0.06	0.68	0.89	10.89	48.32
HP	0.30	0.22	0.46	0.21	2.39	11.40
DEC	0.53	0.31	0.57	0.20	3.40	–
NCR	0.32	0.27	0.52	0.24	4.76	20.00
Wang	0.41	0.31	0.69	0.10	1.21	4.04
Data General	0.61	0.28	0.53	0.48	2.43	–
Amdahl	0.37	0.23	0.44	0.50	2.09	33.41
Non-excellent companies						
Honeywell	0.21	0.19	0.34	0.29	6.38	31.75
Sperry	0.23	0.28	0.32	0.11	3.55	23.35
Control Data	0.30	0.34	0.49	0.09	3.44	3.21
Burroughs	0.31	0.35	0.66	0.12	4.17	37.58
Commodore	0.19	0.33	0.31	0.23	2.10	–
Prime Computer	0.45	0.19	0.89	0.12	1.14	–
Cray Research	0.64	0.47	0.56	0.30	1.36	–

(Source: Compustat Data Base.)

Table 12 *The power of the discriminant function to distinguish excellence*

As classified by Peters and Waterman	As classified by discriminant function		
	Excellent	Non-excellent	Total no. of observations
Excellent	93	23	116
Non-excellent	35	64	99
Total	128	87	215

Summary table of misclassification

Excellent firms			Non-excellent firms		
Name	No. of years in which misclassified	Percentage of years misclassified	Name	No. of years in which misclassified	Percentage of years misclassified
1 Wang	7	41	1 Cray Research	7	100
2 NCR	8	40	2 Prime Computer	8	89
3 IBM	7	35	3 Honeywell	8	40
4 Amdahl	1	12	4 Burroughs	7	35
	23		5 CDC	2	10
			6 Sperry	2	10
			7 Commodore	1	5
				35	

Note: Overall misclassification 58 out of 215 or 27 percent.

The discriminant function was strongly supportive of the 'excellence' of Hewlett Packard, DEC, Amdahl, and Data General. Similarly, it was able to discern the 'non-excellence' of Sperry, Control Data, and Commodore.

The real value of the discriminant function, however, is not in its ability to correctly classify 'excellent' and 'non-excellent' firms. A measure like the *Z* factor, for example, yielded comparable results. But unlike the *Z* factor or other naive performance measures discussed earlier, the discriminant function has a better theoretical rationale. Its variables are measures of a firm's slack sources and uses. It is through the management of these and other slack variables that a firm can ensure its long-term survival. The contribution of this study is in showing that 'slack' variables are important discriminators of strategic performance.

Conclusions

This study sought to identify key measures of performance that are associated with 'excellent' firms. Table 13 (overleaf) recapitulates some of the important measures that were discussed. No single profitability measure seems capable of discriminating excellence. Moreover, accounting data that are typically used to construct these measures capture past performance or historical trends. Strategic performance needs a more futuristic measure.

While Market to Book value or more sophisticated financial-market based measures of performance can alleviate the above problem, financial market may experience difficulties and delays in fully comprehending the ability to adapt to future environments that managers of 'excellent' companies continuously nurture with their slack resources. At any rate M/B ratio was a poor discriminator of 'excellence' in this study.

Moreover, the preponderant attention in the performance literature to maximizing stockholder wealth needs to be tempered with a concern for other stakeholders of the firm. The role of top management is to ensure the continued cooperation of all stakeholders by providing them at least minimal satisfaction (Barnard, 1938). This would suggest that 'excellence' is not reflected in the maximization of performance along any single dimension, but rather in the ability of the firm to simultaneously maintain several performance parameters within safe limits (Ashby, 1971).

Financial criteria such as ROI, ROE, M/B ratio or the Z factor define one set of necessary conditions for 'excellence'. An 'excellent' company's financial performance should be above average for the industry, and definitely above any bankruptcy threshold (e.g. $Z > 3$). The satisfaction of the firm's key stakeholders defines the other set of necessary conditions. Exemplar companies like IBM and Hewlett Packard did not excel on many of the performance screens that were used in this study. For example, their mean Z score and M/B ratio were lower than that of other firms in the sample (Table 13). But they performed at or above industry average on all criteria, and they were also adept at keeping their multiple stakeholders satisfied (Table 8).

While the criteria discussed above are necessary conditions for excellence, they are not sufficient. A firm is excellent only if it has, in addition, the ability to transform itself in response to changes in its environment. The attempt made in this study to operationalize the adaptive ability of a firm by measuring the slack resources generated and invested by it was admittedly rudimentary. However, it is clear that a firm needs slack resources to ensure its flexibility in the future. 'Excellent' firms in our sample were able to generate more slack resources than 'non-excellent' firms (Table 10). The former group also invested a significantly higher proportion of their revenues in research and development (Table 10). This is in keeping with their propensity to invest in options for the future.

A limitation of this study is that it merely examined how a firm had chosen to invest its slack. And yet it is the value of future options that an 'excellent' firm accumulates through current investment of slack that really distinguishes it from the rest of its competitors. For example, higher investment in R&D is no guarantee that it will generate new businesses in the future. Evaluating the economic worth of such an investment is difficult (Myers, 1984). Moreover, not all of the slack invested by a firm can be quantified.

Table 13 *Performance profile of the sample firms*

	Performance attribute				
		Financial performance (mean 1964–83)			
Company	Stakeholder satisfaction (overall score) 1984	Profitability Z score	M/B	Dept/ equity	Future options (mean 1964–83) R/D sales
Excellent companies					
IBM	8.44	9.40	4.72	0.09	0.04
HP	8.08	10.90	4.86	0.01	0.10
DEC	6.86	13.45	7.29	0.09	0.09
NCR	6.07	2.99	1.54	0.49	0.04
Wang	7.07	9.75	10.03	0.42	0.04
Data Control	–	11.04	4.27	0.17	0.10
Amdahl	–	4.79	2.87	0.15	0.13
Non-excellent companies					
Honeywell	5.78	3.41	2.18	0.32	0.04
Sperry	5.00	3.20	1.39	0.33	0.05
Control Data	5.50	2.55	2.26	0.56	0.04
Burroughs	5.33	3.69	2.98	0.35	0.05
Commodore	–	4.58	5.00	0.36	0.04
Prime Computer	–	5.54	5.36	0.77	0.08
Cray Research	–	11.02	5.46	0.16	0.16

Despite some of its failings, the study points nevertheless to the naivete of both researchers and managers in relying solely on financial outcomes such as ROI or Market/Book ratio for measuring a firm's strategic performance. Maximizing performance on these measures does not guarantee excellence, and on occasion may even detract from it. The firm may have alienated its stakeholders in order to satisfy its stockholders, or may have compromised its ability to adapt to future environments.

Acknowledgements

Portions of this paper were presented at the third annual conference of the Strategic Management Society, Paris, 1983. Professors Edward Bowman and Johannes Pennings, as well as two anonymous reviewers, provided valuable suggestions for its revision. Research for this paper was supported by the Reginald H. Jones Center for Management Policy, Strategy, and Organization of the Wharton School.

References

Abernathy, W.J., Clark, K.B. and Kantrow, A.M. (1983) *Industrial Renaissance: producing a competitive future for America.* Basic Books, New York.

Altman, E.I. (1971) *Corporate Bankruptcy in America.* Heath Lexington Books, Lexington, MA.

Argenti, J. (1976) *Corporate Collapse: the causes and symptoms.* John Wiley, New York.

Ashby, W.R. (1971) *An Introduction to Cybernetics.* Chapman & Hall, London.

Bagozzi, R.P. and Phillips, L.W. (1982) 'Representing and testing organizational theories: a holistic construal', *Administrative Science Quarterly*, Vol. 17, pp. 459–489.

Barnard, C.I. (1938) *The Functions of the Executive.* Harvard University Press, Cambridge, MA.

Benson, J.K. (1974) 'Comment on Price's "The study of organizational effectiveness"', *Sociological Quarterly*, Vol. 14, pp. 273–276.

Bettis, R.A. (1983) 'Modern financial theory, corporate strategy, and public policy: three conundrums', *Academy of Management Review*, Vol. 8, pp. 406–415.

Bourgeois, L.J., III (1981) 'On the measurement of organizational slack', *Academy of Management Review*, Vol. 6, pp. 29–40.

Bowman, E.H. (1978) 'Strategy, annual reports and alchemy', *California Management Review*, Vol. XX, No. 3, pp. 64–71.

Buzzell, R.D., Gale, B.T. and Sultan, R.G.M. (1975) 'Market-share – a key to profitability', *Harvard Business Review*, Vol. 53, No. 1, pp. 97–106.

Cameron, K.S. and Whetten, D.A. (1983) *Organizational Effectiveness: a comparison of multiple models.* Academic Press, New York.

Carroll, D.T. (1983) 'A disappointing search for excellence', *Harvard Business Review*, Vol. 61, No. 6, pp. 78–88.

Chakravarthy, B.S. (1981) *Managing Coal: a challenge in adaptation.* SUNY Press, Albany, NY.

Chakravarthy, B.S. (1982) 'Adaptation: a promising metaphor for strategic management', *Academy of Management Review*, Vol. 7, pp. 35–44.

Chakravarthy, B.S. and Lorange, P. (1984) 'Managing strategic adaptation: options in administrative systems design', *Interfaces*, Vol. 14, No. 1, pp. 34–46.

Chandler, A.D. (1962) *Strategy and Structure: chapters in the history of the American Industrial Enterprise.* MIT Press, Cambridge, MA.

Child, J. (1974) 'Management and organizational factors associated with company performance – Part I', *Journal of Management Studies*, Vol. II, pp. 175–189.

Child, J. (1975) 'Management and organizational factors associated with company performance – Part II', *Journal of Management Studies*, Vol. 12, pp. 12–27.

Christenson, C. J. (1973) 'The "contingency theory" of organization: a methodological analysis', Harvard University, Graduate School of Business Administration Working Paper 73-36.

Cyert, R.M. and March, J.G. (1963) *A Behavioral Theory of the Firm.* Prentice-Hall, Englewood Cliffs, NJ.

Dearden, J. (1969) 'The case against ROI control', *Harvard Business Review*, Vol. 47, No. 3, pp. 124–135.

Donaldson, G. and Lorsch, J.W. (1983) *Decision Making at the Top.* Basic Books, New York.

Evan, W.M. (1976) 'Organization theory and organizational effectiveness: an explorating analysis', *Organization and Administrative Sciences*, Vol. 7, pp. 15–28.

Fortune (Claire Makin) (1983) 'Ranking corporate reputations', 10 January, pp. 34–44.

Fortune (Nancy J. Perry) (1984) 'America's most admired corporations', 9 January, pp. 50–62.

Fortune (Patricia Sellers) (1985) 'America's most admired corporations', 7 January , pp. 18–30.

Freeman, R.E. (1984) *Strategic Management: a stakeholder approach.* Pitman, Marshfield, MA.

Ghorpade, J. (1970) *Assessment of Organization Effectiveness*. Goodyear, Santa Monica, CA.

Goodman, P.S. (1979) 'Organizational effectiveness as a decision making process'. Paper presented at the 39th Annual meetings of the Academy of Management, Atlanta.

Goodman, P.S. and Pennings, J.M. (1977) *New Perspectives on Organizational Effectiveness*. Jossey-Bass, San Francisco, CA.

Hannan, M.T. and Freeman, J. (1977) 'The population ecology of organization', *American Journal of Sociology*, Vol. 82, pp. 929–964.

Henderson, B.D. (1979) *Henderson on Corporate Strategy*. Abt Books, Cambridge, MA.

Hirsch, P.M. (1975) 'Organizational effectiveness and the institutional environment', *Administrative Science Quarterly*, Vol. 20, pp. 327–344.

Keats, B.N. (1983) 'On the measurement of strategic performance'. Paper presented at the third annual conference of the Strategic Management Society, Paris.

Kimberly, J., Norling, R. and Weiss, J.A. (1983) 'Pondering the performance puzzle: effectiveness in interorganizational settings', in Hall, R.H. and Quinn, R.E. (eds) *Organizational Theory and Public Policy*, pp. 249–264. Sage Publications, Beverly Hills, CA.

Lawrence, P. and Dyer, D. (1983) *Renewing American Industry*. The Free Press, New York.

Lawrence, P. and Lorsch, J. (1967) *Organization and Its Environment*. Harvard University Press, Boston, MA.

Lenz, R.T. (1981) 'Determinants of organizational performance: an interdisciplinary review', *Strategic Management Journal*, Vol. 2, pp. 131–154.

Magnet, M. (1984) 'How to compete with IBM', *Fortune*, 6 February, pp. 58–71.

McGuire, J. and Schneeweis, T. (1983) 'An analysis of alternate measures of strategic performance.' Paper presented at the third annual conference of the Strategic Management Society, Paris.

Miles, R.E. and Snow, C.C. (1978) *Organizational Strategy, Structure and Process*. McGraw-Hill, New York.

Miles, R.H. (1982) *Coffin Nails and Corporate Strategy*. Prentice-Hall, Englewood Cliffs, NJ.

Mintzberg, H. and Waters, J.A. (1983) 'The mind of the strategist(s)', in Srivastva, S. (ed.) *The Executive Mind*. Jossey-Bass, San Francisco, CA.

Myers, S.C. (1984) 'Finance theory and financial strategy', *Interfaces*, Vol. 14, No. 1, pp. 126–137.

Old, B.S. (1982) 'Corporate directors should rethink technology', *Harvard Business Review*, January–February, pp. 6–14.

Pascale, R.T. and Athos, A.G. (1981) *The Art of Japanese Management*. Warner Books, New York.

Peters, T.J. and Waterman, R.H. (1982) *In Search of Excellence: lessons from America's best run companies*. Harper & Row, New York.

Porter, M.E. (1980) *Competitive Strategy*. The Free Press, New York.

Rappaport, A. (1981) 'Selecting strategies that create shareholder value', *Harvard Business Review*, Vol. 3, No. 59, pp. 139–149.

Reece, J.S. and Cool, W.R. (1978) 'Measuring investment center performance', *Harvard Business Review*, Vol. 56, No. 3, pp. 28–46.

Rumelt, R.P. (1974) *Strategy, Structure and Economic Performance*. Harvard University Press, Cambridge, MA.

Spray, S.L. (1976) *Organizational Effectiveness: theory, research and application*. Kent State University Press, Kent, OH.

Steers, R.M. (1977) *Organizational Effectiveness: a behavioral view*. Goodyear, Santa Monica, CA.

Thorelli, H. (1977) 'Organizational theory: an ecological view', in Thorelli, H. (ed.) *Strategy + Structure = Performance: the strategic planning imperative*. Indiana University Press, Bloomington, IN.

Tukey, J.W. (1953) 'The problem of multiple comparisons'. Unpublished manuscript, IMS, Chicago.

Vancil, R.F. (1972) 'Better management of corporate development', *Harvard Business Review*, Vol. 50, No. 5, pp. 53–62.

Vancil, R.F. (1979) *Decentralization: managerial ambiguity by design*. Dow-Jones Irwin, Homewood, IL.

Woo, C.Y. and Willard, G. (1983) 'Performance representation in business policy research: discussion and recommendation'. Paper presented at the 23rd Annual National Meetings of the Academy of Management, Dallas.

Zammuto, R.F. (1982) *Assessing Organizational Effectiveness: systems change, adaptation, and strategy*. SUNY-Albany Press, Albany, NY.

13
Foundations of corporate success – How business strategies add value*

John Kay

What is corporate success, and how is it measured? In this article I explore the strengths and weaknesses of common performance measures by comparing six British supermarket chains. Some people judge success by size. They look at a firm's sales, its market share, and its value on the stock market. Sometimes performance is assessed by reference to rate of return. This can be measured as return on equity, on investment, or on sales. And sometimes success is measured by growth, reflected in increase in output, movements in earnings per share, or prospectively, the firm's price-earnings ratio.

All of these are aspects of successful performance. But I argue in this article that the key measure of corporate success is added value. Added value is the difference between the (comprehensively accounted) value of a firm's output and the (comprehensively accounted) cost of the firm's inputs. In this specific sense, adding value is both the proper motivation of corporate activity and the measure of its achievement.

This article defines and develops the objective of added value. It introduces the added value statement and the analysis of the value chain as means of making a quantitative appraisal of a firm's operating activities. This contrasts with the usual financial statements which concentrate, appropriate for their purpose, on returns to investors. In the final part of the article I use the added value criterion to identify the most successful European companies of the last decade.

Introduction

Glaxo is not the largest public company in Europe. Depending on the criterion used – turnover, employment, net output – that title goes to Royal Dutch Shell, Europe's largest oil company, to Daimler-Benz, the German engineering conglomerate which owns Mercedes, or to British Telecom. Shell's sales are twenty times those of Glaxo, and Daimler-Benz, with nearly 400,000 employees, has a workforce ten times larger.

The difference in earnings is less marked, but BT's profits are twice those of Glaxo and Shell's twice those of BT. Glaxo's return on capital employed is exceptional – around 40 per cent. But there are many smaller companies which post higher rates of return. And pharmaceutical companies generally show a

* This article was first published in *Foundations of Corporate Success – How business strategies add value* (1993), Chapter 2. Oxford University Press.

return on capital which is abnormally high since neither their principal investments (in research and development) nor their principal assets (the value of their drug portfolio) are recorded in their balance sheets.

Glaxo has done well for its shareholders. Money invested in the company in 1980 would have been worth thirty times as much in 1990. But the stock market provides the market's estimate of success. It is not itself the measure of success. You would have done better still to invest your money in Polly Peck over that same period but you would subsequently have learnt that the company's chief executive had been arrested on fraud charges and that your shares were, in fact, worthless. It is unwise to rely on market performance alone as a guide to corporate effectiveness.

So what defines a successful company? Success is intrinsically a relative concept. The best way to understand what it means is to compare the performance of different firms in the same line of business.

British supermarkets

Food retailing in Britain is dominated by six chains. The oldest and largest is Sainsbury's. John Sainsbury opened the company's first grocery store in south London over a century ago, and the family tradition and the philosophy of good quality products at competitive prices have remained central to the firm ever since. Conservatively managed, the company came to the stock market only in 1973 and since then has expanded steadily from its loyal, and mostly southern, customer base.

Tesco came into existence as an aggressive discounter and the slogan coined by its colourful founder Jack (eventually to be Lord) Cohen – 'pile 'em high, sell 'em cheap' – still hangs around the company's neck. It is a slogan the company would like to forget because from 1977 the firm executed a bold strategic move. Tesco decided to shift market position and attract a different target customer. It offered higher price, higher quality products more like those of Sainsbury's and put a much greater emphasis on fresh foods and on own label goods. Today Tesco rivals Sainsbury's in both market position and market share.

Both Gateway and Argyll were created by amalgamations between weaker chains. Argyll's most important move was the purchase of the UK operations of the US Safeway corporation, and it has since focused its own shops around Safeway's business concept. Gateway was created by the acquisitive ambitions of Alec Monk, an aggressive chief executive whose star fell as rapidly as it had risen. His sprawling retail conglomerate was taken over in 1989 by a highly leveraged investor consortium, Isosceles, which has not found it easy to rationalize its operations into a profitable business.

Asda emerged from Associated Dairies, which distributed milk and dairy products in the north of England. The company pioneered large out-of-town superstores at a time when these were strongly resisted by established shopkeepers and planning authorities. Thereafter, the company began to lose its way. It diversified unsuccessfully into furniture retailing. It attempted to match Tesco's shift of position but its commitment to the change was signalled less clearly. Asda still has more non-food sales than any of the other stores, and this can be seen in its higher net margins. In 1991 Asda faced serious financial difficulties, embarked on a major fund-raising operation and appointed a new chief executive. With Asda's move up-market, the mantle of 'pile 'em high, sell 'em cheap' fell on Kwik Save, a chain of discount shops selling a limited range of branded goods at low prices from basic stores mostly in secondary locations.

The performance of these companies can be compared in many ways (Table 1). Sainbury's has the largest market share, closely followed by Tesco. The profits of the companies, and their value on the stock market, follow broadly the order of their size. Kwik Save, although the smallest of the chains, is very profitable – its returns on investment and on equity are the highest in the sector. The firm does not do quite so well on either gross or net margin – gross margins are lower in a 'no frills' operation and its net margin is held back by its low-price, high-volume strategy. Asda, with a high proportion of more profitable non-food sales, comes out well here.

Table 1 *Performance of supermarkets, 1989*

	Asda	Gateway	Argyll	Tesco	Sainsbury's	Kwik Save
Size (Ecus m)						
Turnover	3,782	6,308	4,889	6,587	7,902	1,649
Profit	218	286	218	383	515	81
Market capitalization	2,678	2,378	2,319	3,281	4,699	1,184
Return (%)						
Gross margin	**9.3*	5.0	5.4	7.3	8.2	6.5
Net margin	**6.2*	3.5	3.6	3.9	4.4	4.1
ROI	18.9	NA	25.6	22.8	20.5	**40.5*
ROE	18.0	17.0	24.0	18.0	21.0	**27.0*
Shareholder return (1 year)	−10	3	−2	3	0	**24*
Shareholder return (10 years)	45	293	**367*	280	326	283
Growth						
Sales growth (%)	10	−12	8	15	18	**27*
EPS growth (%)	14	16	23	17	23	**36*
PE ratio	13	14	14	17	18	**23*
Efficiency						
Sales/Ecus per square foot	759	NA	1,146	771	**1,323*	NA
Stock turnover	13	NA	13	**24*	20	19

NA Not available. * Italicized figures show best performer on each measure.

(Source: Own calculations on data derived from Micro Extel and company annual reports.)

Sainsbury's and Tesco show lower returns on investment or equity than either Kwik Save or Argyll. Yet this is more a warning that these are unreliable indicators than a comment on the performance of the companies. Supermarkets have usually sold goods for cash at the checkout before they have paid their suppliers, and working capital for all these companies is actually negative. Little is needed in the way of fixed assets, beyond shop fittings and delivery vehicles, since the stores themselves may be leased. Kwik Save's return on capital is very high because there is very little capital employed in the Kwik Save business.

Sainsbury's and Tesco – the chains which have dominated the sector for many years – have chosen to reinvest heavily in building their own superstores. This would be a foolish thing for them to have done if they could have earned returns as high as those of Argyll and Kwik Save by developing the business in some other way. But they could not. The return on capital is simply a ratio of two numbers, not a guide to what you will earn by investing more in the business, and Tesco and Sainsbury's have been using their capital as effectively as they can. It is worth their while to invest in stores so long as they can earn more from building stores than the 10 per cent or so return on capital they would have got from the bank. It mostly is worth their while, because the Sainsbury's or Tesco name adds value to a site (which a Kwik Save logo does not) and the stores needed for a Tesco or Sainbury's style of operation are relatively specialist in nature. Ownership is a means by which Sainsbury's and Tesco can retain the whole of the added value their activities create. This reinvestment has the effect of driving down their return on capital but it makes them, taken as a whole, more profitable businesses not less.

What of return to shareholders? In 1989 only Kwik Save did well. This is not because the other businesses were doing badly but because the stock market (correctly) anticipated a recession which would favour Kwik Save's trading approach and damage the sales of other retailers. On a ten-year timescale, the outstanding performers are Argyll (which was a tiny company at the beginning of the decade) and Sainsbury's.

Kwik Save is the fastest growing of the chains – no surprise there, since it is also the smallest. Kwik Save also shows the most rapid growth in earnings per share. The price–earnings ratio is a measure of market analysts' evaluation of the quality of the company's earnings and their expectations of their security and growth. This measure divides the sector clearly into three groups. Kwik Save is on its own, with the highest PE ratio. Sainsbury's and Tesco each have similar ratings. Argyll, Asda and Gateway have much lower market evaluations.

All these are financial measures of performance. What of the technical efficiency of these firms? Sainsbury's sells more goods per square foot than anyone else. Sainsbury's and Tesco turn over their stock most rapidly, but so they should, given their emphasis on fresh produce. In this light, Kwik Save, which relies heavily on packaged goods, comes out particularly well. All these measures tell us something about these companies. None, in itself, gives a complete picture.

The added value statement

What underpins the success of firms such as Glaxo, Sainsbury's, or Kwik Save is their ability to add value to the inputs they use. Table 2 sets this out for Glaxo. In 1990 the company bought materials worth 1,528m Ecus. Its wage and salary bill was 901m Ecus and the cost of the capital which the company used – premises, factories, machinery, and equipment – was 437m Ecus. The resulting product was sold for 3,985m Ecus – 1,120 m Ecus more than it cost.

That figure of 1,120m Ecus is a measure of the added value which Glaxo created. It is the difference between the market value of its output and the cost of its inputs. It is a measure of the loss which would result, to national income and to the international economy, if Glaxo were to be broken up and the resources it uses deployed in other firms. Adding value, in this sense, is the central purpose of business activity. A commercial organization which adds no value – whose output is worth no more than the value of its inputs in alternative uses – has no long-term rationale for its existence.

This assessment of added value is one which accounts comprehensively for the inputs which Glaxo used. It includes not only the depreciation of its capital assets but also provides for a reasonable return on the capital invested in them. (The most appropriate means of charging for capital costs is a complex question. The calculations in this article simply impose a rate of return on operating assets of 10%.) So added value is less than the *operating* profit of the firm – the difference between the value of output and the value of material and labour inputs (but not capital inputs). It is also less than the net output of the firm – the difference between the value of its sales and the cost of its inputs of materials (but not its inputs of labour or capital).

The strength of Glaxo's competitive advantage can be measured by looking at the ratio of added value to the firm's gross or net output. Each unit of Glaxo's sales costs only 0.72 units to produce. Glaxo's net output is the 2,457m Ecus difference between the cost of the materials it bought and the value of the output it sold. It achieved this with only 1,338m Ecus of labour and capital, representing a cost of 0.54 Ecus per Ecu of net output.

Figure 1 looks at the UK supermarket industry in the same way. The added value created by the industry as a whole is small at just over 1 per cent of gross output because some individual chains, like Asda and Gateway, are struggling,

Table 2 *Added value statement: Glaxo, 1990*

Relationships with	Financial flow	Value (m Ecus)
Customers	Revenues	3,985
Labour	Wages and salaries	901
Investors	Capital costs	437
Suppliers	Materials	1,528
	Added value	1,120

(Source: Glaxo plc annual report and accounts)

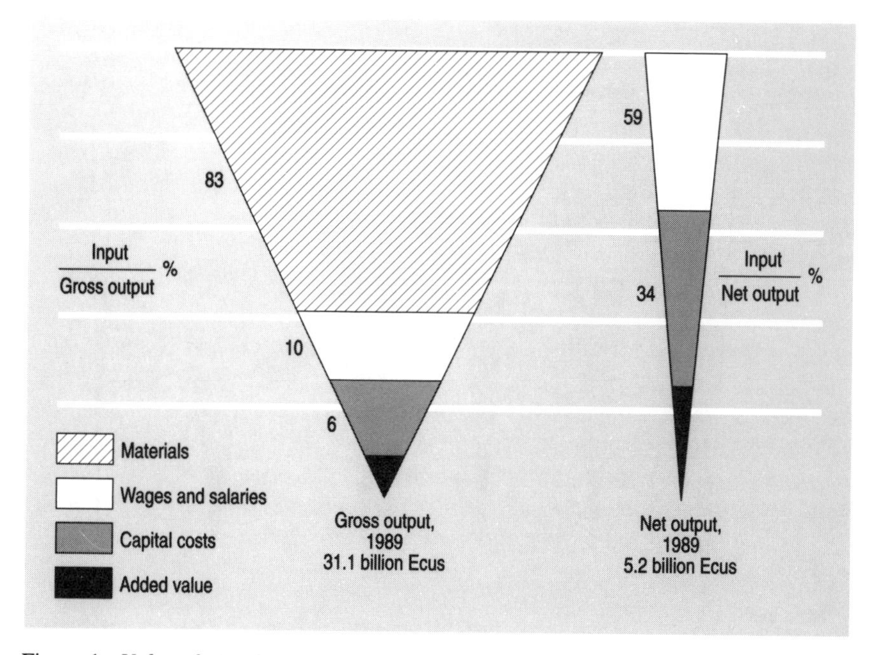

Figure 1 *Value chains for UK supermarket sector, 1989*

and partly because five-sixths of the industry is accounted for by the cost of supplies. This is hardly surprising for self-service retailers. A comparison of added value and net output brings out the performance differences more clearly and this is done in Figure 2 (overleaf).

There are two clearly outstanding performers in the sector – Sainsbury's and Kwik Save. The width of the sections in Figure 2 reflects the size of the company. Sainsbury's adds most value overall, Kwik Save the most per unit of input. Each Ecu of Asda's output costs it 1.01 Ecus. Each Ecu of Kwik Save's, 0.82 Ecus. In a contestable market, characterized by rivalry and easy entry and exit, a firm with no competitive advantage will sell a unit of inputs for precisely one unit. So these ratios measure the strength of Kwik Save's competitive advantage. As Kwik Save grows – Figure 3 – it is likely, perhaps inevitable, that it will move into markets or market segments where its competitive advantage is less strong. But so long as it has some competitive advantage, the added value created by the business as a whole will continue to increase. For a more mature business – like Sainsbury's – overall competitive advantage is less but added value greater.

Glaxo's competitive advantage is stronger than that of any supermarket. By this criterion, Kwik Save's added value is 18 Ecus for each 100 Ecus of output, Glaxo's 46 Ecus per hundred. That results from the different market conditions the latter company faces. In its principal market – that for anti-ulcerant drugs – its main competitors are Tagamet and a more recent therapy with a different pharmacological approach, Losec, manufactured by the Swedish company Astra. But Zantac is widely thought to be superior to Tagamet. Losec must compete with Zantac's established record and reputation with doctors and their patients. The market is not very sensitive to price.Sufferers will readily pay a premium for what

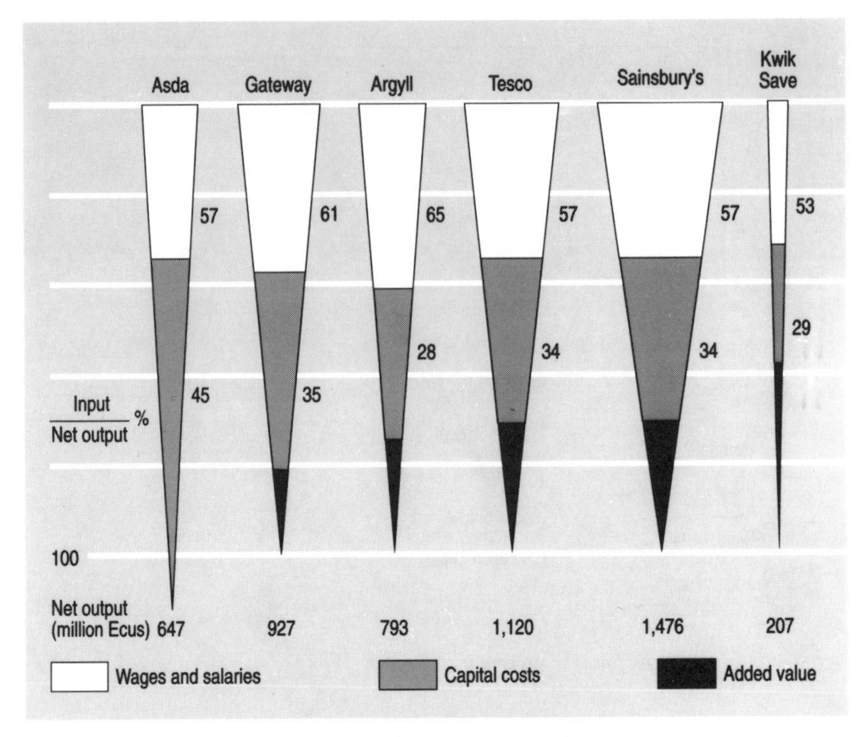

Figure 2 Value chains for individual UK supermarkets, 1989

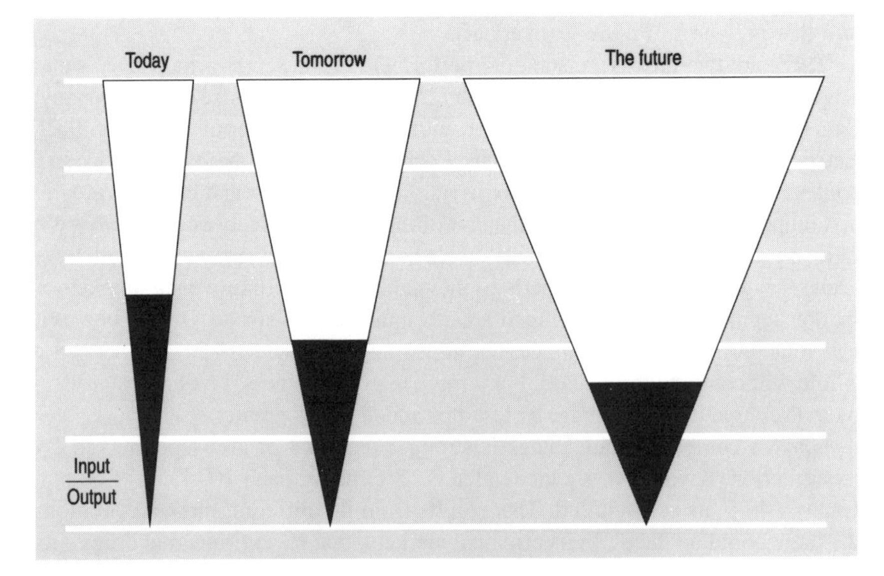

Figure 3 Growing the business: how a growing firm adds more value

their doctors think is a better product and in many geographic markets much of the cost is in any case borne by the government or by insurers. Glaxo's competitive advantage in this market will diminish as other drugs become available and more familiar and as the end of patent protection allows more direct competition from generic versions of Zantac itself. But for the moment, Glaxo's competitive advantage remains strong.

Not all firms succeed in adding value. Table 3 shows the added value statement for the Dutch electrical giant Philips. Each Ecu of Philips's output cost it 1.08 Ecus to produce. It was unable to cover the full costs of its activities in the competitive markets it faced. Philips is a striking case because it is a firm with enormous strengths and clear distinctive capabilities. Its record of innovation in consumer electronics is second to none – the company invented the compact cassette and pioneered the compact disc (CD) and video-cassette recorder (VCR). Yet it has repeatedly failed to translate these innovations into its own commercial success. The contrast between Glaxo and Philips, like that between Glaxo and EMI, is a measure of the importance of strategy in translating distinctive capability into competitive advantage.

Table 3 *Added value statement: Philips, 1990 (m Ecus)*

Revenues	24,247
Wages and salaries	7,666
Capital costs	2,932
Materials	15,716
Added value	(2,067)

(Source: Philips NV annual reports and accounts)

European winners

By the criterion of added value, Glaxo is a success, and Philips a failure. Table 4 shows the European Community's 'top ten' firms of the 1980s measured by the ratio of added value to net output. Most of the companies in that list are household names. Benetton is famous for its knitwear, sold through franchised retail outlets around the world. Reuters began as a news service, providing syndicated material to newspapers, but its principal operations and profits are now derived from providing on-screen information in financial markets. Petrofina is Belgium's oil company with a range of upstream and downstream interests. LVMH is a French conglomerate focused on luxury goods. The company's title reflects three: Louis Vuitton luggage, Moët et Chandon champagne, and Hennessey cognac. Guinness produces not only the famous Irish stout, but also controls many leading brands of Scotch whisky – Johnnie Walker, Bell's – and other branded drinks such as Gordon's Gin.

Table 4 *Europe's most successful companies, 1981–1990*

Position	Company	Activity	Country	Costs per unit of net output	Sales (m Ecus)
1	Glaxo	Pharmaceuticals	UK	.54	3,498
2	Benetton	Textile	Italy	.57	1,019
3	Reuters	Information	UK	.67	1,206
4	Petrofina	Oil	Belgium	.67	13,979
5	Kwik Save	Food retailing	UK	.68	1,609
6	LVMH	Luxury goods	France	.70	2,583
7	Guinness	Drinks	UK	.71	3,875
8	Cable and Wireless	Telecom	UK	.72	1,959
9	BTR	Conglomerate	UK	.74	7,404
10	Marks & Spencer	Retailing	UK	.74	7,678

(Source: Own calculations based on Euroequities database. Chosen from non-financial companies with sales in excess of 1 billion Ecus.)

Cable and Wireless is a British-based international telecommunications company. It holds the franchise for local telephone services in Hong Kong, owns Mercury, the second licensed public telecommunications operator in the UK, and provides international services around the world. BTR is an acquisitive, wide-ranging manufacturing conglomerate which has earned large returns both by trading in business and by squeezing additional profits from the firms it has taken over. Marks & Spencer is a British retailer, now increasing its operations in continental Europe, most famous for its range of reliable clothing at value for money prices.

The list contains a disproportionate number of UK companies and Table 5 attempts to redress this balance by identifying the leading companies in each of the main regions of the European Community. Some common characteristics are clearly apparent among the companies represented in both the overall European list, and in these regional lists – brands and reputation, customer and supplier relationships, market dominance and control of strategic assets. These are key elements in successful strategies.

Corporate success is not measured by size, or market dominance. Corporate success is not simply about the magnitude of profits. Shell and British Telecom earned much larger profits than any company in Table 4 but they did so because they are very large companies. But nor is success just about the rate of return on capital. You can run a drug company with very little capital employed but not an oil business or a telephone network. Size, market share, and profitability are aspects of corporate success, but success is not any one of these alone. The reason I believe it is appropriate to describe Glaxo as the most successful European

Table 5 *European companies by region, 1981–1990*

Position	Company	Activity	Costs per unit of net output	Sales (m Ecus)
UK/Ireland				
1	Glaxo	Pharmaceuticals	.54	3,498
2	Reuters	Information	.67	1,206
3	Kwik Save	Food retailing	.68	1,609
Italy				
1	Benetton	Textiles	.57	1,019
2	Eridania	Food	.88	3,449
3	Mondadori	Printing	.90	1,092
Benelux				
1	Petrofina	Oil	.67	13,979
2	Hunter Douglas	Household goods	.82	1,001
3	Unilever NV	Consumer goods	.85	31,992
Spain/Portugal				
1	Tabacalera	Tobacco	.91	3,780
2	Cepsa	Oil	.92	4,235
Germany				
1	Wella	Toiletries	.83	1,091
2	BMW	Cars	.84	11,079
3	Porsche	Cars	.85	1,558
France				
1	LVMH	Luxury goods	.70	2,583
2	Bongrain	Food	.83	1,065
3	Pernod Ricard	Drinks	.84	1,699

(Source: Own calculations based on Euroequities database.)

company of the 1980s is that, more than any other major company, Glaxo added value to the resources it used. It is that achievement in adding value which underpins the financial returns, provides the basis for its future development, and explains the remarkable returns which its shareholders have enjoyed.

14
Degree results: differences between universities*

Jill Johnes and Jim Taylor

Introduction

One of the primary outputs of the university sector is graduates. Resources such as teaching staff are employed for the specific purpose of disseminating knowledge to every institution's student entrants and a high proportion of these will ultimately obtain a degree or diploma. The *quantity* of graduates, however, is only one aspect of each university's contribution to the creation of human capital since the *quality* of education may vary between institutions. But if the quality of education at different institutions is to be measured, this raises the critical question of how to measure the quality of graduates. The most obvious (but by no means the only) approach is to construct a measure of output based upon the degree results obtained by each university's annual output of graduates. Degree results are an attractive variable for measuring the quality of education since a degree is the most obvious outcome of teaching activity.

This points in the direction of using the degree results achieved by graduates in each institution as a performance indicator. It will be shown in this article that the proportion of graduates gaining a first or an upper second varies considerably between UK universities and it therefore seems appropriate to investigate the extent to which this variation in degree results reflects the quality of tuition. Are universities which award a high proportion of firsts and upper seconds more efficient than universities which produce a low proportion? Do they provide better tuition? Or is it simply that differences in the quality of the raw material (i.e. the innate academic ability of students) explain these inter-university disparities in degree results? Answers to these questions are of interest not only to the universities themselves but also to those who fund them (i.e. taxpayers) and to potential students. Universities will be interested in comparing the performance of their own students in final degree examinations with those of other institutions while potential students will be interested in discovering how their chance of obtaining a 'good' degree varies between universities.

The purpose of this article is to investigate why degree results vary between universities. Attention is concentrated specifically on first degrees since this represents the bulk of each institution's teaching output. It is particularly important to undertake such an investigation in view of the fact that degree results have been proposed as a performance indicator. This is made clear in the 1987 White Paper:

* This article was first published in *Performance Indicators in Higher Education* (1990), pp. 102–120, The Society for Research into Higher Education/Open University Press, Buckingham.

> Academic standards and the quality of teaching in higher education need to be judged by reference mainly to students' achievements. The numbers and class distribution of degrees awarded provide some measure as, conversely, do non-completion rates.
>
> (DES, 1987, p. 28)

But if degree results are to be used as a performance indicator it is important to know why they differ between institutions. If they differ because of factors such as differences in the innate ability of student entrants, any comparisons in degree results between institutions will be worthless unless such factors are taken into account. Ideally this means that any performance indicator based on degree results will have to be 'corrected' to allow for inter-university differences in degree results which are due to factors unrelated to the teaching process – since it is the effectiveness of the teaching process which degree results are supposedly measuring.

This article is in four sections. The first section discusses two alternative methods of measuring degree results at the institutional level and provides these for every UK university for the period 1976–88. The second suggests why degree results might vary between universities, distinguishing between student-related and university-related factors. This is followed in the third section by a statistical analysis of inter-university variations in degree results. Multiple regression analysis is used to estimate the effect of various factors on degree results. The fourth section proposes a method of constructing a performance indicator for each university based upon degree results.

Two measures of degree results

Two alternative measures of degree performance are used in this article. They are as follows:

$$\text{DEGREE RESULT} = \frac{\text{I} + \text{II.1}}{G - \text{II}} \times 100$$

$$\text{DEGREE SCORE} = \frac{(75 \times \text{I}) + (65 \times \text{II.1}) + (60 \times \text{II}) + (55 \times \text{II.2}) + (45 \times \text{III}) + (40 \times \text{PASS/ORD})}{G}$$

where

I	=	number of graduates with a first class honours degree
II.1	=	number of graduates with an upper second class honours degree
II	=	number of graduates with an undivided second class honours degree
II.2	=	number of graduates with a lower second class honours degree
III	=	number of graduates with a third class honours degree
PASS/ORD	=	number of graduates with a pass or ordinary degree
G	=	total number of graduates

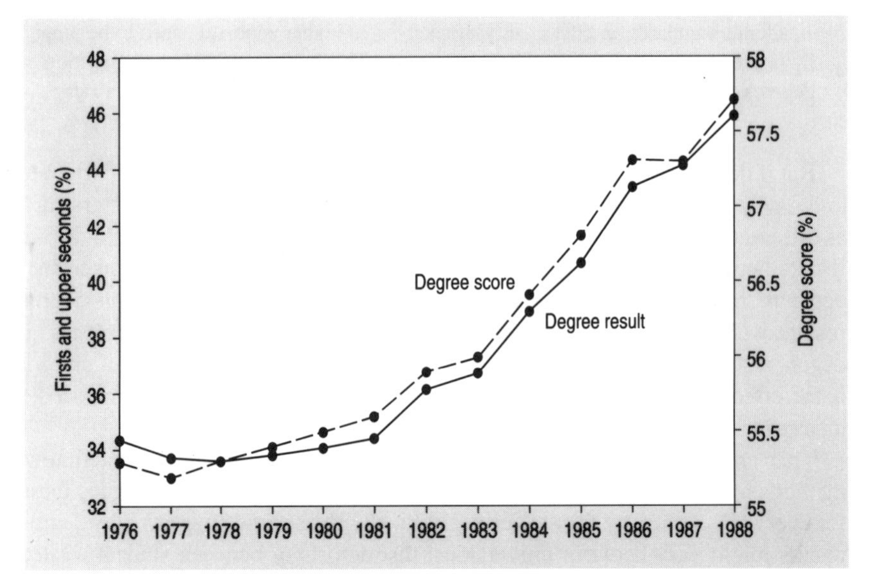

Figure 1 *DEGREE RESULT and DEGREE SCORE: all UK universities, 1976–88*
(Source: Universities' Statistical Record, Cheltenham – unpublished data)

DEGREE RESULT and DEGREE SCORE turn out to be closely correlated in practice. This can be seen from Figure 1, which shows DEGREE RESULT and DEGREE SCORE for the UK university sector as a whole for the period 1976–88. The correlation between DEGREE RESULT and DEGREE SCORE is 0.99. The correlation between these two measures of degree results is also very high across universities (r = 0.92 for 1988).

A major problem arises in any comparisons of degree results which involve Scottish universities. The latter offer two quite separate degree schemes: a three-year non-honours degree and a four-year honours degree. It is important to note that the non-honours scheme is valued in its own right and is recorded as an ordinary degree. Scottish universities point out that the ordinary degree is different from a pass degree on an honours degree scheme. In 1988, for example, pass or ordinary degrees constituted 34 per cent of total degrees awarded by Scottish universities (ranging from 16 per cent at St Andrews to 48 per cent at Glasgow) compared with only 9 per cent in the rest of the UK. This raises the question of whether ordinary degrees should be equated with pass degrees in measuring degree results. In practice, any decision about how to treat ordinary degrees is ultimately arbitrary and there seems little alternative but to group ordinary degrees with pass degrees. (They are in fact grouped together in the data supplied by the Universities Statistical Record, Cheltenham.)

Information on degree results for all UK universities is provided in Table 1 for the period 1976–88. (Oxford is included only from 1986 onwards since second class honours degrees were undivided until 1986.) From Table 1, it can be seen that the proportion of graduates gaining firsts or upper seconds varies considerably between universities. The proportion of firsts and upper seconds at Bath,

Table 1 *Percentage of graduates with a first or upper second class honours degree in UK universities, 1976 to 1988*

	DEGREE RESULT												
University	1976	1977	1978	1979	1980	1981	1982	1983	1984	1985	1986	1987	1988
Aston	31.4	33.1	29.7	28.4	29.5	31.4	34.7	36.3	38.1	43.8	48.1	55.4	58.7
Bath	39.6	38.4	42.0	41.6	40.7	45.6	44.8	45.6	49.1	56.7	57.7	60.3	59.8
Birmingham	34.8	30.3	30.7	31.4	30.8	29.7	33.0	35.6	36.7	36.7	43.3	41.6	39.5
Bradford	37.6	42.0	37.9	37.2	36.8	37.9	37.0	41.2	42.1	39.6	41.9	46.1	45.6
Bristol	39.2	40.3	43.2	44.3	44.2	44.6	43.3	47.1	49.1	47.6	52.1	51.9	53.2
Brunel	35.1	32.5	41.8	41.8	38.4	42.0	41.3	42.1	44.1	45.7	45.9	47.3	45.6
Cambridge	61.6	63.6	61.9	64.4	63.6	63.1	65.7	66.5	67.4	66.0	66.2	68.6	69.3
City	32.0	35.0	35.0	32.5	34.3	32.2	34.8	34.5	37.6	41.5	45.3	42.8	48.1
Durham	37.0	38.4	36.8	35.6	32.9	34.8	40.0	43.9	43.3	47.9	47.8	45.9	49.0
East Anglia	36.8	36.2	36.2	35.0	32.3	29.3	29.0	32.8	39.8	42.0	42.9	51.1	48.8
Essex	41.9	39.0	35.3	37.4	35.3	34.2	38.6	41.2	38.5	44.5	43.5	48.9	48.2
Exeter	38.8	39.9	37.9	36.7	37.6	36.6	40.0	41.0	42.8	45.3	45.1	43.7	47.4
Hull	31.5	32.3	29.8	29.6	28.5	29.9	34.4	29.9	30.6	37.4	41.9	44.5	44.4
Keele	37.3	33.9	36.2	37.1	39.8	32.8	36.0	37.4	38.9	38.3	42.5	45.2	46.4
Kent	32.2	32.2	27.7	29.8	28.1	30.3	35.5	38.3	36.1	36.7	43.6	47.3	51.1
Lancaster	38.7	34.5	36.0	31.0	32.0	33.1	36.4	36.6	41.3	41.0	43.5	49.0	53.6
Leeds	37.5	29.8	29.7	28.9	32.0	34.1	34.1	32.1	35.3	36.3	37.8	37.0	41.6
Leicester	38.9	35.7	39.4	41.5	36.1	36.6	34.3	35.5	40.3	39.1	42.4	41.9	45.4
Liverpool	32.3	30.7	30.6	30.1	29.2	30.3	31.3	32.9	33.8	33.6	35.0	37.4	37.4
London	33.5	33.5	32.7	33.8	34.7	34.2	35.8	35.7	39.2	40.7	43.2	42.2	43.3
Loughborough	32.1	30.7	32.1	29.7	33.6	35.2	39.5	42.3	45.2	47.2	47.2	50.4	51.1
Manchester	33.4	35.6	33.5	33.9	36.8	35.5	38.2	38.0	39.2	42.9	40.7	43.9	45.8
UMIST	36.5	38.7	34.6	33.0	36.9	34.3	37.7	37.0	34.7	40.0	42.3	41.2	43.0
Newcastle	25.5	29.3	28.2	28.9	26.9	29.3	29.4	29.6	31.9	35.9	35.2	37.8	40.2
Nottingham	41.8	40.0	41.9	43.1	44.1	42.8	44.5	44.8	47.6	47.1	47.3	51.8	52.5
Oxford	–	–	–	–	–	–	–	–	–	–	56.8	58.6	58.8
Reading	38.7	40.6	37.1	38.7	37.0	40.0	42.8	41.2	42.7	42.5	51.1	48.3	52.6
Salford	28.3	28.6	29.2	26.5	27.4	28.7	28.2	31.0	32.4	37.9	43.9	42.4	50.5
Sheffield	36.4	36.8	34.6	36.2	35.8	34.4	35.6	39.0	36.9	41.2	41.4	44.5	46.4
Southampton	37.6	37.1	38.9	40.2	38.6	40.1	41.1	41.9	45.6	44.1	43.4	43.7	45.4
Surrey	38.2	36.0	37.6	37.1	36.0	38.0	36.5	42.3	44.9	45.1	43.6	44.2	47.4
Sussex	44.1	40.8	41.9	43.8	42.4	42.8	42.1	45.3	41.4	42.8	44.1	44.9	44.8
Warwick	37.1	35.7	33.2	34.3	30.9	33.2	32.8	34.8	38.2	41.3	47.7	47.1	48.9
York	45.2	48.3	45.1	49.1	48.9	43.7	48.7	51.0	51.2	52.9	54.0	56.4	58.5
Aberdeen	22.2	22.6	23.8	24.1	26.1	25.2	27.7	26.0	27.5	33.1	33.3	31.1	35.8
Dundee	22.3	17.0	20.9	18.9	20.0	21.7	26.0	25.8	27.1	25.4	31.8	29.7	30.7
Edinburgh	–	–	–	–	–	30.9	33.6	31.0	36.3	38.0	37.7	37.6	42.2
Glasgow	16.6	15.9	17.5	–	–	–	–	–	23.5	27.1	29.8	27.0	28.8
Heriot-Watt	18.8	22.8	23.3	21.5	19.7	22.2	25.7	25.0	29.8	26.6	28.2	33.1	35.6
St Andrews	35.0	30.7	30.3	36.2	33.6	38.8	38.8	38.2	38.2	44.8	47.8	44.0	50.0
Stirling	18.8	18.9	17.6	21.7	17.9	20.6	24.3	21.0	26.7	30.3	32.5	33.7	37.9
Strathclyde	20.3	18.5	20.8	21.3	22.7	24.6	21.6	24.1	27.1	33.6	39.1	39.3	41.4
Queen's	25.2	22.3	21.7	24.5	29.0	26.2	27.2	29.7	32.2	31.9	33.4	34.9	36.3
Ulster	35.3	35.1	32.0	32.0	37.3	34.2	33.7	30.8	29.4	28.2	33.3	32.7	36.4
Wales	33.8	32.5	32.5	32.6	32.4	31.5	33.8	33.7	35.3	37.8	39.1	38.6	41.8

Note:

The precise definition of DEGREE RESULT is given in the text. Several universities were awarded undivided seconds during 1976–88. DEGREE RESULT has not been calculated in cases where the percentage of graduates awarded undivided seconds exceeds 20 per cent.

(Source: Universities' Statistical Record, Cheltenham)

Bristol, Cambridge, Nottingham, Sussex and York, for example, has been consistently higher than in most other universities. At the opposite end of the scale are Hull, Leeds, Liverpool, Newcastle, Salford and Ulster.

Further scrutiny of Table 1 indicates that the variation in degree results *between* universities during any single year is far greater than the variation *within* universities over time. This is the case despite the fact that there has been a significant – and in some cases very substantial – increase in the percentage gaining a first or upper second over time. At Loughborough, for example, the percentage increased from an average of 32.2 per cent during 1976–81 to 46.1 per cent during 1982–88. Increases at other universities were less dramatic but have still been considerable, particularly since 1981. Another significant feature of the percentage gaining a first or upper second is the remarkably stable pattern across universities over a long period of time. This is reflected by the very high correlation in the percentage gaining a first or upper second (within each university) in adjacent years. Indeed, there is a high correlation in the percentage of firsts and upper seconds awarded by universities over the entire study period (J. Johnes and Taylor, 1987).

The stability of the percentage of graduates gaining a first or upper second (within universities) over time strongly suggests the existence of some underlying causal factors which determine the inter-university pattern of degree results. One reason for this stability may be that the percentage of firsts and upper seconds in any one year is predetermined by 'an institution's preconception of the appropriate percentage' (Bee and Dolton, 1985). In other words, the past determines the present. An alternative view is that the variation in degree results between universities is a result of fundamental differences in factors such as the ability of students, standards of teaching and the facilities available to both students and staff at each institution. It is this second view which we investigate in the remainder of this article.

Some explanations of inter-university differences in degree results

This section investigates the view that variations in degree results between universities can be explained by factors which relate either to each university's students or to the universities themselves. Students are the essential raw material inputs which universities convert into graduates through teaching and related processes. It is therefore appropriate to search for measurable variables which can be used to describe those aspects of student-related inputs and university-related processes which are likely to have an effect on each university's degree results. *Only those variables for which data can be readily obtained are considered here.* It is useful to distinguish between those factors which relate to the raw material input (the students) and those which relate to the inputs provided by each institution in support of the teaching process.

Student-related factors

Several student-related factors may be expected to affect their degree results. First, degree results are likely to be better for those with high academic ability.

There is plenty of evidence to demonstrate that the academic ability of *individual* students (measured by school qualifications) has a positive effect on their degree result, although the relationship is often only weak (Freeman, 1970; Kapur, 1972; Entwistle and Wilson, 1977; Tarsh, 1982; Crum and Parikh, 1983; Sear, 1983). The only available measure of the academic ability of each university's annual intake of new students is their average A level score, which is expected to be positively related to the average degree result obtained by each university's graduates. A-level score is by no means a perfect indicator of academic ability since it will depend on quality of schooling, support from parents and the personality traits of each individual student. On average across all student entrants in an institution, however, it seems likely that average A level score will be an adequate proxy of the academic ability of each university's annual intake of students.

The use of A level score as an explanatory variable in a model to explain degree results is supported by the high positive correlation between these two variables at national level. Allowing for a three-year lag of the percentage obtaining a first or upper second (DEGREE RESULT) behind A level score, the correlation between these two variables was 0.98 for the period 1979–88 (see Figure 2). Similarly a correlation of 0.98 was obtained between DEGREE SCORE and A level score. Moreover, the regression of DEGREE RESULT on A level score indicates that a one-point increase in A level score has been associated with a 7.5 percentage point increase in the percentage of graduates obtaining a first or upper second (at national level). Further support for using A level score as an explanatory variable is provided by data obtained from the National Survey of Graduates and Diplomates. Table 2 (overleaf) indicates a clear positive relationship between degree class and A level score.

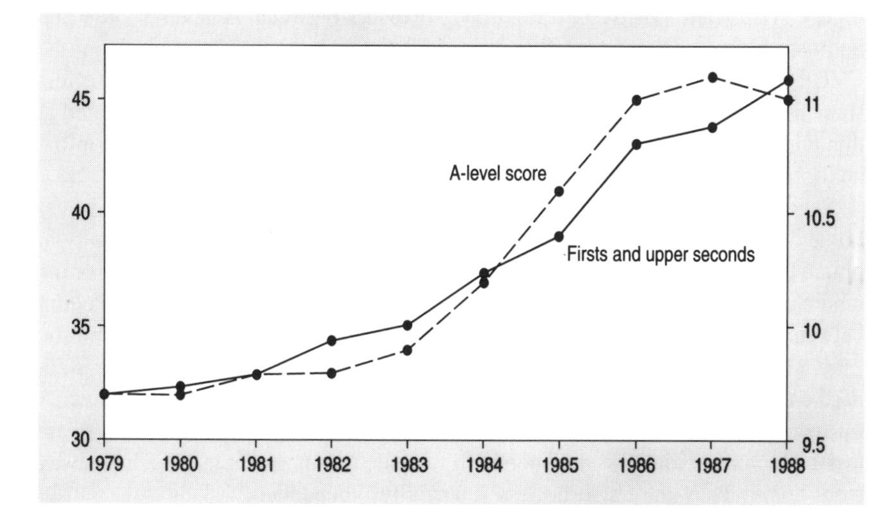

Figure 2 *Degree results v. A level score: UK universities, 1979–88*
(Source: Universities' Statistical Record, Cheltenham – unpublished data)

Table 2 *Mean A level (or equivalent) score by degree classification: graduates of UK universities (1980)*

Degree class	A level score
First	12.8
Upper second	10.8
Undivided second	11.8
Lower second	9.1
Third	8.3
Pass, ordinary or other	3.9
All classes	9.6

Note:
1 A level score is calculated by awarding the following numerical marks to each grade: A = 5, B = 4, C = 3, D = 2, E = 1; and for Scottish highers: A = 3, B = 2, C = 1.
2 Sample size = 4864.

(Source: National Survey of 1980 Graduates and Diplomates, 1987)

One of the problems with using A level score as an indicator of academic ability is that the majority of entrants into Scottish universities take Scottish highers and not A levels. Since any method of converting Scottish highers into A level equivalents would be arbitrary, the A level score of A level qualified entrants is used as a measure of academic ability of all entrants to Scottish universities in spite of obvious problems with this approach. The existence of a highly significant positive correlation, however, between A level scores and Scottish highers across Scottish universities (using data obtained from the CVCP's *University Management Statistics and Performance Indicators*) offers some support for the use of A level score as a proxy variable. It may be noted at this point, however, that the statistical analysis of degree results reported in the next section is undertaken both with and without Scottish universities.

Second, degree results may be affected by whether or not a student lives at home during term time. Students who live at home may have less opportunity to obtain the full benefit of university facilities (such as the library, computers or the laboratories) because a greater proportion of their time may be spent travelling between home and university or they may become more involved in domestic (non-academic) activities. This may consequently result in work of lower standard compared to those students who live away from home during term time. A further possibility is that students who live at home during their degree course are less adventurous and less independently minded than students who live away from home. They may also be less financially independent.

Third, students whose first language is not English may be at a disadvantage in taking a degree in the UK and may therefore achieve a poorer degree as a consequence. Working in the opposite direction is the possibility that students from abroad may have more initiative, ambition and self-reliance than students who study in their home country. The way in which the percentage of each

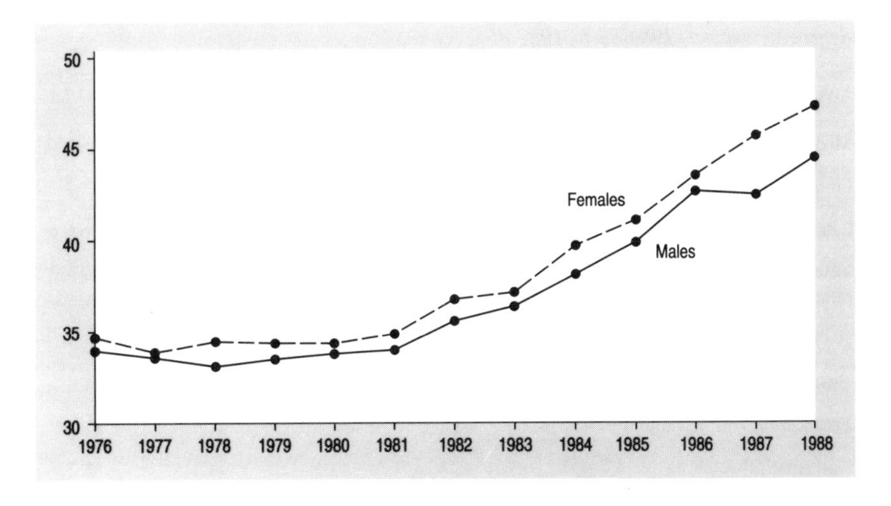

Figure 3 *Percentage of graduates obtaining a first or upper second: males and females, 1976–88*

(Source: Universities' Statistical Record, Cheltenham – unpublished data)

university's graduates who come from overseas will affect its degree results is therefore uncertain.

Fourth, since a higher proportion of female graduates obtain a first or an upper second on average than male graduates for the UK as a whole (see Figure 3), it is worth testing whether the ratio of male to female graduates plays any part in explaining inter-university differences in degree results.

University-related factors

A university-related factor which may be expected to have considerable impact on degree results is the quality of each institution's teaching. Since no direct measure of teaching *quality* is available at the institutional level, it is necessary to fall back upon *quantitative* measures such as the student/staff ratio. Students at universities with a high student/staff ratio may receive less personal tuition than students at universities in which the student/staff ratio is low. The student/staff ratio can therefore be expected to be negatively related to degree results.

A second factor which may influence a university's degree results is its subject mix (Nevin, 1972). Table 3 (overleaf) indicates very wide variations between subjects at national level in the percentage of firsts and upper seconds. Moreover, these intersubject differences are highly correlated over time. It follows that the subject mix of an institution can be expected to affect its degree results. Universities with a high proportion of subjects in which a high proportion of first and upper seconds are awarded can be expected to have a higher than average proportion of firsts and upper seconds.

Third, degree results may vary between different types of universities. The new greenfield universities and the ex-colleges of advanced technology (ex-CATS)

Table 3 *Percentage of graduates who obtained a first or upper second honours degree by subject, 1984/85 to 1987/88*

Subject group	1984/85	1985/86	1986/87	1987/88
Medicine and dentistry	14.6	16.5	14.8	16.3
Librarianship and information science	22.9	24.8	35.8	47.2
Education	25.3	29.1	30.4	36.6
Veterinary science, agriculture and related studies	34.2	34.9	35.5	39.4
Architecture and related studies	34.6	31.1	31.7	35.3
Business and financial studies	37.8	41.1	41.0	44.2
Engineering and technology	41.1	42.3	41.5	42.2
Mathematical sciences	41.6	43.2	44.4	46.0
Physical sciences	42.1	46.0	45.9	47.2
Creative arts	42.3	46.1	46.1	46.4
Social sciences	43.3	46.1	47.6	48.2
Studies allied to medicine	47.9	50.6	55.1	58.3
Languages and related studies	49.1	52.0	55.6	56.6
Biological sciences	49.2	53.2	53.5	55.2
Humanities	50.1	52.5	53.3	55.3

Note:
The formula for calculating the percentage of graduates with a first or upper second class honours degree is given in the text.

(Source: Unpublished data, Universities' Statistical Record, Cheltenham.)

established in the 1960s, for example, have developed along different lines from the older 'civic' universities and this may have an effect on degree results. Both the ex-CATs and the new greenfield universities have been keen, for example, to introduce a substantial coursework element into their assessment procedures. Whether these procedures differ substantially from those used in the older civic universities, however, is unknown since many universities have shifted towards the incorporation of coursework assessment into the determination of their degree results in recent years. In addition, Scottish universities require separate treatment since they award a far larger proportion of ordinary degrees than other UK universities.

Finally, several other university-related factors which may have an effect on degree results are included in the statistical analysis in the next section. These additional variables are the age of a university, its size, library expenditure as a percentage of total expenditure, and the UFC research rating of universities for 1984–88. Thus students at universities which spend a high proportion of their income on their libraries may provide better access to relevant books and articles and they may be expected to improve their prospects of gaining a good degree.

The effect of a university's commitment to research on its teaching is uncertain. On the one hand, universities in which the staff are highly committed to research may have less time for undergraduates and this could result in less intensive tuition and consequently poorer degree results. On the other hand, good quality research might actually improve teaching effectiveness and hence the quality of degrees obtained (Voeks, 1962; Hammond *et al.*, 1969; Hayes, 1971; Harry and Goldner, 1972; Aleamoni and Yimer, 1973; Linsky and Straus, 1975; Dent and Lewis, 1976). Any attempt to suggest how the age or the size of a university might affect degree results would be purely speculative.

Statistical analysis of inter-university differences in degree results

Multiple regression methods were used to estimate the extent to which differences in degree results between universities could be explained (statistically) by the student-related and university-related factors identified in the previous section. Two variables have been used to measure the average degree result in each university. These are the mean degree score (DEGREE SCORE) and the percentage of firsts and upper seconds (DEGREE RESULT) as defined above.

The regression analysis was undertaken for four separate years 1983–86 inclusive. Both DEGREE SCORE and DEGREE RESULT were used as dependent variables. The main results obtained from the statistical analysis are as follows. First, over 80 per cent of the variation in DEGREE SCORE and DEGREE RESULTS is explained by six explanatory variables. These are:

1. the mean A level score of entrants
2. the percentage of students who live at home
3. library expenditure as a percentage of total expenditure
4. whether or not a university is an ex-college of advanced technology
5. whether or not a university is one of the new greenfield universities established in 1964/65
6. whether or not a university is located in Scotland.

The second main result obtained from the regression analysis is that each of the explanatory variables has a similar effect on degree results in all four years. This means that the results appear to be robust. Third, several explanatory variables were found to be *unrelated* to both DEGREE SCORE and DEGREE RESULT. These are the percentage of students from overseas, the ratio of male to female graduates, the student/staff ratio, the subject mix, the age and size of each university and the UFC rating of each university's research over the period 1984–88.

One of the most interesting results obtained from the regression analysis is the highly significant positive relationship between A level score and degree results. This indicates that the academic ability of each university's student entrants has a substantial impact upon their subsequent degree results. The equations using DEGREE RESULT as the dependent variable imply that a one-point increase in A level score is associated with an increase of between three and four percentage points in the proportion of graduates with a first or an upper second. This result is very firm and is not disturbed when either Scottish universities or Oxford and Cambridge (where A level scores are very high) are excluded from the analysis.

The importance of A level score as an explanatory variable conflicts with previous research which indicates at best only a weak positive relationship between A level score and degree result for individual students (e.g. Sear, 1983). The most likely explanation for these conflicting results is that many of the factors which affect an *individual's* degree results (such as motivation and commitment to study) will cancel out when the relationship is being tested at the *institutional* level (as in the present study). The absence of a strong statistical relationship between A level score and degree results in the cross-sectional analysis of *individual* graduates may therefore be consistent with the highly significant relationship found in the present highly aggregated analysis of degree results for *entire institutions.*

Third, very little evidence could be found to indicate that inter-university variations in degree results were associated with corresponding variations in subject mix. This is a surprising result in view of the substantial differences in degree results across subjects. The only finding of interest as far as subject mix is concerned is that universities with a high proportion of arts graduates tend to have poorer degree results. But this relationship is statistically rather weak.

Fourth, there is considerable evidence that degree results vary significantly between different broad types of universities. The regression results indicate that the percentage of firsts and upper seconds is about six to seven percentage points lower in Scottish universities (on average), six percentage points higher in the ex-CATs, and about four percentage points higher in the new greenfield universities than in the older civics. The lower percentage of firsts and upper seconds in Scottish universities is a direct consequence of the long tradition of awarding ordinary degrees for three-year courses in Scotland (as explained earlier). Exactly why the ex-CATs and the new greenfield universities should award a higher proportion of firsts and upper seconds is uncertain, but it is possible that it has something to do with different methods of assessing students in these institutions compared to the civics.

Finally, two other variables were found to be significantly related to DEGREE RESULT and DEGREE SCORE: the percentage of students who live at home is negatively related to degree results; and library expenditure as a proportion of total spending is positively related to degree results. Degree results therefore tend to be better in those universities which give library expenditure a relatively high priority (or perhaps can afford to do so) and which have a high proportion of their students who do not live at home during term time. It should also be noted that none of the statistical results is disturbed when Scottish universities are excluded from the regression analysis.

Construction of a performance indicator based upon degree results

It was shown in the previous section that differences in degree results between universities are strongly influenced by both student-related and university-related factors. As far as can be ascertained, however, none of these is specifically related to the quality of teaching at each institution. The student/staff ratio, for example, was found to be unrelated to inter-university variations in degree results. This was not the case, however, for A level scores: the highly significant coefficient on the A level score variable clearly indicates that a university's degree results are likely to be strongly affected by the A level scores achieved by its student entrants. It would therefore be entirely inappropriate *not* to take differences in A level scores into account when comparing degree results between universities since individual universities have only limited control over the mean A level score of their students. This is because universities *generally* aim to attract students with as high an A level score as they can (in spite of the fact that many academics and university administrators believe that there is very little correlation between A level scores and the degree results ultimately obtained by students).

The substantial influence of a university's average A level score on its degree results suggests that each university's degree results should be compared not with the average for all universities (when assessing its performance) but with a *standardized* value of degree results for each university based upon the variables which explain inter-university variations in degree results. The difference between the *actual* and the *standardized* degree result for each university can then be used to indicate the extent to which differences in degree results between universities have *not* been explained by the variables included in the model. Thus for the percentage of firsts and upper seconds, the performance indicator would be given by:

DEGREE RESULT – DEGREE RESULT*

where DEGREE RESULT* (the standardized degree result) is computed for each university by substituting actual values of each explanatory variable into the appropriate regression equation. For example, the standardized degree result for each university's 1986 graduates would be calculated as follows:

DEGREE RESULT* = –3.26 + (3.26 × A LEVEL) –
(0.05 × LIVEHOME) + (7.05 × EXCAT) + (2.88 × NEW) –
(6.85 × SCOTTISH) + (2.94 × LIBRARY)

The explanatory variables are as defined in the Appendix. This performance indicator for degree results is given for UK universities for 1983–86 in Table 4 (overleaf). The most interesting result is the low correlation between:

DEGREE RESULT
and DEGREE RESULT – DEGREE RESULT*.

The correlation coefficient does not exceed 0.42 in any year. Inter-university comparisons in *actual* degree results are therefore unlikely to be helpful in evaluating the performance of individual institutions. Whether inter-university comparisons in DEGREE RESULT – DEGREE RESULT* are useful for this purpose, however, is also questionable. It is by no means clear that inter-university variations in this indicator can be attributed entirely to corresponding variations in teaching quality. Indeed, this would be a rash assumption. It should be remembered that a very high proportion of the variation in degree results between universities is accounted for by factors which do *not* include a measure of teaching quality. The fact that the variation in DEGREE RESULT – DEGREE

Table 4 *A performance indicator based upon the percentage of graduates with a first or upper second*

	DEGREE RESULT – DEGREE RESULT*			
University	1983	1984	1985	1986
Aston	2.4	0.4	3.7	2.4
Bath	–6.5	–4.1	0.8	1.8
Birmingham	–1.3	–2.4	–2.4	0.5
Bradford	3.6	2.5	–2.9	–3.2
Bristol	0.6	1.9	0.5	4.8
Brunel	3.5	2.1	2.7	1.3
Cambridge	8.4	7.4	1.7	4.2
City	–3.1	–0.7	–1.4	–0.6
Durham	–4.0	–7.2	–4.0	–3.6
East Anglia	–5.4	0.8	0.1	–0.8
Essex	7.2	4.7	7.0	1.8
Exeter	–1.6	–1.3	–1.1	–3.7
Hull	–3.6	–5.7	–3.5	0.1
Keele	3.2	2.9	1.4	–0.2
Kent	–0.2	–4.2	–5.4	–2.5
Lancaster	–2.4	0.2	–0.3	–0.7
Leeds	–3.2	–1.0	–2.0	–1.3
Leicester	–1.6	0.8	–2.8	–0.4
Liverpool	0.2	–0.9	–2.4	–2.8
London	0.3	3.1	2.6	2.2
Loughborough	–2.7	–1.4	–0.6	–2.7
Manchester	0.8	0.6	2.9	–0.9
UMIST	–1.3	–4.1	–2.0	–1.5
Newcastle	–4.3	–3.6	–1.9	–4.5
Nottingham	5.1	5.4	4.9	3.4
Oxford	–	–	–	–5.0
Reading	2.6	2.9	2.6	8.8
Salford	1.0	–1.5	0.3	1.3
Sheffield	0.2	–3.1	0.2	–2.3
Southampton	–0.6	2.0	–0.0	–1.2
Surrey	2.3	1.0	–2.0	–1.5
Sussex	1.8	–2.4	–2.0	–2.5
Warwick	–7.6	–3.0	–3.4	2.7
York	4.4	3.2	6.4	4.8
Aberdeen	0.3	1.4	1.9	0.7
Dundee	2.5	–0.0	–2.3	–0.8
Edinburgh	–1.2	1.0	0.8	0.6
Glasgow	–	–4.6	–2.4	–3.9
Heriot-Watt	–1.5	3.4	–2.7	–3.8
St Andrews	0.9	–1.0	2.9	5.0
Stirling	–3.2	–2.6	–2.1	–4.3
Strathclyde	2.3	2.5	4.0	6.6
Queen's	–1.6	1.2	–1.9	–2.3
Ulster	–0.3	0.3	0.7	2.5
Wales	3.7	3.1	3.6	1.7

Note:

See text for definition of DEGREE RESULT and DEGREE RESULT*. Values of DEGREE RESULT – DEGREE RESULT* are missing in cases where the percentage of undivided seconds awarded exceeds 20 per cent.

RESULT* is far smaller than in DEGREE RESULT alone suggests that there is relatively little scope for using degree results as a performance indicator once inter-university variations in the various explanatory variables (such as mean A level score) have been taken into account.

A further interesting result to emerge from inter-university comparisons in DEGREE RESULT – DEGREE RESULT* is that this variable is highly correlated with itself for the four years for which it has been calculated. Thus the stability over time in DEGREE RESULT – DEGREE RESULT* suggests that at least one other important explanatory variable which has had a consistent effect on degree results has been omitted from the regression model. Whether this missing variable is teaching quality is unknown. The general problems with using a regression residual as a performance indicator are also applicable here.

Conclusion

The performance of graduates in final degree examinations varies considerably between UK universities. Some universities consistently award a high proportion of firsts and upper seconds, for example, while others consistently award a much lower proportion. In other words, there is a high degree of stability in the university 'league table' of degree results over many years.

Since the government has indicated that variations in degree results between universities should be used as a performance indicator (presumably to reflect inter-university differences in the quality of teaching), it is important that these variations in degree results should be carefully and thoroughly investigated. It would be entirely wrong to use degree results as a performance indicator in the absence of a detailed statistical inquiry into why degree results vary between institutions. The purpose of this article was therefore to investigate the causes of inter-university variations in degree results since this is a necessary first step towards constructing a performance indicator based upon this variable. Using regression analysis, it was found that over 80 per cent of the variation between universities in degree results can be explained (statistically) by a set of plausible explanatory variables, the main one being the mean A level score of each university's student entrants.

Although the importance of A level score as an explanatory variable is hardly surprising, it is nevertheless an important result for those intent on using degree results as a performance indicator. In particular, it would clearly be wrong to compare degree results between universities without taking into account differences in the mean A level score of each university's student entrants. Other variables also played an important part in explaining inter-university differences in degree results. These include the percentage of students living at home during term time and type of university (i.e. ex-CATs, new greenfield universities, civics and Scottish universities).

Since a substantial proportion of the inter-university variation in degree results can be explained by a set of explanatory variables which do not include a direct measure of teaching inputs, it is tempting to assume that the remaining unexplained variation must be due to inter-university variations in the quality of teaching. But this would be an entirely speculative conclusion since the unexplained variation may be a result of other factors in addition to variations in teaching quality. Thus although a performance indicator can be constructed based upon the variation in degree results *not* accounted for by explanatory variables such as A level score, it is by no means certain that such an indicator would be useful for measuring performance.

Finally, a further problem of using degree results as a performance indicator needs to be underlined. Degree results are under the direct control of each university's examining body, and although these are advised by independent external examiners there may nevertheless be a strong temptation for universities to award more 'good' degrees if those with unfavourable degree results are seen to be penalized in the allocation of funds. This would inevitably result in a general upward trend in degree results and a narrowing of differences between universities. It may therefore be inappropriate to use degree results as a target variable since this variable is itself determined by those who are affected by it.

Appendix

Estimated regression equations: dependent variable = DEGREE SCORE

Explanatory variables	1982/83		1983/84		1984/85		1985/86	
	(1)	(2)	(1)	(2)	(1)	(2)	(1)	(2)
CONSTANT	47.71	48.82	47.87	47.60	47.49	49.35	50.25	51.31
	(37.49)	(37.56)	(38.66)	(37.68)	(29.45)	(34.02)	(28.60)	(29.09)
ALEVEL	0.65	0.57	0.64	0.67	0.66	0.59	0.50	0.48
	(6.28)	(5.49)	(6.49)	(6.89)	(5.15)	(5.28)	(3.38)	(3.28)
LIVEHOME	−0.071	−0.081	−0.061	−0.060	−0.048	−0.070	−0.051	−0.075
	(−6.14)	(−4.93)	(−5.84)	(−4.02)	(−3.55)	(−4.16)	(−3.38)	(−3.60)
EXCAT	2.61	2.34	2.33	2.09	2.20	2.03	2.08	1.82
	(6.90)	(6.41)	(6.97)	(6.63)	(5.62)	(6.14)	(4.90)	(4.64)
NEW	0.91	1.09	0.91	1.15	0.70	1.03	0.60	0.90
	(2.20)	(2.55)	(2.52)	(3.14)	(1.58)	(2.62)	(1.25)	(1.88)
SCOTTISH	−4.02		−3.66		−3.46		−3.24	
	(−10.26)		(−10.34)		(−7.96)		(−6.56)	
LIBRARY	0.79	0.73	0.76	0.76	0.82	0.57	0.66	0.51
	(5.21)	(4.75)	(5.42)	(5.69)	(4.17)	(3.40)	(3.53)	(2.84)
$\bar{R}^2$	0.91	0.80	0.91	0.82	0.87	0.79	0.82	0.70

Notes

1 () = *t*-ratios

2 Oxford is excluded from the regression analyses for 1982/83, 1983/84 and 1984/85 since a large proportion of seconds were undivided until 1985/86.

3 Scottish universities are excluded from equation (2) in all three years.

4 For further results see J. Johnes and Taylor (1987).

5 Definition of variables

DEGREE SCORE = as defined in text

ALEVEL = average A level score of A level qualified undergraduate entrants three years previously: A = 5, B = 4, C = 3, D = 2, E = 1

LIVEHOME = percentage of each university's students living at home

EXCAT = binary variable for ex-colleges of advanced technology; EXCAT = 1 for ex-CATS and 0 otherwise

NEW = binary variable for new greenfield universities; NEW = 1 for new university and 0 otherwise

SCOTTISH = binary variable for Scottish universities; SCOTTISH = 1 for universities located in Scotland and 0 otherwise

LIBRARY = recurrent library expenditure (excluding wages and salaries) as a percentage of total recurrent expenditure

(Source: J. Johnes and Taylor, 1987)

Estimated regression equations: dependent variable = DEGREE RESULT

Explanatory variables	1982/83		1983/84		1984/85		1985/86	
	(1)	(2)	(1)	(2)	(1)	(2)	(1)	(2)
CONSTANT	−7.34	−5.32	−7.84	−10.95	−11.15	−9.50	−3.26	−3.18
	(−1.28)	(−0.81)	(−1.45)	(−1.72)	(−2.08)	(−1.54)	(−0.57)	(−0.52)
ALEVEL	3.85	3.73	3.89	4.13	3.76	3.78	3.26	3.45
	(8.22)	(7.05)	(9.30)	(8.48)	(8.83)	(7.92)	(6.84)	(6.79)
LIVEHOME	−0.10	−0.15	−0.14	−0.11	−0.06	−0.08	−0.05	−0.06
	(−1.76)	(−1.80)	(−3.07)	(−1.45)	(−1.43)	(−1.07)	(−1.01)	(−0.87)
EXCAT	8.50	8.26	7.87	7.32	8.25	7.95	7.05	6.62
	(5.15)	(4.46)	(5.41)	(4.61)	(6.35)	(5.67)	(5.13)	(4.86)
NEW	4.60	4.40	3.98	4.56	2.42	3.44	2.88	4.17
	(2.54)	(2.04)	(2.52)	(2.46)	(1.64)	(2.05)	(1.86)	(2.50)
SCOTTISH	−8.25		−7.08		−6.41		−6.85	
	(−4.85)		(−4.59)		(−4.44)		(−4.29)	
LIBRARY	2.03	1.96	2.24	2.34	3.37	2.88	2.94	2.38
	(3.10)	(2.53)	(3.69)	(3.46)	(5.18)	(4.06)	(4.86)	(3.85)
$\bar{R}^2$	0.80	0.71	0.83	0.77	0.84	0.80	0.80	0.78

Notes

1 See notes to previous table

2 A *t*-ratio ≥ 1.96 indicates significance at the 5% level or less; a *t*-ratio ≥ 2.58 indicates significance at the 1% level or less (using a two-tailed test)

3 Definition of variables

DEGREE RESULT = percentage or graduates with a first or upper second (see text for precise definition)

(Source: J. Johnes and Taylor, 1987)

References

Aleamoni, L.M. and Yimer, M. (1973) 'An investigation of the relationship between colleague rating and student rating, research productivity and academic rank in rating instructional effectiveness', *Journal of Educational Psychology*, Vol. 64, No. 3, pp. 274–7.

Bee, M. and Dolton, P. (1985) 'Degree class and pass rates: an inter-university comparison, *Higher Education Review*, Vol. 17, pp. 45–52.

Crum, R. and Parikh, A. (1983) 'Headmasters' reports, admissions and academic performance in Social Sciences', *Educational Studies*, Vol. 9, pp. 169–84.

Dent, P.L. and Lewis, D.J. (1976) 'The relationship between teaching effectiveness and measures of research quality', *Educational Research Quarterly*, Vol. 1, No. 3, pp. 3–16.

Department of Education and Science (1987) *Higher Education: Meeting the Challenge*, Cmnd 114. London, HMSO.

Entwistle, N.J. and Wilson, J.D. (1977) *Degrees of Excellence: The Academic Achievement Game*. London, Hodder and Stoughton.

Freeman, P.R. (1970) 'A multivariate study of students' performance in the university examinations', *Journal of the Royal Statistical Society, Series A*, Vol. 133, pp. 38–55.

Hammond, P.E., Meyer, J.W. and Miller, D. (1969) 'Teaching versus research: sources of misperceptions', *Research Policy*, Vol. 40, pp. 682–90.

Harry, J. and Goldner, N.S. (1972) 'The null relationship between teaching and research', *Sociology of Education*, Vol. 45, pp. 47–60.

Hayes, J.R. (1971) 'Research, teaching and faculty fate', *Science*, Vol. 172, pp. 227–30.

Johnes, J. and Taylor, J. (1987) 'Degree quality: an investigation into differences between UK universities', *Higher Education*, Vol. 16, pp. 581–602.

Kapur, R.L. (1972) 'Student wastage at Edinburgh University', *Universities Quarterly*, Vol. 26, pp. 353–77 and 483–96.

Linsky, A.S. and Straus, M.A. (1975) 'Student evaluations, research productivity, and eminence of college faculty', *Journal of Higher Education*, Vol. 46, pp. 89–102.

Nevin, E. (1972) 'How not to get a first', *Economic Journal*, Vol. 82, pp. 658–73.

Sear, K. (1983) 'The correlation between A level grades and degree results in England and Wales', *Higher Education*, Vol. 12, pp. 609–19.

Tarsh, J. (1982) 'The labour market for new graduates', *Employment Gazette*, Vol. 90, pp. 205–15.

Voeks, V.W. (1962) 'Publications and teaching effectiveness', *Journal of Higher Education*, Vol. 33, pp. 212–18.

15
Operational performance of airlines: an extension of traditional measurement paradigms*

Michael Schefczyk

This study presents a new approach for measuring operational performance, an important facet of performance missing in the current literature concerned with international airline strategy. International performance assessments of airlines from published financial information are difficult, because (1) most airlines lease a substantial fraction of their aircraft, and (2) different accounting and taxation rules in various countries result in different impacts of leased assets on profit and balance-sheet information. A possible solution are nonfinancial data. For example, the number of available ton kilometers may reflect aircraft capacity more accurately than flight equipment depreciation. However, different units of measurement introduce new difficulties. Drawing on data from 15 airlines, this study utilizes 'Data Envelopment Analysis' as a technique to analyze and compare operational performance of airlines. The study concludes with an analysis of strategic factors of high profitability and performance in the airline industry.

Introduction

For the airline industry, the years 1989–92 were a period of challenge and transition due to an industry-wide downturn that began in 1989 (Air Canada, 1991). During this period, short-term problems, such as the Gulf War and an economic recession plus long-term difficulties, such as cost, regulatory, competitive, and environmental issues have caused substantial uncertainties for airlines around the world. Despite the presence of uncertainties, the airline business requires extremely long-term decision making. The reason is that most cost factors besides fuel and labor, e.g., acquisition of aircraft, construction of facilities, and development of route systems have a multi-decade character. Because of the extensive use of capital assets, such as aircraft and facilities, capital cost is considered an important long-term factor in airline operations. An issue of rising importance has been the ongoing environmental and safety discussion. For example, low noise emission is considered a prerequisite for expanding service at many airports.

Current research with the potential of supporting the necessary long-term decision making usually falls into one of two categories. One predominant

* This article was first published in *Strategic Management Journal*, Vol. 14, pp. 301–317, 1993.

category is classical strategy research that addresses strategic variables, such as core business focus, internalization, load factors, and productivities only in broad terms and usually in the context of regulation (Frentz, 1992; Levine, 1987). The other major category is productivity research that utilizes econometric methods to assess airline productivities, usually comparing US airlines (Caves, Christensen, and Tretheway, 1983; Cornwall, Schmidt, and Sickles, 1990). These two directions of research have two gaps. First, productivity research is typically limited to an airline based in a single country. Hence, the scope of such research needs to be broadened to better reflect the global nature of the airline business. Second, operational efficiency or the efficiency of the 'internal factory' of an airline is not usually addressed in strategy research. Therefore, the outcome of productivity research suitable to assess operational efficiency at an international scope needs to be linked to strategic questions.

Objectively assessing operational performance of international airlines from published information is difficult, because most airlines lease a substantial fraction of their aircraft. Especially in connection with different accounting and taxation rules in various countries, a high fraction of leased assets decreases the comparability of profit and loss account and balance sheet based information. A possible solution is the use of published nonfinancial information. For example, the number of available ton kilometers may reflect aircraft capacity much more accurately than flight equipment depreciation and amortization. Then, however, different units of measurement, e.g., US$ costs, kilometers, and US$ assets, introduce new difficulties. This study utilizes 'Data Envelopment Analysis' as a technique to analyze and compare operational performance of international airlines despite the difficulties mentioned. Finally, this study explores key strategic determinants of high profitability and performance based on the comparison of international airlines.

The next sections proceed along the following outline. In the section 'Performance measurement of airlines,' the fundamentals of performance analysis are reviewed and a basic model of airline operations is described. In the section 'Review of past performance,' classical performance measures for airlines are reviewed. In the section entitled 'Data envelopment analysis,' Data Envelopment Analysis (DEA) is described as an approach to measure productivity. DEA is a nonparametric methodology, because it does not require an explicit formulation of the underlying functional relationship of inputs and outputs. In the section 'Analysis of operational performance of airlines', airline performance analysis is carried out using DEA and the results are interpreted. In the final section, the results are summarized.

Performance measurement of airlines

In order to operate profitably, airline companies are motivated to administer their activities as cost effectively, reliably and rapidly as possible. Performance analysis is a process used to evaluate the cost efficiency, reliability, and timeliness of corporate management and design. The purpose of performance analysis is to identify areas of improvement in these activities as well as to aid strategic decision making. This paper is concerned with performance analysis, especially cost efficiency.

Knowledge provided by nonsubjective quantitative assessments is essential to keep planning and decision making in line with the goal of improving efficiency. Potential deficiencies in existing measures include bias and inconsistency with corporate objectives. Measures might be inconsistent with corporate objectives. An airline may focus on load factors as a basis for its performance measurement, while its corporate strategy features aggressive growth. Or, measures might be biased. Measures used to evaluate overall performance of entities often consider resources and services only partially. For example, an operating profit margin may not fully reflect the cost of leased assets, because capital leases have financially motivated terms. Applied in the wrong context; such a measure can misguide the decision maker. Providing objective quantitative performance assessments is especially difficult on an international scale, where, for example, different accounting and taxation rules exist.

To analyze airline operations, a model that fundamentally connects the services provided by an airline to the resources consumed in providing these services is required. One purpose of such a model is to define a common view of airline operations. Another reason is to clearly define the objects within an airline that are appropriate for measurement.

Figure 1 contrasts operations against other building blocks of airline business activity. 'Operations' does not include the core activity of marketing airline services. For modeling purposes, it is assumed that operations 'sells' revenue passenger kilometers and other services to marketing, which then, among other things, determines the pricing structure and sells the airline's products to customers. 'Operations' also does not include the core activity of financing an aircraft. For modeling purposes, it is furthermore assumed that finance/purchasing 'sells' available ton kilometers and other inputs to operations.

Figure 2 represents essential inputs and outputs of airline operations. The inputs can broadly be classified into asset-related inputs and cost-related inputs. Asset-related inputs are those inputs that represent capital goods and current assets. Such inputs contribute to costs only indirectly through depreciation, amortization, and interest. Cost-related inputs include labor, fuel, commissions and related items. The main output for a typical passenger focused airline are the revenue passenger kilometers, respectively the funds marketing generates selling tickets. Further outputs are represented by cargo and other revenues.

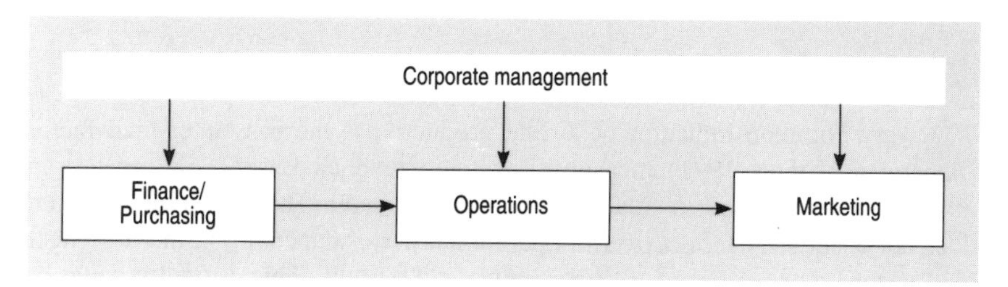

Figure 1 *Scope of operations*

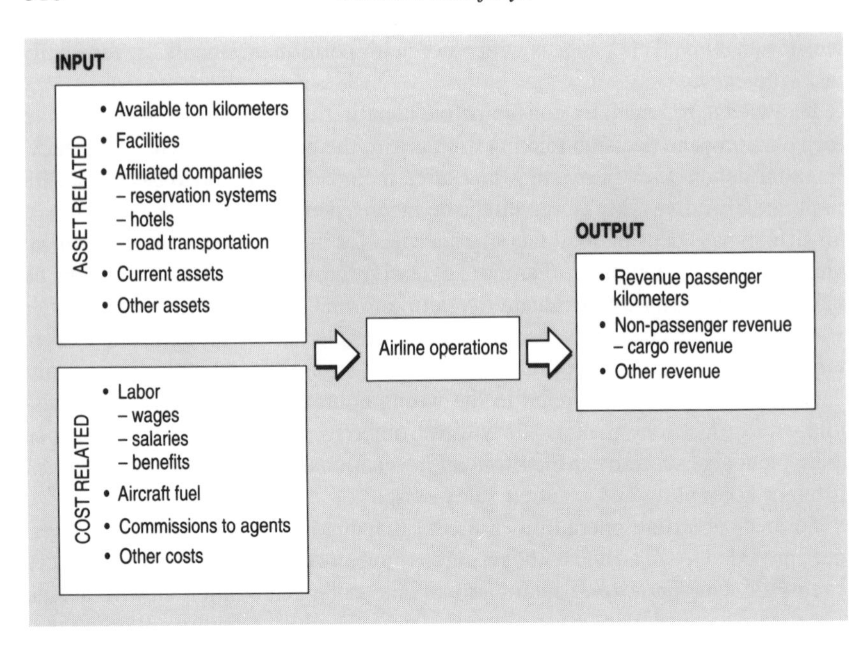

Figure 2 *Airline operations*

The link between inputs and outputs is the external demand for services which creates an internal demand for inputs. Satisfying the demand for outputs with minimum consumption of inputs is an airline management objective. Enabling managers to make decisions leading to higher achievement levels of this objective is a central purpose of airline performance analysis.

Review of past performance measures

Performance analysis is the measurement and comparison of actual levels of achievement of specific objectives. Possible objectives include having the lowest costs, having the highest load factor, or being able to respond the fastest to ticket requests. To numerically evaluate airline performance across countries, measures must be developed for the levels of achievement of airlines, regardless of their country of incorporation.

One candidate management objective is to produce a given output with minimum consumption of a resource. To measure this, the value of outputs produced is divided by the value of input resources consumed (Krajewski and Ritzman, 1990):

$$\text{Productivity} = \frac{\text{Output}}{\text{Input}}$$

A very common indicator of airline productivity, the passenger load factor (American Airlines, 1991), measures how many revenue passenger kilometers an airline can generate per available passenger kilometer. This measure, however, does not adequately reflect overall operational performance. First, the passenger load factor ignores all nonpassenger inputs and outputs. This difficulty could be resolved by changing the basis from passenger kilometers to ton kilometers. One would have to determine, however, whether passengers and cargo are weighted adequately. Second, load factors ignore most inputs besides aircraft capacity. For example, facilities, affiliated companies (reservation systems, hotels, etc.), and current assets (i.e., representing resource consumption for the purpose of generating revenue passenger kilometers) are being ignored. This difficulty cannot be corrected easily, because the inputs mentioned have different units of measurement. They can neither be added to compute total input, nor can they be easily priced to obtain additivity in an international comparison. Third, differences in factor costs are also ignored by load factors. For example, different labor costs in different countries are not reflected in load factors. Hence, load factors are not fully adequate as measures of operational productivity. While they link an output with an input, their scope remains limited to utilization analysis.

Computing valid operational productivity measures for international airlines based on the above definition is difficult. Initially, one may expect the profit and loss account of an airline to reflect inputs (i.e., costs) and outputs (i.e., revenues). However, to give just one example, the use of the same type of aircraft may have very different impacts on the profit and loss account of two different airlines. One airline may own the aircraft and depreciate it over its expected life. In this situation, resulting depreciation and interest expenses would imply efficient use of the aircraft. Another airline, due to different taxation rules, may prefer to acquire the aircraft through a wholly-owned subsidiary in a country with low corporate taxes. To maximize accumulation of equity in the low-tax subsidiary and to minimize total tax liabilities, the parent company may obtain the aircraft from its subsidiary through a capital lease with an artificially high rate. In this case, the resulting expenses would imply inefficient use of the aircraft. Furthermore, the details of such a transaction would not be published. Nevertheless, major international airlines have the capabilities to undertake such transactions. For example, Cathay Pacific Airways Limited, Hong Kong, owns three subsidiaries in the Bermudas with aircraft leasing as the stated principal activity, with capital of US$ 12,000 issued and paid up, per company (Cathay Pacific Airways Limited, 1991). Therefore, profit and loss accounts may not reflect inputs and outputs of international airlines sufficiently well, due to distorted pricing of some inputs and outputs.

Airline productivity measures proposed in literature also suffer from the pitfalls described above. Thuong (1986), among others, proposes an operating efficiency based on the Cobb–Douglas production function. First, the author does not provide a rationale explaining why the Cobb–Douglas function adequately represents the correct type of efficiency frontier (including scale effects) for airlines. Second, the author represents the input of seat capacity acquisition by 'annual depreciation of owned flight equipment and amortization of capital leases'. This may be appropriate for comparing airlines based in one single country, but for the reasons stated above, the methodology cannot be expanded to international comparisons. Hence, the challenge as well as the contribution of this study is to define an improved representation of operational performance of airlines that can be applied in international comparisons.

Productivity alone, however, does not reflect overall airline performance. Specifically, productivity does not consider customer and competition issues well enough. The new competitive pressures stated in the introduction also increase the importance of quality and timeliness in service. Both business and private customers are often willing to pay premiums for reliable service of high quality. However, these factors are beyond the scope of this article, which is limited to operational performance or the cost efficiency aspect of performance analysis.

Data envelopment analysis

A *production function* indicates the maximum output obtainable from a given set of inputs that are used as efficiently as possible. One way to measure a firm's efficiency would then be to compare its observed output level to the output determined by the production function. Let $X = (x_1, x_2, \ldots, x_J)$ denote a vector of J inputs (e.g., labor, equipment, and space) consumed by a firm, let y denote the observed output, and let f(X) denote the production function. In mathematical terms, the *output efficiency* of the firm is y/f(X). For example, a firm or 'Decision Making Unit' (DMU) might have an actual output of 120 units while the production function specifies 150 units as the maximum output for the same input. This leads to 120/150 = 0.8 as an output efficiency. Alternatively, it is possible to use a production function to assess *input inefficiency*, by determining the scale by which inputs can be reduced and still achieve the same output level as before.

Knowledge of a production function is obviously useful for computing efficiencies in situations where there are multiple inputs. In parametric analysis, an explicit functional form for the production function is posited *a priori*. One popular example is the Cobb–Douglas production function (Ghobadian and Husband, 1990). Nonparametric analysis, on the other hand, uses data to determine implicitly the production function without requiring a functional form and without estimating parameters.

In this article 'Data Envelopment Analysis' (DEA) is used, which is a recently developed nonparametric approach due to Charnes, Cooper, and Rhodes (1978). It was introduced as a method to compute multiple-output, multiple-input productivities without requiring preassigned weights for outputs and inputs (Banker, 1984) and it may therefore be viewed as a generalization of single-output to single-input productivity ratios. A variety of DEA models have appeared in the literature (Banker, Charnes, and Cooper, 1984; Charnes *et al*., 1985; Charnes *et al*., 1978).

Technical assumptions

Let $X_j = (x_{1j}, \ldots, x_{ij}, \ldots, x_{Ij})$ denote the vector of observed inputs and $Y_j = (y_{1j}, \ldots, y_{rj}, \ldots, y_{Rj})$ denote the vector of observed outputs for firm j. In DEA the technology is defined by the *production possibility set* as $T = \{(X,Y) \mid Y \geq 0$ can be produced from $X \geq 0\}$. The first assumption of DEA is that the set T is *convex*, i.e., if $(X_j, Y_j) \in T, j = 1, \ldots, J$, and $\lambda_j \geq 0$ are non-negative scalars such that $\Sigma\lambda_j = 1$, then $(\Sigma\lambda_j X_j, \Sigma\lambda_j Y_j) \in T$. The second assumption is *allocative efficiency*, meaning that, if $(X, Y) \in T$ and $X' \geq X$, then $(X', Y) \in T$, and if $(X, Y) \in T$ and $Y' \leq Y$, then $(X, Y') \in T$. Allocative efficiency has two aspects, one corresponding to inputs and one corresponding to outputs. For a multiple-input, one-output case, the input aspect of allocative efficiency represents the notion that increasing inputs does not decrease output. A third assumption is that T exhibits *constant returns to scale*, i.e., if $(X, Y) \in T$ and $k > 0$, then $(k X, k Y) \in T$, too. If this assumption is not invoked, then the DEA technology definition is referred to as a *variable returns to scale* technology.

To interpret graphically the third assumption of DEA, the single-input, single-output DEA model is used in Figure 3, illustrating both variable returns to scale and constant returns to scale. The efficient frontier, an arbitrary production function that satisfies the assumptions regarding convexity and allocative efficiency, represents a variable returns to scale model. Using this model, DMUs A, B and C are technically efficient because they lie on the efficient frontier. In contrast, the ray through the DMU A represents the constant returns to scale model.

In the variable returns to scale model, one can distinguish between increasing and decreasing returns to scale. The segment of the efficient frontier to the right of DMU A exhibits decreasing returns to scale. For example, DMU C requires 60 percent (16/10 = 1.6) more input than DMU A while its output is only 50 percent (12/8 = 1.5) above the level of DMU A. Accordingly, the productivity of A is equal to 0.8 (= 8/10) while the productivity of C is equal to only 0.75 (=12/16). Likewise, the segment of the efficient frontier to the left of DMU A exhibits increasing returns to scale. For example, DMU A requires one quarter (10/8 = 1.25) more input than DMU B. Nevertheless, A produces one-third (8/6 = 1.33) more output than B produces. Accordingly, the productivity of B is equal to only 0.75 (= 6/8). Since increasing returns to scale exist for points on the efficient frontier with input levels below 10 units, it is attractive to scale these points up to DMU A. Beyond DMU A, decreasing returns to scale exist for points on the efficient frontier. Because of this property, DMU A has the optimal scale size.

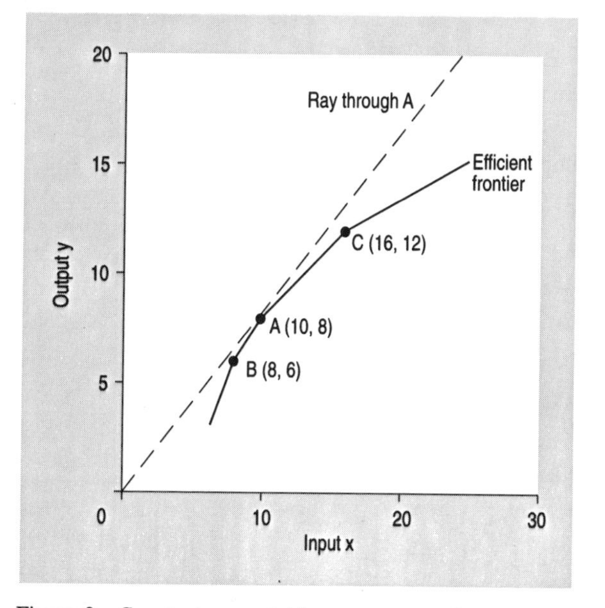

Figure 3 *Constant vs variable returns to scale*

Multiple-input, multiple-output DEA

Figure 4 illustrates how to represent graphically the input efficiency for the two-input case. In this graph the combined consumption of inputs can be measured in terms of the distance of a DMU from the origin. Here, DMU A is inefficient, because it lies above the efficiency frontier and consumes the same fractions of labor and equipment as A. In detail, A is 15 units away from the origin while the efficient DMU A' is only 10 units away from the origin. The input efficiency score for DMU A is recorded as 2/3 (= 10/15).

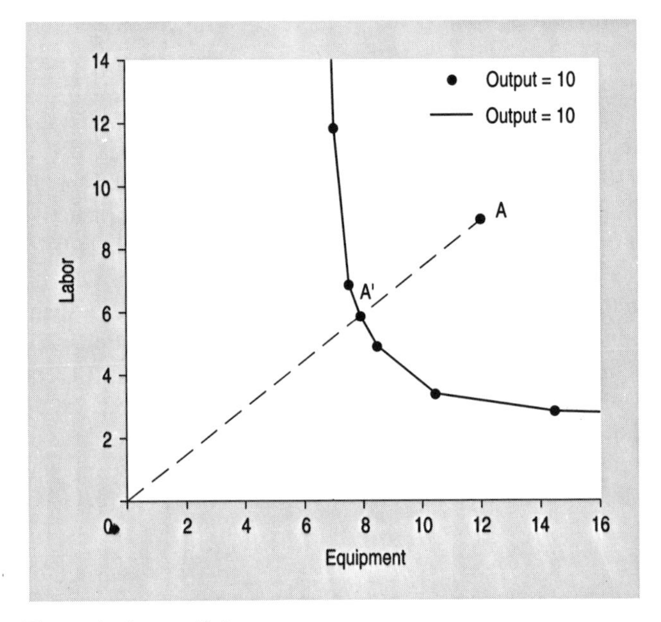

Figure 4 *Input efficiency*

A basic multiple-input multiple-output DEA model is (Ali and Lerme, 1991):

$CRS_P\,(Y_j, X_j, u^j, v^j)$: min $-\,(u^js + v^je)$(1)

$$\text{s.t. } Y\lambda - s = Y_j$$

$$-X\lambda - e = -X_j$$

$$\lambda \geq 0, e \geq 0, s \geq 0$$

$CRS_D(Y_j, X_j, u^j, v^j)$:(2)

$$\max \mu Y_j - \nu X_j$$

$$\text{s.t. } \mu Y - \nu X \leq 0$$

$$\mu \geq u^j;\ \nu \geq v^j$$

$$u_r^j \equiv 1/y_{rj};\ v_i^j \equiv 1/x_{ij}$$

with $j = 1, \ldots, J;\ r = 1, \ldots, R;\ i = 1, \ldots, I$

with J decision making units, I inputs and R outputs. In this model, $X_j = (x_{1j}, \ldots, x_{ij}, \ldots, x_{Ij})$ denotes the vector of observed inputs and $Y_j = (y_{1j}, \ldots, y_{rj}, \ldots, y_{Rj})$ denotes the vector of observed outputs for firm j. The model follows directly from the definition of the constant returns to scale (CRS) envelopment surface consisting of hyperplanes R^{I+R} that are particular facets of the complex polyhedral cone determined by the vectors (Y_j, X_j). A facet

$$\mu y - \nu x = \sum_{r=1}^{R} \mu_r y_r - \sum_{i=1}^{I} \nu_i x_i = 0 \quad (3)$$

of the cone is a facet of the CRS envelopment surface if and only if

$$\mu Y_j - \nu X_j = \sum_{r=1}^{R} \mu_s y_{sj} - \sum_{i=1}^{I} \nu_j x_{ij} \leq 0 \quad (4)$$

for all j = 1, …, J, with equality for at least one j.

The parameters u^j and v^j determine the specific lower bounds on the multipliers μ and ν. For the model to be units invariant (Ahn, Charnes, and Cooper, 1988), the conditions $u_r^j \equiv 1/y_{rj}$; r = 1, …, R, $v_i^j \equiv 1/x_{ij}$; i = 1, …, I have to be satisfied. An optimal solution is then given by the output vector μ^j and the input vector ν^j. Note that performing DEA requires the solution of a linear programing model for each decision-making unit j. Each of the J sets of values given by μ^j, ν^j, j = 1, …, J are the coefficients of hyperplanes that define facets of the envelopment surface.

In the primal formulation, the vectors u^j and v^j define the directions of the projection, which are the basis for evaluating efficiency. To measure input efficiency, a ratio is required that represents the minimum factor which when applied to the input vector and given the relative prices μ^j and ν^j would yield the current level of outputs assuming that the entire hyperplane represents a facet of the envelopment surface. The definition of a ratio measure ι^j of total input efficiency is (Ali and Lerme, 1991):

$$\iota^j = \frac{\mu^j Y_j}{\nu^j X_j} \quad (5)$$

The inequalities $\nu^j \geq v^j > 0$, $\mu^j \geq u^j > 0$, $Y_j > 0$, $X_j > 0$, imply $0 < \iota^j \leq 1$. The point (Y_j, X_j) lies on the facet-defining plane, $\mu^j y - \nu^j x = 0$ if and only if $\iota = 1$. The measure can be interpreted as the reduction of inputs – proportionate and residual – required to make a DMU efficient. For example, $\iota = 0.95$ means that one would have to reduce the inputs of the corresponding DMU to 95 percent of current inputs to make it efficient.

Analysis of operational performance of airlines

Operational efficiency scores

In this section, the efficiencies of airlines are compared, using DEA measures. A set of industry data is the basis for measuring operational performance. Criteria for selecting the airlines for this study are size of the carrier, international operations, and public availability of data. The reference data set contains 1990 information on 15 large international airlines. Fourteen of these airlines are major passenger carriers with more than 15 million passenger kilometers per year for which published data exists. Federal Express was included as an all-cargo airline to get a more extreme fix on a 'non-passenger revenue' decision making unit. The data are based on company annual reports and published IATA materials.

For the analysis, constant returns to scale are assumed. Airlines, unlike, for example, municipal subway systems, have the opportunity to influence their own scale over a time frame of a few years. To do so they can engage in mergers and acquisitions or undertake divestitures. Furthermore, airlines are less limited to a specific operating region through regulation. Therefore, airlines should not be credited for deviations from the optimal scale. This is best expressed through a constant returns to scale model. From a different perspective, a constant returns to scale model has certain analytical advantages. Especially in the case of small sample sizes, too high a fraction of DMUs could lie on the production function if a variable returns to scale model was used. Figure 3 shows why more DMUs will be efficient in a variable returns to scale model. As stated above, a variable returns to scale model could favor an airline that is too small to compete.

The definitions of inputs and outputs are derived from the model of airline operations as described in Figure 2:

- Available ton km (ton km, input)

  = available ton km scheduled services

  + available ton km charter services

  This figure reflects aircraft capacity obtained.
- Operating cost (op. cost, input)

  = total operating expenses

  – aircraft rent

  – depreciation and amortization

  This figure reflects operating cost excluding capital and aircraft cost reflected in available ton km. Monetary conversions are based on 1990 annual average exchange rates (OECD, 1991).
- Nonflight assets (n.f. assets, input)

  = total assets

  – flight equipment, at cost

  + accumulated depreciation for flight equipment

  – purchase deposits for flight equipment

  – flight equipment under capital leases, at cost

  + accumulated amortization for flight equipment under capital leases

  This figure reflects all assets not already reflected by available ton km (e.g. facilities, reservation systems, current assets).
- Revenue passenger km (p. km, output)

  = revenue passenger km scheduled services

  + revenue passenger km charter services

  This figure reflects the passenger-flight related output.

- Nonpassenger revenue (n.p. rev., output)
  = total operating reveune
  – passenger revenue
  This figure reflects all output that is not passenger-flight related.

For the computation of DEA efficiency scores in this study, a current commercial algorithm (1 Consulting, 1992) is used. With this algorithm, scalar input efficiency scores denoted ι are computed. The interest is in input efficiencies because from an operations perspective, the output of an airline may be regarded as a target value that is specified by management. The objective of operational airline management is then to meet this target with minimum consumption of resources. Table 1 contains a summary of inputs, outputs and efficiency scores.

Four airlines, Cathay Pacific, Federal Express, Singapore, and UAL appear efficient. The characteristics of these airlines vary widely. Both a relatively small airline in terms of passenger revenue km in this sample, Cathay Pacific, and the second largest, UAL, appear efficient. An example of an inefficient airline is KLM. KLM's efficiency score of 0.73 indicates that it theoretically would have to reduce its resource consumption to 73 percent of the current level to become efficient.

The efficiency of Federal Express, the only all-cargo carrier included in the sample data, may partially be due to its uniqueness among passenger-focused peer carriers. Such an airline, describing an extreme case within the production possibility set, should less likely be dominated in terms of its efficiency by another airline producing a mix of passenger and nonpassenger output. If Federal Express is removed from the sample data, Lufthansa and Korean become efficient.[1] Hence, Federal Express dominates these carriers. Especially Lufthansa is a highly diversified carrier with an emphasis on cargo. Its ratio of non-passenger revenue to available ton km is surpassed only by Federal Express. Therefore, if Federal Express was not included in the sample data, Lufthansa itself would gain an extreme position within the production possibility set. This demonstrates the limitations of the concept of relative efficiency for decision making units with extreme properties.

Another key limitation of DEA becomes evident immediately. With a small sample size relative to the number of inputs and outputs, too many DMUs can appear efficient. Reducing the number of inputs and outputs is not a solution to this problem, because the model would lose its conceptual power and the analysis would become very similar to classical ratio based productivity measurement (Schefczyk, 1990). Substantially increasing the sample size is also difficult because the number of large international airlines for which published data exist is limited. Perhaps the sample size could be doubled, but further increases appear unrealistic.

Table 1 *Input/output variable values and DEA input efficiencies for 15 airlines*

	Inputs			Outputs		IOTA
	Available ton km	Operating cost	Nonflight assets	Revenue pass. km	Nonpass. revenue	Input efficiency
Airline	ton km	op. cost	n.f. assets	p. km.	n.p. rev.	ι
Air Canada	5723	3239	2003	26677	697	0.817
All Nippon Airways Co.	5895	4225	4557	33081	539	0.758
American Airlines, Inc.	24099	9560	6267	124055	1266	0.896
British Airways Plc	13565	7499	3213	64734	1563	0.907
Cathay Pacific Airways	5183	1880	783	23604	513	1.000
Delta Air Lines, Inc.	19080	8032	3272	95011	572	0.893
Federal Express	10884	6730	3934	0	7688	1.000
IBERIA Lineas Aereas	4603	3457	2360	22112	969	0.793
Japan Airlines	12097	6779	6474	52363	2001	0.724
KLM Royal Dutch Airlines	6587	3341	3581	26504	1297	0.734
Korean Air	5654	1878	1916	19277	972	0.847
Lufthansa	12559	8098	3310	41925	3398	0.878
Quantas	5728	2481	2254	27754	982	0.917
Singapore Airlines	4715	1792	2485	31332	543	1.000
UAL Corporation	22793	9874	4145	122528	1404	1.000

Analysis of operational performance

To further analyze the operational performance of the airlines in the sample data set, a few statistical variables are computed, as displayed in Table 2.

- Return on equity (ret. on eq.)

  = income after income taxes/common stockholders equity

  Weighted average of 1990, 1989, and 1988 figures (5: 3: 2).
- Gross margin (gr. margin)

  = income before income taxes/total operating revenue

  Weighted average of 1990, 1989, and 1988 figures (5: 3: 2)
- Passenger load factor (p. load f.)

  = revenue passenger km (scheduled and charter)/available passenger km (scheduled and charter)

  This figure represents aircraft utilization.
- Percentage of passenger revenue (% p. rev.) = passenger revenue/total operating revenue

  This figure represents the passenger-focus of an airline.

Table 2 *Airline statistics*

	Return on equity	Gross margin	Pass. load factor	% pass. revenue	Nonflight assets/tkm	Revenue growth	% int'l pass. km
Airline	ret.on eq.	gr. margin	p.load f.	% p. rev.	nfa/tkm	rev. grow.	% int'l km
Air Canada	0.024	0.021	0.714	0.794	0.350	0.032	0.572
All Nippon Airways Co.	0.056	0.035	0.725	0.894	0.773	0.100	0.215
American Airlines, Inc.	0.061	0.032	0.623	0.885	0.260	0.111	0.195
British Airways Plc	0.144	0.047	0.701	0.822	0.237	0.026	0.941
Cathay Pacific Airways	0.365	0.202	0.741	0.798	0.151	0.092	0.942
Delta Air Lines, Inc.	0.069	0.036	0.612	0.936	0.171	0.088	0.137
Federal Express	0.048	0.024	–	0.000	0.361	0.207	–
IBERIA Lineas Aereas	-0.007	-0.015	0.693	0.737	0.513	0.005	0.704
Japan Airlines	0.042	0.035	0.732	0.741	0.535	0.076	0.767
KLM Royal Dutch Airlines	-0.027	-0.013	0.696	0.640	0.544	0.037	0.996
Korean Air	0.022	0.012	0.728	0.590	0.339	0.040	0.870
Lufthansa	0.021	0.015	0.648	0.621	0.264	0.076	0.925
Quantas	0.087	0.028	0.682	0.663	0.394	0.050	1.000
Singapore Airlines	0.193	0.259	0.751	0.786	0.527	0.043	1.000
UAL Corporation	0.188	0.046	0.662	0.873	0.182	0.057	0.290

- Nonflight assets per available ton km (nfa/tkm)

  = non flight assets/available ton km

  Low values indicate a high core business focus.
- Revenue growth (rev. grow.)

  Compound annual growth rate of total operating revenues 1987–90, adjusted for inflation.
- Percentage of international km (% int'l km)

  = international passenger km/revenue passenger km

  This figure represents the international focus of an airline.

First, it is investigated whether there is a relationship between operational performance and profitability. Figure 5 (overleaf) displays a regression analysis between iota (ι) and return on equity.

$$\text{ret. on eq.} = 0.72\iota - 0.55$$
$$\text{with } R^2 = 0.49,\ F = 12.50,\ p < 0.0037 \qquad (6)$$

Variable	Iota
Std. Coeff.	0.70
t-Value	3.54
$p > \|t\|$	0.0037

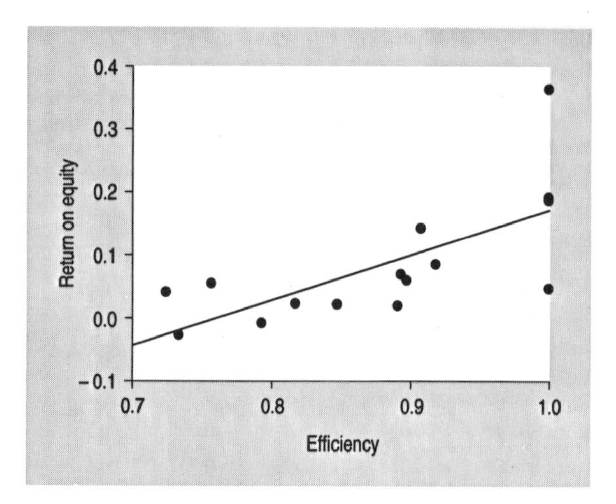

Figure 5 *Relationship of efficiency and profitability*

The regression analysis confirms a positive relationship between return on equity and efficiency. Obviously, the coefficient of determination (R^2) is relatively low for this relationship. This is not surprising in light of the model of airline operations as illustrated in Figure 2. An airline may operate efficiently while, for example, acquiring its aircraft at too high a price or selling tickets at too deep a discount. Furthermore, different corporate tax rates and taxation rules in various countries may lead to different profitabilities of otherwise equal firms. Also, the efficient airlines have very different profitabilities. For example, Cathay Pacific has a return on equity of 37 percent while Federal Express has a return on equity of 4.8 percent. In such a situation, the sum of least squares method used in regression analysis must lead to low coefficients of determination because of its sensitivity to outliers.

The statistical data reveal another disadvantage of DEA. Korean, for example, generates only 59 percent of its revenues from what is perceived as the core business of a typical airline: passenger transportation. DEA does not focus exclusively on any one output. Nonpassenger revenue may be as important an output in the production function of an airline as passenger revenue km. To further analyze this difficulty, it can, however, be determined whether it is advantageous for an airline to be focused on its core business.

Next, the key factors of high performance were analyzed. For this analysis, Federal Express is excluded from the regression data, because the study emphasizes passenger-focused airlines and because of the missing data for Federal Express in all passenger related categories. Nevertheless, Federal Express remains part of the efficient frontier determining input efficiencies. By means of stepwise regression ($F_{IN} = 4.000$; $F_{OUT} = 3.996$), an explanatory relationship for efficiency is determined:

$$\iota = -0.31 \text{ nfa/tkm} + 0.73 \text{ gr. margin} + 0.95$$

$$\text{with } R^2 = 0.79,\ F = 20.28,\ p < 0.0002 \qquad (7)$$

Variable	nfa/tkm	gr. margin
Std. Coeff.	−0.59	0.60
t-Value	4.23	4.31
$p >$ |t|	0.001	0.001

The above relationship indicates that low nonflight assets per available ton km and a high gross margin, in other words a profitable core business, predict high efficiency. The coefficient of determination for this relationship of 0.79 appears relatively high in light of the findings from the regression analysis between profitability and efficiency. The partial *t*-tests indicate that the level of nonflight assets per available ton km as well as the gross margin clearly have a significant relation to operating efficiency.

The relationship implies that being lean and focused on the core business tends to increase efficiency.[2] The first part of the relationship is directly plausible from the model of airline operations as described in Figure 2. Many of the nonflight assets, such as facilities, reservation systems, and current assets do not directly contribute to generating revenues. They are merely means to support the overall operating activities of airlines. Therefore, minimizing such assets should increase operating productivity. This minimization strategy finds its limits where non-flight assets are essential for conducting business or for establishing competitive advantages. The second part of the regression relationship, that a high gross margin supports high efficiency, has some similarity to the relationship between return on equity and efficiency illustrated in Figure 5. Here, it is difficult to determine which factor has the greatest influence on which other factors. The profit margin is highly likely depending on operational efficiency.

Having analyzed the factors of high productivity, a stepwise regression is utilized ($F_{IN} = 4.000$; $F_{OUT} = 3.996$) to determine the factors of high profitability. Again, Federal Express is excluded from the regression data, so that variables, such as passenger load factor, can be included in the analysis.

$$\text{ret. on eq.} = 0.84\iota + 1.04 \text{ p. load f.} + 0.20 \ln (\% \text{ p. rev.}) - 1.31$$
$$\text{with } R^2 = 0.83, F = 16.31, p < 0.0004 \quad (8)$$

Variable	Iota	p. load f.	ln (% p. rev.)
Std. Coeff.	0.77	0.44	0.28
t-Value	5.67	3.24	2.02
$p >$ |t|	0.0002	0.009	0.071

This relationship indicates that high operational efficiency, high passenger load factors, and high percentages of passenger revenue predict high profitability. In other words, an efficient, well utilized, and passenger-focused airline is most likely profitable. The partial *t*-tests indicate that all regressor variables have a significant influence on profitability at least at the $p = 0.071$ level.

The impacts of operational efficiency and passenger load factor on profitability are obvious. Both factors state that the consumption of resources has to be optimized relative to the output generated. The relationship between percentage of passenger revenue and profitability indicates an increased likelihood of operating profitably by being passenger-focused. This reiterates, from an output perspective, the advantages of a focus on the core business, as expressed by the previous regression analysis. Furthermore, a positive influence of growth on profitability exists. Revenue growth would be the next variable to enter the regression relationship, if the criteria were relaxed slightly. This means that most airlines in the sample set have remained within the limits of advantageous, reasonable growth that did not come at the expense of low profitability (e.g., because of a decrease in utilization). This relationship, however, is not supported at the same level of statistical significance as the other relationships.

Finally, the reasons for, and symptoms of, low performance of two example airlines, All Nippon (inefficient, ι = 0.758) and UAL (efficient, ι = 1.000) are investigated. This analysis is based on the slack inputs as displayed in Table 3. First, the distribution of slack operating cost is studied. All Nippon theoretically had slack operating costs, excluding depreciation and amortization, of US$ 1.8 billion in 1990, or 42 percent of total operating costs. All Nippon's operating costs equal 12.8 cents per revenue passenger km, while UAL, another passenger and domestic focused carrier, had operating costs equal to only 8.1 cents per km. In other words, All Nippon's operating costs per km are 58 percent higher than UAL's operating costs. In 1990, efficient airlines with a high passenger-focus (e.g., Cathay Pacific, Singapore Airlines, and UAL) had operating costs, excluding depreciation, amortization and aircraft rent of between 5.7 and 8.1 cents per revenue passenger km. Airlines with a lower passenger-focus, such as Korean and Lufthansa, do not fit in this comparison, because the costs of nonairline businesses, such as hotels and road transportation, could bias this ratio.

Table 3 *Slack and excess variables*

	Slack			Excess		IOTA
Airline	ton km	op. cost	n. f. assets	p. km	n. p. rev.	ι
Air Canada	0	639	0	0	584	0.817
All Nippon Airways Co.	0	1766	1602	0	682	0.758
American Airlines, Inc.	0	0	0	0	1470	0.896
British Airways Plc	0	1352	0	0	506	0.907
Cathay Pacific Airways	0	0	0	0	0	1.000
Delta Air Lines, Inc.	0	270	0	0	1037	0.893
Federal Express	0	0	0	0	0	1.000
IBERIA Lineas Aereas	0	1404	145	0	315	0.793
Japan Airlines	0	1177	797	0	1885	0.724
KLM Royal Dutch Airlines	0	218	540	0	998	0.734
Korean Air	1116	0	625	0	0	0.847
Lufthansa	0	2494	594	0	0	0.878
Quantas	0	79	0	0	278	0.917
Singapore Airlines	0	0	0	0	0	1.000
UAL Corporation	0	0	0	0	0	1.000

Furthermore, on a nonconsolidated basis, All Nippon theoretically had slack nonflight assets of US$ 1.6 billion in 1990, or 35 percent of the total nonflight assets. All Nippon's nonflight assets equal US$ 138 per 1000 revenue passenger km, while UAL had nonflight assets equal to only US$ 34 per 1000 km. Hence, All Nippon's nonflight assets per km are fourfold UAL's nonflight assets. More than a fifth of this difference is due to different cash levels alone. All Nippon holds US$ 25 of cash per 1000 km, while UAL holds only US$ 1.8 per 1000 km. Other reasons include All Nippon's higher property and equipment, prepaid expenses, and securities levels per km. Strategic reasons, for example the preparation for a corporate acquisition, may justify large cash holdings. In the case of All Nippon, however, the cash level remained relatively stable over the past years. In 1990, efficient airlines with a high passenger-focus (e.g., Cathay Pacific, Singapore Airlines and UAL) had nonflight assets of between US$ 33 and US$ 79 per 1000 revenue passenger km.

Conclusions

Within its methodological limits, DEA is a viable tool for international benchmarking of operational airline performance. The scope of operations includes the core task of producing passenger revenue km from available ton km. It does not include either the acquisition of resources through financing and purchasing or the marketing and sales activities. Based on this model of airline operations, DEA can provide nonsubjective assessments of operational performance, in other words, the ability to produce given outputs with minimum consumption of resources.

For the analysis of performance, an input efficiency score based on available ton km, operating cost, and nonflight assets as inputs and revenue passenger km and nonpassenger revenue as outputs was computed. Furthermore, statistics were computed, such as return on equity, measures of core-business focus, and passenger load factors. Then regression analysis was used in seeking to determine the relationship between profitability and performance as well as the influence of structural characteristics on both performance and profitability. Finally, an example was given to compare two airlines in slightly more detail.

An important question to be answered is the set of reasons for preferring DEA over other analytical methods for strategy research. The holistic view that can be taken through applying DEA is perceived as the key advantage. Basis for this conclusion are the deficiencies of classical measures as identified in the section 'Review of past performance measures' vs. the advantages of DEA as discussed in the section entitled 'Analysis of operational performance of airlines'. DEA remains as the only viable methodology that links *all* factors of efficiency by evaluating the relationships between each input and output to arrive at a scalar measure of performance. In so doing, DEA overcomes the difficulties described in the introduction: limited international comparability of financial information and variety of units of measurement in nonfinancial information.

The analysis indicates that high operational performance is a key factor of high profitability. Other factors, of course, include efficient resource acquisition and marketing and sales activities. The fourteen passenger airlines in the sample data display increasing performance with strong focus on the core business of passenger transportation. Obviously, high passenger load factors support high profitability. Finally, growth also stimulated profitability for the airlines in the sample.

A specific comparison showed that efficient, passenger-focused airlines tend to have operating costs, excluding depreciation, amortization and aircraft rent, not exceeding 8 cents per revenue passenger km. Furthermore, the nonflight assets of such airlines do not exceed US$ 80 per 1000 revenue passenger km.

Further research should strive for maximizing the sample size of studies assessing operational performance of airlines in order to draw most valid conclusions of strategic factors of high profitability and performance. For increased strategic relevance, future measures should cover longer time spans than the 1- to 3-year measures used in this study. To better link research with management practice, and to minimize the uncertainties connected to the use of published information, further studies should include active participation of senior airline management, possibly represented by strategy and corporate development departments. A trade-off of such an approach would be, that the use of proprietary information would constrain the possibilities for publication of such a study. Nevertheless, increased certainty and validity of conclusions combined with publication of a partially anonymous benchmarking exercise should adequately serve both the research community and management practice.

Acknowledgements

The author expresses his appreciation to Dr Gunter P. Sharp, Associate Professor at the School of Industrial and Systems Engineering at the Georgia Institute of Technology, who provided guidance and support. An acknowledgement is extended to Dr Torsten J. Gerpott, Senior Associate, Booz-Allen & Hamilton Inc., for giving valuable advice.

Notes

1 The efficiency of Lufthansa and Korean under this condition appears counter-intuitive in [the] context of profitability. To further investigate this, a single-input single-output productivity ratio describing how many passenger revenue km an airline can generate per available ton km is computed. Lufthansa and Korean reach levels of 3.3 and 3.4, respectively, while Singapore Airlines achieves 6.7. From this perspective, Lufthansa and Korean appear inefficient. Another such productivity ratio describes how much nonpassenger revenue an airline can generate per US$ of operating cost. Lufthansa and Korean generate US$ 0.42 and US$ 0.52, respectively, while Cathay Pacific reaches a level of only US$ 0.27 nonpassenger revenue per US$ of operating cost. From this perspective, Lufthansa and Korean appear efficient. This reveals one disadvantage of this DEA model: in a multiproduct case, the production function can neither associate specific inputs with specific outputs, nor can it determine the relative importance of individual outputs for performance.

2 Omitting Federal Express not only from the regression data, but also from the DEA reference set yields an additional relationship. Thereby, a high international focus supports high efficiency. This is a statement that cannot be verified from the model of airline operations. Possible explanations include higher load factors on international flights and scale effects resulting from longer flights (i.e., lower relative impact of resource-intensive departure and arrival activities). Market related aspects, such as more lead-time and certainty of international reservations may also influence operational performance. Naturally, the measure 'percentage of international km' introduces a bias towards airlines incorporated in small countries with marginal home markets.

References

Ahn, T., Charnes, A. and Cooper, W.W. (1988) 'A note on the efficiency characteristics obtained in different DEA models', *Socio-Economic Planning Sciences*, Vol. 6, pp. 253–258.

Ali, A.I. and Lerme, C.S. (1991) 'Data envelopment analysis models: A framework', Working Paper. School of Management, The University of Massachusetts at Amherst, Amherst, MA.

Banker, R.D. (1984) 'Estimating most productive scale size using data envelopment analysis', *European Journal of Operational Research*, Vol. 17, pp. 35–44.

Banker, R.D., Charnes, A. and Cooper, W.W. (1984) 'Some models for estimating technical and scale inefficiencies in data envelopment analysis', *Management Science*, Vol. 30, pp. 1078–1092.

Caves, D.W., Christensen, L.R. and Tretheway, M.W. (1983) 'Productivity performance of US trunk and local service airlines in the era of deregulation', *Economic Inquiry*, Vol. 21, pp. 312–324.

Charnes, A., Cooper, W.W. and Rhodes, E. (1978) 'Measuring the efficiency of decision making units', *European Journal of Operational Research*, Vol. 2, pp. 429–444.

Charnes, A., Cooper, W.W., Golany, B., Seiford, L. and Stutz, J. (1985) 'Foundations of data envelopment analysis for Pareto-Koopmans efficient empirical production functions', *Journal of Econometrics*, Vol. 30, pp. 91–107.

1 Consulting (1992) *Integrated Data Analysis System Version 5.0.1*. Amherst, MA.

Cornwell, C., Schmidt, P. and Sickles, R.C. (1990) 'Production frontiers with cross-sectional and time-series variation in efficiency levels', *Journal of Econometrics*, Vol. 46, pp. 185–200.

Frentz, M. (1992) 'Daedalus 1992, Strategische Wettbewerbsvorteile der Luftverkehrsindustrie im liberalisierten Europäischen Markt', *Zeitschrift für Betriebswirtschaft*, Vol. 62, pp. 415–434.

Ghobadian, A. and Husband, T. (1990) 'Measuring total productivity using production functions', *International Journal of Production Research*, Vol. 28, pp. 1435–1446.

International Air Transport Association (1991) *World Air Transport Statistics*, Number 35, June.

Krajewski, L.J. and Ritzman, L.P. (1990) *Operations Management: strategy and analysis*. Addison-Wesley, Reading, MA.

Levine, M.E. (1987) 'Airline competition in deregulated markets: theory, firm strategy, and public policy', *Yale Journal of Regulation*, Vol. 4, pp. 393–494.

OECD (1991) *OECD Economic Outlook*, Number 49, July.

Schefczyk, M. (1990) Warehouse performance analysis: techniques and applications', *MHRC Report Series* TD-90-11, July. Georgia Institute of Technology, Atlanta, GA.

Thanassoulis, E., Dyson, R.G. and Foster, M.J. (1987) 'Relative efficiency assessments using data envelopment analysis: an application to data on rates departments', *Journal of the Operational Research Society*, Vol. 38, pp. 397–411.

Thuong, L.T. (1986) 'Coping with adverse economic conditions under a regulated versus competitive environment: a study of domestic trunk airlines', *Akron Business and Economic Review*, Vol. 17, pp. 62–67.

Annual Reports

Air Canada, *1990 Annual Report,* Montreal, 1991.

All Nippon Airways Co. Ltd., *1991 Annual Report,* Tokyo, 1991.

American Airlines, Inc., *Form 10-K Annual Report Pursuant to Section 13 or 15(d) of the Securities Exchange Act of 1934 for the fiscal year ended: December 31, 1990,* Fort Worth, 1991.

British Airways Plc, *Reports & Accounts 1990–91*, Hounslow, 1991.

Cathay Pacific Airways Limited, *Annual Report 1990,* Hong Kong, 1991.

Delta Air Lines, Inc., *1991 Annual Report,* Atlanta, GA, 1991.

Federal Express Corporation, *1991 Annual Report*, Memphis, 1991.

IBERIA Lineas Aereas de España, *1990 Annual Report*, Madrid, 1991.

Japan Airlines, *Annual Report 1990–1991*, Tokyo, 1991.

KLM Royal Dutch Airlines, *Annual Report 1990/91,* Amstelveen, 1991.

Korean Air, *Annual Report 1990*, Seoul, 1991.

Lufthansa Aktiengesellschaft, Deutsche, *Geschäftsbericht 1990*, Köln, 1991.

Quantas, *Annual Report 1990–91*, Sydney, 1991.

Singapore Airlines, *Annual Report 1990–91*, Singapore, 1991.

UAL Corporation, Form 10-K Annual Report Pursuant to Section 13 or 15(d) of the Securities Exchange Act of 1934 for the fiscal yar ended: December 31, 1990, Chicago, IL, 1991.

Appendix: Airline data sources and comments

Airline	Variable	Value (m)	Source	Comment
Air Canada (consolidated)	available ton km	5723	IATA	
Air Canada (consolidated)	operating cost	3239	Ann.Rep.	includes staff reduction and retirement cost
Air Canada (consolidated)	nonflight assets	2003	Ann.Rep.	
Air Canada (consolidated)	revenue pass. km	26677	IATA	
Air Canada (consolidated)	nonpass. revenue	697	Ann.Rep.	
All Nippon Airways (company)	available ton km	5895	IATA	fiscal year ending March 31st
All Nippon Airways (company)	operating cost	4225	Ann.Rep.	fiscal year ending March 3lst
All Nippon Airways (company)	nonflight assets	4557	Ann.Rep.	flight equipment accumulated depreciation estimated at Yen 525 billion
All Nippon Airways (company)	revenue pass. km	33081	IATA	fiscal year ending March 31st
All Nippon Airways (company)	nonpass. revenue	539	Ann.Rep.	fiscal year ending March 31st
American Airlines (company)	available ton km	24099	IATA	
American Airlines (company)	operating cost	9560	Form 10-K	
American Airlines (company)	nonflight assets	6267	Form 10-K	
American Airlines (company)	revenue pass. km	124055	IATA	
American Airlines (company)	nonpass. revenue	1266	Form 10-K	
British Airways (consolidated)	available ton km	13565	Ann.Rep.	computed from annual report to account for fiscal year ending March 31st
British Airways (consolidated)	operating cost	7499	Ann.Rep.	fiscal year ending March 31st
British Airways (consolidated)	nonflight assets	3213	Ann.Rep.	fiscal year ending March 31st
British Airways (consolidated)	revenue pass. km	64734	Ann.Rep.	computed from annual report to account for fiscal year ending March 31st

British Airways (consolidated)	nonpass. revenue	1563	Ann.Rep.	fiscal year ending March 31st
Cathay Pacific (consolidated)	available ton km	5183	IATA	
Cathay Pacific (consolidated)	operating cost	1880	Ann.Rep.	
Cathay Pacific (consolidated)	nonflight assets	783	Ann.Rep.	
Cathay Pacific (consolidated)	revenue pass. km	23604	IATA	
Cathay Pacific (consolidated)	nonpass. revenue	513	Ann.Rep.	
Delta Air Lines (consolidated)	available ton km	19080	IATA	
Delta Air Lines (consolidated)	operating cost	8032	Ann.Rep.	average of 1991 and 1990 value to account for fiscal year ending June 30th
Delta Air Lines (consolidated)	nonflight assets	3272	Ann.Rep.	average of 1991 and 1990 value to account for fiscal year ending June 30th
Delta Air Lines (consolidated)	revenue pass. km	95011	IATA	
Delta Air Lines (consolidated)	nonpass. revenue	572	Ann.Rep.	average of 1991 and 1990 value to account for fiscal year ending June 30th
Federal Express (consolidated)	available ton km	10884	IATA	fiscal year ending May 31st
Federal Express (consolidated)	operating cost	6730	Ann.Rep.	fiscal year ending May 31st
Federal Express (consolidated)	nonflight assets	3934	Form 10-K	fiscal year ending May 31st
Federal Express (consolidated)	revenue pass. km	0		fiscal year ending May 31st
Federal Express (consolidated)	nonpass. revenue	7688	Ann.Rep.	fiscal year ending May 31st
Iberia (consolidated)	available ton km	4603	IATA	
Iberia (consolidated)	operating cost	3457	Ann.Rep.	
Iberia (consolidated)	nonflight assets	2360	Ann.Rep.	
Iberia (consolidated)	revenue pass. km	22112	IATA	
Iberia (consolidated)	nonpass. revenue	969	Ann.Rep.	

Japan Airlines (company)	available ton km	12097	Ann.Rep.	computed from annual report to account for fiscal year ending March 31st
Japan Airlines (company)	operating cost	6779	Ann.Rep.	fiscal year ending March 31st
Japan Airlines (company)	nonflight assets	6474	Ann.Rep.	fiscal year ending March 31st
Japan Airlines (company)	revenue pass. km	52363	Ann.Rep.	computed from annual report to account for fiscal year ending March 31st
Japan Airlines (company)	nonpass. revenue	2001	Ann.Rep.	fiscal year ending March 31st
KLM (consolidated)	available ton km	6587	Ann.Rep.	computed from annual report to account for fiscal year ending March 31st
KLM (consolidated)	operating cost	3341	Ann.Rep.	fiscal year ending March 31st
KLM (consolidated)	nonflight assets	3581	Ann.Rep.	fiscal year ending March 31st
KLM (consolidated)	revenue pass. km	26504	Ann.Rep.	computed from annual report to account for fiscal year ending March 31st
KLM (consolidated)	nonpass. revenue	1297	Ann.Rep.	fiscal year ending March 31st
Korean (consolidated)	available ton km	5654	IATA	
Korean (consolidated)	operating cost	1878	Ann.Rep.	
Korean (consolidated)	nonflight assets	1916	Ann.Rep.	flight equipment accumulated depreciation estimated at Won 1355 billion
Korean (consolidated)	revenue pass. km	19277	IATA	
Korean (consolidated)	nonpass. revenue	972	Ann.Rep.	
Lufthansa (company)	available ton km	12559	IATA	
Lufthansa (company)	operating cost	8093	Ann.Rep.	
Lufthansa (company)	nonflight assets	3310	Ann.Rep.	
Lufthansa.(company)	revenue pass. km	41925	IATA	
Lufthansa (company)	non-pass. revenue	3398	Ann.Rep.	

Quantas (consolidated)	available ton km	5728	IATA	
Quantas (consolidated)	operating cost	2481	Ann.Rep.	average of 1991 and 1990 value to account for fiscal year ending June 30th
Quantas (consolidated)	nonflight assets	2254	Ann.Rep.	average of 1991 and 1990 value to account for fiscal year ending June 30th
Quantas (consolidated)	revenue pass. km	27754	IATA	
Quantas (consolidated)	nonpass. revenue	982	Ann.Rep.	average of 1991 and 1990 value to account for fiscal year ending June 30th
Singapore Airlines (company)	available ton km	4715	Ann.Rep.	computed from annual report to account for fiscal year ending March 31st
Singapore Airlines (company)	operating cost	1792	Ann.Rep.	fiscal year ending March 31st
Singapore Airlines (company)	nonflight assets	2485	Ann.Rep.	fiscal year ending March 31st
Singapore Airlines (company)	revenue pass. km	31332	Ann.Rep.	computed from annual report to account for fiscal year ending March 31st
Singapore Airlines (company)	nonpass. revenue	543	Ann.Rep.	fiscal year ending March 31st
UAL (consolidated)	available ton km	22793	IATA	
UAL (consolidated)	operating cost	9874	Ann.Rep.	
UAL (consolidated)	nonflight assets	4145	Ann.Rep.	
UAL (consolidated)	revenue pass. km	122528	IATA	
UAL (consolidated)	nonpass. revenue	1404	Ann.Rep.	

Index